TRANSACTIONS OF THE
ROYAL HISTORICAL SOCIETY

FIFTH SERIES

VOLUME 33

LONDON

OFFICES OF THE ROYAL HISTORICAL SOCIETY

UNIVERSITY COLLEGE LONDON, GOWER ST., WC1E 6BT

1983

British Library Cataloguing in Publication Data

Transactions of the Royal Historical Society
5th series, Vol. 33
1. History—Periodicals
905 D1

ISBN 0-86193-099-1

Made and printed in Great Britain by Butler & Tanner Ltd, Frome and London

CONTENTS

TRANSACTIONS OF THE
ROYAL HISTORICAL SOCIETY

IDEAS OF THE STATE IN THIRTEENTH AND FOURTEENTH-CENTURY COMMENTATORS ON THE ROMAN LAW

By Joseph P. Canning, M.A., Ph.D., F.R.Hist.S.

READ 5 FEBRUARY 1982

THE late thirteenth and fourteenth-century civilians made a distinctive contribution to the theory of the state, because they were seeking to apply a specific juristic language to account for the existence of contemporary territorial states. Fully worked out state concepts are to be found in the works of Bartolus and Baldus, although elements necessary for the construction of a concept of the state exist in earlier Commentators. The theories of Bartolus and Baldus are prime illustrations that the concept of the state is historically fluid: they do not possess *our* concept of the state; indeed their theories are highly complex, combining aspects which are distinctively late medieval with others which can justifiably be termed elements of a modern idea of the state.

It is fundamental to any idea of the state that it is understood to exist within an essentially this-worldly, and specifically political dimension; and that the state exists for its own political ends, which its government seeks to achieve, and is composed of human beings understood as essentially political animals. In the historical development of this view the rediscovery of Aristotelian political concepts in the mid-thirteenth century has conventionally been accorded pride of place by modern scholars. Indeed this aspect of the second reception of Aristotle in the Middle Ages made possible the re-establishment of political science as an autonomous discipline, and provided much of its basic language, including the concept of the naturalistic state. It is, however, misleading simply to maintain that the concept of the state was established in the late Middle Ages through the rediscovery of Aristotelian political ideas, because the Aristotelian concept of the state is only *a* concept of the state; it is not *the* concept of the state. And indeed medieval interpretations of the Aristotelian view diverge from the original meaning. Nor was Aristotle the sole source for medieval ideas of the state. The *Corpus Iuris Civilis* was also a major source. It provided an articulated language for the public dimension of human activity necessary for a concept of political life: the whole structure of civil law was divided between *ius publicum* and *ius privatum*; and the public dimension in an ordered community was contained in the basic terms of the *respublica* and the *utilitas publica* themselves. Furthermore it set forth a secular model both in the sense that much of its language concerning the community and its government was this-worldly in tone, and in the sense that the aspect of Caesaropapism it contained was the epitome of lay control over the Church. This is not to deny that the language of Roman public law could be used in hierocratic and theocratic theories of government which permitted no true idea of the state, since they envisaged both temporal and spiritual rulership as existing within the overall body of the Church: after all in the early and high Middle Ages papal theory made great use of Roman governmental terms. The point, however, remains that the medieval jurists, when they confronted the problem of the emerging territorial states from the last decade of the twelfth century onwards, were able to draw on Roman law concepts of government, and of law (such as *ius naturale*, *ius gentium*, and *ius civile*) in moving towards the idea of the territorial state, an idea lacking in the *Corpus Iuris Civilis* itself. In this process the Commentators, building on the achievements of canonists and Glossators, came to produce a theory of the territorial state whose points of reference were very clearly rooted in this world.

It is the major distinguishing mark of the whole school of the Commentators that they did not seek to produce a merely academic elucidation of the Roman law, but to apply its terms and principles to contemporary reality in order to work out a living law for their own times. They focused their attention on facts: human relationships and actions in so far as they pertained to a legal dimension. That these jurists had a fundamentally this-worldly orientation becomes obvious in any study of their works; it is also avowed by them. Thus for instance Cynus da Pistoia reports as established opinion that, 'The subject or material (of legal science) is nothing other than the acts of men.'[1] Baldus gives a magisterial statement of this view: 'Every art takes nature for its material ... but the jurist takes the works of man for his material ... He interprets them; and thus our law is founded upon accidentals, that is on cases which emerge ... for laws are born of facts ... But the common material (of legal science) is not concerned with the works of nature, but of man.'[2] To this human subject-matter

[1] 'Subiectum sive materia (legalis scientie) nihil aliud est quam actus hominum', ad Digestum vetus, Proem, n. 8, f. 2v (edn. Frankfurt, 1578).

[2] 'Omnis ars assumit sibi naturam pro materia ... sed legista pro materia assumit sibi facta hominum ... Item ipsa interpretatur, et sic ius nostrum est fundatum super

the Commentators applied a legal science which, following Ulpian, they considered to be a true philosophy (*vera philosophia*),[3] that is an autonomous discipline with its own technical language.[4] Universally they defined jurisprudence as being a subdivision of moral philosophy, constantly referring back to the Glossator Azo's statement in relation to the *Codex*, 'It belongs to ethics, because it deals with morals, just like all the books of legal science also do.'[5] Aristotelian political science was, of course, also considered to be a distinct branch of moral philosophy; thus it and the jurisprudence of the Commentators (in so far as it was concerned with public law) can validly be seen as running on parallel lines. The language of the Commentators was Aristotelian in the sense that it employed Aristotelian logical categories and forms of argument, and is thus validly seen as one of the major disciplines of late medieval and Renaissance scholasticism; yet the terms it employed for what may be called political matters and concepts were derived from the *Corpus Iuris Civilis*, and the *Libri Feudorum*, with only a gradual and partial assimilation of Aristotelian political terms. The jurists' technical language, and, as we shall shortly see, the precise way in which they dealt with political reality, demands a distinction between jurists and the exponents of *scientia politica* as such, be they theologians, philosophers or publicists. Within the technical language of the Commentators there developed a recognition of political facts which amounted to a political dimension of discourse in effect, but not originally at least in name. Both late medieval *scientia politica* and civilian jurisprudence produced systems for the discussion of ordered society and its government within a human dimension: the subject for both of them was man as he is in this world.

The best way to appreciate the factual political view of the Commentators is to approach it through their solutions to the most fundamental problem which at first sight might appear to prevent them from developing any concept of the territorial state at all. On the basis of the *Corpus Iuris Civilis* a universal sovereignty could be claimed for the emperor as *dominus mundi* (lord of the world).[6] As civilians the Commentators were not at liberty simply to ignore this claim. If,

---

accidentibus, id est super casibus emergentibus ... nam iura ex factis nata sunt ... Communis vero materia non versatur in factis nature, sed in factis hominum', ad D.1.1.Rubr., f. 4r (edn. Lyon, 1498).

[3] 'Ius est ars boni et aequi. Cuius merito quis nos sacerdotes appellet: iustitiam namque colimus et boni et aequi notitiam profitemur ... veram nisi fallor philosophiam, non simulatam affectantes' (D.1.1.1).

[4] See, for instance, D. R. Kelley, 'Civil Science in the Renaissance: Jurisprudence Italian Style', *Hist. Jnl.*, xxii, 4 (1979), 783.

[5] 'Supponitur ethice, quia tractat de moribus, sicut et omnes libri legalis scientie', Summa Codicis, ad v. 'Incipit materia ad codicem', f. 25r (edn. Speyer, 1482).

[6] D.14.2.9.

however, they accepted it, then they would appear to be denying the external sovereignty of territorial city-states and kingdoms, and since external sovereignty is fundamental to any concept of the state they would thus be unable to extend true statehood to such bodies. It was not just Roman law texts which posed them this problem: it had some basis in political reality. Although the imperial claim to lordship of the world was in practical terms ridiculous after the death of Frederick II, it did throughout the fourteenth century (and indeed into the fifteenth) retain some real force in Italy north of the papal patrimony, in that the emperor was in fact recognised as a form of overlord with powers to legitimise republican and signorial regimes. It is only necessary to recall the confirmation of their liberties which many cities such as Florence and Perugia purchased from Charles IV on his visit to Italy for his imperial coronation in 1355, and the many imperial vicariates bought by *signori* to legitimise their rule, culminating in the grant of a dukedom in 1395 to Giangaleazzo Visconti by Wenceslas, King of the Romans.[7] Nevertheless, despite this ultimate overlordship of the emperor there were city-republics and *signorie* in north and central Italy which in practical terms amounted to territorially sovereign states, quite apart from the French, English and Spanish kingdoms whose sovereignty was not in doubt.

Amongst the Commentators two forms of solution emerge, both of which provide juristic justifications for these territorial states. The first is the more radical one and is very well known: it involves a denial of the universal sovereignty of the emperor, and treats independent kingdoms as existing on the same basis as the territorially restricted empire. This view approaches a modern state concept because it advocates a plurality of territorially sovereign bodies. It major expression is to be found in the works of Neapolitan jurists, notably Marinus da Caramanico in the thirteenth century and Andreas de Isernia who died in 1316. The Neapolitan view is also ably supported by Oldradus da Ponte in his famous *Consilium*, 69, where he justifies Robert of Naples' rejection of imperial overlordship.[8] The Neapolitan theory

[7] For extensive details on both cities and *signori* see F. Ercole, *Dal comune al principato: saggi sulla storia del diritto pubblico del rinascimento italiano* (Florence, 1929), esp. 273–328; and for *signori* in particular see P. J. Jones, 'Communes and Despots: the City-State in Late-Medieval Italy', *Trans. Roy. Hist. Soc.*, 5th series, 15 (1965), 71–96.

[8] The views of the Neapolitan jurists are extensively dealt with in F. Calasso, *I Glossatori e la teoria della sovranità*, (3rd edn., Milan, 1957), where the text of the Proem of Marinus da Caramanico on the *Liber Constitutionum* of Frederick II is provided (176–205). For Oldradus da Ponte see E. Will, *Die Gutachten des Oldradus de Ponte zum Prozesse Heinrichs VII. gegen Robert von Neapel* (Berlin, 1917), 51–62, and E. M. Meijers' review of this (*Etudes d'histoire du droit*, ed. R. Feenstra and H. F. W. D. Fischer, iii (Leiden, 1966), 195–6). W. Ullmann discusses the views of the Neapolitans and Oldradus in 'The development of the medieval idea of sovereignty', *Engl. Hist. Rev.*, lxiv (1949) at 19–33.

attains a general significance because its arguments, directed primarily to establishing the complete independence of the king of Sicily from the emperor, have in the main a wider application suitable for any independent monarchy. Amongst the range of arguments produced one in particular has special importance for our enquiry: that kingdoms derive their independent existence from the *ius gentium.* This is of course prominently stated in D.1.1.5.[9] For justifying the fact of the independence of kingdoms this argument has overwhelming advantages. It circumvents any imperial claims over kingdoms because the *ius gentium* antedated the Roman empire, which was the product of Roman civil law. Thus Marinus is able to describe a political perspective in which 'long before the empire and the Roman race from of old, that is from the *ius gentium* which emerged with the human race itself, kingdoms were recognised and founded'.[10] For him the Romans established only a *de facto* empire, with the contemporary contraction of which kingdoms are able to regain their original rights under the *ius gentium.*[11] The *ius gentium* was very often seen by jurists as a form of natural law in the sense that it was understood to be that fundamental law created by human reason;[12] and on the basis of this view Oldradus is able to demonstrate that kings have a more secure right to their dominion than the emperor has to his empire, based as it is only on Roman civil law:

> From the primeval law of nature there are neither kingdoms nor an empire ... From the *ius gentium* which is also called natural ... from this law dominions are made distinct through occupation and kingdoms founded (D.1.1.5.). And thus, since kings exist from this law, and emperors only existed from civil law, that is through the Roman people, kings, as will be made clear below, possess a juster title,

---

For more modern treatments of the pro-Neapolitan view see P. Costa, *Iurisdictio. Semantica del potere politico nella pubblicistica medievale 1100–1433*, Università di Firenze pubblicazioni della Facoltà di Giurisprudenza, 1 (Milan, 1969), 333–41; and B. Paradisi, 'Il pensiero politico dei giuristi medievali', in *Storia delle idee politiche economiche e sociali*, ed. L. Firpo, ii (Turin, 1973), 57–76.

[9] 'Ex hoc iure gentium introducta bella, discretae gentes, regna condita, dominia distincta ...'.

[10] 'Longe ante imperium et romanorum genus ex antiquo, scilicet iure gentium quod cum ipso humano genere proditum est, fuerunt regna cognita, condita' (edn. Calasso, 17, p. 196).

[11] Edn. cit., 17, pp. 196–7.

[12] This identification between *ius naturale* and *ius gentium* derived ultimately from Gaius (D.1.1.9), although Ulpian's contrary view distinguishing between the two (D.1.1.1) also found expression in the works of medieval jurists. For the origins of the Commentators' views in the theories of the Glossators and Decretists see R. Weigand, *Die Naturrechtslehre der Legisten und Dekretisten von Irnerius bis Accursius und von Gratian bis Johannes Teutonicus*, Münchener Theologische Studien, iii. Kanonistische Abteilung, 26 (Munich, 1967), esp., 62–4.

> since it remains firm and immutable forever by a form of natural law (which was set up by divine providence).[13]

This *ius gentium* argument is clearly an advanced contribution to the development of the established juristic concept of the *rex qui superiorem non recognoscit*. The argument is strictly speaking not a contribution to the development of the idea that *rex in regno suo est imperator regni sui*, because the emperor is emphatically *not* seen as the model of sovereignty.[14] Marinus is, however, willing to apply to the king of Sicily within his kingdom all the legal rights and powers which the *princeps* enjoys in Roman law; but he does this on the grounds that Roman law, provided that it does not conflict with Sicilian constitutions and customs, has validity in Sicily, not because of any pretensions of the emperor, but in so far as it is accepted by the custom of the people of the kingdom (an argument from simple fact), and has been given effect by the will of the Sicilian monarchy which expressly appropriated elements from Roman law in the *Liber Constitutionum*.[15] The fundamental meaning of the argument that *rex in regno suo est imperator regni sui* is that the king in his territory has the same power of jurisdiction as the emperor possesses in the empire as a whole. The pro-Neapolitan *ius gentium* argument envisages a world of a plurality of kingdoms where the empire is only one territorial body amongst several. Thus Andreas de Isernia does indeed maintain that a king in his kingdom possesses the same power as the emperor in the empire; but he means by this that a kingdom and the empire are in essence the same kind of territorial body, and that therefore the world had returned to its pristine condition before the conquests of Rome:

> With cause another king will be able to do in his kingdom what the emperor can in the land of the empire, which is small these days. In Italy he possesses only Lombardy, and not all of that, and part of Tuscany; the rest belongs to the Church of Rome, like the kingdom of Sicily also. The first lords were kings as Sallust says, and is clear from (D.1.2.2,3) ... and (Nov., 47). The provinces therefore (which have a king) have returned to the pristine form of having kings,

[13] 'De iure naturali primevo, nec sunt regna nec imperium ... De iure gentium quod etiam naturale vocatur ... de iure isto per occupationem distincta sunt dominia, et regna condita (D.1.1.5). Et sic cum de iure isto sint reges, et imperatores solum fuerunt de iure civili, quia per populum romanum, ut infra patebit reges iustiorem titulum habent, cum a iure quodammodo naturali (quod divina providentia constitutum est) semper firmum atque immutabile perseverat', Cons., 69, n. 5, f. 24r (edn. Lyon, 1550).

[14] These two expressions were in origin distinct, although they were soon very often combined: see the recent highly pertinent discussion in W. Ullmann, 'This Realm of England is an Empire', *Journal of Eccles. Hist.*, xxx, 2 (1979), 188, n. 48.

[15] Edn. cit., 19, pp. 198–9.

which is easily done (D.2.14.17). Free kings have as much in their kingdoms as the emperor in the empire.[16]

In parenthesis the kingdom of Sicily's feudal subjection to the papacy to which Andreas alludes here, and which was of a unique kind, was not understood by this school of jurists to constitute a real infringement of their king's sovereignty within his kingdom.[17]

In this *ius gentium* argument the idea of territorial sovereignty crucial to a state concept clearly emerges. These jurists did not, however, necessarily quite reach this concept because they were primarily concerned to demonstrate the territorial sovereignty of their king rather than of an entity such as the kingdom itself. Certainly their views can rightly be seen as a most important contribution towards the development of the idea of the territorial state.

In contrast the mainstream of French and Italian Commentators retained the *de iure* universal sovereignty of the emperor and had in consequence greater difficulty in accommodating the fact of the existence of territorial states. Their set of solutions should, therefore, be seen as distinct also from the canonistic tradition which from the last decade of the twelfth century had developed a general theory of the *de iure* sovereignty of kings, and from those thirteenth and early fourteenth-century French publicists who had elaborated a special theory for the *de iure* sovereignty of the king of France in particular.[18]

Two stages can be discerned in the response of these mainstream Commentators. Although it is arguable, but not totally clear, that Johannes de Blanosco and Guilelmus de Cuneo held that the king of France at least enjoyed a *de iure* independence from the emperor,[19] the major representatives of the School of Orléans, Jacobus de Ravannis

[16] 'Cum causa rex alius poterit in regno suo quod imperator potest in terra imperii, que hodie modica est. In Italia non habet nisi Lombardiam, et illam non totam, et partem Thuscie; et alia sunt ecclesie Romane, sicut et regnum Sicilie. Primi domini fuerunt reges, ut dicit Sallustius, et patet (D.1.2.2,3) ... in auth. "Vt preponatur imperatoris nomen" (Coll.5.3=Nov.,47) in princ.. Reddite ergo sunt provincie (que regem habent) forme pristine habendi reges, quod de facili fit (D.2.14.27). Liberi reges tantum habent in regnis suis quantum imperator in imperio', ad Feud., 2.56, n. 2, f. 286r (edn. Lyon, 1579).

[17] See, for instance, Paradisi, 'Il pensiero politico', 71–6, and Costa, *Iurisdictio*, 335–6.

[18] The modern literature is vast. H. G. Walther, *Imperiales Königtum, Konziliarismus und Volkssouveränität* (Munich, 1976), 65–111, and 135–59, through discussing both a large amount of source material and a wide range of opinions of modern historians provides a highly useful survey of the contribution of both canonists and French publicists together with the views of Neapolitan jurists and early mainstream publicists. For the significance of the contribution of the French publicists and jurists Ullmann, 'Medieval idea of sovereignty', remains fundamental.

[19] See Meijers, *Etudes*, iii, 192–3, and especially Guilelmus de Cuneo ad D.1.11.1, f. 11v (Bodl., MS. Can. Misc. 472), 'Dico quod omnes tribuni erant sub rege Romano sicut omnes reges sunt hodie sub imperatore excepto rege Francie qui non habet

and Petrus de Bellapertica, maintained that the king of France's independence only existed on a *de facto* basis. Thus Jacobus de Ravannis for instance says, 'Some say that France is exempted from the empire. This is impossible *de iure*. You have it in C.1.27.2,2 that France is subject to the empire ... If the king of France does not recognise this, I do not care.'[20] Likewise the Italian jurist, Cynus da Pistoia, inspired by Petrus de Bellapertica in particular only admits in his commentary on the *Codex* a *de facto* independence for those who do not recognise the emperor's authority.[21]

The second stage was introduced by Bartolus and developed by his pupil and colleague, Baldus de Ubaldis, the two most important Italian jurists of the fourteenth century, and indeed the major luminaries of the whole school of the Commentators. For them the retention of the *de iure* universal sovereignty of the emperor reflected contemporary imperial claims to overlordship in the *terrae imperii* in Italy north of the papal patrimony. Furthermore they considered that the universal empire had been initiated on the human level by the Roman

---

superiorem' ('I say that all tribunes were under the Roman king just as all kings are to-day under the emperor with the exception of the king of France who does not have a superior').

[20] 'Quidam dicunt quod Francia exempta est ab imperio; hoc est impossibile de iure. Et quod Francia sit subdita imperio habes ... C.1.27.2,2. Si hoc non recognoscit rex Francie, de hoc non curo', ad Digestum Vetus, Proem, f. 2r, MS. Leiden, d'Ablaing 2 (as quoted in Meijers, *Etudes*, iii, 192). Cp. id. ad C. Rubr. 'De emendatione Iustiniani Codicis', ad v. 'Augustus', f. 1v (edn. Paris, 1519), 'Non recognoscens superiorem de facto non prescribit dominium ... Et hoc valet contra regem yspanie et regem francie qui non recognoscunt superiorem de facto. Tamen lex est expressa dicens quod ipsi sunt sub imperatore. Vnde de iure se non possunt tueri prescriptione, quia (C.1.27.2,2) ibi dicit quod imperator misit quendam ut preesset in yspaniam et franciam. Ergo de iure sunt subiecti imperio, quia semel fuerunt subiecti' ('He who does not recognise a superior *de facto* does not prescribe *dominium* ... And this is valid against the king of Spain and the king of France who do not recognise a superior *de facto*. There is, however, a law which expressly says that they are under the emperor, and as a result they cannot defend themselves *de iure* through prescription, because (C.1.27.2,2) says that the emperor sent someone to be in authority over Spain and France. *De iure*, therefore, they are subject to the empire, because they were once subject').C.1.27.2,2 provides the *locus classicus* for the argument that the French and Spanish kings are subject to the emperor.

[21] The first words of *l. Cunctos populos* (C.1.1.1)—'Cunctos populos, quos clementie nostre regit imperium' (edn. Venice, 1498)—invited the application of the *de iure-de facto* distinction to the relationship between the emperor and lesser rulers. Was 'quos' to be taken '*declarative*' thus signifying that all peoples were under the emperor's rule, or was it to be understood '*restrictive*' indicating that only his subjects were? In their commentaries on C.1.1.1 Petrus de Bellapertica (n. 3, p. 8, edn. Frankfurt, 1571) and Cynus (n. 3, f. 1v, edn. Frankfurt, 1578) hold that, while the emperor is *de iure* lord of the world, Justinian had intended 'quos' to be taken in a restrictive *de facto* sense so as to avoid making his laws a laughing-stock through trying to apply them to peoples not worthy to be ruled by them.

people's grant of its authority through the *lex regia* (for Baldus an irrevocable measure from the start, but for Bartolus one which had become irrevocable in time);[22] that this empire had then been confirmed by divinity and was thus understood to derive from God also;[23] and that in consequence the empire was the basic and perpetual constitution of Christendom, in the context of which any theory of territorial states had to be developed. The emperor was the symbol of legitimacy and the model of sovereignty. Indeed Bartolus, on the grounds that Christ had confirmed the empire, described as heretical any denial that the emperor was *dominus mundi*;[24] and Baldus held that it was simply impossible for any human power to suppress the empire because it was and continued to be a divine institution: 'And again that supreme dignity is instituted by God; and therefore it cannot be suppressed by man. It is for this reason that the empire is sempiternal.'[25] Thus Bartolus and Baldus gave the firmest possible support to the *de iure* claims of the emperor, firmer indeed than those jurists, notably Jacobus de Ravannis, who had held that the *lex regia* was revocable.[26]

It was Bartolus however who introduced a crucial innovation into the *de iure–de facto* distinction, which was ancient in medieval political theory before he used it. Previously full legitimacy had been accorded only to the *de iure* authority: thus apologists for the French king in the thirteenth century were anxious to prove his *de iure* independence from the emperor, and the Neapolitan jurists we considered accorded *de iure* sovereignty to kings. Bartolus, however, maintained that independent states could obtain fully independent powers of jurisdiction *de facto*: that, in short, *de facto* authority was not mere power without legitimacy.[27] This was such a highly significant step because it marked a full acceptance that legal rights, duties and authority emerge from the facts of human existence: it was in short the prime example of the

[22] See Baldus ad D.1.2.2,11, f. 13r (edn. Lyon, 1498); id. ad C.8.47.2, f. 323r (edn. Lyon, 1498); and Bartolus ad C.1.14.12, n. 3–4, f. 29r (edn. Turin, 1577).

[23] See Baldus ad C.1.14.4, f. 50v (edn. Lyon, 1498), and ad C.7.37.3, f. 196v (edn. Lyon, 1498).

[24] Ad D.49.15.24, n. 7, f. 228r (edn. Turin, 1577).

[25] 'Et item illa dignitas suprema est a deo instituta, unde per hominem supprimi non potest. Hinc est quod imperium semper est', ad Digestum Vetus, Proem, ad v. 'Quoniam omnia', f. 1v (edn. Lyon, 1498).

[26] See Jacobus de Ravannis ad C.1.14.12, f. 36v (edn. Paris, 1519); cp. Azo, *Summa Codicis*, ad C.1.14 (edn. Pavia, 1484), and Odofredus ad D.1.4.1, n. 1, f. 17v (edn. Lyon, 1550). For the *dissensiones dominorum* on this point see Cynus ad C.1.14.12, n. 4, f. 29r (edn. Frankfurt, 1578).

[27] This theme runs throughout C. N. S. Woolf, *Bartolus of Sassoferrato—his Position in the History of Medieval Political Thought* (Cambridge, 1913); but see esp. 195–6. Q. Skinner, *The Foundations of Modern Political Thought* (2 vols., Cambridge, 1978), i: *The Renaissance*, 9–12, lays considerable stress on this aspect of Bartolus' achievement.

this-worldly view characteristic of the Commentators. Baldus developed this *de facto* argument maintaining that, as he put it, the *de iure* empire remained universal, but was in fact not whole since there were gaps in the spread of the emperor's jurisdiction where the legitimate sovereignty of territorial powers was operative.[28]

The treatment accorded by Bartolus and Baldus to city-states can conveniently be considered first. As regards city-republics, *that* some Italian cities recognised no superior (particularly those in Lombardy) had on a few occasions been recognised by jurists before Bartolus: by Hostiensis and Jacobus de Ravannis in the thirteenth century and by Oldradus in the fourteenth;[29] and Petrus de Bellapertica and Cynus had referred generally, but without approbation, to *populi* who did not recognise the emperor's sovereignty.[30] It was Bartolus who had produced a full-scale *justification* for the independence of these cities from external control. His fundamental argument is very well known: the constitutive element of consent in the people's customs and statutes is perceived to culminate in the non-recognition of any superior, and indeed to accord to an independent city (which is in the position of a *populus liber*) the same jurisdictional powers within its territory as the emperor enjoys in the empire as a whole, a sure indication of its status as a territorial state.[31] Bartolus was in essence accepting the facts of political life. Baldus followed Bartolus' argument, but went beyond him in examining why such cities are sovereign states. On one level he develops the *de facto* argument in purely juristic terms: he applies the *ius gentium* argument to independent cities. On this basis Baldus with city-republics specifically in mind is able to maintain that peoples come into existence through the operation of their members' natural reason, and that the government of these communities (without which they cannot subsist) is derived from the same source. What is impor-

[28] 'Respondeo omnes sunt subiecti (i.e. imperatori) de iure, et merito; sed non omnes sunt subiecti de consuetudine; et peccant sicut Francigene et multi alii reges ... et licet regnum Francorum non sit de Romano imperio, tamen non sequitur, ergo imperium non est universale, nam aliud est dicere universale, aliud integrum, ut no. (D.50.16.25)' ('I reply all are subject (to the emperor) *de iure*, and rightly so; but not all are subject by custom, and they sin like the French and many other kings ... and although the kingdom of the French is not of the Roman empire, it does not however follow that the Empire is not therefore universal, for it is one thing to say "universal", and another "whole", as (D.50.16.25) notes'), ad Feud., 2.53, f. 74r (edn. Pavia, 1495).

[29] See Hostiensis ad X.1.31.3, f. 147r (edn. Paris, 1512); Jacobus de Ravannis ad C.7.33.12, f. 344v (edn. Paris, 1519); and Oldradus, Cons., 69, n. 6, f. 24r (edn. Lyon, 1550).

[30] See Petrus de Bellapertica ad C.1.1.1, n. 3, p. 8 (edn. Frankfurt, 1571), and Cynus, ibid., n. 3, f. 1v (edn. Frankfurt, 1578).

[31] See W. Ullmann, 'De Bartoli sententia: concilium repraesentat mentem populi', in *Bartolo da Sassoferrato—studi e documenti per il VI centenario* (2 vols., Milan, 1962), ii, 707–33.

tant is that there is no necessity for the involvement or authorisation of a superior.[32] Baldus' structure of argument has its own internal logic in purely juristic terms; but he also employs some of the language of Aristotelian political science. He does this because he realises that civilian jurisprudence and *scientia politica* consider as their subject-matter man in an essentially this-worldly dimension. Thus Baldus defines the aims of jurisprudence according to Aristotelian categories: 'The final cause (of our art) is three-fold, namely within man, in relation to man, and in relation to the *respublica*. Within man, so that he may be good; and this belongs to ethics. In relation to man, so that someone may rule his family well; and this belongs to economics. In relation to the *respublica*, so that it may be ruled healthily; and this belongs to politics.'[33] Most importantly Baldus overtly uses the Aristotelian concept of natural political man, and maintains that man as a result of his political nature forms cities: 'If he is considered in congregation, then natural man would be made political; and the people is created out of many men come together, as in (D.41.3.30). This people is sometimes girt by walls, and inhabits a city; and as such it is properly called political from "polis", which means "city".'[34] Such cities have no need for the involvement of a superior in their formation, or indeed for the continuance of their government. In this usage of Aristotelian political conceptions Baldus was partly anticipated by Guilelmus de Cuneo, who used the term, *homo politicus*, to denote man understood in a public dimension living within a community ruled by law. Guilelmus gives a classic exposition of the this-worldly political dimension of human life as the subject-matter of jurisprudence: 'Is political man, therefore, the subject-matter (of jurisprudence)? I say here that he is, because he is principally treated in the law as a man, since all laws are made for the sake of men (above D.1.5.2). I say however concerning this that the subject-matter should be ruled well, because man living in a civil community can be said to be the subject-matter.'[35] This passage exploits the community of terms,

[32] Ad D.1.1.9 (f. 9r); see also id. ad D.1.1.5 (f. 7v), and D.1.1.1,4 (f. 5v), edn. Lyon, 1498.

[33] 'Causa finalis (artis nostre) est triplex, scilicet in homine, ad hominem, et ad rempublicam. In homine, ut bonus sit; et hoc pertinet ad ethicam. Ad hominem, ut quis bene regat familiam; et hoc pertinet ad economicam. Ad rempublicam, ut respublica salubriter regatur; et hoc pertinet ad politicam', ad D.1.1.Rubr, f. 4r (edn. Lyon, 1498).

[34] 'Si consideratur in congregatione tunc homo naturalis efficeretur politicus, et ex multis aggregatis fit populus ut (D.41.3.30). Iste populus quandoque muris cingitur, et incolit civitatem; et idem proprie dicitur politicus a polis quod est civitas', ad C.7.53.5, f. 236r (edn. Lyon, 1498).

[35] 'Nunquid ergo homo politicus est subiectum (i.e. legalis scientie)? Hic dico quod sic, quia ideo principaliter tractatur in iure ut homo; cum gratia hominum omnia iura

such as *civis*, *civitas* and *civilis* which existed between Roman law and medieval versions of Aristotelian political ideas, a road which Baldus was to explore further. The *Digest* at D.1.3.2 (*l. Nam et Demosthenes*) contains in the original Greek the following statement: 'Law should be the rule of the just and the unjust and of those by nature political animals.'[36] The translation in the *littera Bononiensis* text used by medieval jurists obscures the overtly political concept: 'Law is the rule of the just and the unjust and of those things which are by nature civil.'[37] Thus Accursius, for instance, glossing this passage, does not recognise its political import: '*Natura sunt civilia.* id est. Naturalis hominis ingenio' ('By the genius of natural man').[38] Nevertheless here the reference to 'natural man' does seem a movement towards the kind of natural dimension in which political conceptions could develop. Baldus, however, is able to bring out the political dimension of the passage: 'Note there, "*Naturalia et civilia*" that man is naturally a civil animal; and law should be similar to a well composed and civil man.'[39] He is employing here William of Moerbeke's translation of the famous statement in Aristotle's *Politics*, 'Man is by nature a political animal':[40] 'homo natura civile animal est'.[41] William's translation of *πολιτικόν* by *civile* permits Baldus a play on the word *civilis*: *lex* is 'civil' in an Aristotelian sense; it is also 'civil' in the sense that enacted law is, in the terminology of Roman law, part of *ius civile*. It is thus with semantic ease that Aristotelian political concepts can be combined with Roman law ideas of law and government. Baldus may be said to have reactivated political man who had as it were been hibernating in the *Corpus Iuris Civilis* itself. There remains however an important difference between Guilelmus de Cuneo's use of *homo politicus* and Baldus'. Guilelmus gives no indication whether his political man is considered to be an active citizen or a passive one, in the sense of being a subject ruled by a superior. Although Baldus' conception of political man can embrace subjects, such as those ruled by the princely government of a *signore*, it is of the greatest significance that the concept of

---

facta sunt, infra (D.1.5.2). Dico tamen circa hoc quod subiectum bene regatur, quia homo civiliter vivens potest dici subiectum', ad Digestum Vetus, Proem, in B. Brandi, *Notizie intorno a Guillelmus de Cunio* (Rome, 1892), 111.

[36] '*δεῖ δὲ αὐτὸν* (i.e. *νόμον*) ... *κανόνα τε ειναι δικαίων καὶ ἀδίκων καὶ τῶν φύσει πολιτικῶν ζωων*'.

[37] 'Lex ... regula est iustorum et iniustorum et eorum que natura civilia sunt', edn. Venice, 1494 (f. 8r).

[38] F. 8r (edn. Venice, 1498).

[39] 'Nota ibi, "naturalia et civilia", quod homo naturaliter est animal civile; et lex similis debet esse homini bene composito et civili', f. 13v (edn. Lyon, 1498).

[40] '*ὁ ἄνθρωπος φύσει πολιτικὸν ζωον*', 1253a.

[41] Ed. Susemihl (p. 7).

natural, political man also forms a fundamental philosophical foundation of his theory of active citizenship operative within sovereign, self-governing, territorial city-states seen as communities of citizens.[42] In contrast Lucas de Penna, Baldus' Neapolitan contemporary who appears to have worked completely separately from him, uses the concept of 'the political' to characterise the relationship between the ruler and the community he rules.[43]

Both Baldus' Aristotelian and his *ius gentium* argument lead to the proposition that independent city-republics do not recognise a superior;[44] but Baldus draws back from the culminating Bartolist statement that such a community is a *civitas sibi princeps*. Strictly speaking Bartolus' formula is not fully logical: the expression is elliptical because the city or free people is not actually the emperor, the *princeps*. Baldus is, I believe, for this reason just a little more circumspect. He refers, for instance, to the election of a judge, 'by a people in the emperor's *place*, because it is the *princeps* in its territory';[45] he says of independent Italian cities that they are peoples which 'have the *place* and *image* of the *princeps*';[46] that 'a city free from superiors can concede a franchise to its inferiors, because in its dominion it takes the *place* of the *princeps*';[47] and that cities with fiscal or regalian rights 'in their territories fill the *place* of the *princeps*'.[48] Baldus is not seeking to convey that the cities are imperial vicars, but that in the gaps caused by the absence of effective imperial jurisdiction in the fourteenth century the cities have had to take the law into their own hands. In a universal and normative sense the emperor is the bearer of sovereign power; but where his power is not operative the city wields sovereign power in the emperor's stead: the city *replaces* the emperor as the bearer of sovereignty. If, however, the emperor should be physically present in the city's territory, then the gap is closed up, and Baldus is perfectly clear that any city statutes would then require imperial confirmation: in

[42] See J. P. Canning, 'A fourteenth-century contribution to the theory of citizenship: political man and the problem of created citizenship in the thought of Baldus de Ubaldis' in *Authority and Power: Studies on Medieval Law and Government Presented to Walter Ullmann on his Seventieth Birthday*, ed. B. Tierney and P.A. Linehan (Cambridge, 1980), 197–212.

[43] See, for instance, Lucas ad C.11.59.7, n. 8, pp. 563–4 (edn. Lyon, 1597).

[44] Ad D.1.8.Rubr., f. 36r (edn. Lyon, 1498).

[45] 'A populo *vice* imperatoris, quia in territorio suo princeps est', ad X.1.29.41, n. 3, f. 143 (edn. Lyon, 1551).

[46] '*Vicem* ergo et *imaginem* principis habent', Cons., 2.49, edn. Brescia, 1490 (=Cons., 4.52, ed. Venice, 1575).

[47] 'Civitas enim francha a superis concedere potest franchisiam inferis, quia *vicem* principis in suo gerit solio', Cons., 5.406, n. 5–6, f. 107r (edn. Venice, 1575).

[48] 'In suo territorio *vice* principis funguntur', ad X.1.2.13, n. 3, f. 28v (edn. Lyon, 1551).

this sense the emperor remains the ultimate sovereign.[49] But in normal circumstances this argument is totally irrelevant because the whole cause of the sovereignty of the cities is the factual weakness and absence of the emperor.[50] The situation, therefore, is that there is a hierarchy of sovereignty with the cities not possessing the ultimate grade, possessed by the emperor, a view also reinforced by Baldus' omission in that he does not accord to independent cities that *potestas suprema* which is possessed by the emperor and the pope.

There are clearly differences of emphasis between Bartolus and Baldus, but they agree on the argument from fact accepting territorially sovereign cities within this framework of a hierarchy of sovereignty. In modern terms the external sovereignty of such cities would appear to be impaired, with the result that true sovereignty would seem to be denied them. Yet the cities' non-recognition of a superior, and their legal identification with the emperor in Bartolus' case, and their replacement of him in Baldus', suggest that the attribution of sovereignty to them is reasonable. It is however a late medieval form of sovereignty within its overall hierarchical structure. As we have noted, the question of the precise nature of these independent cities' sovereignty clearly relates to the question of whether they may truly be termed states. One would suggest that Bartolus and Baldus do consider them to be states located in a peculiarly medieval way in the hierarchy of sovereignty: that is to say their form of statehood matches their form of sovereignty. In this respect neither jurist has in mind a modern idea of the state. Their view is, for example, quite distinct from the Neapolitan solution which, as we have seen, envisages a plurality of territorial states of which the empire forms but one, and has no universal, encompassing existence. The hierarchy of empire and territorial city-states also has another aspect. It accepts that two fundamentally different kinds of justification for political authority co-exist. Bartolus and Baldus consider that there exist territorially sovereign states which derive their existence and justification from simple political reality, that is within a purely this-worldly dimension, whereas the empire is a divinely confirmed institution. Neither form of justification exludes the other.

In both jurists' treatment of monarchies the same form of hierarchy emerges: beneath the *de iure* overlordship of the emperor there exist *regna* with an essentially *de facto* independence. Despite Bartolus' major discussion of monarchy in his tract, *De regimine civitatis*, it remains true that Baldus throughout his commentaries and in his *consilia* gives a far more extensive treatment to monarchy. Although for both jurists the

[49] Ad C.1.14.8, f. 54v (edn. Lyon, 1498).

[50] Ad Auth., 'Sed omnino' (ad C.4.12.4), f. 228r (edn. Lyon, 1498); and ad D.1.8.Rubr., f. 36r (edn. Lyon, 1498).

source of the monarchies' independence is political fact, they accept both theocratic and *de facto* justifications for the monarch's authority; thus Bartolus is able to say, 'Every king is elected by God either indirectly or directly, or by electors inspired by God . . . And note from this that rulership through election is more divine than that through succession . . . And thus the election of the emperor who is the universal king is made through the election of prelates and princes, and does not proceed through succession . . . For God constituted this empire from heaven . . . Particular kings however are more from human constitution, as in (D.1.1.5).'[51] Baldus explains how free peoples deriving their existence from the *ius gentium* can elect their monarch on this basis,

> The question is asked whether a province today could elect itself a king? And it seems that it could not, for provinces are under the natural dominion of the emperor, therefore they cannot confer *merum imperium* on anyone, in Auth., 'De defensoribus civitatum' (Coll.3.2,1 = Nov.15,1). But you should say that it can, if it is such a province which is not subject to the emperor, like Spain. For if the lordship of Castile were to become totally defunct, the inhabitants of the kingdom could elect themselves a king through the *ius gentium*, as here. Were jurisdictions therefore introduced through the *ius gentium*? Say that they were, because a king indicates the possession of jurisdiction; since therefore there were kings through the *ius gentium*, there were also jurisdictions.[52]

The picture that emerges is that Baldus envisages a this-worldly origin for kingdoms and kingship, but that within this context he is willing also to apply theocratic language to the authority of a king: he is *vicarius dei*,[53] and '*in regno suo tanquam quidam corporalis deus*'.[54] On the hierarchical scale Baldus places independent *regna* below the empire

[51] 'Omnis rex aut mediate aut immediate a deo eligitur vel ab electoribus inspirante deo . . . Et ex hoc nota quod regimen quod est per electionem est magis divinum quam illud quod est per successionem . . . Et ideo electio principis qui est rex universalis fit per electionem prelatorum et principum; non autem vadit per successionem . . . Hoc enim imperium deus de celo constituit . . . *Reges vero particulares sunt magis ex constitutione hominum*, ut (D.1.1.5)', *De regimine civitatis*, n. 22–3, f. 157r (edn. Turin, 1577).

[52] 'Queritur an hodie provincia possit sibi eligere regem? Et videtur quod non, nam provincie sunt sub naturali dominio imperatoris, ergo non possunt conferre alicui merum imperium, in auth., "De defensoribus civitatum" (Coll.3.2,1 = Nov.,15,1). Sed tu dic, quod sic, si est talis provincia que non subsit imperatori, ut Hispania. Nam si dominus Castelle deficeret in totum, regnicole possent sibi eligere regem de iure gentium, ut hic. Nunquid ergo iurisdictiones fuerunt introducte de iure gentium? Dic quod sic, quia rex significat se habere iurisdictionem; cum ergo de iure gentium fuerint reges, ergo et iurisdictiones', ad D.1.1.5, f. 7r (edn. Lyon, 1498).

[53] As for instance ad X.1.29.38, n. 5, f. 141r (edn. Lyon, 1551).

[54] Ad Feud., 2.55, f. 86r (edn. Pavia, 1495).

but above autonomous city-republics. As a sign of this he is willing to accord *suprema potestas* to sovereign kings,[55] the reason perhaps being that although they are in the empire in the widest sense of Christendom, they unlike the Italian cities are not in the *regnum italicum* where the empire could claim a more direct jurisdiction, nor with the exception of Sicily in the lands of the Church. This may also explain why he has no hesitation in applying the formula *rex in regno suo est imperator regni sui* to sovereign kings,[56] while he hesitates to employ the formula, *civitas sibi princeps*. I am not suggesting that Bartolus also places *regna* above sovereign cities: in his commentaries there appears to be insufficient information on kingship to make this judgment. As an example of the incomplete nature of Bartolus' treatment of kingship it would appear that there are in his works only a few approaches to the basic formula, *rex in regno suo est imperator regni sui*, of which he was nevertheless acutely well aware, and which clearly provided the model for his *civitas sibi princeps*.[57] It might furthermore still be objected that, although it has been shown that both Bartolus and Baldus accepted the territorial sovereignty of kings on a hierarchical scale, insufficient evidence has so far been presented for maintaining that their *kingdoms* can be termed territorial states. The treatment of kingdoms as such as states will become clear shortly when juristic corporation theory is considered.

It has been necessary to concentrate at such length on the mainstream Commentators' application of the *de iure–de facto* distinction in their treatment of the relationship between universal imperial authority and the jurisdiction of territorial powers because it forms a fundamental organising principle of their whole structure of public law. It is possible, for instance, to discuss as separate topics Baldus' and Bartolus' ideas of sovereign, territorial states; but it is fundamentally misleading if the ultimate context of a divinely approved imperial jurisdiction, the umbrella as it were beneath which all else exists, is forgotten. At the beginning of this paper a distinction was made between the Aristotelian tradition in late medieval political science, and that of civilian jurisprudence, which although scholastic and to that extent Aristotelian in method experienced only a very gradual and partial influx of Aristotelian political concepts. The quite distinctive character of the Commentators' usage of the *de iure – de facto* distinction illustrates why it is justifiable to treat their political theory in a separate category. The point remains that Bartolus and Baldus

[55] As for instance ad D.1.2.2,2, f. 12v (edn. Lyon, 1498).

[56] Ad C.4.19.7, f. 241r (edn. Lyon, 1498); ad X.Proem, ad v. 'Rex pacificus', n. 15, f. 5r (edn. Lyon, 1551); ad X.2.27.23, n. 5, f. 344r (ead. ed.); and ad X.1.33.6, n. 1, f. 158r (ead. ed.).

[57] See Woolf, *Bartolus*, 107–12.

(as had the Neapolitans and Oldradus in their different way) achieved the this-worldly concept of the sovereign, territorial state through using Roman law terms quite distinct from Aristotelian political terms, although Baldus (and to some extent Gulielmus de Cuneo before him) realising the basically similar this-worldly orientation of civilian jurisprudence and Aristotelian political science adopted the Aristotelian concept of a city-state composed of natural political men. My point concerns the idea of the state and does not bring into question the extent to which there seeped into civilian jurisprudence other ultimately Aristotelian political ideas, such as Bartolus' adopting the Aristotelian division of forms of government as an organising principle of his tract, *De regimine civitatis*, and using Aristotelian ideas on tyranny in his tract, *De tyrannia*.

In comparing the approaches of late medieval Aristotelian political science and the Roman law Commentators two major points remain: one of similarity and one of difference. The civilians and the Aristotelians were above all medieval, and thus both groups of writers accepted that man and the whole of creation depended ultimately upon God. In this sense their views could not be totally secular. But the point is that for both Aristotelians and civilians the main focus of their discussion of government, law and politics was on man as he is in this world. Out of many possible illustrations of this view from the Commentators I select this revealing quotation from Guilelmus de Cuneo: 'I ask what is the final cause (of legal science). I say that it is two-fold. One cause is proximate, and this can be called the good government of men, as in (C.1.14.3; Inst. Proem, 7), for the *whole* purpose of laws is that the *respublica* should be governed well ... Again there can be another remote final cause, which can be called that eternal bliss to which end all sciences are ordained.'[58] The point of difference between the civilians and the Aristotelian political thinkers concerns specifically how they looked at this world. The mature theory of Bartolus and Baldus was a triumph in nothing less than twisting the public law concepts of Roman law to fit the facts of contemporary political conditions, for which of course they had never been originally intended. If ever a political theory was dominated by the facts it was theirs: it was a theory developed specifically to accommodate the facts of their political world. In contrast in late medieval *scientia politica* Aristotelian political concepts were adopted as a ready-made general explanation of the world as it is in its political dimension. One

[58] 'Quero que sit causa finalis, dico quod duplex est; una proxima et ista potest dici bonum regnum hominum, ut (C.1.14.3; Inst.Proem, 7), totus enim est finis iurium, ut bene regatur res publica ... Item potest esse alia causa finalis remota, que potest dici beatitudo eterna ad quam omnes scientie ordinantur finaliter', ad Digestum Vetus, Proem (ed. Brandi, 112).

would suggest that the prize for mental gymnastics should go to the jurists.

Although the relationship between universal imperial jurisdiction and that of territorial states is the basic problem in the Commentators' theory of statehood, there remains the question of the relationship between the Church and these states. These jurists' treatment of the Church is, needless to say, an immense subject, and I have space only very briefly to mention certain aspects which modify and complete what I have already said. In giving such attention to the Church, and the papacy in particular, the Commentators were simply mirroring the reality of contemporary ecclesiastical jurisdiction: the power and authority of the Church were facts which they could not ignore.

As regards the external sovereignty of territorial states, the vast number of words, which the Commentators poured forth on the question of whether the pope enjoyed any superiority over the emperor in terms of temporal jurisdiction, was not directly relevant. In any case there was no uniformity of view among the Commentators: their opinions ranged from imperialist denials of any papal jurisdiction over the emperor to extreme hierocratic statements. Notable changes of mind and contradictions exist in the writings of individual jurists. Thus Cynus in his commentary on the *Codex*, and in his fragmentary lecture on the *Digestum Vetus* (as printed for instance in the Frankfurt, 1578, edition), puts forward a dualist view denying that the emperor was in any sense subject to the pope in temporal matters,[59] and then in his long-lost *Lectura super Digesto Veteri* (rediscovered in manuscript by Domenico Maffei) expresses classically hierocratic views.[60] Bartolus' treatment is also contradictory.[61] Baldus' well-argued view is that, while the pope possesses an ultimate form of universal sovereignty, in the sense that he has the right to confirm and crown the emperor, and depose him in extreme crisis,[62] the emperor also enjoys a real universal sovereignty which is the necessary basis of the fundamental constitutional law of Christendom, and which remains valid whatever the ultimate relationship of emperor and pope.[63] This view of Baldus is

[59] Ad C.7.37.3, n. 5, f. 446r-v (edn. Frankfurt, 1598); ad D.1.1.5, n. 4 (f. 4v); and ad D.1.4.3, n. 1 (f. 8r).

[60] See Maffei, *La 'Lectura Super Digesto Veteri' di Cino da Pistoia. Studio sui MSS Savigny 22 e Urb. Lat. 172* (Milan, 1963), 48–56.

[61] See Woolf, *Bartolus*, 72–100.

[62] Cons., 3.283, f. 88r, edn. Brescia, 1491 (=Cons., 1.333, edn Venice, 1575); *De Pace Constantie*, ad v. 'Hoc quod nos', f. 90r (edn. Pavia, 1495); and ad C.1.14.12, f. 55r (edn. Lyon, 1498).

[63] See, for instance, Baldus ad Digestum Vetus, Proem, ad v. 'Quoniam omnia', f. 1r (edn. Lyon, 1498), where he maintains that the hierocratic view of papal supremacy found in canonist writings, in order to be acceptable, has to be interpreted in such a way that the temporal sovereignty of the emperor is retained.

not a dualist one but, again, rather a form of hierarchy of sovereignty unacceptable to imperialists or hierocrats.

It was however in the lands of the Church (the *terrae ecclesiae*), that is the papal patrimony and the kingdom of Sicily, that church jurisdiction had immediate relevance to the external sovereignty of territorial states, for in these territories the papacy was either direct temporal ruler or overlord. The mature doctrine of the Commentators, as represented by Bartolus and Baldus, considered that temporal jurisdiction in general was divided territorially between the emperor and the pope: that Christendom was geographically separated into the *terrae imperii* and the *terrae ecclesiae*.[64] Bartolus offered two contradictory explanations of this state of affairs: that the lands of the Church were part of the Roman empire which had been given over to the Church through the Donation of Constantine;[65] and that the papacy through the *translatio imperii* had handed most of the Roman empire over to the emperor for temporal government, but had retained temporal rule in the *terrae ecclesiae*, a view preeminently expressed in his classic hierocratic statement in his commentary on *Ad reprimendum*.[66] Baldus argued consistently that papal temporal jurisdiction in the patrimony was not derived from spiritual authority, but from imperial grant through the Donation of Constantine.[67] He considered (as had Bartolus in his commentary on D.49.15.24)[68] that papal temporal jurisdiction was of essentially the same kind as the imperial; that is to say, supreme authority remained identical in both territories, but in the one was operated by the emperor and in the other by the pope: the pope in short had taken over imperial authority in the patrimony, or as Baldus put it, 'The emperor has an empire divided with the pope, so that the lands of the Roman church are not subject to the

[64] See Bartolus, *Ad reprimendum*, ad v. 'Per edictum', f. 5r (edn. Venice, 1497), and Woolf, *Bartolus*, 99; and Baldus, Cons., 2.37, f. 11v, edn. Brescia, 1490 (=Cons., 4.40, edn. Venice, 1575).

[65] Ad D.49.15.24, n. 4, f. 228r (edn. Turin, 1577). By common consent Bartolus' treatment of the Donation is one of the weaker parts of his political theory. Because of his *caveat* in two crucial passages that he wishes to please the Church in whose territories he is speaking, Domenico Maffei maintains that it is impossible to make out Bartolus' true opinion (*La donazione di Costantino nei giuristi medievali*, repr. Milan, 1969, 185–90).

[66] Ad v. 'Totius orbis', f. 1r (edn. Venice, 1497).

[67] See for instance Baldus ad Feud., Proem, ad v. 'Expedita', f. 2v (edn. Pavia, 1495), and ad X.2.24.33, n. 4, f. 315r (edn. Lyon, 1551).

[68] n. 4, f. 228r (edn. Turin, 1577), where he says of the papal patrimony, 'In those lands the Roman Church exercises the jurisdiction which belonged to the Roman Empire, and they (i.e. the peoples of the patrimony) acknowledge this; they do not therefore cease to be members of the Roman people, but the administration of those provinces is conceded to another person' ('Ecclesia romana exercet illis in terris iurisdictionem, que erat imperii romani, et istud fatentur; non ergo desinunt esse de populo romano, sed administratio istarum provinciarum est alteri concessa'—I have emended 'ill*as* in terr*as*' and 'imperi*o* ro.' in this edn.).

emperor either directly or indirectly.'[69] Whatever the justification employed, both Bartolus and Baldus, through accepting the basic distinction between the *terrae imperii* and the *terrae ecclesiae*, placed the kingdom of Sicily and those cities not recognising a superior in the *terrae ecclesiae* in the same relationship to the pope as that which independent states in the *terrae imperii* enoyed with the emperor. Cities such as Perugia and Bologna would be in question. Thus precisely the same hierarchical considerations apply in the *terrae ecclesiae* as we saw applying in the *terrae imperii* with the same implications for the statehood of independent territorial bodies. We may therefore refine our conception of these jurists' view of the constitutional structure of Christendom: they justify the sovereignty of territorial states within this overall context of a universal temporal jurisdiction divided between the emperor and the pope. In contrast, the pro-Neapolitan school of jurists, while it accepted a form of hierarchy of sovereignty between the papacy as feudal overlord and the king of Sicily, did so specifically within the general context of a plurality of territorially sovereign states and the consequent denial of the universality of imperial jurisdiction.

It is, of course, axiomatic to any modern concept of the state that the supreme authority within it should have a monopoly of law-making power within its borders. The Commentators however remain clearly medieval in their outlook because they accept the jurisdictional immunities of the clergy and the whole structure of autonomous ecclesiastical courts. In modern terms this means that the internal sovereignty of the *civitates* and *regna* is infringed with the result that they cannot be considered states in a modern sense. That the Commentators should accept the validity of the claims of canon law can cause no surprise because they are reflecting contemporary legal reality. We find mirrored in their works both the real jurisdictional power and authority of the Church, and the attempts of contemporary secular governments to limit ecclesiastical immunities. These jurists do not feel free to develop a Marsilian form of argument in which the clergy, as far as the state is concerned, are treated simply as citizens; rather the reverse—there is no evidence that the Commentators feel attracted to this view. The concept of the subjection of the clergy to state authority is of course readily available in the *Corpus Iuris Civilis*: the *ius publicum* covered sacred persons and property.[70] The Commentators are well aware of this, as Albericus de Rosciate shows in his commentary on D.3.4.1 where he draws the conclusion that the clergy should

[69] Cons., 2.37, f. 11v, edn. Brescia, 1490 (= Cons., 4.40. edn. Venice, 1575).

[70] 'Publicum ius in sacris, in sacerdotibus, in magistratibus consistit', D.1.1.1,2 (Ulpian).

not be treated legally in a way any different from other members of the citizen-body:

> The *ius publicum* consists more of things sacred and priests, see above, D.1.1.1,2 ... Again the philosophers of old (even pagan ones) ... divided all religion into three parts, of which the first they called sacred, the second public, and the third private, as the philosopher narrates in the second book of the Politics, chapter 4 about the middle. As parts of the whole they should not therefore be counted under a different law, see above (D.41.3.23). And thus a priest should be counted as part of the community and have access to its advantages (*Decr. Grat.*, D.10.7; and *Decr. Grat.*, C.12.q.1.c.7). It is no obstacle that a priest and ecclesiastical persons should enjoy many privileges, for they are not on this account any less part of the community, for decurions and senators also enjoy many privileges both in their persons and their property (D.48.19.9,11; and C.9.41.11; and C.10.53.6), and they are nonetheless part of the community and the people, as in (Inst., 1.2,4), therefore so is a priest.'[71]

The references to Ulpian and Aristotle are notable; but this whole passage in the context of Albericus' commentary on D.3.4.1 as a whole is more in the form of a line of argument, rather than his considered conclusion. This illustrates the point that the Commentators do not follow up this aspect of the *ius publicum* in constructing their overall view of the position of the clergy. Their consistent opinion is that clergy and laity constitute two distinct groups within any community with the clergy being superior to the laity in that laymen cannot validly make law for clergy, although the clergy can benefit from lay customs and statutes if they so wish (Albericus does not agree on this last point however).[72] In general they accept the *privilegium fori* but with detailed differences of opinion on matters such as taxation of clerical possessions and the extent of the application of ecclesiastical jurisdiction *ratione peccati*, differences which reflect the attempts of contemporary governments to limit the privileges of the Church. Even

[71] 'In istis sacris et sacerdotibus magis consistit ius publicum, supra (D.1.1.1,2) ... Item philosophi antiqui etiam pagani ... omnem religionem diviserunt in tres partes, quarum unam sacram, aliam publicam, tertiam privatam appellaverunt, ut narrat philosophus, secundo Politicorum, iiii. c. circa medium. Non debent ergo sicut partes totius diverso iure censeri, infra (D.41.3.23). Et ideo sacerdos sicut pars universitatis debet censeri, et eius commodis uti, pro hoc (*Decr. Grat.*, D.10.7; et *Decr. Grat.*, C.12.q.1.c.7). Non obstat quod sacerdos et ecclesiastice persone multis privilegiis gaudeant; non enim per hoc est minus esse partem universitatis, nam et decuriones et senatores multis gaudent privilegiis, tam in personis quam in rebus, infra (D.48.19.9,11; et C.9.41.11; et C.10.53.6), et tamen sunt de universitate et populo, ut (Inst., 1.2,4), ergo et sacerdos', n. 6–7, f. 228v (edn. Lyon, 1545).

[72] Ad D.1.3.32, n. 138, f. 43v (edn. Lyon, 1545).

Cynus, who in his commentary on the *Codex* clearly opposes himself to the overextension of ecclesiastical jurisdiction, nevertheless in his commentary on C.8.52.2 has to admit the validity of separate clerical jurisdiction: 'The third question is, whether the people's custom binds clerics? And we say that it does not, for two reasons. In the first place because there are two peoples, which is clear because there are two judges ... In the second place because clerics are greater than laymen ... But the statutes of inferiors do not bind superiors ... therefore etc., unless the clerics shall have so wished it.'[73] And Albericus himself adopts the same view as his major position on this topic.[74] The idea that clergy and laity constitute *duo populi* (expressed about 1160 by the canonist Stephen of Tournai)[75] for these jurists derives directly from St Jerome's view, 'duo sunt genera Christianorum', as quoted in Gratian's *Decretum* (C.12.q.1,c.7). As regards Italy this general attitude of the Commentators with its respect for the rights of ecclesiastical jurisdiction reflected those city-statutes which protected the *libertas ecclesiae* (such as the vulgar statutes of Perugia of 1342,[76] and the statutes of Milan of 1351),[77] rather than those which consciously infringed it (such as the communal legislation of Padua between 1270 and 1290, and the Florentine Statutes of the Captain of the People of 1322).[78] On this question Baldus' opinions are a very interesting case. Throughout his works he is a staunch defender of the jurisdictional rights of the clergy as a distinct and independent group in any community. Yet in one *consilium* written towards the end of his life he expressly accepts Giangaleazzo Visconti's legislation specifically including the clergy amongst his subjects taken as a whole; indeed Baldus says, 'Again clerics are also part of the city, and indeed its most honourable component, and are not if at all distinct from the corporate body (of the city), because their honour is increased.'[79] As Luigi

[73] 'Tertio queritur, nunquid consuetudo populi liget clericos? Et dicimus, quod non, duabus rationibus. Vna quia duo sunt populi, quod patet quia duo sunt iudices ... Alia quia clerici sunt maiores respectu laicorum ... Sed statuta minorum non ligant maiores ... ergo etc., nisi clerici voluerint', n. 27, f. 525v (edn. Frankfurt, 1578).

[74] Ad D.1.3.32, n. 138, f. 43v (edn. Lyon, 1545); and *De statutis*, 2, q. 2, ad v. 'Ex predictis oritur', n. 16–17, f. 28v (edn. Lyon, 1552).

[75] See F.L. von Schulte, *Die Summa des Stephanus Tornacensis über das Decretum Gratiani* (Giessen, 1891), Introductio, 1.

[76] See *Statuti di Perugia dell' anno MCCCXLII*, Corpus statutorum italicorum, 4, ed. G. degli Azzi (2 vols., Milan, 1913–16), ii, 451 (Lib. 4, cap. 157).

[77] See L. Prosdocimi, *Il diritto ecclesiastico dello Stato di Milano dall'inizio della signoria viscontea al periodo tridentino (sec. XIII–XVI)*, repr. Milan, 1973, 24–5.

[78] See N. Rubinstein, 'Marsilius of Padua and Italian Political Thought of his Time', in *Europe in the Late Middle Ages*, ed., J.R. Hale, J.R.L. Highfield, and B. Smalley (repr. 1970), 47–8.

[79] 'Item et clerici pars civitatis sunt et quidem honorabilissimum membrum, nec si omnino ab universali corpore alieni, quia auctus sit honor eorum', Cons., 1.442, f. 134v, edn. Brescia, 1490 (=Cons., 3.241, edn. Venice, 1575).

Prosdocimi has shown, this legislation of Giangaleazzo developed earlier and far less extensive Viscontean measures which had been taken in response to requests from the clergy of Milan to enjoy certain legal advantages as *subditi* of the state rather than remain in the category of *non subditi*.[80] This late opinion of Baldus goes further than his statement in his commentary on the *Liber Decretalium* written shortly before he died, that clerics are part of the whole *populus* in the sense that they can benefit from lay legislation;[81] but it is only an isolated expression of view. In general, however, the Commentators' treatment of ecclesiastical jurisdiction only serves to underline that they definitely did not possess a modern view of the state in that they considered that independent cities and kingdoms were in their external relations located in a hierarchy of sovereignty, and were in their internal affairs ruled by governments which lacked a monopoly of law-making and had incomplete control over a highly important part of their population.

There is, however, a major sense in which the Commentators did contribute to the development of the early modern idea of the state. It is generally accepted that a necessary part of any such modern conception is the idea of the state as an abstract entity distinct from its government and its members. Quentin Skinner, for instance, has recently examined this point at length and located the acquisition of this concept in the second half of the sixteenth century.[82] It appears however that this part of the modern state concept was in fact developed in the thirteenth and fourteenth centuries by the school of the Commentators as part of their corporation theory, and that it is their most important contribution to the idea of the state.

The Commentators viewed the territorial state in two ways: both as a congregation of men, and as an abstract entity distinct from its members.[83] Their argument is elaborated in their juristic language, and is thus to that extent distinct from other late medieval treatments of the state. Whereas the Glossators had almost universally identified the corporation with its members (in Accursius' famous formulation, for instance, 'the corporation is nothing other than the individual men who are there'),[84] the Commentators on the other hand viewed it as a distinct unitary entity as well as the plurality of men who composed

[80] *Diritto ecclesiastico*, 28–9, and 288–96.

[81] Ad X.1.2.7, n. 7, f. 17 (edn. Lyon, 1551).

[82] *Foundations*, ii, 352–8.

[83] For extended discussion of the political aspect of their corporation-theory see J.P. Canning, 'The corporation in the political thought of the Italian jurists of the thirteenth and fourteenth centuries', *Hist. of Pol. Thought*, i, 1 (1980), 9–32.

[84] 'Vniversitas nil aliud est nisi singuli homines qui ibi sunt', ad D.3.4.7, col. 409–10 (Antwerp, 1575).

it. Developing the formulation of Innocent IV that the corporation was a *persona ficta* (fictive person) the Commentators maintained that through legal fiction the state as a corporation was a *persona* in law, that is to say, through a legal construction they attributed to the state in its abstract aspect legal existence and capacity—legal personality in short. Overt use of the term, *persona*, to denote a legal person was an invention of the thirteenth-century jurists: *persona* was not used in that sense in the *Corpus Iuris Civilis*, although that usage was anticipated to some extent in theological terms by the Augustinian identification of Christ as the *persona ecclesiae*.[85] The juristic approach was characterised by the constructive use of fiction in order to create a state-entity with a purely legal existence. In the full-scale theory of sovereign city-states elaborated by Bartolus and Baldus the *populus* in its abstract aspect is deemed to be an immortal entity which is understood to be able to act through the instrumentality of its mortal members through a structure of councils and elective representative officers: that is to say, it consents and acts in its corporeal aspect, but that consent and action is imputed to the *populus* as an abstraction.[86] It is Baldus who gives the most elaborate application of corporation theory to sovereign kingdoms. While in one aspect the *regnum* is identified with its members ('the nations and peoples of the kingdom themselves collectively are the kingdom'),[87] in its abstract and perpetual aspect as *universitas* or *respublica regni* it is distinct from them. This undying corporation of the kingdom sets up an abstract and thus also perpetual royal office or *dignitas* which is operated by each individual as ruler. There are thus two different kinds of person in the king: the human person and an abstract legal person (his *dignitas*). The human king is no more than the instrument or organ of his *dignitas*, which thus appears as the principal agent in royal actions. There is thus a clear distinction between the kingdom and the royal office, which are legal persons, and the individual king who acts on their behalf.[88] The corporational view of the territorial state produced in the mature theory of the Commentators is clearly a distinctive contribution to political thought couched in a specific juristic language. Its very distinctiveness is made

[85] See M.J. Wilks, *The Problem of Sovereignty in the Later Middle Ages—the Papal Monarchy with Augustinus Triumphus and the Publicists*, Cambridge Studies in Medieval Life and Thought, 2nd ser., 9 (Cambridge, 1963), 24; and id., 'Corporation and representation in the Defensor Pacis', *Studia Gratiana*, xv (1972), 258.

[86] See Canning, 'The corporation', 14, and 27–32.

[87] 'Ipse gentes regni et ipsi populi collective regnum sunt', Cons., 1.359, f. 109v, edn. Brescia, 1490 (=Cons., 3.159, edn. Venice, 1575).

[88] Ibid. for full details of Baldus' theory; but see also especially Cons., 1.417, f. 129r, edn. Brescia, 1490 (=Cons., 3.217, edn. Venice, 1575); Cons., 1.322, f. 98r, edn. Brescia, 1490 (=Cons., 3.121, edn. Venice, 1575); and his commentaries ad C.6.51.1,6 (f. 152v), C.7.55.1 and C.7.61.3 (f. 252v), edn. Lyon, 1498.

even clearer when this juristic view is compared with some contemporary ideas of the state. The Aristotelian tradition tended to identify the state with its members. Thus in the view, for instance, of Walter Ullmann, the major effect of the rediscovery of Aristotelian political ideas in the thirteenth century was the acquisition of the concept of the state in the sense of a congregation of natural political men, of citizens.[89] Aquinas certainly identified the state with its members;[90] even when he stressed the unitary aspect of a community by saying, 'In civil matters all those who belong to one community are considered as if one body, and the whole community as if one man,'[91] he was not thereby considering it as an entity distinct from its members. Michael Wilks has shown how Marsilius' conception of the *universitas civium* as a corporate entity distinct from individual citizens was derived from juristic sources.[92] Ockham, of course, identifying any group only with the human beings who composed it, expressly rejected the *persona ficta* concept of the jurists.[93] Indeed Bartolus conceded that civilian corporation theory was opposed, as he saw it, to current philosophical conceptions of the individual and the group:

> Is a corporation other than the men who compose that corporation? Some say it is not ... and all philosophers and canonists hold this, maintaining that the whole does not differ in reality from its parts. The truth is that if indeed we were to speak really, truly, and properly, they speak the truth. For a corporation of scholars is nothing other than the scholars; but according to the fiction of the law they do not speak the truth. For a corporation represents one person, which is different from the scholars or from the men of the corporation ... and this is clear because even though all those scholars may depart, and others take their place, it nevertheless remains the same corporation. Again when all the members of a people have died and others taken their place it is the same people; and thus according to a fiction of the law the corporation is something other than the persons who compose the corporation, because it is a represented person.[94]

[89] See, for instance, *Medieval Foundations of Renaissance Humanism* (1977) 94-5.

[90] See, for instance, T. Gilby, *Principality and Polity: Aquinas and the Rise of State Theory in the West* (1958), 253-60; and E. Lewis, *Medieval Political Ideas* (2 vols., 1954), i, 206-7.

[91] 'In civilibus omnes qui sunt unius communitatis reputantur quasi unum corpus, et tota communitas quasi unus homo', *ST*, 1a2ae, 81,1. ('Leonine' edn., Rome, 1892, 88).

[92] 'Corporation and representation', esp. 254-6.

[93] See *Tractatus contra Benedictum*, c.8, in *Guillelmi de Ockham opera politica*, iii, ed. J.G. Sikes, R.F. Bennett, and H.S. Offler (Manchester, 1956), 189.

[94] 'An universitas sit aliud quam homines universitatis? Quidam dicunt quod non, ut no. (D.3.4.7,1, et D.47.22.1 in fine), et hoc tenent omnes Philosophi et Canoniste, qui tenent, quod totum non differt realiter a suis partibus. Veritas est, quod si quidem

What we find in sum in the corporation theory of Bartolus and Baldus is a distinctive, systematic and articulated theory of the state as an abstract entity distinct from its government or ruler, and its human members, be they subjects or citizens.

The choice of title for this paper expressly indicates the Commentators' *ideas* of the state in order to reflect the variety of views amongst them, notably that concepts which appear identical to aspects of a modern idea of the state, that is to say the pro-Neapolitan view of a plurality of states with the empire being but one of several, and the corporational theory of the state as an abstract legal person, coexist with views which appear clearly medieval: the hierarchical view and the autonomy of ecclesiastical jurisdiction. Whatever the divergence among their ideas, the whole this-worldly orientation of the Commentators, and the articulation (where it occurs) of theories justifying non-recognition of a superior by cities and kingdoms indicate that it is justifiable to consider that they were thinking in terms of territorial states. Certainly it would appear that Bartolus and Baldus operated with a concept of the territorial state: a body which was sovereign, perpetual, territorial, possessed of this-worldly objectives, composed of men, whether citizens or subjects, understood on a political level (overtly so in the case of Baldus), and also distinguished as an abstract entity from its rulers and members; but theirs was a view of the state which was on the whole medieval rather than modern because of their acceptance of a hierarchy of sovereignty and ecclesiastical immunities.

The firm possession of a concept is obviously best shown by the employment of an agreed term; and the Commentators certainly did not possess one for 'the state'—they did not, for instance, use the word, *status*, as meaning 'the state' in any sense recognisable in political thought, but rather 'well-being' or 'standing' as in *status regni* or *status reipublicae*. The absence of any such agreed term is not fatal because a concept can exist without it; indeed the lack of one agreed term for the state appears generally characteristic of theories of the state produced from the mid-thirteenth to the early sixteenth century. It seems in sum that the term, 'the state', can justifiably be employed in interpreting the political thought of the Commentators so long as modern scholars realise the limitations within which that term can be

---

loquamur realiter vere et proprie, ipsi dicunt verum. Nam nil aliud est universitas scholarium quam scholares; sed secundum fictionem iuris ipsi non dicunt verum. Nam universitas representat unam personam, que est aliud a scholaribus seu ab hominibus universitatis (D.46.1.22), quod apparet quia recedentibus omnibus istis scholaribus et aliis redeuntibus eadem tamen universitas est. Item mortuis omnibus de populo et aliis subrogatis idem est populus, et sic aliud est universitas quam persone que faciunt universitatem secundum iuris fictionem, quia est quedem persona representata, d. (D.46.1.22)', ad D.48.19.16,10, n. 3-4, f. 200r (edn. Turin, 1577).

used; and that the variety and content of contributions made by the Commentators to ideas of the state only serve to underline that there is no one idea of the state, but that it is a term with a somewhat fluid historical meaning.

GOVERNMENT IN PROVINCIAL ENGLAND UNDER THE LATER STUARTS

By G. C. F. Forster, B.A., F.S.A., F.R.Hist.S.

READ 23 APRIL 1982

IN a paper presented on St George's day one may be forgiven for thinking of England, and not even simply of England as a nation but of provincial England, described by Professor Everitt as 'a union of partially-independent county states'. He and other historians have paid fruitful attention to the 'county communities'—and the urban communities too—of Tudor and Stuart England. But much of their research has been devoted to the period before 1660, and most of what little we know about the provinces under Charles II and James II is concerned with economic change, landownership, the professions, political faction and religious persecution. Recent work on government in the localities during the Interregnum has suggested that, contrary to earlier suppositions, 'changes are often hard to seek' and that local authorities carried out their duties 'in much the same way as their predecessors'. Nevertheless, the impression survives that after the Restoration provincial government, like *Punch*, was not what it had been, that it did not recover from the upheavals of the 1640s and 1650s, that local governors were left to their own devices, and that inertia set in largely because of 'the long decline in central interference in local administration'.[1]

The purpose of this paper is to test these impressions by offering a preliminary survey—tentative in places, for there is still work to be done—of provincial government in later Stuart England, confining our attention largely to the efforts of the county justices, the activities of town corporations, and the contacts between the localities and the central government. The first task is to examine the performance of the local authorities during the months following the Restoration and then to consider how effectively they undertook their main duties: the enforcement of statutes and the provision of a few rudimentary public services.

[1] A. M. Everitt, *The Local Community and the Great Rebellion* (Historical Association, 1969), 8; G. E. Aylmer, *The State's Servants* (1973), 305–17; G. C. F. Forster, 'County Government in Yorkshire during the Interregnum', *Northern History*, xii (1976), 104; M. Beloff, *Public Order and Popular Disturbances 1660–1714* (Oxford, 1938), 2; J. R. Western, *The English Militia in the Eighteenth Century* (1965), 27.

The political upheavals of the early months of 1660 temporarily halted the normal processes of local government, as is shown by interruptions in the sequence of meetings of quarter sessions and town corporations and is reflected in the widespread and clear efforts made, especially by J.P.s, to reestablish the routine of government once assemblies of local governors had restarted, usually during the late summer of that year. The first thing to be settled, however, was the identity and authority of the office-holders themselves. There was much uncertainty about the government of corporate towns. The titles to office of aldermen and other corporators, even the status of recently granted borough charters, were open to question, but an additional difficulty was that town corporations themselves, by charter, filled the vacancies on their own governing bodies. To some extent individual action had produced a solution. The mayor of Maidstone, a participant in the trial of Charles I, prudently fled. At High Wycombe all the acting corporation resigned on the day Charles II landed, to make way for those members displaced during the Interregnum. Local agreements at Shrewsbury and Great Yarmouth allowed excluded aldermen to resume office, and at Chester three aldermen were dismissed without acrimony. In other towns proceedings were less amicable. There was a fierce dispute between ex-Royalist and ex-Cromwellian factions at Newcastle. Charges of obstruction were made at Warwick, and royal pressure for an accommodation was required at York and Lincoln before ex-aldermen could resume their places. Whatever was accomplished by these means it remained true that town corporations all over the country were still in the hands of men whose loyalty to the restored monarchy was by no means certain. The government therefore devised the Corporation Act which imposed oaths and a sacramental test on municipal office-holders; those refusing to conform were expelled, and even some conformers lost office on the grounds of public safety. By these means sweeping changes were made in the governing bodies of towns, and a useful precedent was set for the future.[2]

In the counties at large the government was of course free to nominate or displace the justices, and it naturally took the first oppor-

[2] For a general account, see: J. H. Sacret, 'The Restoration Government and Municipal Corporations', *Engl. Hist. Rev.*, xlv (1930), 232–59; W. A. H. Schilling, 'The Central Government and the Municipal Corporations in England, 1642–1663', (Ph.D. thesis, Vanderbilt University, 1970). For individual towns, see: A. M. Johnson, 'Politics in Chester during the Civil Wars and the Interregnum, 1640–62', in *Crisis and Order in English Towns 1500–1700*, ed. P. Clark and P. Slack (1972), 228–31; R. Howell, *Newcastle upon Tyne in the Puritan Revolution* (Oxford, 1967), 185–6; P. Styles, 'The Corporation of Warwick, 1660–1835', *Transactions of the Birmingham Archaeological Society*, lix (1938), 29–31; G. C. F. Forster, 'York in the 17th century', in V.C.H., *City of York*, 174, 176; J. W. F. Hill, *Tudor and Stuart Lincoln* (Cambridge, 1956), 171–4.

tunity to remodel the commissions of the peace. The changes were extensive. In the West Riding, of seventy-six justices (excluding dignitaries) in the last commission of the Interregnum only fourteen were named in the first commission of the Restoration; in the North Riding eleven of fifty-seven J.P.s were reappointed; in the East Riding only eight of fifty-five. Similar figures are found elsewhere. In Warwickshire only ten justices were appointed to both the pre-Restoration and the post-Restoration lists; in Lincolnshire only one fifth of the J.P.s of the later '50s survived; in Sussex thirty-five justices were dropped; in Wiltshire forty-six met a similar fate. The most extreme case was Shropshire, where only one of the Interregnum justices was reappointed in 1660.[3] The commissioned justices predictably included a considerable proportion of former Royalists, some of them bent on revenge, with an admixture of 'Presbyterians' and moderate Cromwellians together with newcomers to the bench. This purge placed magisterial authority largely in untried hands although in some counties—Sussex and the three Ridings of Yorkshire, for example—the return to the bench of pre-war J.P.s to join the handful of survivors from the 1650s no doubt brought some measure of administrative experience to the justices' proceedings.

In county government the urgent need was to return to normal, and throughout 1660–2 the emphasis was on businesslike methods and continuity with the pre-war era. Thus when regular meetings of quarter sessions were resumed the justices quickly sought to reassert discipline over subordinate office-holders, and to fill vacancies, although there are few signs of a purge. The J.P.s also tried to trace monies lately levied for national, county or parochial purposes by calling receivers of public funds to account for their receipts during the 1650s. This task was not easy: in the West Riding the J.P.s were still trying to recover such accounts for audit in 1665, and similar delays in recovering arrears were reported in Devon. In an attempt to settle local rating disputes the justices of Wiltshire and the North and West Ridings decided to use the pre-war rate-book, cancelling all changes made in the 1650s.[4] Unfortunately no move of that kind

[3] Forster, 'County Government in Yorkshire during the Interregnum' p. 103; *Warwick County Records*, ed. S. C. Ratcliff and H. C. Johnson, iv, pp. xvi–xvii; C. Holmes, *Seventeenth-Century Lincolnshire* (Lincoln, 1980), 219; A. Fletcher, *A County Community in Peace and War: Sussex, 1600–1660* (1975), 134; J. Hurstfield, 'County Government c. 1530–c. 1660', in V.C.H., *Wiltshire*, v. 109; D. C. Cox, 'County Government 1603–1714', in V.C.H., *Shropshire*, iii. 92.

[4] West Yorkshire Record Office (henceforth W.Y.R.O.), West Riding (henceforth W.R.) Sessions Order Book, F, ff. 8, 13–16, 21, 27, 31–2, 49, 61, 62, 75; G, f. 4; North Yorkshire Record Office (henceforth N.Y.R.O.), QSM 2/11, ff. 271, 306 ff; A. H. A. Hamilton, *Quarter Sessions from Queen Elizabeth to Queen Anne* (1878), 207–8; W. R. Ward, 'County Government, 1660–1835', in V.C.H., *Wilts.*, v. 190.

could solve a major difficulty which always underlay their work: shortage of money. The sums required—for poor relief, the houses of correction or bridges—were raised *ad hoc*, on a wholly unco-ordinated basis, and there was ample opportunity for argument, evasion and delay. Local benches spent much time in trying to enforce payment, with limited success, and this aspect of their duties expanded because of the excise and the hearth tax. From time to time they found themselves checking lists of chargeable hearths, helping collectors by putting pressure on defaulters or, alternatively, dealing with complaints against the extortionate methods of excise collectors or 'chimney-men'.[5]

Magisterial support for government officials was, of course, not new, and in much of the work of J.P.s under Charles II and James II there is a striking degree of continuity with earlier times. Thus the most important routine task of the J.P.s remained the maintenance of law and order and the punishment of petty crime; more serious offences were left to assizes. During the period serious breaches of public order—riots and attacks on officials, for example—broke out sporadically but were firmly dealt with.[6] Scandalous words against the regime or, more seriously, plotting and open disaffection drew the interest not only of J.P.s and sheriffs but also of the government, keen to counter any public defiance.

Two dissident groups called for particular measures. Fear and hatred of Popery had long been reflected in records of the courts. The conviction of Roman Catholic recusants by quarter sessions had continued at intervals until the Civil War but then seems for the most part to have lapsed. The old procedures were slowly revived after 1660 (as Dr Miller has shown) but in the early years very little happened beyond occasional presentments of recusants in quarter sessions and assizes, or calls for the disarming of Papists. On the whole the J.P.s proved unwilling to enforce the recusancy laws—often against their kinsmen, friends and neighbours—without specific government orders. These came in 1673–4 and resulted in lengthy presentments, fines and some confiscations in the years following. Still the 'recusant service' was undermined by the familiar difficulties revealed in county records: the failure of officers to make presentments, or to levy fines; obstruction by juries; confusion about the technicalities of procedure on the part of magistrates and sheriffs. About 1680 the Popish Plot goaded central and local authorities into more vigorous action against recusancy but although lengthy presentments were again made, even

[5] W.Y.R.O., W.R. Sessions Order Book, F, ff. 96, 155; G, f. 58; N.Y.R.O., QSM 2/14, f. 281; 2/15, ff. 113, 115; *North Riding Quarter Sessions Records*, ed. J. C. Atkinson (1884–9), vi, 270, 277–8, 280; vii. 2–3; Hamilton, *Quarter Sessions*, 203–5, 224.

[6] Beloff, *Public Order*, 76, 92–4.

during the tense years 1679–81 the J.P.s often showed some reluctance to act, and the results seem to have fallen short of intentions. Moreover the pressure against the Roman Catholics was reduced even before James II's reign began and in the face of strong royal discouragement the campaign slackened soon afterwards.[7]

Repressive moves against Nonconformity also alternated with periods of relaxation. The task of persecution probably appealed to loyal Anglican gentry lately returned to the magistracy and motivated by a strong spirit of revenge, and some J.P.s—in Lincolnshire and the West Riding, for example—gained notoriety for their harshness; on the other hand some moderate J.P.s and sympathetic parish officers were able to temper the effects of the law. In Yorkshire and elsewhere the tense early 1660s, especially the years 1664–7, saw one peak of persecution backed by enthusiasm for the provisions of the so-called Clarendon Code, but the number of prosecutions fluctuated from year to year, partly no doubt as a reflection of national politics; in the West Riding the Quakers were often the worst sufferers. For a time after Charles II's abortive Declaration of Indulgence the prosecution of Noncomformists for attending conventicles ran in parallel with the attack on recusants, but the onslaught faltered in the late 1670s, perhaps because of preoccupation with the Papists. A renewed offensive, stimulated by a Privy Council order, began in 1681, and everywhere there was mounting pressure on Dissenters for some four years: the suppression of conventicles and illicit meeting-houses; searches by militia officers of homes and seizure of papers; long lists of prosecutions in court. By 1686, however, this onslaught too had faltered and effective persecution of Nonconformists—in Yorkshire, Lincolnshire, Wiltshire, Warwickshire and probably other counties too—was at an end.[8]

Apart from these spasmodic and centrally enforced campaigns against recusants and Nonconformists, however, little attention was now paid to private beliefs and behaviour by the local courts. Judicial enforcement of Sabbatarian rules had gone out of fashion; personal morality was left to the ecclesiastical authorities. Only heavy drink-

[7] W.Y.R.O., W.R. Sessions Order Book, G, ff. 66, 73; I, ff. 18ff, 189; K, f. 105; N.Y.R.O., QSM 2/14, ff. 87 ff; 2/16, ff. 98b, 122, 161 ff, 165, 185; Hamilton, *Quarter Sessions*, 179, 182–6, 222; *Warwick County Records*, vii, pp. lxix, lxxii–lxxvii; J. Miller, *Popery and Politics in England 1660–1688* (Cambridge, 1973), chap. 3.

[8] W.Y.R.O., W.R. Sessions Order Books, F–K, *passim*; N.Y.R.O., QSM 2/17, f. 11; Leeds City Archives, Mexborough MSS., Reresby Correspondence, 18, ff. 15, 21, 85, 96; 28 ff. 8, 21–2; R. M. Faithorn, 'Nonconformity in Later Seventeenth-Century Yorkshire' (M.Phil thesis, Leeds University, 1982), chaps. 8 and 9; Hamilton, *Quarter Sessions*, 179–80, 182–6, 188–9, 192–6, 197–8, 222, 241; Holmes, *Lincolnshire*, 220–2, 228–34, 247; Ward, V.C.H., *Wilts.*, v. 183; *Warwick County Records*, vii, pp. lxix, lxxvii, lxxxi; ibid., viii, p. lxv.

ing—always linked in the minds of magistrates with misconduct of all kinds—still attracted their attention.

Much of the threat to domestic peace arose from poverty, unemployment and hunger, exacerbated temporarily by bad harvests, trade depression and plague. As before 1642 the authorities' actions showed a counterpoint of repression and relief. Measures in the early '60s to collect arrears of rates and force parish officers to fulfil their duties were an important step. Because repression of the undeserving poor was usually cheaper, and easier to organise, than relief it tends to bulk larger in the records. Harsh treatment for the parents of bastards continued to be ordered by justices out of sessions. The unending problem of vagrancy too was similarly met by attempts at repression. From time to time, as local circumstances (or a general fear of disorder at times of political tension) demanded, there was an energetic campaign against vagrants: in Middlesex, for example, during the '60s, and in all three Ridings of Yorkshire during the '70s and early '80s, when the J.P.s ordered regular searches for vagrants and the traditional 'whipping campaign'.[9] In part these measures against vagrants and 'undersettlers' (lodgers or squatters) were attempts to meet local difficulties about settlement rights and uncertainties about identifying the 'poor of the parish' who were entitled to parochial poor relief. The provisions of the Poor Law (or Settlement) Act of 1662 concerning the conditions for removal of those likely to become chargeable to the parish in which they had arrived codified existing practice. By legalising the removal of newcomers, subject to an appeal to quarter sessions, the Act neverthelesss greatly added to the burden on local magistrates and parish officers. Disputes about settlement and removal undoubtedly multiplied and a growing stream of appeals came before sessions: in the North Riding, for example, they became more frequent after 1671, and during the 1680s the West Riding magistrates were considering an average of eighteen settlement disputes a year.[10]

By statute and earlier practice, relief for the deserving poor took several forms but by the Restoration period, if not before, one, the provision of raw materials and tools to enable the workless poor to work and support themselves, had dropped out of use in most counties: it was difficult to organise and economically impracticable. Instead parish officers gave some weekly sums to those in need. If they proved

[9] E. G. Dowdell, *A Hundred years of Quarter Sessions* (Cambridge, 1932), 69–70; W.Y.R.O., W.R. Sessions Order Book, G, f. 36; H, ff. 18, 72, 177; K, ff. 87, 95, 96, 105; N.Y.R.O., QSM 2/13, ff. 74 ff; 2/15, ff. 180–1; G. C. F. Forster, *The East Riding Justices of the Peace in the Seventeenth Century* (East Yorkshire Local History ser., 30, York, 1973), 48.

[10] W.Y.R.O., W.R. Sessions Order Books, I and K, *passim*; N.Y.R.O., QSM 2/13 and 14, *passim*.

reluctant quarter sessions took a hand, and at most sessions in Yorkshire, Warwickshire, and Middlesex three or four orders for weekly relief were made during the '60s and '70s; the North Riding was one of the counties where these provision cases rose markedly in number during those decades, and where J.P.s were specially active in poor relief. Very occasionally justices used funds to pay for pauper apprenticeship or provide a cottage on the waste; they also continued to enforce the obligations of parish officers and the payment of local poor rates.[11]

One persistent and growing burden on scarce public monies was the provision of pensions for lame soldiers. During the '50s the number of lame soldiers' pensions and the size of the lame soldiers' funds had inevitably grown everywhere as ex-Parliamentarian soldiers were admitted to relief. They were all dropped in 1660 and were replaced by Royalist soldiers clamouring for pensions. In all the counties where information is available the demand for pensions grew, to the evident alarm of justices: the number in the West Riding tripled between 1660 and 1667. Frequent checks, more stringent rules, the removal of doubtful cases, were all to no avail; the obligation was unavoidable and was not reduced—by peace and natural causes—until the 1680s.[12] Other deserving poor continued to receive relief as occasion demanded—the victims of fire, or other personal disaster, or distressed people in places stricken by the plague; the sums provided were neither large nor regular, the J.P.s often showing a greater will to enforce quarantine precautions when plague threatened than to relieve sufferers when it spread.[13]

Although in these years much poor relief was mainly supervised by justices out of sessions, poor law administration continued to occupy much time at quarter sessions: petitions for relief, rating and settlement appeals, orders for the discharge of parochial responsibilities. But the government now exercised very little pressure for the enforcement of the law and left J.P.s to themselves. They issued few general orders, preferring to deal with poor relief business piecemeal. In Yorkshire and other parts of the country much depended on local initiative and local economic difficulties. The range of poor law matters administered by the J.P.s therefore tended to contract, to occasional cam-

[11] W.Y.R.O., W.R. Sessions Order Book, G, ff. 15, 27, 60, 66, 83–4, 162–4; H, ff. 74, 75, 79; see also Order Books, I, K, L, *passim*; N.Y.R.O., QSM 2/14, ff. 311 ff; 2/15, ff. 102, 115, 180–1; *Warwick County Records*, vii, *passim*; Dowdell, *A Hundred Years*, 44–5, 55–8, 61–2, 86–8; Ward, V.C.H., *Wilts.*, v. 182; Cox, V.C.H., *Shropshire*, iii. 104.

[12] W.Y.R.O., W.R. Sessions Order Book, F, ff. 21–2, 35, 72, 73, 74, 123, 168; G, ff. 5, 6, 7, 8, 45, 78 ff, 142; I, ff. 9–10, 60, 99; N.Y.R.O., QSM 2/12, ff. 30–2, 40–1, 61; 2/13, f. 63; 2/16, ff. 218, 239.

[13] W.Y.R.O., W.R. Sessions Order Book, F, f. 160; G, ff. 13, 17, 24, 36; *North Riding Quarter Sessions Records*, vi. 92–3; Hamilton, *Quarter Sessions*, 219.

paigns against vagrants, enforcement at the parish level, orders for individual relief and consideration of appeals about settlement and removal.

Statutory economic controls aimed, like the poor laws, at social stability and public order had given the J.P.s extensive powers of interference in industry, employment and markets. As in earlier decades the J.P.s' response showed that much of the law was most likely to be applied in emergencies, or when it met clear local needs, however temporary. Thus the complicated industrial controls were almost a dead letter, less so in cloth producing areas, but even in Wiltshire and the West Riding there was not much action. Apprenticeship regulations, always more important in town than in county jurisdictions, were only enforced occasionally as the trickle of offenders in court records shows.[14] Economic developments were no doubt undermining the law.

The same could probably be said for much of the time about wage assessments and the enforcement of contracts of service. Yet it has long been clear (from Professor Kelsall's study and local records) that from time to time wage schedules were issued by justices; the courts then sought to enforce the wages assessed; and the J.P.s also tried to insist on the fulfilment of contracts of service between masters and men. The familiar case of the concerted enforcement in 1679 and after of a wage schedule in the North and East Ridings and Lincolnshire during a temporary labour shortage due to a local epidemic of agues, as well as other similar evidence, suggests the likelihood that all over the country, by the later seventeenth century at least, the J.P.s' interest in wage and service controls was stimulated more by abnormal labour conditions than by paternalism.[15]

The J.P.s were also charged by statute with the regulation of market dealing and with responsibility for supplying markets in times of dearth. The law could have given quarter sessions plenty of business but in practice now rarely did so, and only a handful of cases appears in post-Restoration records; for example in Wiltshire 'scarcity' orders in 1662 and 1675 reflected a local shortage of corn. In the absence of both central pressure and any prolonged, widespread dearth to impart a sense of urgency the laws about markets and trade were generally falling into disuse, to be used only when a local emergency arose.[16] The same could hardly be said, however, about the regulation of

[14] W.Y.R.O., W.R. Sessions Order Book, F, ff. 63, 118; H, ff. 80, 163, 194; Dowdell, *A Hundred Years*, 159, 173.

[15] W.Y.R.O., W.R. Sessions Order Book, F, ff. 72, 76; G, ff. 128, 136, 170; H, ff. 35 ff, 72, 94; I, ff. 162, 183; K, f. 123; N.Y.R.O., QSM 2/12, ff. 76, 78, 87; 2/16, ff. 149, 164, 184, 192–4, 195–6; R. K. Kelsall, *Wage Regulation under the Statute of Artificers* (1938), 7, 11, 16–18, 29–30, 93–5, 96–8.

[16] Ward, V.C.H., *Wilts.*, v. 184.

alehouses, those 'nurseries of naughtiness' in Lambard's words. The J.P.s made continuing efforts to enforce the licensing laws, and to discourage 'inordinate drinking'. On their initiative occasional campaigns were undertaken against unlicensed alehouses and efforts were made to stop their proliferation, especially at politically tense times (when they could be used for suspect gatherings). Perhaps the most important measure made at this time, however, was the step taken by J.P.s in many counties to counteract abuses in ale-selling by concentrating the business of licensing in special alehouse sessions.[17]

Road and bridge repairs also called for unremitting activity. In supervising parochial road repairs, the justices in and out of sessions seldom made any general orders or supplied any initiative. Instead they fined defaulters, whether individuals or parishes, and imposed suspended (or conditional) fines, large enough to be an incentive to the fulfilment of parochial obligations. In the '70s the temporary road rate instituted by statute was widely administered but magistrates had to wait until the act of 1691 for permanent permission to raise a road rate when necessary. In the meantime the frequency of road repair cases at sessions shows that the system of statute labour was far from satisfactory. In connection with bridge repairs the justices had wider powers and more direct responsibilities. Bridge repairs were an unending and expensive problem: considerable sums had to be levied for work done; and the repeated presentment of some bridges as 'decayed' is a sign of inadequate surveying, repair and supervision. As bridge rates became, therefore, an insistent burden on county finance it is not surprising that in many counties J.P.s began to dispense with legal formalities, to arrange regular inspections, undertake work in advance of court orders and even establish a permanent bridge fund.[18]

As the records of several counties show, this innovation is only one of the newer methods of county administration being adopted during the later seventeenth century. Another is the rapid spread of, and the extensive delegation of business to, petty (or divisional) sessions, a development of earlier practice apparently favoured by Lord Chancellor Clarendon himself. Petty sessions assisted with the 'sifting and settling' of local business and gave justices a more direct and immediate control over the parishes and their officers. Parallel to petty sessions were special licensing sessions (whose value has already been

[17] N.Y.R.O., QSM 2/14, f. 19–21, 96 ff, 317; 2/16, f. 118; *Warwick County Records*, vii, pp. lxvi–lxvii; Ward, V.C.H., *Wilts.*, v. 179.

[18] 22 Charles II, c. 12 and 3 William and Mary, c. 12; W.Y.R.O., W.R. Sessions Order Book, F, ff. 8, 13–16, 75, 105, 124, 170; G, ff. 56, 142; H, ff. 78, 196; K, ff. 81–2, 118, 145, 155; N.Y.R.O., QSM 2/11, ff. 271, 306 ff; 2/15, f. 179; 2/17, ff. 31, 69; 2/18, f. 23; Dowdell, *A Hundred Years*, 95–6, 102–3; B. E. Harris, 'County Government 1660–1888', in V.C.H., *Cheshire*, ii. 69–70; Ward, V.C.H., *Wilts.*, v. 173, 175; Cox, V.C.H., *Shropshire*, iii. 101, 103.

mentioned). Another development was the use of committees of justices for audit and other purposes; they reduced the burden on quarter sessions and speeded up their work. In some counties there are signs of greater formality in the court's proceedings and even the use of printed forms for routine paperwork. Above all—in Shropshire, Wiltshire, Devon, Warwickshire, Cheshire and the West Riding, at least—there were experiments with a regular, permanent general fund for various county purposes to make collection and accounting easier, as well as the beginnings of a permanent, or semi-permanent, salaried county treasurer. Such innovations provided more flexibility and a better administrative routine, but they were as yet by no means fully or permanently established—in some counties the 1690s seem to have been a crucial period—and otherwise there were no far-reaching changes in structure or procedure.[19]

Moreover if the county magistrates held the initiative in some matters, in others their time was either spent in compelling subordinate officers to do their duty or in settling disputes. They issued (as we have seen) few general enforcement orders, and sessions dealt almost entirely with individual cases: in Professor Ward's words 'piecemeal business, piecemeal decisions'. Inevitably, perhaps, given the small funds and inadequate bureaucracy, the tendency noted even in the early decades of the seventeenth century for the J.P.s' work to become narrower in scope was by now more marked. They tended to concentrate on a few particularly pressing local problems: petty crime and punishment, vagrancy, bastardy, settlement, deserving claims for poor relief, aleselling, roads, bridges, rating disputes and the supervision of parish and other local officers. Wider controls of economic activity and social or religious regulations were enforced chiefly under the stimulus of circumstances in each county or in response to central pressure.[20] Otherwise a limited number of tasks was partly tackled regularly, partly with occasional bouts of enthusiasm rather than sustained initiative: much of the J.P.s' work was of a reflex nature prompted by the pressure of local circumstances which could be stronger and more effective than central supervision.

The governing bodies of the corporate towns enforced the same statutes and shared some of the same concerns as the county justices.

[19] W.Y.R.O., W.R. Sessions Order Book, G, ff. 45, 46; I, ff. 55, 69, 93; H and K, *passim*; W.R. Sessions Rolls, 1680–85; *Warwick County Records*, vii, pp. xxxviii–xl; Ward, V.C.H., *Wilts.*, v. 173–5, 180–1; Cox, V.C.H., *Shropshire*, iii. 98, 100, 101, 103; Harris, V.C.H., *Cheshire*, ii. 69; S. K. Roberts, 'Participation and Performance in Devon Local Administration, 1649–1670' (Ph.D. thesis, Exeter University, 1980), 184, 185, 273, 277.

[20] Ward, V.C.H., *Wilts.*, v. 183; cf., G. C. F. Forster, 'The English Local Community and Local Government, 1603–1625', in *The Reign of James VI and I*, ed. A. G. R. Smith (1973), 195–213.

Study of a sample of town records and histories shows that they perhaps had a closer interest in some governmental tasks: in the regulation of dealers, markets and fairs; in apprenticeship and gild ordinances for local handicrafts. Some towns, like Bedford and Coventry, showed an independent attitude to the persecution of Nonconformists. On the other hand there remained a stronger vein of paternalism and control in town government: towns were more tightly knit communities (at least until late in the seventeenth century) than counties, and this made the regulation of their citizens' behaviour easier. So too did their much smaller areas of jurisdiction, frequent council meetings, paid officials and (in many towns) rating powers. It is perhaps a commonplace that many towns provided important municipal services: piped water supplies, fire precautions, scavenging and health regulations, market halls, and extra market places. Town corporations also actively upheld local interests and jurisdiction but because they were, in the conduct of much of their business, free of the shackles of legal procedures, they were able to do more. Countless examples of municipal enterprise could be cited, but a few must suffice: Worcester's elaborate 'improvements' for a royal visit (which never took place); Exeter's scheme to reconstruct the canal and repair the quay, as well as Lincoln's plans for the navigability of the Fossdyke; Leeds's attempt to unify poor relief in all the chapelries of the huge parish; numerous urban schemes to provide work for the poor; Ipswich's campaign to attract immigrant craftsmen; the decision of Coventry in 1678 to establish the town waits and institute the Lady Godiva procession, which became a focus of local patriotism. There were municipally encouraged changes of a negative kind too: in some towns there was declining emphasis on gild membership and freedom, which probably came to mean less; municipal protectionism was being slowly dismantled in the face of economic development and as a consequence of the apparent decrease in the frequency of prolonged dislocation of town economies. It seems clear that town governors were adaptable and usually mindful of their civic duties and of the general interests of their towns.[21] Town and county government alike was nevertheless

[21] M. Mullett, 'The Internal Politics of Bedford 1660–1688', (Bedfordshire Hist. Rec. Soc., 59, 1980) 3–7, 11, 17; P. Styles, 'The Corporation of Bewdley under the later Stuarts' and 'The City of Worcester during the Civil Wars, 1640–60', in P. Styles, *Studies in Seventeenth Century West Midlands History* (Kineton, 1978), 45–57, 256–7; W. B. Stephens, *Seventeenth Century Exeter* (Exeter, 1958), 90–1, 95–9; Hill, *Tudor and Stuart Lincoln*, 206–9, 214; G. C. F. Forster, 'The Early Years of Leeds Corporation', *Publication of the Thoresby Society*, liv (1977), 256–60; E. M. Hampson, *The Treatment of Poverty in Cambridgeshire, 1597–1834* (Cambridge, 1934), 61–5; Forster, V.C.H., *York*, *passim*; M. Reed, 'Seventeenth-century Ipswich', in *Country Towns in pre-industrial England*, ed. P. Clark (Leicester, 1982), 120–3, 125; D. K. Bolton, 'Social history to 1700' (Coventry), in V.C.H., *Warwickshire*, viii. 219; C. R. Elrington *et al.*, 'Tewkesbury Borough', in V.C.H., *Gloucestershire*, iii. 149.

hampered by the same familiar failings: negligent officers, undemanding supervision, shortage of money, delays and obstruction, collusion between officers and local people to evade obligations or the law. Much of their work was, moreover, tempered by localism, giving priority to the supposed needs and interests of the local community at some cost to wider concerns: localism could undermine efficiency—as it did, for example, in the prolonged dispute about the liability to the hearth tax of the Yorkshire cutlers' forges[22]—and it was not easy to combat.

A great deal of work was nevertheless done by town corporations and J.P.s. Between 1665 and 1685, for example, the West Riding Quarter Sessions alone issued an average of about two hundred administrative orders a year; this leaves out of account strictly criminal cases and the orders of petty sessions and single justices.[23] It is a total which could no doubt be matched elsewhere. Much of the work was done on their own initiative, without central direction, and it is not hard to understand why. First, although many J.P.s seem never to have attended quarter sessions—that criticism does not apply to aldermen in town corporations—a considerable number did and many appeared regularly: attendances of fifteen to twenty J.P.s at a single session were not uncommon. Consequently the county benches all had groups of particularly industrious J.P.s.[24] These men, with their counterparts in the governing bodies of towns, therefore shouldered the main burden of local government in the English provinces. However mixed their motives may have been—and in this period social and political aggrandisement and religious antagonism must not be overlooked—they clearly had a strong sense of public duty. During the later seventeenth century there seem to have been far fewer complaints about idle justices than under Elizabeth or James I. There were too some notable figures on Restoration commissions: Sir Daniel Fleming, the indefatigable Westmorland justice; Henry Townshend in Worcestershire; Sir Peter Leicester with his well informed sessions charges; Sir John Reresby in Yorkshire. Reresby, admittedly a hot-tempered fellow, was a deputy lieutenant before he had undertaken any other public service, an active high sheriff and governor of York, a very conscientious J.P., who postponed being sworn until he had read some law, who attended quarter and petty sessions with some

[22] *The Memoirs of Sir John Reresby*, ed. A. Browning (Glasgow, 1936), 104–5, 348; J. D. Purdy, 'The Hearth Tax Returns for Yorkshire' (M.Phil. thesis, Leeds University, 1975), chap. 2.

[23] The figures are derived from W.Y.R.O., W.R. Sessions Order Books, F to K and N.Y.R.O., QSM 2/14 and 15.

[24] Harris, V.C.H., *Cheshire*, ii. 62; Cox, V.C.H., *Shropshire*, iii. 95; Ward; V.C.H., *Wilts.*, v. 177; see also note 23.

regularity, and initially used his considerable influence in support of the cutlers of his native South Yorkshire in the hearth-tax dispute; he was active in political and military affairs too.[25]

Reresby's wish to read the law provides a second clue. No one who held public office could be unmindful of parliamentary statutes. County benches bought published collections of statutes, and they—if not yet perhaps all town corporations—were advised by legally-trained clerks of the peace. They could also refer to the many legal manuals available since the later sixteenth century; of these Dalton's *Countrey Justice* and Shephard's *Sure Guide for his Majestie's Justices of the Peace* were perhaps the best known.[26]

The law of the land was one of the major links between local governors and central government, and in this period important legislation like the Settlement Act, the Clarendon Code and the Game Law materially added to the labour of magistrates. There were other means, of varying effectiveness, by which national government could influence the conduct of local affairs: the royal judges on assize; lords lieutenant; the new standing army; the Privy Council in general and the Secretaries of State in particular. The assize judges were, of course, crucially important in the field of crime and punishment, and their advice on legal technicalities, as well as their adjudication of difficult problems like the apportionment of rates, was probably welcome to local authorities. As the 1680s showed, they could be a formidable means of government influence, given the will. But there were limitations, sometimes forgotten: their twice-yearly visits to any one county were of short duration (usually two or three days), and they themselves were dependent on instructions. After the Restoration the central government, for the most part, made less use of them as a means of central pressure than before. Consequently the judges issued fewer general administrative orders at assizes; they became less important in routine government, and even their role in supervising and reporting on the magistrates was being partly left to the lords lieutenant.[27]

[25] A. Macfarlane, *The Justice and the Mare's Ale* (Oxford, 1981); 'Henry Townshend's "Notes of the Office of a Justice of the Peace", 1661-3', ed. R. D. Hunt, in *Miscellany*, ii (Worcestershire Hist. Soc., new ser., v, 1967), 68-137; *Charges to the Grand Jury at Quarter Sessions, 1660-1677, by Sir Peter Leicester*, ed. E. M. Halcrow (Chetham Soc., 3rd ser., v, 1953); Reresby, *Memoirs, passim.*

[26] M. Dalton, *The Countrey Justice* (1661 and other editions); W. Shephard, *A sure guide for his Majecties Justices of the Peace* (1663).

[27] P.R.O., PC 2/65/123; PC/67/24, 29, 64; PC/68/475; Ass. 24/23, 28; J. S. Cockburn, *A History of English Assizes, 1558-1714* (Cambridge 1972), chap. 8; Cox, V.C.H., *Shropshire*, iii. 90; Ward, V.C.H., *Wilts.*, v. 172. For the less close association between the judges and the Lancashire J.P.s during the assizes, see *Proceedings of the Lancashire Justices of the Peace at the Sheriff's Table during Assize Week, 1578-1694*, ed. B. W. Quintrell (Lancashire and Cheshire Rec. Soc., cxxi, 1981).

On the reconstitution of the lieutenancy at the Restoration the lords lieutenant, as Court magnates in many cases, with strong local connections, resumed their pre-war role as a channel of influence, patronage and pressure in local affairs. Much of their importance lay in their command of the county militias, re-established under Charles II, and their Court connections could mean that contact between the central government and the local militias was closer than with civil administrators. The militia's prime task, as the late Professor Western has shown, was that of police, and although there was little pressure on lords lieutenant to organise regular training, the lieutenancy establishment was quickly stimulated to action by the Privy Council when its interest was aroused by political tensions, plots and threats to public order. To these periodic bouts of activity several lieutenancy books bear witness: seizure of arms and arrest of suspects gave the militia successes in frustrating uprisings in the tense '60s (notably in Yorkshire) as well as in the repression of disaffection and in attacks on conventicles later on. The militia even played a useful part in containing Monmouth's Rebellion, although by that time it was being overtaken in its policing function by the new standing army. Under Charles II the regiments and garrisons played an effective but limited role in collaboration with the lieutenancy, the militia and the justices. The army's activities expanded considerably under James II, undermining the militia (which was allowed to decay), lengthening and strengthening the reach of the central government, and enforcing law and order in the King's interest.[28]

The mainsprings of military activity and policing were the initiative and pressure of a frequently nervous government. If threats to public order attracted the close attention of the Privy Council and the Secretaries of State so too did religious disloyalty. The local campaigns against Dissent and Popery were galvanised into action by Privy Council orders and royal proclamations supported by growing numbers of letters to local governors, although there seems to have been no heavy pressure for reports on results. The campaigns at different times against political and religious disaffection alone show that the Privy Council had not lost the ability to enforce its will in the conduct of local government. But apart from security and religious persecution, in the wider and less sensitive fields of local affairs the Council was no doubt hampered by the diminution of its coercive powers caused by the abolition of Star Chamber and the Council in the North and the reduction of the Council of Wales to the status of a civil court. Nevertheless, contrary to the belief of some historians, the central govern-

[28] Beloff, *Public Order*, 141–50; Western, *English Militia*, chaps. 2 and 3; N.Y.R.O., Wombwell MSS., DV, viii; J. C. R. Childs, *The Army, James II and the Glorious Revolution* (Manchester, 1980), 6–10, 84–5, 100–12.

ment maintained an interest in the actions of local authorities. The records are full of detailed advice to J.P.s, sheriffs, and corporations about a host of social and economic matters—petty crime, tax collection, plague precautions, smugglers, tobacco growing, woollen burials—together with innumerable petitions for help and redress of grievances.[29] Small beer, no doubt; but certainly not complete detachment from the work of local office-holders. Central intervention was, however, spasmodic and usually no more than a response to individual or localised difficulties: it was 'piecemeal' government again. Undoubtedly economic development and the absence of prolonged periods of widespread dearth obviated the necessity for Books of Orders on scarcity or poor relief. But the intermittent issue of a very limited range of proclamations and general enforcement measures reflects a distinct diminution in government initiative. On many matters government supervision had always been negative rather than positive, but after 1660 conciliar interest in general direction and control waned and more was left to the decisions of local governors themselves. About those measures however, in which the later Stuart regime had the strongest interests, experience showed that even with heavy central pressure the government did not find it easy to secure a rapid response: its expressed wishes could easily fall on the deaf ears of local governors.

As James, when Duke of York, commented it was 'an age to try men and know them'.[30] In part of its programme of centralisation and the extension of royal authority during the 1680s, therefore, the government began to focus attention on office-holders themselves. Thanks to the researches of Dr Glassey no detailed treatment of the remodellings of the commission of the peace is needed here. Suffice it to say that although there was nothing new about 'purges' of individual J.P.s for inactivity or political opposition—the precedents of the 1650s and 1660 were still within living memory—the changes in the commissions in 1679–81 and 1687–8 were not partial or routine, they were *general* remodellings conducted by the government for all, or almost all, counties together; in 1687–8 they were complicated by further alterations introduced by the 'regulators'. By the autumn of 1688 the commissions of the peace were no longer dominated by Tory-Anglican gentry but included significant numbers of Catholics, Dissenters and ex-Exclusionists, whose commissioning was an unwise step which

[29] These comments are based upon a sampling of P.R.O., PC 2/55 to 73; see also *Royal Proclamations of the Tudor and Stuart Sovereigns, 1485–1714*, ed. R. Steele, i (Bibliotheca Lindesiana, v, Oxford, 1910), *passim.*

[30] H.M.C., *Dartmouth*, i. 72.

strained the loyalty, and undermined the authority, of the traditional leaders of the county communities.[31]

In parallel with the remodelling of the commissions of the peace Charles II's government turned its attention to the corporations. The provincial towns posed two problems. One was the extent of the religious and political disaffection in some of them, including York, Coventry and Chester. The other was their independent powers of self-government which reduced royal authority and impeded the policy of centralisation. Historians have usually seen the 'borough campaign' of the 1680s as an attempt to tamper with the borough electorate in preparation for parliamentary elections. Without wishing to question that view one can fairly argue that, in the context of the times, the governmental aspect of the 'borough campaign' was at least as important as the political. A warrant of May 1661 provides an early clue: by its requirement for a measure of royal approval for future holders of municipal office it implied intrusion on borough independence. The workings of the Corporation Act gave, as we have seen, ample precedent for a general purge of unreliable office-holders. Moreover, however impressive the upheavals in the governing bodies of major towns during 1662–3 they may well have fallen short of what the royal government even then intended: royal remodelling of borough charters and constitutions was a prerequisite for control of municipal office-holders, magistracy, courts and administration. However, from the mid-1660s royal interference in the boroughs was mainly limited to occasional attempts to enforce the oaths and sacramental test required by the Corporation Act.[32] There are also signs of official pressure on towns to renew their charters, and when they did so the Crown usually nominated the first aldermen, recorder and town clerk in the new charters and reserved a right of veto over future nominees to the two last-named posts.[33] In 1680 there was renewed government pressure for town office-holders to take the required oaths and soon afterwards one of the judges, Sir Francis North (the future Lord Guilford), seems to have recommended a campaign to remodel borough charters and thereby enable the Crown to take control of nominations to aldermanships and the other major borough offices.[34]

The outcome was the *quo warranto* campaign against the boroughs,

[31] L. K. J. Glassey, *Politics and the Appointment of Justices of the Peace, 1675–1720* (Oxford, 1979), chaps. 2 and 3; *Warwick County Records*, viii, pp. xv, xvii–xx; Cox, V.C.H., *Shropshire*, iii. 92–3, 95.

[32] *Calendar of State Papers, Domestic, 1660–61*, 582; *Commons Journals*, viii. 310–12; *C.S.P.Dom. 1663–4*, 185; P.R.O., PC 2/56/338; PC/57/18, 130, 217, 268; PC/61/42–3, 46; *C.S.P.Dom. 1667–8*, 145; ibid., *1668–9*, 110, 111.

[33] P.R.O., PC 2/56/338; *C.S.P.Dom. 1663–4*, 185; *Sacret, E.H.R.*, xlv. 232–59.

[34] B.L., Add. MS. 32, 518, ff. 183–4; R. North, *Lives of the Norths*, ed. A. Jessopp (1890), i. 150 ff, 165–6.

some 120 of which were reincorporated with remodelled charters before the end of 1685. The Crown thereby achieved the power to purge the corporations along political and religious lines, nominating aldermen, clerks and recorders, with a right of veto over future nominees, and gaining the right to displace borough officers—elective or feed—in the future; in short, control of municipal administration and the borough courts. All the traditional means of central intervention were deployed against the towns. There were detailed government instructions.[35] Apart from hearing *quo warranto* proceedings in King's Bench judges on assize used direct pressure. Riding the northern circuit Lord Chief Justice Jeffreys put heavy pressure on corporations to surrender their charters and seek new ones: York failed to succumb to his notorious powers of persuasion, but 'Judge' Jeffreys successfully encouraged several other places—Newcastle, Lincoln, Pontefract, Liverpool, Preston, Carlisle—to follow his advice.[36] In other towns the county lieutenancy brought pressure to bear: all but one of eighteen Cornish corporations took new charters through the agency of Lord Bath, and Lord Yarmouth made Norwich the first major city to surrender. Some towns—including Beverley and York—were threatened by deputy lieutenants searching for conventicles and seizing arms. Even county magistrates played a part, having been encouraged officially to investigate governmental abuses in towns and infringements which called existing charters into question: Berwick, Salisbury, Ipswich are examples.[37] Finally, perhaps the most notorious and unprecedented encroachments on urban liberties were made by governors of military garrisons usually (as in the familiar cases of Hull, York and Chester) in collaboration with Tory factions in the towns themselves.[38] In some towns the remodelling involved heavy purges of

[35] P.R.O., PC 2/68/439, 455; Sacret, *E.H.R.*, xlv. 233, 240, 258.

[36] Forster, V.C.H., *City of York*, 174–5, 176; Leeds City Archives, Mexborough MS., Reresby Corr., 26, f. 18; Bodleian Library, Rawlinson MS., D. 850, f. 143; Hill, *Tudor and Stuart Lincoln*, 188–9; B.L., Add. MS. 12,037, f. 30 ff; M. Mullett, 'The Politics of Liverpool, 1660–88', *Transactions of the Hist. Soc. of Lancashire and Cheshire*, 124 (1973), 47 and 'The Search for Agreement in Preston Politics, 1660–90', ibid., 125 (1975), 75; *Some Municipal Records of the City of Carlisle*, ed. R. S. Ferguson and W. Nanson (Cumberland and Westmorland Ant. and Arch. Soc., extra ser., 1887), 17; H.M.C., 9th *Report*, i. 200.

[37] J. R. Jones, *The Revolution of 1688 in England* (1972), 161; J. T. Evans, *Seventeenth-century Norwich* (Oxford, 1979), 281–92; Forster, V.C.H., *City of York*, 174–5, 176, 193–4; Yorkshire Arch. Soc. Library, MS. DD 149, ff. 125–6; Reresby, *Memoirs*, 330; *C.S.P.Dom. 1683–4*, 143–4, 156–7, 168–9, 215–16; ibid., *1680–81*, 201, 505–6; ibid., *1684–5*, 11–12; *Beverley Borough Records, 1575–1821*, ed. J. Dennett (Yorkshire Arch. Soc. Rec. Ser., lxxxiv, 1933), 106, 170–2.

[38] G. C. F. Forster, 'Hull in the 16th and 17th centuries', V.C.H., *East Riding*, i, *City of Kingston upon Hull*, 114–15, 118–19; Forster, V.C.H., *City of York*, 174–5, 176, 193–4; Reresby, *Memoirs*, *passim*; *C.S.P.Dom. 1680–1*, 141; ibid., *1682*, 402, 420, 449, 458, 472; ibid., *1683–4*, 166; ibid., *1684–5*, 38–9.

the corporations (e.g. at Liverpool and York); in others (e.g. Hull, Chester and Oxford) only small changes were involved; in Leeds no serving alderman was omitted.[39] No doubt the extent of the remodelling depended on local politics and rivalries as well as on the availability of suitable replacements, but further investigation of the point is needed. There was unquestionably a legacy of bitterness in some towns—Norwich, Newcastle, Liverpool, Preston and Bewdley among others—faction, and franchise disputes.[40] Moreover the powers of interference gained by the Crown in the borough campaign of 1681–5 left the remodelled corporations defenceless against James II's regulators in 1687–8. Their measures, recently described in detail by Professor J. R. Jones, were no mere epilogue: hundreds of corporators lost office and thirty-five borough charters were forfeited.[41]

The remodelling of town constitutions and county commissions shows what could be done by a determined government armed with its own powers, able to use paid agents, and prepared to mobilise one local institution against another. But the results were widespread inefficiency and confusion, for by the late summer of 1688 it was difficult to know who was in office and who out; not surprisingly the resentment of gentry and leading townsmen was intensified. The confusion was compounded by the King's decision to make concessions. Yet another general remodelling of the commissions led to an 'incomplete reversal' of the recent displacements.[42] In the towns the restoration was also incomplete: in most of them the constitution reverted to that of 1679 but legal technicalities gave rise to exceptions, and although the charters of York, Chester, Exeter and Winchester were reinstated by proclamation about a score of towns still had charters of questionable status at the end of the year.[43] By that time local government had fallen into chaos: there was much uncertainty in the magistracy and some refusals to serve; newly-chosen sheriffs lacked the legal power to act; the lieutenancy was under-

[39] Mullett, 'Politics of Liverpool', 47 ff; Forster, V.C.H., *City of York*, 175, 176; Forster, V.C.H., *City of Hull*, 118–19; *C.S.P.Dom. 1684–5*, 38–9; H. T. Dutton, 'The Stuart Kings and Chester Corporation', *Journal of the Chester Arch. Soc.*, 2nd ser., xxviii (1929), 194–203. V.C.H. *Oxfordshire*, iv, *City of Oxford*, 124; Forster, 'Leeds Corporation', 256.

[40] Evans, *Norwich*, 297, 317; R. Howell, 'Newcastle and the Nation: the seventeenth-century experience', *Archaeologia Aeliana*, 5th ser., viii (1980), 26–9; Mullett, 'Liverpool Politics', 47 ff and 'Preston Politics', 75 ff; Styles, *Studies*, 54–62.

[41] Jones, *Revolution of 1688*, chap. 6; R. H. George, 'The Charters Granted to English Parliamentary Corporations in 1688', *E.H.R.*, lv (1940), 47–56.

[42] Glassey, *Justices of the Peace*, 91–9.

[43] Jones, *Revolution of 1688*, 263–4; P.R.O., PC 2/72/752, 785, 786; George, *E.H.R.*, lv, 47–56.

mined by frequent dismissals and paralysed by the run-down of the militia.[44]

The extent of the breakdown in routine local government in 1688–9 is not always easy to discern because of the general confusion, repeated changes in personnel and short-lived commissions and charters. What follows can only be a brief and tentative estimate. 'Business as usual' probably lasted until the autumn of 1688: the records show regular meetings and much of the normal routine, thanks perhaps to the efforts of experienced local governors and clerks who had survived successive remodellings. In Shropshire quarter sessions did not meet for twelve months after Easter 1688 but elsewhere the interruptions began later; in the West and North Ridings and Devon the justices conducted less business than normal in 1688 and then failed to hold sessions until the summer of 1689; in Warwickshire sessions met earlier than that but recorded few decisions. An immediate task for the new regime was clearly the re-establishment of routine in county government. Protestant loyalists were nominated to lord lieutenancies and shrievalties, and after some delay new, politically neutral, commissions of the peace were issued, based less on central discrimination, more on local advice and influence. When sessions' meetings were resumed they turned again to the familiar tasks; the only novelties noted in the records were oath-taking to the monarchy and the licensing of Nonconformist chapels.[45] In most towns, however, the resumption of normal government took place earlier, for extruded corporators simply re-entered their places, but in some boroughs—including Salisbury, Bewdley, and Warwick—constitutional uncertainties about the charters were not legally removed for several years.[46] Despite the political factiousness sometimes engendered, there was no further threat to municipal administrative independence.

The campaign of the 1680s against the autonomy of the localgovernors was not the least serious attack on their position during the seventeenth century for it meant interference not with measures but with men. As such, it posed a fundamental threat to the standing, 'interest', and influence of gentry and leading townsmen, to the position of estab-

[44] Jones, *Revolution of 1688*, 266–7; Miller, *Popery and Politics*, 251–2; Glassey, *Justices of the Peace*, 97–9, 268–9.

[45] Glassey, *Justices of the Peace*, 92–4, 97–9, 263; Cox, V.C.H., *Shropshire*, iii, 96; Harris, V.C.H., *Cheshire*, ii. 83–4; W.Y.R.O., W.R. Sessions Book, L, ff. 69–147; N.Y.R.O., QSM 2/18, ff. 46, 56; *North Riding Quarter Sessions Records*, vii. 84–104; Reresby, *Memoirs*, 542–3; Hamilton, *Quarter Sessions*, 246; Holmes, *Lincolnshire*, 250–3.

[46] M. E. Ransome, 'City Government 1612–1835' (Salisbury), in V.C.H., *Wilts.*, vi. 106; Styles, *Studies*, 57–70, and 'Warwick Corporation', 16–17, 38–9; R. W. Dunning, 'Political and Administrative History 1545–1835' (Warwick), in V.C.H., *Warwickshire*, viii. 498–9.

lished ruling families. The collapse of that campaign, and especially the rapid stabilisation of local government in 1689–90 after the concentrated upheavals in local office-holding, testified to the force of custom and the strong spirit of local independence.

Tensions between central and local were an unavoidable part of government in seventeenth-century England—perhaps they still are. But with the limited means at its disposal—legal, bureaucratic, personal—the pressure of the central government on the localities was rarely long sustained even before 1642, or during the 1650s. For much of the time government, after 1660 as before, limited itself to routine, to haphazard involvement in the affairs of local officers, courts and people; bursts of central pressure were short and concentrated on matters of crucial importance—finance, security, religion. But the government had no free hand: it needed local cooperation and when that was forthcoming the system worked with least difficulty or opposition. Thus J.P.s and town corporations went on their own way for much of the time, cooperating with the government on a basis, no doubt, of the calculated advantages for their own districts. Local initiative was not simply permitted, it was expected to solve local problems in town and county: hence the striking continuity in some aspects of local administration. For their part local rulers seem to have accepted central pressure but defied centralisation, which undercut their interests and damaged the supposed interests of their localities. In carrying out their duties they were influenced by law and custom and very often by a sense of duty too. The county, and for that matter the town, communities enjoyed an independence tempered by wider concerns: if they were units of local autonomy they were, as the Webbs said long ago, also units of national obligation.[47]

[47] S. & B. Webb, *The Parish and the County* (1963), 40–1, 305–10.

ARBITRATION AND THE LAW IN ENGLAND IN THE LATE MIDDLE AGES

The Alexander Prize Essay

By Edward Powell, M.A., D.Phil.

READ 28 MAY 1982

THE central problem facing the student of public order in England in the late middle ages is to reconcile two conflicting lines of research. On one hand the institutional historians, through their studies of the central courts at Westminister, the provincial circuits of assize and gaol delivery and the justices of the peace and coroners in the counties, have proved beyond doubt the sophistication of the late-medieval legal system.[1] On the other hand the historians of crime have shown equally clearly that the courts were often incapable of keeping the peace or of doing justice.[2] Indeed the late-medieval period has long been notorious as one of widespread uncontained disorder. Reviewing the secondary literature on the subject Professor Bellamy concluded: 'Not one investigator has been able to indicate even a few years of effective policing in the period 1290–1485.'[3]

In seeking to explain the failure of the elaborate machinery of royal justice, historians have put forward two connected arguments. First, the demise of the general eyre and the rise of the J.P.s have been taken to signify a loosening of royal control over local government. According to this view judicial authority in the provinces was delegated from full-time justices in royal service to magnates and gentry whose own rivalries and conflicts created much of the disorder they were appointed to suppress.[4] Secondly it is argued that the institutions and

[1] A few of the more important works are: M. Blatcher, 'The Workings of the Court of King's Bench in the Fifteenth Century' (Ph.D. thesis, London Univ., 1936); M. Hastings, *The Court of Common Pleas in Fifteenth-Century England* (New York, 1947); R. F. Hunnisett, *The Medieval Coroner* (Cambridge, 1961); *Proceedings before the Justices of the Peace in the Fourteenth and Fifteenth Centuries*, ed. B. H. Putnam (Ames Foundation, 1938).

[2] J. G. Bellamy, *Crime and Public Order in England in the Later Middle Ages* (1972); E. L. G. Stones, 'The Folvilles of Ashby-Folville, Leicestershire, and their Associates in Crime', *Trans. Roy. Hist. Soc.*, 5th ser., vii (1957), 117–36; R. L. Storey, *The End of The House of Lancaster* (1966).

[3] Bellamy, *Crime and Public Order*, 3–4.

[4] Ibid., 2; A. R. Myers, *England in the Late Middle Ages* (2nd edn., Harmondsworth, 1963), 51–3; cf. B. A. Hanawalt, 'Fur-Collar Crime: the Pattern of Crime among the Fourteenth-Century English Nobility,' *Jnl. Soc. Hist.*, viii (1974–5), no. 4, 1–17.

processes of justice were systematically perverted to serve the ends of those whose wealth or might was the greatest—usually the very magnates and gentry who filled the commissions of the peace.[5]

In the past such an interpretation carried additional weight because it confirmed the prevailing picture of the late middle ages as a period of economic decline, political stagnation and royal weakness.[6] But as the traditional view of the period is called increasingly into question,[7] so too the problem of public order is coming to be reassessed.[8] The simplest but most fundamental point was made by the late K. B. McFarlane, when he refuted the opinion that the late middle ages saw a decline in standards of public order and law enforcement relative to those of previous centuries, so questioning whether the period deserves its reputation for exceptional disorder.[9] If McFarlane is right,[10] we can no longer dismiss the state of public order in late-medieval England as a temporary aberration attributable to short-term conditions, and the need to understand the functions and apparent inefficiency of the law courts becomes all the more acute.

The starting-point is to appreciate the limitations of royal power to enforce the law. Throughout the middle ages the Crown lacked the resources to maintain the standing army or salaried police force which would have been necessary to enforce a primarily punitive system of justice. The administration of justice depended instead on the co-operation of local society at all levels, with the scope for graft and inefficiency this entailed. In such circumstances, where the coercive apparatus serving the courts was weak and the influence of the local community powerful, it was inevitable that the mediatory, restitutive functions of justice would prevail over the punitive. Even today, as Dr Baker notes, '... the vast majority of cases commenced in the central courts never reach trial; the issue of a writ is as much an inducement to compromise as it is a threat to pursue the law to its conclusion'.[11]

The particular relevance of this observation to the late middle ages

[5] Bellamy, *Crime*, 12–29; cf. Hastings, *Common Pleas*, chap. 15, 'Delays and Hindrances to Justice'.

[6] The classic statement of this orthodoxy is to be found in W. Holdsworth, *A History of English Law* (1922–38) ii (4th edn., 1936), 406–18.

[7] e.g. by A. R. Bridbury, *Economic Growth: England in the Later Middle Ages* (1962); F. R. H. DuBoulay, *An Age of Ambition: English Society in the Late Middle Ages* (1970).

[8] See M. T. Clanchy, 'Law, Government and Society in Medieval England', *History*, lix (1974), 73–8; T. A. Green, 'The Jury and the English Law of Homicide, 1200–1600', *Michigan Law Review*, lxxiv (1976), 413–99.

[9] K. B. McFarlane, *The Nobility of Later Medieval England* (Oxford, 1973), 114–15.

[10] Research into thirteenth-century homicide suggests a level of violent disorder as high, and conviction rates as low as in the late middle ages: J. B. Given, *Society and Homicide in Thirteenth-Century England* (Stanford, 1977), 33–40, 91–9.

[11] *The Reports of Sir John Spelman*, ed. J. H. Baker (Selden Soc., xciii–xciv, 1976–7) ii. 91.

is evident from the failure of all but a tiny proportion of lawsuits initiated during the period to come to judgement. Dr Blatcher's studies of the court of King's Bench show that while twenty per cent of Crown Pleas heard in the court reached verdict, barely one per cent of private suits did so.[12] Similarly, in Common Pleas, Dr Hastings found that the overwhelming majority of entries on the plea roll recorded the non-appearance of parties summoned.[13] As a general estimate Dr Guth suggested that in Henry VII's reign less than ten per cent of suits initiated in King's Bench and Common Pleas came to judgement.[14] On the criminal side rates of appearance in court and of conviction were only a little better.[15] The irresistible conclusion is that in the late middle ages the vast majority of lawsuits were not terminated by a court judgement. We must seek their resolution elsewhere.[16]

Violent self-help is the only form of extra-judicial remedy for the settlement of disputes which has attracted much notice from historians. We have become familiar with a pattern of late-medieval dispute in which interminable and inconclusive litigation is punctuated by short bursts of violence and intimidation.[17] This traditional picture remains incomplete, however, for it takes little account of peaceful procedures for reaching a settlement out of court; its inadequacy is reflected in the unsatisfactory conclusion reached by Professor Bellamy, that '... many disputes ended only because the parties were bored, exhausted or dead'.[18] Between self-help and resort to law lay a variety of methods for extra-judicial compromise which have yet to receive the attention they deserve. Disputes could be settled by direct negotiation, by the mediation of third parties or by submission to the award of elected arbitrators.[19] Legal proceedings might therefore be

[12] Blatcher, 'King's Bench,' 216–19.

[13] Hastings, *Common Pleas*, 183.

[14] D. J. Guth, 'Enforcing Late-Medieval Law: Patterns in Litigation during Henry VII's Reign', in *Legal Records and the Historian*, ed. J. H. Baker (1978), 87.

[15] J. B. Post estimates that thirty per cent of offenders indicted at peace sessions appeared for trial: 'Criminals and the Law in the Reign of Richard II' (D.Phil. thesis, Oxford Univ., 1976), 15. Professor R. B. Pugh calculated that the conviction rate of those appearing at Newgate gaol deliveries during Edward I's reign averaged thirty per cent: 'Some Reflections of a Medieval Criminologist', *Proceedings of the British Academy*, lix (1973), 89.

[16] Cf. Guth, *loc. cit.*, 87: 'Most claims for trespass and debt [in King's Bench and Common Pleas] were never intended for judicial resolution. They merely armed plaintiffs with royal record and gave the means for formal, serious confrontations between parties out of court.'

[17] Bellamy, *Crime*, 117–19; A. Harding, *The Law Courts of Medieval England* (1973) 93–4; see R. Jeffs, 'The Poynings-Percy Dispute', *Bull. Inst. Hist. Res.*, xxxiv (1961), 148–64, for a detailed case study of such a dispute.

[18] *Op. cit.*, 117–18.

[19] Cf. Y. Bongert, *Recherches sur les Cours Laïques du Xe au XIIIe Siècle* (Paris, 1949), 98–111.

accompanied not merely by armed confrontation but also by peaceful deliberations leading to a settlement.

The aim of this paper is to reassess the functions of litigation in late-medieval England in the light of these alternatives, by exploring the use of arbitration procedures in conjunction with legal action. The occurrence during this period of arbitration, whereby the parties to a dispute agree to be bound by the award of certain mutually acceptable persons, has often been noted in passing,[20] and there can be little doubt of its widespread use throughout late-medieval society. The King, the Chancellor and the Council often resorted to it in their efforts to settle disputes which involved leading magnates or the great urban and ecclesiastical corporations of the realm. Cases of this kind include the Gloucester–Beaufort dispute of 1426,[21] the Devon–Bonville feud in the west country which was submitted to arbitration in 1441,[22] and the jurisdictional conflicts between the bishop of Ely and the abbot of Bury St Edmunds in 1418 and between the bishop and city of Exeter in 1447–8.[23] Arbitration was also popular among the county gentry for the resolution of property disputes,[24] and for the establishment of compensation for physical assault and homicide.[25] Canon law formally encouraged arbitration,[26] and the monastic and episcopal records of the time reveal that the Church frequently favoured the 'way of peace' over litigation.[27] The Chancellor of Oxford University was particularly active in arranging for civil suits within

[20] e.g. Storey, *House of Lancaster*, 87–8, 101, 113, 121, 125, 155, 185, 226–7; J. T. Rosenthal, 'Feuds and Private Peace-Making: a Fifteenth-Century Example', *Nottingham Medieval Studies*, xiv (1970), 84–90; A. J. Pollard, 'The Richmondshire Community of Gentry during the Wars of the Roses', in *Patronage, Pedigree and Power in Later Medieval England*, ed. C. D. Ross (Gloucester, 1979), 50–1.

[21] *Chronicles of London*, ed. C. L. Kingsford (Oxford, 1905), 88–94.

[22] Storey, *House of Lancaster*, 87–8.

[23] *Memorials of St. Edmund's Abbey*, ed. T. Arnold (Rolls series, 1896), 188–211; *Letters and Papers of John Shillingford*, ed. S. A. Moore (Camden Soc., New ser., ii, 1871).

[24] *Plumpton Correspondence*, ed. T. Stapleton (Camden Soc., iv, 1839), li–lii, lxxxix–xcv, cxix–cxxii, 22 n., 32 n., 98 nn., 210–11, 219–20 n., 221 n., 222–3 n.; *The Langley Cartulary*, ed. P. R. Coss (Dugdale Soc., xxxii, 1980), nos. 70, 444; *The Hylle Cartulary*, ed. R. W. Dunning (Somerset Rec. Soc., lxviii, 1968), nos. 156, 190.

[25] Storey, *House of Lancaster*, 155; *Plumpton Correspondence*, 3–4; Rosenthal, 'Private Peace-Making', 88–90.

[26] P. Caspers, 'Der Güte- und Schiedsgedanke im kirchliche Zivilgerrichtsverfahren' (Iur. Diss., Mainz, 1954).

[27] There is a vast body of evidence for ecclesiastical arbitration. See, for example, *Vetus Registrum Sarisberiense*, ed. W. H. R. Jones (R. S., 1884), i. 256–9; ii. 79–80. *The Coucher Book of Furness Abbey*, ed. J. Brownbill (Chetham Soc., New ser., lxxvi, 1916), 295–6, 353–4; *Gesta Abbatum Monasterii Sancti Albani*, ed. H. T. Riley (R. S., 1867–9) i. 423–5; ii. 13–16, 27–8, 163–70; iii. 246–8, 516–17, 528–9. *Register of Edmund Lacy, Bishop of Exeter, 1420–55*, ed. G. R. Dunstan (Canterbury and York Soc., 1963–72), i. 144–7, 167–75, 195–6; ii. 134–9; iii. 245–55, 271–2, 290–6, 311–15.

his jurisdiction to go to arbitration, but this was a duty incumbent upon any ecclesiastical judge.[28] In a similar way, city and borough courts were active in promoting arbitration, whether in disputes between private litigants or between craft and religious gilds.[29] Such procedures were especially suitable for settling commercial matters, particularly when one party was a foreign merchant or when business had taken place overseas.[30] Relations between master and apprentice or employer and wage-earner might also be regulated by arbitration,[31] and even, on occasion, those between landlord and tenant or lord and serf.[32]

What significance should we attach to this evidence? Two recent commentators, Professor Bellamy and Professor Storey, have interpreted resort to arbitration in the late middle ages as a temporary expedient forced on litigants by the paralysis of the legal system, and have adduced examples from the mid-fifteenth century as evidence of the collapse of royal authority during the Wars of the Roses.[33] There is reason, however, to doubt whether it was just a late-medieval, still less a purely fifteenth-century phenomenon. Well before our period, and long after it, arbitration was clearly in evidence as an alternative or supplement to litigation.

The forms and terminology characteristic of arbitration in the fourteenth and fifteenth centuries were developed by canon lawyers, under the influence of Roman law models, in the late twelfth century, and soon came into common use within the Church.[34] The two essen-

[28] *Registrum Cancellarii Oxoniensis, 1434–69*, ed. H. E. Salter (Oxford Hist. Soc., xciii–xciv, 1932), *passim.*

[29] *Calendar of Plea and Memoranda Rolls of the City of London*, ed. A. H. Thomas and P. E. Jones (Cambridge, 1926–61), *1323–64*, 20, 41, 158–9, 267; *1364–81*, 49–50, 86, 137, 169–70, 179–80, 201–2, 251–2; *1381–1412*, 75, 77, 82, 83, 108, 121–2, 136, 140–2, 146, 162–3, 179, 192, 207–8, 231, 239, 245, 274–5, 278–9, 302, 307, 314. *York Memorandum Book, 1388–1493*, ed. M. Sellers (Surtees Soc., cxxv, 1915), 14–17, 25–7, 35–7, 67–8, 70–3, 82–3, 93–4, 125–8, 162–4, 179–82, 219, 242–5, 270–1, 288–9, 296–7.

[30] *Cal. Plea and Mem. Rolls London, 1323–64*, 258–9; *1364–81*, 75–6, 158, 278, 279–80; *1381–1412*, 136. *Select Cases Concerning the Law Merchant, 1239–1633*, ed. H. Hall (Selden Soc., xlvi, 1930), 34–9, 53–62.

[31] *Cal. Plea and Mem. Rolls London, 1323–64*, 268, 278; *1364–81*, 280–1; *1381–1412*, 127–8. *Year Books of Richard II: 12 Richard II, 1388–89*, ed. G. F. Deiser (Ames Foundation, 1914), 37–8.

[32] *Gesta Abbatum S. Albani*, ed. Riley, ii. 163–70; *Calendar of Close Rolls, 1272–1485* (1892–1954), *1461–68*, 230–4; R. H. Hilton, *The English Peasantry in the Later Middle Ages* (Oxford, 1975), 67–8; *Year Books of Richard II: 11 Richard II, 1387–88*, ed. I. D. Thornley (Ames Foundation, 1937), 168–74.

[33] Bellamy, *Crime*, 118–19; Storey, *House of Lancaster*, 121–2.

[34] L. Fowler, 'Forms of Arbitration', *Proceedings of the Fourth International Congress of Medieval Canon Law* (1972), ed. S. Kuttner, 133–47; A. R. Julien, 'Evolutio Historica Compromissi in Arbitros in Iure Canonico', *Apollinaris*, x (1937), 187–232.

tial stages of arbitration procedure at canon law were the *compromissio*, or submission to arbitration, through which the parties bound themselves to observe the award of specified arbitrators, usually on pain of a large sum of money; and the arbitrators' award itself, the *arbitrium* (or *arbitratus*).[35] From an early date both stages were almost invariably committed to writing, and drafted in precise, formulaic terms designed to survive any subsequent challenge to the award in court. The *compromissio* defined the arbitrators' powers and the form of arbitration, identified the issues in dispute and usually set a term for completion of the award.[36] Procedure was in general left to the discretion of the arbitrators, and came to be loosely based on the main principles of trial procedure at canon law.[37] An early English example of canon law arbitration is provided by the dispute between the bishop of Worcester and Oseney abbey, referred to arbitrators by the bishop of Exeter, papal judge-delegate in the case, in 1173.[38]

The Church soon came to use these procedures in its dealings with the laity, as in the dispute of 1227 between Richard Harcourt and the dean and chapter of Salisbury over their respective rights in the church of Sherston.[39] An arbitration of this kind, involving the abbot of Fountains and Richard Percy on one side and William Percy on the other, is notable in that it sought to regulate affairs, not merely between the abbot and the Percys, but between the two Percys (uncle and nephew respectively) as well. Completed in 1219, the award was made by ten arbitrators, including three clerics, and was one of a number of attempts to resolve an inheritance dispute which had ranged Richard and William on opposite sides in the northern rebellion against King John.[40]

The spread of such procedures to disputes among the laity continued throughout the thirteenth and early fourteenth centuries, as is evidenced by cases from the *Curia Regis* rolls and early Year Books.[41]

[35] A distinction was recognised at canon law between an *arbitrium*, performed by *arbitri* whose award adhered closely to legal principles and could not be appealed; and an *arbitratus*, performed by *arbitratores* who might take equitable considerations into account and whose award could, in certain circumstances, be subject to appeal: Fowler, *loc. cit.*, 135–44. In practice, however, this distinction tended to become blurred: cf. H. Janeau, 'L'Arbitrage en Dauphiné au Moyen Age', *Revue Historique de Droit Français et Étranger*, 4th ser., xxiv–xxv (1946–7), 246.

[36] William de Drokeda, *Summa Aurea*, ed. L. Wahrmund (Quellen zur Geschichte des Römisch-Kanonischen Processes im Mittelalter, Bd. II, Heft II, Innsbruck, 1914), 189–90.

[37] Janeau, *loc. cit.*, 255–7; Bongert, *Cours Laïques*, 175–82.

[38] *Cartulary of Oseney Abbey*, ed. H. E. Salter (Oxford Hist. Soc., 1929–36), v. 3–4.

[39] *Vet. Reg. Sarisberiense*, ed. Jones, ii. 79–81.

[40] *The Percy Chartulary*, ed. M. T. Martin (Surtees Soc., cxvii, 1911), 54–7; cf. J. C. Holt, *The Northerners*, (Oxford, 1961), 21–2, 67.

[41] *Select Cases in the Court of King's Bench*, ii, ed. G. O. Sayles (Selden Soc., lvii, 1938),

During this period, however, these are comfortably outnumbered by examples of ecclesiastical arbitration drawn from monastic and episcopal records.[42] Only after 1350 does the evidence for secular arbitration increase dramatically, but since much of this evidence is to be found in those very sources whose abundance has given the late-medieval era such a bad name—the administrative and legal records of the Crown—it would be rash to equate such an increase with a comparable growth in the frequency of resort to arbitration.[43] Nor should it be implied that with the supposed restoration of order by the Tudors, arbitration procedures became unnecessary and fell into disuse. On the contrary, they enjoyed continued popularity at every level of society in the sixteenth and seventeenth centuries.[44] We must therefore resist the temptation to dismiss arbitration in the late middle ages merely as a product of the shortcomings of the legal system. Instead it should be considered in the longer perspective as one phase of a vigorous and durable tradition of extra-judicial settlement.

The long-standing popularity of arbitration in medieval and early-modern England should occasion no surprise, for it possessed several advantages which made it an attractive alternative to litigation. As an antidote to the elaborate formalism of the common law and the delays and expenses this often entailed, arbitration offered a well-designed, adaptable procedure notable for its flexibility, simplicity and speed. Since submission to arbitration—the *compromissio*—was a voluntary undertaking, the participants enjoyed considerable discretion as to the detailed arrangements, especially regarding the selection of arbitrators and the nature and extent of the issues to be decided. With certain exceptions,[45] the legal system offered a very restricted choice of judges, whereas the choice of arbitrators was left entirely to the parties themselves.[46] Similarly, while the rigid structure of the forms of action constrained the judge to consider the facts of the case only insofar as they related to the legal issue at hand, the arbitra-

cvi, n. 2 (I am grateful to Dr P. R. Hyams for this reference). *Year Books of Edward II: 5 Edward II, 1312*, ed. W. C. Bolland (Selden Soc., xxxiii, 1916), 178, 214–16; *The Eyre of Kent, 6 and 7 Edward II, 1313–14*, ed. W. C. Bolland and others (Selden Soc., xxvii, 1912), 23–7.

[42] See above, footnote 27.

[43] McFarlane, *Nobility*, 114.

[44] J. A. Guy, *The Cardinal's Court* (Hassocks, 1977), 97–105; M. J. Ingram, 'Communities and Courts: Law and Disorder in Early Seventeenth-Century Wiltshire', in *Crime in England, 1500–1800*, ed. J. S. Cockburn (1977), 125–7; *Somerset Assize Orders, 1629–40*, ed. T. G. Barnes (Somerset Rec. Soc., lxv, 1959), *passim*.

[45] R. W. Kaeuper, 'Law and Order in Fourteenth-Century England: the Evidence of Special Commissions of Oyer and Terminer', *Speculum*, liv (1979), 758–61.

[46] Janeau, *loc. cit.*, 245–6; B. Guenée, *Tribunaux et Gens de Justice dans le Bailliage de Senlis a la Fin du Moyen Age* (Paris, 1963), 117–20.

tors could, if the parties so wished, examine the broader context of the dispute. In this respect arbitration offered a far better prospect of achieving a lasting settlement because it allowed the disputants to air all their grievances and did not confine them to a single point of conflict which might merely be symptomatic of deeper divisions.[47]

The voluntary nature of arbitration was also important in shaping a simple and unencumbered mode of procedure. It was assumed from their free submission that the parties desired a quick resolution of the dispute, and for this reason no dilatory devices were permitted, nor any appeal allowed against the final award.[48] Here the backing of the courts was essential, for without their recognition resort to arbitration would have been futile. The common law provided unequivocal support by accepting the plea of arbitration as a bar to further legal action. In addition there were various legal remedies available, if necessary, to enforce the obligations incurred through arbitration.[49]

Simplicity of procedure made for speed of execution, and speed was of the essence in arbitration, both to prevent the escalation of disputes and to keep costs to a minimum. The secular *compromissio*, which in general took the form of mutual bonds with conditional defeasance,[50] usually followed its canon law model in setting a term for the completion of the award.[51] There was of course the risk that the term might run out, and the arbitrators' powers thus expire, before the award had been completed. This was not uncommon, but in most cases the impasse was broken by the negotiation of fresh arrangements for arbitration.[52] If the brevity of arbitration procedure helped to keep down expenses, they were reduced still further by savings on court costs and lawyers' fees. John Wheathampstead, abbot of St Albans in 1431, boasted that he had saved his house a thousand marks by avoiding litigation with William Fleet of Rickmansworth and opting instead for arbitration.[53]

Without question the use of arbitration also had its disadvantages, notably the problem of enforcing an award with which either party felt dissatisfied. When informal social pressures were ineffective, the

[47] Cf. S. D. White, '"Pactum ... Legem Vincit et Amor Judicium." The Settlement of Disputes by Compromise in Eleventh-Century Western France', *American Journal of Legal History*, xxii (1978), 281–308.

[48] In certain circumstances, appeal from arbitration to the ecclesiastical courts was, however, permitted at canon law: see above, footnote 35.

[49] See below, 63–6.

[50] Ibid., 63–4.

[51] *Cal. Close Rolls, 1409–13*, 69, 187; *1413–19*, 369; *1429–35*, 157.

[52] As, for example in the Meryng–Tuxford and Paston–Aslake disputes, below, 57–8, 61–2.

[53] Johannes Amundesham, *Annales Monasterii Sancti Albani*, ed. H. T. Riley (R.S., 1870–1), i. 273.

only sanctions available to compel observance of awards were to be found in the courts, which of course the whole process was designed to avoid. Nor, according to contemporary observers such as Langland and Wyclif, was arbitration any more impervious to corruption and intimidation than the law.[54] Indeed, there were occasions when love-days ostensibly appointed for the conclusion of arbitration degenerated into armed brawls between the supporters of the disputing parties.[55] Such hazards were not peculiar to arbitration, however, but were fundamental elements in the conduct of disputes as long as the coercive powers of the government remained relatively weak. The problem of enforcement and the ease with which disputes escalated into violence gave still greater urgency to the search for genuine conciliation and compromise which was the main function of arbitration.

When examined more closely, therefore, arbitration in late-medieval England proves to be a popular and well-established institution, whose speedy and straightforward procedures were adaptable to all manner of disputes at every social level. But perhaps the most striking feature of arbitration in late-medieval England is the frequency with which it occurs in conjunction with litigation. The evidence does not suggest simply that frustrated litigants rejected the ponderous inefficiency of the law courts in favour of the more effective remedies of arbitration. Rather it reflects their sophisticated appreciation of the tactical possibilities offered by the co-ordinated use of law and arbitration as part of a general strategy (which might often include self-help) to secure the favourable resolution of a dispute. In the same way as war and diplomacy, the two went hand in hand. Legal proceedings, like a military campaign, might be protracted, costly and inconclusive, but with the threat that a tactical error could bring total defeat; whereas arbitration, like diplomacy, offered the safer if less spectacular alternative of peaceful negotiation.

Not all disputants, then, embarked on legal action with the single-minded intention of pursuing the law to its conclusion. Their primary purpose might rather be to persuade the opposing party to negotiate by threatening him with the expenses, risks and inconvenience of a lawsuit. A well-documented example is the case of *Meryng v. Tuxford*, which first comes into view as the result of a broken loveday in 1411.[56] Alexander Meryng and John Tuxford had conflicting claims to a

[54] J. W. Bennett, 'The Medieval Loveday', *Speculum*, xxxiii (1958), 364–5.

[55] *Rotuli Parliamentorum* (1783–1832), iii. 649–50; *Memorials of London and London Life*, ed. H. T. Riley (1868), 156–62.

[56] P.R.O., KB 9 (King's Bench, Ancient Indictments)/204/2, mm. 6, 10. For the Meryng family, see A. Cameron, 'Meering and the Meryng Family', *Transactions of the Thoroton Society of Nottinghamshire*, lxxvii (1973), 41–52.

portion of the manor of Little Markham in Nottinghamshire, the former's based on a grant by his maternal grandfather, the latter's on a grant in favour of his wife by Alexander's father Francis.[57] The failure of attempted mediation at the loveday led Tuxford to occupy the land by force; Meryng responded in kind, and the resulting disturbances led to the indictment and trial of both parties and their supporters in King's Bench.[58] With Tuxford still in control of the land, Meryng brought an action of novel disseisin against him early in 1412. The case came before the assize justices of the Midland circuit, headed by Robert Tyrwhitt; but in October, while the action was still pending, both sides submitted to the arbitration of Tyrwhitt, Chief Justice William Gascoigne and William, Lord Roos, which was to be completed by the octave of Hilary following.[59] This award was not made within the stipulated term, however, and in February 1414 Meryng obtained a royal order to proceed anew with the assize.[60] After further inconclusive litigation the two sides again agreed to arbitration in November 1416, and an award was successfully concluded in which the disputed lands were divided equally between the disputants.[61]

As the evenhandedness of the award suggests, Meryng and Tuxford were well-matched opponents whose wealth, status and local support were roughly comparable. Many disputes, however, were not so evenly balanced. In such circumstances the stronger party might bombard his adversary with a battery of lawsuits in the hope of forcing him to accept arbitration under unfavourable conditions. At the beginning of Henry V's reign the abbey of Crowland was involved in two disputes with the inhabitants of townships in the Lincolnshire fens. The men of Moulton and Weston in one case, and of Spalding and Pinchbeck in the other, claimed rights of common in tracts of fenland which the abbey held to be part of its lordship of Crowland.[62] For a year or more the villagers exercised the rights they claimed in the disputed lands. The abbot responded, in May 1415, by securing two special commissions of *oyer et terminer* against their incursions, and by filing a petition in Chancery against the inhabitants of Spalding

[57] *Cal. Close Rolls, 1413–19*, 50–4.

[58] P.R.O., KB 27 (King's Bench, Plea Rolls)/614, Rex, mm. 9, 12; 616, Rex, mm. 17d, 28d.

[59] *Calendar of Patent Rolls, 1216–1509* (1891–1916), *1408–13*, 431–2; *Cal. Close Rolls, 1409–13*, 397.

[60] *Cal. Close Rolls, 1413–19*, 50–4.

[61] Ibid., 373–4; *Cal. Pat. Rolls, 1416–22*, 54–5.

[62] *Historiae Croylandensis Continuatio*, ed. W. Fulman (Rerum Anglicarum Scriptores Veteres, i, Oxford, 1684), 500–12; *Ingulph's Chronicle of the Abbey of Croyland*, trsld. H. T. Riley (1854), 366–87.

and Pinchbeck.[63] Should temporal measures prove ineffective, the abbot also excommunicated his opponents in all four villages.[64] These actions quickly persuaded the townships to compromise, and by the late summer of 1415 both disputes had been submitted to arbitration. The Crowland chronicler attributed the villagers' change of heart to the intervention of St Guthlac, so beneficial was it to the abbey.[65] Separate panels of arbitrators were elected for each dispute, those named in the Spalding and Pinchbeck case being chosen from the Council of the Duchy of Lancaster.[66] The abbey presented a huge body of documentary evidence in support of its claims, to which the villagers could make little response. The two awards which followed provided a complete vindication of the abbey's rights. In the case of Moulton and Weston the offending villagers were also ordered to pay the abbey four hundred marks in damages.[67]

To the disputant who went to court considering compromise, a lawsuit had the added advantage of bringing the case before judges who might agree to act as arbitrators out of court. The common-law judge, unlike his canon-law counterpart,[68] was not formally obliged to encourage litigants to explore all avenues of compromise before proceeding with legal action; there is evidence, nevertheless, that on occasion he did take an active role in arranging arbitration. In January 1462, for example, Sir Richard Bingham, a justice of King's Bench, wrote to Sir William Plumpton advising him that Henry Pierrepont had agreed to submit to the arbitration of Bingham and Sir John Markham concerning the homicide of his father Henry by Robert Green, a relative of Plumpton's.[69] This followed an appeal of homicide lodged in King's Bench against Green by the widow of Henry Pierrepont senior.[70] Bingham's letter suggested a time and place for the parties to meet and asked Plumpton's approval of these arrangements.[71] In a similar way the dispute between Sir John Trussell and William Porter over the manor of Colleyweston, Northamptonshire,

[63] *Cal. Pat. Rolls, 1413–16*, 406; P.R.O., C 1 (Early Chancery Proceedings)/6 no. 272. The dispute with Spalding also appears to have been heard before the Duchy of Lancaster Council: P.R.O., DL 41 (Duchy of Lancaster, Miscellanea)/42, no. 3.

[64] *Hist. Croyland*, 501.

[65] Ibid., 502.

[66] Ibid., 502, 506.

[67] Ibid., 502–12. The award against Moulton and Weston is calendared in *Cal. Pat. Rolls, 1413–16*, 375–6. In view of these penal settlements it is not surprising that the disputes continued throughout the fifteenth century: P.R.O., C 1/12, no. 53; *Ingulph's Chronicle*, 393–5, 506–7.

[68] See above, 52–3.

[69] *Plumpton Correspondence*, 3–4.

[70] P.R.O., KB 27/802, m. 5d.

[71] The parties finally submitted to Bingham's arbitration in May 1462: *Plumpton Correspondence*, 3 n.

was submitted to the arbitration of the Chancellor in September 1416 after coming before him as an equitable suit in Chancery.[72] In order for a judge to act as arbitrator it was of course not essential that the case should first have appeared before him in court; but since royal justices were in great demand as arbitrators by virtue of their high position and legal expertise, this was an obvious course for the less well-connected disputant seeking an authoritative award.[73]

If an arbitration award was successfully completed, the parties often returned to the courtroom, on the arbitrators' instructions, to confirm the settlement through collusive legal action. A dispute between Sir John Bagot and Burton abbey over lands in Abbots Bromley in Staffordshire was settled by arbitration in 1428, the lands in question being awarded to Burton in exchange for a substantial cash payment.[74] An action of novel disseisin, brought by Bagot against the abbey, was still pending at the time of the award: the arbitrators ordered that the assize be continued in Bagot's name by attornies named and supervised by the abbot, who was to bear the costs of the lawsuit and bring it to the conclusion he desired.[75] In other cases, arbitrators made provision for collusive litigation but left its execution to the discretion of the beneficiary of the settlement, as in the Archbishop of York's award resolving a dispute between Thomas Lacy and Thomas Stapleton over the manor of Quarmby in Yorkshire in 1487.[76]

Arbitration used in combination with litigation might therefore prove a quick and effective means of dispute settlement in the late middle ages. But of course this was not always so, and we must beware of over-emphasising straightforward examples of successful arbitration, such as those given above, for fear of presenting too simple and schematic a view of the procedure and its relation to legal action. Many disputes were far more complex and untidy, giving rise to protracted litigation in several different courts and resisting repeated attempts at settlement by arbitration. A classic example was the dispute between the Catesbys and Cardians over the manor of Ladbroke in Warwickshire, which lasted from 1383 until 1399. Before its eventual resolution by arbitration, it was heard in the courts of King's

[72] P.R.O., C 1/6, no. 257; *Cal. Close Rolls, 1413–19*, 369; *Cal. Pat. Rolls, 1413–16*, 223–4; *1416–22*, 111. The other arbitrator was the duke of Clarence. For the importance of arbitration in the rise of the Chancellor's equitable jurisdiction, see below, 64–6.

[73] For royal justices as arbitrators or umpires, see Amundesham, *Annales S. Albani*, i. 266–72; *Rot. Parl.*, iii. 649–50; *Cal. Close Rolls, 1385–89*, 437–8; *1409–13*, 59, 183–5, 211, 222, 227, 235, 319, 330, 338–9, 397; *1447–54*, 63, 173–4, 264, 360; *Cal. Pat. Rolls, 1416–22*, 183–95.

[74] Burton-on-Trent Public Library, D. 27, no. 654.

[75] For another example, see *Cal. Close Rolls, 1413–19*, 197.

[76] *Yorkshire Deeds, III*, ed. W. Brown (Yorks. Arch. Soc. Rec. Ser., lxiii, 1922), 91–2.

Bench and Assize, of Common Pleas and Chancery, before the King's Council and the councils of four leading magnates.[77]

Another case, from the Paston letters, confirms how involved and intricate the workings of the disputing process could be.[78] The differences between William Paston and Walter Aslake in the 1420s allegedly began when Paston acted as legal counsel to the prior of Norwich in a suit between Aslake and the prior over the advowson of Sprowston in Norfolk. In August 1424 Aslake and his servants posted bills in Norwich threatening Paston's safety; Paston responded by demanding surety of the peace from Aslake before the Norfolk J.P. Sir Thomas Erpingham, and by lodging an action of trespass against him in the city court of Norwich. Aslake brought in the required surety before Erpingham, who tried to dissuade Paston from pursuing his trespass suit, arranging instead for the dispute to go to arbitration. Paston agreed to submit to this award, but insisted upon continuing his action, ostensibly for reasons of prestige, while promising, according to Aslake, 'that the sayd Walter schuld noght be damaged ine hys body ne hys goodes, qwatsumeuer the qwest sayd'.[79] The accounts of Aslake and Paston differ on the course of the lawsuit: Paston claimed it proceeded in due and lawful form, while Aslake alleged that a packed jury was empanelled at dead of night with the assent of corrupt officials to ensure his conviction. Both versions agreed, however, on the outcome: the jury found for Paston and awarded £120 in damages against Aslake, who was committed to gaol in Norwich. As a result, the attempted arbitration arranged by Erpingham broke down late in 1424.

After a lull of several months, negotiations resumed between the parties, and in the spring of 1425 Erpingham persuaded the duke of Gloucester to organise a second arbitration, which was to be concluded by August of that year.[80] Meanwhile Aslake secured his release from Norwich gaol through a writ of *corpus cum causa* in Chancery, and in July submitted a petition against Paston to Parliament. Paston countered with a bill of account in the Exchequer for the damages owed him by Aslake.[81] Despite this continued litigation, the arbitration arranged by Gloucester was completed at Norwich in August 1425. According to Paston's account, Aslake, newly released from gaol, refused to observe its provisions and took his grievances against

[77] 'Courts, Councils and Arbitrators in the Ladbroke Manor Dispute, 1382–1400', ed. J. B. Post, in *Medieval Legal Records Edited in Memory of C. A. F. Meekings*, ed. R. F. Hunnisett and J. B. Post (1978), 290–339.

[78] Two conflicting versions of this dispute appear in *Paston Letters and Papers of the Fifteenth Century*, ed. N. Davis (Oxford 1971, 1976), i. 7–12; ii. 505–7.

[79] Ibid., ii. 506.

[80] Ibid., i. 9.

[81] Ibid., ii. 506–7.

Paston to the duke of Norfolk. This proved a most effective strategy, causing Norfolk, on Paston's own admission, 'to be hevy lord to the seyd William'.[82] On Norfolk's instructions Paston twice agreed to further efforts at arbitration in the spring of 1426, although both were unsuccessful. Having seized the initiative, Aslake kept up the pressure, bringing actions against the jurors who convicted him on Paston's suit of trespass and petitioning the Leicester Parliament of 1426.[83] After a fifth inconclusive submission to arbitrators late in 1426,[84] the matter was finally settled by the award of the duke of Norfolk in June 1428: Paston was ordered to pay Aslake £50 in return for a release of all personal actions.[85]

The foregoing examples illustrate the close interdependence of law and arbitration in the late middle ages, and reveal that legal action was often pursued, not as an end in itself, but as a tactical preliminary or accompaniment to arbitration. They suggest that in many disputes compromise and negotiation must have provided a powerful counterpoint to the familiar themes of violence and litigation. On the other hand arbitration procedures were clearly influenced by the pervasive effects of the legal system. The form and conduct of arbitration was inevitably affected by such factors as the prominence of judges and lawyers as arbitrators, the use of collusive litigation to confirm the terms of an award, and the tendency of litigation to redefine the issues of a dispute by acquiring a momentum of its own (as in the Paston–Aslake dispute). It is arguable, indeed, that the methods of arbitration characteristic of late-medieval England, far from reflecting the failure of the legal system, as some have claimed, [86] represent rather a measure of its success. The widespread imitation of the precise, legalistic formulae of canon-law arbitration, suitably adapted for the requirements of the common law, implies a recognition on the part of disputants that a settlement made out of court would only endure if it proved unassailable to a subsequent challenge in court. The resources of the law were thus harnessed to provide support and protection for arbitration. While not yet supervised by the common-law courts, arbitration in the late middle ages functioned in an unmistakably legal context, its effectiveness ultimately guaranteed by the law courts. This helps to explain the enormous growth of documentary evidence for the practice which takes place after 1350.[87] The rising tide of paper-

[82] Ibid., i. 10.

[83] Ibid., i. 11–12. Aslake's parliamentary petition of 1426 is the one published by Davis in the *Paston Letters:* see above, footnote 78.

[84] Paston's memorandum to arbitrators on the dispute apparently survives from this attempt: *Paston Letters*, ed. Davis, i. 7–8.

[85] *Cal. Close Rolls, 1422–29*, 393–4, 406.

[86] See above, 53.

[87] Ibid., 55.

work does not prove that arbitration was becoming more popular; it may suggest, however, that greater formality and better record-keeping were required of the process as the law grew more complex, litigation more commonplace and lawyers more sophisticated.

The common-law courts did not make direct provision for the enforcement of arbitration, and unlike their urban and ecclesiastical counterparts were not actively engaged in its promotion.[88] Perhaps their most significant contribution was passive—the acceptance of arbitration, pending or concluded, as a plea in bar to further legal action.[89] The dissatisfied party to a completed award could escape its provisions only by showing that he had agreed to arbitration under duress.[90] Nevertheless, when arbitration broke down, or when either party refused to accept its terms, certain remedies were available through the actions of debt and detinue. The characteristic form of *compromissio* after 1350 was the conditional bond, whereby each party acknowledged himself in debt to the other for a specified sum in a sealed deed whose defeasance was conditional upon observance of the award.[91] The bonds were entrusted to a neutral third party, and if one side defaulted the other could claim them and sue his opponent for debt.[92] If the custodian of the bonds refused to deliver them to the injured party, the latter had a remedy against him in detinue. In Michaelmas term 1414, for example, Edmund Ferrers of Chartley in Staffordshire brought an action of detinue against Walter Bullock, clerk, for bonds of arbitration made between Ferrers and Hugh Erdswick of Sandon, and entrusted to Bullock pending completion of the award. The bonds were made for the sum of five hundred marks, and their defeasance was conditional upon observance of the award of six named arbitrators and the maintenance of peace between the parties until the day of the award. The attempted arbitration broke down

[88] See *Cal. Plea and Mem. Rolls London, 1381–1412*, xxix–xxx, for the involvement of urban courts in arbitration; for ecclesiastical courts, see above, 52–4.

[89] 'Ladbroke Manor Dispute', ed. Post, 294–5 and n. 36; *Year Books 12 Richard II*, ed. Deiser, 37–8, 164–6; *Year Books of Richard II: 13 Richard II, 1389–90*, ed. T. F. T. Plucknett (Ames Foundation, 1929), 20–2, 104–5; P.R.O., KB 27/640, m. 12 (*Huse v. Dethick*).

[90] *Year Books of Richard II: 11 Richard II, 1387–88*, ed. I. D. Thornley (Ames Foundation, 1937), 168–74; *Year Books of Henry VI: 1 Henry VI, 1422*, ed. C. H. Williams (Selden Soc., l, 1933), 42–7.

[91] A. W. B. Simpson, 'The Penal Bond with Conditional Defeasance', *Law Quarterly Review*, lxxxii (1966), 392–422. E.g. *Cal. Close Rolls, 1409–13*, 56–7, 69, 85, 96, 187, 202, 204, 211, 227, 294, 297, 298, 310, 311, 319, 324, 325, 330, 331, 334, 353, 395, 397, 400–2, 408, 416, 418; *1476–85*, 22, 23, 76, 84–5, 108, 114, 168, 221, 223, 232, 243, 279, 286, 336, 357, 364–5, 394, 406–7, 414, 421.

[92] *Year Book Eyre of Kent*, ed. Bolland, 23–7; *Year Books 12 Richard II*, ed. Deiser, 70–1; *Year Books of Edward IV: 10 Edward IV and 49 Henry VI, 1470*, ed. N. Neilson (Selden Soc., xlvii, 1931), 56–8.

before completion, and Ferrers' action against Bullock was based on an allegation that Erdswick's men had broken the conditions of the bond by an assault on one of his servants before the day set for the award.[93] An action of debt could also be used to enforce an arbitration award which ordered the payment of a specific sum by one party to the other.[94] In such circumstances the sum awarded was often smaller than the value of the bond, and to avoid collusion in usury the courts allowed the action to lie only on the final award.[95]

The remedies available at common law were, however, too cumbersome and indirect to provide a satisfactory resolution of all the issues which arose from unsuccessful arbitration. In particular they failed to address the problem of the arbitrator who neglected to perform his duties, and made no provision to compel specific performance of an award which did not involve cash payments. In this respect, as in others, the old forms of action proved poorly suited to change and adaptation, and were inadequate to meet the new demands of litigants.[96] Their limitations encouraged the search for other resorts, and led in the late-fourteenth and fifteenth centuries to the growth of the equitable jurisdiction of the court of Chancery. The Chancellor's jurisdiction could be invoked by petition in cases where justice could not be had because of the power and influence of an opponent, or where the common law offered insufficient remedy because of its technical or procedural limitations.[97]

Studies of this court have shown that its early growth was based on two main categories of business: urban and mercantile litigation, arising especially from commercial practices unenforceable at common law,[98] and actions involving enfeoffments to use, which the common law did not recognise.[99] To these should be added a third category comprising cases which arose from arbitration, a frequent source of Chancery proceedings throughout the fifteenth century. The

[93] P.R.O., CP 40 (Court of Common Pleas, Plea Rolls)/615, m. 342, calendared in *William Salt Archaeological Society*, xvii (1896), 51. For more on the Erdswick-Ferrers dispute, see E. Powell, 'Public Order and Law Enforcement in Shropshire and Staffordshire in the Early Fifteenth Century' (D.Phil. thesis, Oxford Univ., 1979), 285-99.

[94] Harvard Law School Library, MS. 162, f. 200 (Year Book, temp. Edward I) (I am grateful to Dr R. C. Palmer for this reference). *Year Book 1 Henry VI*, ed. Williams, 12-13.

[95] *Year Book Eyre of Kent*, ed. Bolland, 27.

[96] Cf. Holdsworth, *History of English Law*, ii. 591-7.

[97] For the early history of the Chancery court of equity, see M. Avery, 'The History of the Equitable Jurisdiction of Chancery before 1460', *Bull. Inst. Hist. Res.*, xlii (1969), 129-44; N. Pronay, 'The Chancellor, the Chancery and the Council at the End of the Fifteenth Century', in *British Government and Administration*, ed. B. H. Hearder and H. R. Loyn (Cardiff, 1974), 87-103.

[98] Pronay, *loc. cit.*, 93-5.

[99] Avery, *loc. cit.*, 130-1; J. L. Barton, 'The Medieval Use', *Law Quart. Rev.*, lxxxi (1965), 562-77.

elements common to virtually all Chancery petitions concerning arbitration are the failure of an award owing to breach of faith, whether by a disputant or an arbitrator, and the petitioner's inability to obtain a common-law remedy. As we have seen, conditional bonds were the principal means for securing compensation at common law for default on an award; but if there were no bonds to show in court—if they had been lost, for example, or if the disputants had made an oral submission to arbitrators—the only recourse was to the Chancellor.[100] Sometimes the beneficiary of an award was trusting or careless enough to deliver a general release of all actions to his opponent before the terms of the award had been fulfilled, thus denying himself access to common law when the latter subsequently defaulted.[101] Another common complaint of petitioners was the pursuit of vexatious litigation against them by the opposing party in disregard of a completed award.[102] The majority of petitions involving arbitration, however, were concerned with biased or obstructive arbitrators, against whom there was no action available at common law.[103] In all these cases the petitioner generally requested writs of *sub pena* summoning the offenders to answer his accusations before the Chancellor.

As well as entertaining such complaints, the court of Chancery was more immediately involved in fostering arbitration. The Chancellor was active in arranging and supervising arbitration to settle disputes which came before him, and the hope of his intervention must have encouraged many petitioners to lodge a suit in Chancery.[104] The Chancellor's readiness to promote the practice stands in marked contrast to the aloofness of common-law justices and calls to mind the behaviour of ecclesiastical judges.[105] A comparison of Chancery proceedings with bonds of arbitration entered on the dorse of the Close rolls reveals a steady stream of cases referred by the court to the award of arbitrators,[106] with the Chancellor himself sometimes acting in this

[100] P.R.O., C 1/10, no. 311 (bonds lost); C 1/9, no. 68 (oral submission to arbitrators).

[101] P.R.O., C 1/9, nos. 237, 476.

[102] P.R.O., C 1/10, no. 243; C 1/33, nos. 191, 332.

[103] P.R.O., C 1/9, nos. 160, 279; C 1/10, nos. 141, 337; C 1/16, no. 260; C 1/33, nos. 22, 327.

[104] Cf. Harding, *Law Courts*, 101–2. The court of Star Chamber was later to exercise a similar function: Guy, *Cardinal's Court*, 97–105.

[105] Throughout the late middle ages the Chancellor was usually a cleric, but his concern to promote arbitration may have derived less from experience as an ecclesiastical judge than from considerations of equity and conscience which were the basis of his jurisdiction in Chancery: see S. F. C. Milsom, *Historical Foundations of the Common Law* (1969), 81.

[106] e.g. P.R.O., C 1/4, nos. 61, 193; *Cal. Close Rolls, 1409–13*, 69; *1419–22*, 117 (*Drax v. Bosvyle*). C 1/16 no. 110; *Cal. Close Rolls, 1409–13*, 187 (*Covert v. Pensford*). C 1/6, nos. 270–1; *Cal. Close Rolls, 1413–19*, 523–4 (*Barstable v. Blount et al.*). C 1/33, no. 210; *Cal. Close Rolls, 1429–35*, 157 (*Herwarde v. Waterman et al.*).

capacity.[107] One example is the case of *Borlas v. Tregoys*, which began about 1436 when Robert Borlas of Cornwall brought a bill in Chancery against Richard Tregoys for unlawfully taking a quantity of tin valued at £100.[108] In May 1436 the parties submitted to the Chancellor's arbitration, and the award was completed, after a local commission of inquiry returned to Chancery, in 1439.[109] The Chancellor awarded that Tregoys should return the tin or pay Borlas its value, but Tregoys was slow to comply, and in the early 1440s Borlas was again suing him in Chancery, this time for debt on the Chancellor's award.[110] Tregoys' claim that he had paid the debt through a third party, Udo Vivian, was shown to be false by an examination of Vivian in Chancery.[111] Finally, in 1448, Tregoys was compelled to submit to arbitration under court supervision, and was discharged from attendance in Chancery only after Borlas confirmed that a settlement had been reached.[112]

Magnate councils exercised an equitable jurisdiction similar to that of Chancery in the late middle ages, and they were equally important in the promotion of arbitration.[113] Of the examples given above, the dispute involving the men of Spalding and Pinchbeck and Crowland abbey was settled by arbitrators from the Council of the Duchy of Lancaster, while the duke of Norfolk's settlement of the Paston–Aslake feud followed the unsuccessful intervention of the duke of Gloucester.[114] The emerging equitable jurisdictions of late-medieval England reveal the interdependence of litigation and arbitration in its most refined form. The two became part of a single process of dispute settlement, as the fluidity of equitable procedure allowed them to be used almost interchangeably. Common-law procedure did not provide such flexibility, but as I have attempted to show, this did not deter disputants from combining law and arbitration in a general strategy to achieve an advantageous settlement.

The evidence for arbitration softens the dichotomy, noted at the beginning of this paper, between the precocity of royal judicial institutions in the late middle ages and their apparent inefficiency. There is no denying the widespread corruption of the law, but this must not be allowed to obscure the important mediatory functions exercised

[107] e.g. *Trussell v. Porter* (see above, 59–60), and *Auncell v. Clerk*: P.R.O., C 1/9, no. 20; *Cal. Close Rolls, 1429–35*, 297; *Cal. Pat. Rolls, 1429–36*, 351, 470.

[108] The bill, now lost, is referred to in *Cal. Close Rolls, 1441–47*, 52–3.

[109] *Cal. Close Rolls, 1435–41*, 67; *1441–47*, 52–3.

[110] P.R.O., C 1/16, no. 196.

[111] *Cal. Close Rolls, 1441–47*, 306; *Cal. Pat. Rolls, 1441–46*, 352.

[112] *Cal. Close Rolls, 1447–54*, 63.

[113] 'Ladbroke Manor Dispute', ed. Post, 292–7; C. Rawcliffe, 'Baronial Councils in the Later Middle Ages, in *Patronage, Pedigree and Power*, ed. Ross, 91–3.

[114] See above, 58–9, 61–2.

by the courts as long as the coercive powers of the Crown remained weak, and the successful resolution of disputes relied largely on conciliation and compromise. Litigation brought pressure to bear on an opponent while allowing ample time for compromise, and many lawsuits were probably filed to strengthen the disputant's bargaining position out of court. Legal action represented only a single phase in the conduct of disputes and often formed a prelude or adjunct to arrangements for arbitration. Only with an understanding of the complementary nature of litigation and arbitration is it possible to make sense of the workings of the law in the late middle ages and to explain the inconclusiveness of the vast majority of legal actions.

BEYOND THE MARKET: BOOKS AS GIFTS IN SIXTEENTH-CENTURY FRANCE

The Prothero Lecture

By Professor Natalie Zemon Davis, B.A., M.A., Ph.D.

READ 7 JULY 1982

I

'SINCE he isn't able to sell his books,' Erasmus said of a fellow scholar in 1518, 'he goes about offering them as gifts to important people; he makes more that way than if he had sold them.' Erasmus's shrewd observation to his friend Tunstall has considerable currency among historians today, anxious as we are about the book market. But writing his *Colloquies* a few years later, the great humanist also envisaged other purposes for giving books. At the end of a banquet, during which the gifts of God and human charity have been discussed, the host presents books to his guests, suiting each one to their learning, piety or vocation. His friends thank him not only for the gifts, but for the advice and compliments that went with them. 'It is I who thank you,' the host insists, 'for being so good about my simple style of living and for refreshing my mind with your conversation.'[1]

These two examples suggest the ways in which printed books could be part of systems of gift and obligation in the sixteenth century, passing beyond the transactions of buying and selling. Up to now, historians have been more interested in the owning of printed books than in their being given away. We have concentrated on the book as commodity rather than on the book as bearer of benefits and duties, on copyright rather than on common right. And this is understandable: the number of books now sold was so many times greater than the number of manuscripts vended by the late medieval stationer that other means of spreading books have seemed unimportant. Apart from library bequests, the only kind of present that has received much

[1] *Opus Epistolarum Des. Erasmi Roterodami*, ed. P. S. Allen, H. M. Allen and H. W. Garrod (Oxford, 1906–58), iii, 424, ep. 886. 'The Godly Feast', in *The Colloquies of Erasmus*, tr. C. R. Thompson (Chicago, 1965), 75–6. I am grateful to the National Endowment for the Humanities and to the Council for the Humanities of Princeton University for gifts which have supported this research.

scholarly attention is the dedicated book in search of patronage—the gift seeking immediate return—and this too is understandable: the evidence is readily available on the book's opening pages and the trade-offs in patronage relationships are familiar.[2] Still, by this limitation, we may have been missing some significant elements in the intentions of authors and publishers and in the experience of readers and book-owners. The printed book may be able to tell us more than we have realised about property and possessiveness, markets and gifts.

Such relations have been central in the anthropological reflection on gifts. Marcel Mauss set his great study of *Le Don* in the context of primitive exchange and reciprocity: every gift created the obligation for a return gift and the event of giving and receiving had many meanings embedded in it, such as the affirmation of peaceful solidarity and the establishment of rank. Though Mauss still saw features of that social form in the 1920s when he was writing (and indeed hoped they would expand), on the whole he thought gift exchange was in tension with market economies and Economic Man. Sir Raymond Firth, while pointing out that the distinction was not a rigid one, has insisted that 'the patterned differences between market process and the passage of gifts are considerable'. So too, the notions that maintained gift-systems were in tension with the ideas of absolute property and with beliefs that disconnected people from their objects and their things. Rather objects carried with them something from the givers—Mauss called it a spirit animating the gift, Annette Weiner sees it as a symbolic representation of kinship obligations—which kept them moving or guaranteed that an equivalent return or replacement would eventually come back to the donors or their children. Marshall Sahlins formulates it as a potentiality for benefits, for fecundity in the given object, which it would be immoral for the recipient to profit from at others' expense.[3]

The question to ask here, then, is what kind of gift is a printed book in the sixteenth century? Is it in tension with buying and selling? Did book-producers and book-owners have any sense of a mixed or qualified property in that object which restrained them from disposing of

[2] Among many studies on the practice and theory of patronage, see E. Rosenberg, *Leicester, Patron of Letters* (New York, 1955); F. Haskell, *Patrons and Painters. Art and Society in Baroque Italy* (2nd edn., New Haven and London, 1980); and *Patronage in the Renaissance*, ed. G. F. Lytle and S. Orgel (Folger Institute Essays, Princeton, 1981).

[3] M. Mauss, *The Gift*, tr. I. Cunnison (1969). Sir Raymond Firth, 'Symbolism in Giving and Getting', in *Symbols, Public and Private* (1973), 368–402. A. B. Weiner, *Women of Value, Men of Renown. New Perspectives in Trobriand Exchange* (Austin, Texas, 1976), chap. 9, and 'Reproduction: A Replacement for Reciprocity', *American Ethnologist*, vii (1980), 71–85. M. Sahlins, *Stone Age Economics* (Chicago, 1972), chap. 4.

it in just any way they saw fit? Did the book carry with it something that generated the need to keep it moving or to pass on the benefits received from it? And if so, to whom? to the donor in Mauss's gift–counter-gift, or rather to someone else in less reciprocal fashion? In answering these questions we will want to consider both how gifts of printed books resembled gifts of manuscripts in the later Middle Ages and how they fit into other systems of gifts in their own day—that is, compare the present of a book in 1540 with the present of a manuscript in 1400, and also with, say, the partridges and hares offered by a seigneur to the royal officer who had granted him the right to hold a weekly fair in his village.

In medieval society, learning was believed to come as a gift and this had implications for what one did with it and how one should be rewarded for it. In the village, most lore was inherited and collective, passed on by the storyteller, whose recompense was gifts of food and a place of honour near the hearth. In the castle, the poet Marie de France spoke of the obligations and returns of knowledge:

> To Whom God has given science
> And the eloquence of good speech
> Must not be silent or conceal it
> But willingly show it.
> When a great good is heard by many
> Then it begins to seed
> And when it is praised by many
> Then it bursts into flower.[4]

In the university, where the store of learning was constantly enlarged by new manuscripts, disputations, commentaries, concordances and reformulations, it was still believed in the thirteenth century that 'knowledge is a Gift of God and cannot be sold' ('Scientia donum dei est, unde vendi non potest'—it has the ring of a proverb). This Greek ideal, fortified by Christ's injunction 'Freely ye have received, freely give' (Matt. 10:8) and now firmly entrenched in the canon law, was applied not only to professors, who were to take no fees for their teaching, but even to the sale of notarial and scribal productions. (Walter Map told the story of an imprisoned Archbishop of Hungary, who refused to accept the papal letters ordering his release because the copyist had been paid one shilling. The Lord then freed him by a miracle.) Fortunately for the teachers and scribes, many of whom had no benefices, the text from Luke that 'the labourer is worthy of his hire' (10:7) was finally used to justify some payments; but the ban-

[4] Marie de France, *Les Lais de Marie de France*, ed. J. Rychner (Paris, 1973), Prologue. See also the Biblical and classical *topoi* given by E. R. Curtius, *European Literature and the Latin Middle Ages*, tr. W. R. Trask (New York, 1963), 85–9.

quets, fruits, sweets and wine presented by students to their professors at Paris and Montpellier in the sixteenth century after examinations and disputations attest to some continuing vitality of the old ideal.[5]

Meanwhile the belief that copying manuscripts was a meritorious and godly act (rubrication was compared to the blood of martyrs) and lending a manuscript an act of mercy, lingered on long after monastic scribes had been supplemented by university stationers, who rented out manuscripts for copying, and by busy lay scriveners, who were paid salaries for their work by authors and would-be owners. The careful regulation of rates for the rental and sale of manuscripts was in part a recognition by university authorities that knowledge was a gift of the Holy Spirit and should not be too dearly sold. When the fixed prices were thought too low, buyers would have to supplement them with presents, not with money. In the early fifteenth century, a few decades before the invention of movable type, the theologian Jean Gerson was reminding princes that they must collect books not just for themselves, but for their companions, 'nedum pro te, sed pro consortibus tuis'.[6]

The point of all this is that sixteenth-century authors, book-producers and book-possessors inherited not only patterns of gifts, but also a belief that property in a book was as much collective as private and that God himself had some special rights in that object. By this argument, the book was at its best when given, should not be sold beyond a just price and never be hoarded.

Could such a cultural ideal survive the sixteenth century? Could God's share, already somewhat eroded, survive the desacralising technology of the printing shop? His gifts were certainly not mentioned when the profit-minded merchant-publisher begged the king for an exclusive privilege to publish an edition for a number of years, but only the *libraire's* own efforts and expenses in finding, preparing, editing and/or illustrating a correct text. And what happened to God's

[5] G. Post, K. Giocarinis and R. Kay, 'The Medieval Heritage of a Humanist Ideal: "Scientia Donum Dei est, Unde Vendi non Potest",' *Traditio*, xi (1955), 195–234. J. Le Goff, *Les Intellectuels au Moyen Age* (Paris, 1962), 104–8. J. W. Baldwin, *Masters, Princes and Merchants. The Social Views of Peter the Chanter and his Circle* (Princeton, 1970), i, 121–30, ii, 83–6. J. K. Farge, 'The Faculty of Theology of Paris, 1500–1536: Institution, Personnel and Activity in Early Sixteenth-Century France' (Ph.D. thesis, University of Toronto, 1976), 37–80. L. Dulieu, *La Médecine à Montpellier* (Avignon, 1975–9), ii, 67–8.

[6] G. H. Putnam, *Books and their Makers during the Middle Ages* (New York, 1962, reprinted from the 1896–7 ed.), i, chaps. 2–4. J. Destrez, *La 'Pecia' dans les mansucrits universitaires de XIIIIe et du XIVe siècles* (Paris, 1935). Curtius, *European Literature*, 315. The tight prescription for payments for letters from royal chancelleries was intended to prevent bribery and injustice, but it also stemmed from the notion that what comes as a gift, here a gift from the king, should not be sold (H. Michaud, *La Grand Chancellerie et les écritures royales au 16e siècle* (Paris, 1967), 113, 335–45). R. F. Green, *Poets and Prince-pleasers. Literature and the English Court in the Late Middle Ages* (Toronto, 1980), 99.

share in the multiplication of trivial or silly books, the kind that Rabelais made fun of in the Library of Saint Victor—*Les Pétarrades* of Copyists and Scribes, to give one of his odoriferous titles—the kind that ended up being sold as scented paper at stalls near the Paris bridges?[7]

On the other hand, there were now many more books to give if one wished to, and with increased literacy more people to read them and read them aloud; possibly the printed book could have more varied use as a present than the rarer illuminated manuscript. However unequally the profits from an edition were divided, the evidence for collective work on it was more manifest than in the manuscript, as both the publisher's and the author's name were prominently displayed on the title page, and throughout much of the sixteenth century that of the printer might be found in the colophon, if he or she were different from the publisher. (Only the journeymen were ignored.) The enhanced sense of self-consciousness of the Renaissance author might be expressed more effectively and honourably in a gift than in a sale.[8] And perhaps the Lord's share could be remembered when tradespeople were bringing out religious texts of all kinds. The printed book could retain some of its privileged status as a gift, a product of 'the divine art'. The reformulation of the medieval saying might be: 'The gifts of God can be sold and given, it depends on the circumstances.'

II

What then of the circumstances for giving books? We can sort them out for purposes of this essay into three categories: the dedicated book, that is, the public gift; the book given to others in the course of one's lifetime; and the book bequeathed at death. The initial diffusion of late-medieval writings was, as we know, through a gift, that is, through the sending of the treatise, the poem, the translation or the freshly corrected text to a person, ordinarily more powerful and wealthier than oneself, who might have commissioned it; who would send one back a gift of money or some other precious object; and who, through his or her reputation, would add to the lustre of the work and defend it against the malicious criticism of the jealous. The manuscript might

[7] François Rabelais, *Pantagruel, Roy des Dipsodes*, chap. 7 in *Oeuvres complètes*, ed. P. Jourda (Paris, 1962), i, 253. *Discours non plus melancoliques que divers, de choses mesmement qui appartiennent a notre France* (Poitiers, 1557), chap. 15. On the impact of printing, see E. L. Eisenstein, *The Printing Press as an Agent of Change* (Cambridge, 1979), i, chap. 2.

[8] On this general question, see S. Greenblatt, *Renaissance Self-Fashioning from More to Shakespeare* (Chicago, 1980).

include an illumination of the author on bended knee presenting the book and a dedicatory letter, which was often included by later copyists, thus making the praise of the patron a part of the text. Nor was one limited to making a single gift of a work: in 1400 Christine de Pisan sent dedicatory copies of her *Epistre qu'Othea ... envoya a Hector* to the Dukes of Orléans, Burgundy and others.[9]

With the printed book in the sixteenth-century context, the character of the dedicated gift changed. More kinds of people dedicated books: authors, relatives of authors, translators, editors, publishers, printers. It is the translator of Alciato's *Emblems* into French who dedicates that work to a Scottish count, not Alciato. It is the printer who dedicates the French translation of Biringuccio's metallurgical work to a military man, not the translator. The learned publisher Guillaume Rouillé dedicated his editions as often as did his authors and translators, his epistles repesenting himself as a *giver* rather than a seller of books, publishing New Testaments to help a Cardinal defend the faith and Italian books to celebrate the glory of Catherine de Medici's ancestors.[10]

Now more kinds of people receive dedications than before and the return gifts and consequences hoped for are more diverse. The quest for patronage continued to be important, or course. Authors and translators were compensated by publishers by copies of their books, by salaries or by a combination of the two. The books were used mostly as presents, as medieval writers had done, but the sixteenth-century transaction had a somewhat different quality to it. The printed epistle now carried the patron's praise far and wide, both adding to the value of the gift to the recipient and taxing the donor's ingenuity in finding ways to multiply patrons for the same work. Erasmus was able to get away with specially prepared dedications for the same book; his recipients were either unsuspecting or were so flattered by the gift from the admired humanist that they did not care

[9] H. J. Chaytor, *From Script to Print* (Cambridge, 1945), chap. 6. G. Mombello, 'Per un' edizione critica dell' Epistre Othea di Christine de Pizan', *Studi Francesi*, viii (1964), 401–17, ix (1965), 1–12. I am gratfeul to Sandra Hindman for this reference.

[10] *Emblemes d'Alciat, De nouveau translatez en François* (Lyon: Guillaume Rouillé, 1549), Dedication of Barthélemy Aneau to Jacques, Conte d'Aran, 3–4. *La Pyrotechnie ou art du feu ... Composée par le Seigneur Vanoccio Biringuccio ... traduite ... en François par feu Maistre Iaques Vincent* (Paris: Claude Frémy, 1556), Dedication by Claude Frémy to Jean de La Marche, Seigneur de Jametz, Captaine de cinquante hommes. *Il Nuovo Testamento di Giesu Christo* (Lyon: Guillaume Rouillé, 1552), Dedication of Rouillé to the Cardinal de Tournon, 3–4. *Prima parte del Prontuario de le Medaglie de Piu Illustri et fulgenti huomini e donne* (Lyon: Guillaume Rouillé, 1553), Dedication of Rouillé to Catherine de Medici, f. a2^{r-v}. N. Z. Davis, 'Publisher Guillaume Rouillé, Businessman and Humanist', in *Editing Sixteenth Century Texts*, ed. R. J. Schoeck (Toronto, 1966), 72–112. Also see M. Lebel, 'Josse Bade, éditeur et préfacier (1462–1535)', *Renaissance and Reformation*, n.s., V (1981), 63–71.

about their competitors. Other authors simply changed the dedicatee with a new edition, while the mathematician Pierre Forcadel of the Collège Royale inserted a fresh dedication at every break in his texts—four for his *Arithmetique* and six for his translation of Euclid. So common were these practices that a late sixteenth-century explicator of the proverb 'D'une fille deux gendres' ('From one daughter two sons-in-law') gave as an example 'learned men who dedicate their works to several princes and seigneurs for the presents they hope for'.[11]

Whatever their hopes, the dedicator now chose among a wider range of identities *vis à vis* the patron and (as befitted a century when there was much reflection on Seneca's treatise on *Benefits*) the language of gratitude was more varied. At one end of the scale, in 1570, printer Antoinette Peronet dedicates the translation she has commissioned of Marcus Aurelius to the noble Governor of Lyon, whose protection she wishes not only for the book but also for her person, poor widow with orphans, against the dangers of civil war; despite her 'petitesse et ignorance', the simplicity of her writing and the 'unworthiness of her gift' compared to his grandeur, she hopes that he will accept the book because of its useful instruction on governance and her good will.[12] At the other end of the scale, Ambroise Paré, the royal surgeon, presents his *Oeuvres* to King Henri III in a volume replete with the author portrait which has long since replaced the kneeling donor picture,[13] with poems from the court poet Pierre Ronsard and others honouring Paré; and with a dedicatory epistle which reviews his own service for three previous kings before he put this, 'his masterpiece', at Henri's feet. In between these examples are dedications like that of the royal

[11] A. Parent, *Les Métiers du livre à Paris au XVIe siècle* (Histoire et civilisation du livre, 6; Geneva, 1974), 100–4. Jean Hoyoux, 'Les moyens d'existence d'Erasme', *Bibliothèque d'humanisme et renaissance* v (1944), 29–59. *Arithmetique entiere et abregee de Pierre Forcadel* (Paris: Charles Perier, 1565), dedications to the Count of Bothwell, Charles de Thelligny, Jean de Morel and Georges Aubert. *Les Six Premiers Livres des Elements d'Euclide, traduicts et commentez par Pierre Forcadel* (Paris: Jérome de Marnef and Guillaume Cavellat, 156— [sic]), dedications to Charles IX, Gaspard de Coligny, Charles de Thelligny, François de La Noue, Pierre de Montdoré, and Monsieur Guetauld. 'Explications morales d'aucuns proverbes communs en la langue francoyse', in *Thresor de la langue francoyse* (Paris, 1606), 17.

[12] *Institution de la vie humaine, Dressee par Marc Antonin Philosophe ... Traduit, par Pardoux du Prat* (Lyon: Widow of Gabriel Cotier, 1570), dedication of Antoinette Peronet to Governor François de Mandelot.

[13] R. Mortimer, *A Portrait of the Author in Sixteenth-Century France* (Chapel Hill, N.C., 1980). In one of Dr. Mortimer's illustrations, the donor, rather than kneeling, is striding energetically, book in hand, up to a seated recipient (Fig. 6). The traditional kneeling position was used by the humanist Guillaume Budé in the portrait for his manuscript *De l'Institution du Prince*, presented to François Ier around 1519. In a work focused around the importance of royal patronage for the new learning, the older style of gift-presentation may have been essential, lest the author appear too self-interested. It was not included in the posthumous printed edition, Arrivour, 1547.

geographer Nicolas de Nicolay to Henri II: it is at the king's command that he has travelled the seas and translated this Spanish work on the *Art of Navigation*; may these galleys and brigantines extend Henri's dominion not only as far as Caesar's and Alexander's, but communicate his light throughout the universe. Here the geographer's gift does not humbly 'venture out under the shade of the wings of the patron', to quote the older but still current phrase, but proudly reflects the patron's glorious sun.[14]

Finally, there are straightforward dedications quite without the language of deference. The jurist and *Parlementaire* René Choppin sends Henri III his commentary on the customs of Anjou with a dedication talking only of royal interest in that duchy; this does not deter the king from sending him 1000 *écus d'or* in return. The Protestant artisan Palissy dedicates a scientific work to a nobleman and simply evokes their philosophical and mathematical discussions together. A certain Jean Massé offers his book on the *Veterinary Art* to a master of the royal stables and after informing him that a horse is the most noble animal after man, tells him of his own skills and that his last employer is now dead.[15]

As interesting as this proliferation in the style of the donor-patron relationship is the appearance of dedications which have quite different purposes. First are those in which a publisher uses the public gift to entice or reward copy from an author or translator. Already Aldus Manutius had tried this in Venice in the opening years of the sixteenth century, and in France Guillaume Rouillé was a master of the art. To a theologian in Spain he dedicates a book, asking him to send him more manuscripts as 'gifts'. To the literary Domenichi in Italy, he dedicates the author's own works: 'Accept this book with the same good heart in which you sent it. You presented it to me in a beautiful script and with pictures made by hand. I return it to you printed in beautiful characters and with engraved illustrations. Think of me,' the rich merchant-publisher says to his author, dissolving the commercial

[14] *Les Oeuvres de M. Ambroise Paré* (Paris: Gabriel Buon, 1575), Dedication of Paré to Henri III. *L'Art de Naviguer de Maistre Pierre de Medine, Espaignol . . . traduict de Castillan en Françoys, avec augmentation . . . par Nicolas de Nicolai . . .* (Lyon: Guillaume Rouillé, 1554), Dedication of Nicolay to Henri II. 'Un essay souz l'ombre de voz fortes ailes' used by the jurist Jean de Coras in the dedication to Henri II of *Des Mariages Clandestinement et irreveremment contractes par les enfans de famille . . .* (Toulouse: Pierre du Puis, 1557).

[15] René Choppin, *De Legibus Andium Municipalibus Libri III . . . Ad Henricum. 3. Regem Franciae et Poloniae* (Paris: Nicolas Chesneau, 1581). 'Dons du roi Henri III', *Archives historiques, artistiques et littéraires*, ii (1890–1), 329–30. Bernard Palissy, *Discours admirables, de la nature des eaux et fonteines* (Paris: Martin Le Jeune, 1580), Dedication to Antoine de Ponts, Capitaine de cents gentils-hommes. Jean Massé, *L'art veterinaire, ou grande marechalerie* (Paris: Charles Perier, 1563), Dedication to François de Knevenoy, chevalier de l'ordre du Roi.

relationship into another kind of reciprocity, 'as your friend and brother.'[16]

Indeed, a significant number of printed books were dedicated to friends, that is, to friends with few of the business ties that linked Rouillé and Domenichi. In the first generation of French humanism, from 1490 to 1520, Eugene Rice has found that the literary men dedicated more of their works back and forth to each other and to university colleagues than to powerful patrons. Erasmus explains why in a 1514 dedication to Pieter Gillis:

> Friends of the commonplace and homespun sort, my open-hearted Pieter, have their idea of relationship, like their whole lives, attached to material things; and if ever they have to face a separation, they favour a frequent exchange of rings, knives, caps and other tokens of the kind, for fear that their affection may cool when intercourse is interrupted or actually die away ... But you and I, whose idea of friendship rests wholly in a meeting of minds and the enjoyment of studies in common [a slight exaggeration, since Gillis helped Erasmus sell his books], might well greet one another from time to time with presents for the mind and keepsakes of a literary description ... Any loss due to separation in the actual enjoyment of our friendship should be made good, not without interest, by tokens of this literary kind. And so I send a present—no common present, for you are no common friend, but many jewels in one small book.

Erasmus then went on to discuss the similes and metaphors from classical authors which he had collected for this edition of his *Parabolae*.[17]

Such gifts continued throughout the century, and in contrast with what is often thought about Renaissance dedications, rival in importance those seeking and rewarding patronage. In 1531 Charles de Bouelles dedicates his collection of *Popular Proverbs* to a friend who was a jurist in Paris; the epistle discusses Erasmus's *Adagia* and other proverbs, that is, it suggests a literary setting for the subject of the book. For the poet and mathematician Jacques Peletier, his *Arithmetique*

[16] M. Lowry, *The World of Aldus Manutius. Business and Scholarship in Renaissance Venice* (Ithaca, 1979), 221–2. *Francisci Sanctii Brocensis ... Commentarius in And. Alciati emblemata* (Lyons: Guillaume Rouillé, 1573), Dedication of Rouillé to Martin Azpilcueta Navaro. *Dialogo dell'Imprese Militari et Amorose di Monsignor Giovio ... Con un Ragionamento de Messer Lodovico Domenichi* (Lyon: Guillaume Rouillé, 1559), f. a2^{v}.

[17] E. F. Rice, Jr., 'The Patrons of French Humanism, 1490–1520', in *Renaissance Studies in Honor of Hans Baron*, ed. A. Molho and J. A. Tedeschi (Dekalb, Ill., 1971), 687–702. Hoyoux, 'Les moyens d'existence d'Erasme', 51–2. *Collected Works of Erasmus* (Toronto, 1974–), iii: *The Correspondence of Erasmus*, tr. R. A. B. Mynors and D. F. S. Thomson, no. 312.

of 1552 was a testimonial to his years of intimacy with Theodore Beza in Paris. Each of its 'proems' to him raised an important issue in regard to mathematics, music and the French language, making known to readers the educational program which they and their circle had talked about late into the night.[18]

The public gift could also be used to give expression to the intimate relations among members of a family, while still calling attention to wider cultural values. Uncles dedicate books to nephews and nephews to uncles. Fathers dedicate instructional works to daughters, urging them to be virtuous and obedient; daughters dedicate works to virtuous fathers showing their obedience. Laurent Joubert, royal physician and chancellor of the University of Montpellier, dedicates his translation of a medieval work on surgery to his elderly mother, Catherine Genas. It was not so much her twenty children and eighty grandchildren he wished to praise, he said, but her role as a practical healer, creator of remedies and salves for the poor and the sick. Her ointment for maladies of the breasts was now known in several provinces. Why should she have no reputation after her death? This remarkable text not only celebrates Joubert's mother, but was also his way of showing his readers the best of folk practice, the best of that practice which he had tried to correct in his widely read *Popular Errors in Regard to Health and Medicine*, the best one could hope for when female skills were kept in their proper domain.[19]

In short, these dedications to friends and family establish a context for the subject of the book, the kind of circle where and the spirit with which the book should be read and its contents discussed. The book

[18] Charles de Bouelles, *Proverbiorum Vulgarium Libri tres* (Paris: Galliot Du Pré, 1531), dedication to Joachim Michon. *L'Aritmetique de Iaques Peletier du Mans, departie en Quatre Livres, A Theodore De Besze* (Poitiers: Jean de Marnef, 1552). On the withdrawal of Beza's name in a subsequent edition when their friendship had cooled, see N. Z. Davis, 'Peletier and Beza Part Company', *Studies in the Renaissance*, xi (1964), 188–222.

[19] Antoine de Masso, *Orationes Duae, Comitus Consularibus, Lugduni habitae* (Lyon: Guillaume Rouillé, 1556), Dedication by de Masso to his uncle François Grolier, a Consul. Juan Luis Vives, *L'Institution de la femme chrestienne . . . traduicte en langue Françoise par Pierre de Changy Escuier* (Lyon: Jean de Tournes, 1543), Dedication to Changy's daughter Marguerite. *Epistre consolatoire de Messire Iean Boccace, envoyee au Signeur Pino de Rossi, traduicte d'Italien en Françoys par Damoiselle Marguerite de Cambis* (Lyon: Guillaume Rouillé, 1556), Dedication of Marguerite to her father Louis de Cambis. Jean de Coras, *De Iure Emphyteutico* (Lyon: Guillaume de Rouillé, 1550), Dedication by Coras to his father Jean de Coras. Jean de Coras, *Arrest Memorable du Parlement de Tolose . . Item, Les Douze Reigles du Seigneur Iean Pic de la Mirandole . . . traduites de Laten en François par ledit de Coras* (Lyon: Antoine Vincent, 1565), Dedication of the translation to Coras' daughter Jeanne. *La Grande chirurgie de M. Guy de Chauliac . . . Restituee . . . par M. Iaurens Ioubert* (Lyon: Etienne Michel, 1579), Dedication of Joubert to his mother Catherine Genas; on Joubert's concerns here, see N. Z. Davis, *Society and Culture in Early Modern France* (Stanford, 1975), 224, 258–61.

must seem to come not only to the dedicatee but also to the buyer as a gift, a service.[20]

The turning of the dedication away from the preoccupations of patronage into more general social or religious uses is one of the most striking features of the sixteenth-century book. Erasmus himself made this distinction in a letter to Cardinal Riario, which he had printed not long after he had sent it; should he dedicate his forthcoming edition of Jerome to William Warham, the Archbishop of Canterbury, 'to whom I owe everything', or to Pope Leo X, where the most important return would be the encouragement of peace, 'the nurse of literary studies'? Erasmus finally opted for Warham, making his *New Testament* a gift to Leo, with an epistle which, while including praise for the archbishop's work in England, stressed how the pope could channel the text to the whole world.[21]

The book in fact had an advantage over the traditional gifts from city governments to monarchs and high officials from whom they sought public benefits. Golden statues, cups, capes and barrels of fine wine did not necessarily carry with them the message about the hoped-for reform or action, and were more likely to be given away or returned than was the presentation copy of a book. In the book, everything could be made explicit and the dedications themselves could draw heavily on the language of gifts and responsibilities. So the town lawyer of Lyon sends his commentary on the privileges and immunities of that city to the Governor: 'you represent in this *pays* the king, who has made the gift of these privileges to us'. I now give the *Privileges* back to you in book form, begging you to protect them and allow the Lyonnais to enjoy them and live in peace. A Catholic canon dedicates his book on *The Providence of God over the kings of France* to Charles IX, pointing out that he, like Clovis, was king by the gift of God. He had the gift to cure scrofula, and in return had the obligation to defend sacred religion, in this particular instance by exterminating the heretics. Protestants, of course, could use the book in a similar way, as in Calvin's dedication of his *Institutes* to François Ier, a gift intended to soften the king's heart toward the evangelical cause. Characteristically, Calvin, with his theological worry about the whole matter of reciprocity, talks less of gift and obligation, than of ministry, office and the duty to serve God's glory.[22]

[20] Sometimes authors talk of their publications as a gift to all their readers (Joachim du Bellay in the 'Au lecteur' of *L'Olive* of 1550 says, 'Je te fay" present de mon Olive'). Prefaces from publishers stress their 'service' to the public, even while the title page may be set up to advertise the virtues of the book to potential buyers.

[21] Erasmus, *Correspondence*, no. 333, no. 384.

[22] Claude de Rubys, *Les Privileges, Franchises et Immunitez Octroyees par les Roys ... aux Consuls, Eschevins, manans et habitans de la ville de Lyon* (Lyon: Antoine Gryphius, 1574), Dedication of de Rubys to François de Mandelot, Governor of Lyon. Gabriel de

The most novel Protestant dedication, however, is that of Robert Olivétan for his translation of the Bible, the beautiful folio edition printed by Pierre de Vingle at Neuchâtel in 1535. He will not follow Dame Custom and trot about here and there to a most liberal Maecenas, to a most attentive Patron. This book needs no Very-illustrious, Very-excellent, Very-magnificent Name; it is not of the stuff which Authors exchange craftily for rich gifts and copious grants. Rather he dedicates it to 'the church of Jesus Christ, poor and little, made up of the true faithful', to whom it properly belongs. He gives them what is theirs, but still remains his. This gift has a different nature from any other: 'it is made only to be given and communicated ... it enriches those to whom it is given, but does not improverish in any way those who give it'.[23]

Fed by new sources, the notion that God's gift must be passed on is here restated; the contrast made, however, is not between giving and selling, but between right giving and crafty giving.

As the last test of some of the things I have been claiming about the book as public gift, let us consider which kinds of editions are rarely thought suitable to include a dedication. In the decades when Protestant polemics were too dangerous for the name of the author and the printer, they were also too dangerous for a gift. But could it be that all other works which are not dedicated are simply regarded as too modest, trivial or ephemeral in content and appearance to have the status of a gift—fit therefore only to be objects of commerce? For example, little pamphlets about meteors, floods and monstrous births have no dedications. But this explanation appears inadequate when one reflects on other categories of books which are virtually never dedicated: royal edicts and decrees of other governmental bodies; Shepherd's Calendars, those unchanging repositories of rural lore, though the editions are of substantial size and illustrated; Books of Hours, even when the publisher has adorned them with new woodcuts; and collections of popular plays, farces and songs, even when they appear for the fist time.[24] Here, quite apart from God's share, are texts

---

Saconay, *De la providence de Dieu sur les Roys de France* (Lyon: Michel Jove, 1568), Dedication from Saconay to Charles IX. Jean Calvin, *Christianae Religionis Institutio ... Praefatio ad Christianissumum Regem Franciae, qua hic ei liber pro confessione fidei offertur* (Basel, 1536).

[23] *La Bible. Qui est toute la Saincte escripture* ... (Neuchâtel: Pierre de Vingle, 1535), ff.* ii^{r-v}: D. Robert Olivetanus lhumble et petit translateur a Leglise de Jesus Christ Salut.

[24] For example, of the many Books of Hours which I have examined the only edition which has a dedication is the *paraphrase* in French by Gilles Cailleau, that is, one that departs from the usual texts: *Paraphrase sur les Heures de nostre Dame ... traduictes de Latin en Françoys, par frere Gilles Cailleau* (Poitiers: Jean and Enguilbert de Marnef), 1542, Dedication to Anne de Poulignac, Comtesse de la Roche Foucault. News reports sometimes have the form of a letter, but not a dedicatory letter.

which are so much common property, so much part of the *res publicae*, so much part of the currency of everyday discussion, that no one has the right to appropriate them even long enough for a gift. Rabelais said in his dedication of a scholarly work in 1534 that a book without a dedicatory epistle was acephalous, a book without a head. Yet there is not even a mock dedication in his pseudononymous *Gargantua* and *Pantagruel*, printed not long before, but only prologues to the readers. Was Rabelais ashamed of what he was publishing, as some have claimed? or was it rather that he wanted the stories he had authored to have this quality of common property?[25]

III

In addition to the public gift of a dedicated book, there was the personal gift of a book, by the author or printer, but more especially by a book-owner during his or her lifetime to another person. The evidence for this is scattered through letters and journals, or caught in the bindings, flyleaves and title-pages of the books themselves. Such informal giving was found with medieval manuscripts, as when books were brought by high-born women to their husbands as part of a dowry, but it became much more common with the more easily replaceable printed book. Sometimes these gifts are part of the world of obligation: in 1519, a publisher of Caen presents the University library with six volumes in hopes that he will be forgiven the late payment of a tax, and in 1542 Nicolas de Herberary, translator of the *Amadis de Gaule*, finds he must provide a secretary at the chancellory with two bound volumes of the series if he wants the privilege delivered for his new editions. (In principle, secretaries were paid their salaries by the king and were to take no fees from petitioners for the simple signing of letters.)[26]

Other times, as with the host's gifts at the end of Erasmus's *Godly Banquet*, they are part of the improvised back-and-forth of friendship and intimacy. Montaigne formed the resolution to send a certain Mademoiselle Paulmier his book quite freely from the first hour he saw her, for as he wrote her, 'I felt that you would do it much honor.' Between the learned Protestant judge Jean de Coras in Toulouse and

[25] Dedicatory epistle of Rabelais to Jean du Bellay for *Topographia antiquae Romae* by G. B. Marliani (Lyon: Sébastien Gryphius, 1534) in Rabelais, *Oeuvres*, ed. Jourda, II, 528.

[26] S. G. Bell, 'Medieval Women Book Owners: Arbiters of Lay Piety and Ambassadors of Culture', *Signs*, VII (1982), 763–5. L. Delisle, *Catalogue des livres imprimés ou publiés à Caen avant le milieu du XVIe siècle* (Amsterdam, 1969), II, xvi-xvii, 85–6. Parent, *Les Métiers du livre à Paris*, 108–9. Michaud, *La Grand Chancellerie*, 112–13.

his wife Jacquette in their country home, there was a constant exchange of gifts and compliments: partridges and homemade garters from the wife and from the husband 'a naughty dress', spices, two pens ('well cut to my taste, just like you') and three books: the Psalms translated into Gascon, his own tale in French of a memorable case he had judged, and Nostradamus's predictions for the next year, foretelling bloody things especially against the Catholic clergy. 'Use each of these books for your recreation, while waiting till I come.'[27]

The arrival of such gifts in the countryside was important because in the absence of well-developed routes for peddlers of books, this was a means of their circulation. So we see noblewoman Anne de Laval exchanging fruits and peas with her sister-in-law from their manor houses in the Poitou and then being asked by Claude for the Sixth Book of *Amadis de Gaule*; Anne cannot give it to her yet because her children's tutor has not sent it from Paris. In the Cotentin of rural Normandy, where an active gift exchange went on in food, game, fish, honey and hunting dogs, books were one of the few presents that a *curé* could offer a local landowner like Gilles de Gouberville. Visiting one priest in Cherbourg, Gilles is given Machiavelli's *Prince*; another brings a law book with him when he comes to dinner at the manor house; with a third Gouberville lends the editions of publisher Guillaume Rouillé back and forth, and then makes a gift of one of them to his cousin not far away.[28]

Giving books rather than other presents allowed one a certain flexibility, so long as the recipient was a reader or part of a household where someone read aloud. One could give a new book, but if one did not wish to wait for it to be bound, one could give one's own copy without it being taken at all amiss (indeed, a personal copy may have had more value as a gift in the sixteenth century than a new one). The printed book also had a sexual and especially a social neutrality about it that many other gifts lacked in that world of encoded objects: for instance, the same book could move from parish priest to seigneur to seigneur in Normandy, while a rose could go only from parish priest to seigneur, and a deer only from seigneur to seigneur to duke.[29] It

[27] Michel de Montaigne, *Oeuvres complètes*, ed. M. Rat (Paris, 1962), 1396, letter 32. Montaigne distinguishes between this gift and the obligation he has toward Mlle Paulmier's father. Archives départmentales de la Haute-Garonne, E916; *Lettres de Coras, celles de sa femme, de son fils et de ses amis*, ed. C. Pradel (Albi, 1880), 12, 15, 17, 21.

[28] Archives Nationales, 1AP251, nos. 67, 98. *Le Journal du Sire de Gouberville*, ed. E. de Robillard de Beaurepaire (Caen, 1893), 28, 136, 231. When Jean de Coras is in the country and his wife in Toulouse, she sends him printed news accounts (*Lettres de Coras*, 31).

[29] Based on an analysis of Gouberville, *Journal*. This relative neutrality gives books some advantage as objects to steal, so long as they have no signatures or distinctive binding on them. See B. Lescaze, 'Livres volés, livres lus à Genève au XVIe siècle', in *Cinq siècles d'imprimerie genevoise*, ed. J. P. Candaux and B. Lescaze (Geneva, 1980), 140–50.

could be given at different times of year, unlike the Christmas cake or eggs of Easter. While New Year's Day had been a favoured moment for the presentation of manuscripts in the Middle Ages, dedications and informal gifts of printed books in France were distributed throughout the year. People knew that the royal surgeon, François Rasse des Neux, was a passionate collector, so whenever there was an occasion for a gift for him, as when he got married or had taken good care of a royal patient, he could simply be offered a book. And a book was a durable good: it would last long after the rabbit and deer had been eaten, bearing witness to the intentions of its donor.[30]

Finally, we have some glimpse of the ritual associated with the gift, the inscription by the new owner. This form of taking possession became common in the fifteenth century,[31] when manuscripts were a more plentiful item of trade, and then was developed in the printed book. The buyer might record the place, date and cost of purchase; the recipient might describe the source of the gift. 'These Hours [printed in Paris in 1491] belong to Jeanne Peltre by gift from her Aunt Damoiselle Hilleiry de Faulx, Widow of the late Hugues des Moynes. Nancy, July 7, 1565.' Jeanne then adds religious sayings in Latin and French and draws a skull. The book is appropriated, but not so strongly that it cannot move on and be signed for once again. A particularly interesting form of sixteenth-century signature, first appearing in an Italian manuscript before 1466, suggests this balance between possessiveness and generosity: this book belongs to Jean Grolier [the celebrated collector] and his friends, 'Joannis Grolieri et Amicorum.' A law student in Toulouse signs his textbook 'Guillaume Maillarde et Amicorum' and writes a list of all the books he has lent out—his *Pantagruel* to one friend and so on. The inscription which best illustrates the mixed sentiments I am describing here begins with a little poem:

[30] Lebeuf, 'Remarques sur les dons annuels faits anciennement aux rois de France de la seconde race', in C. Leber, *Collection des meilleurs dissertations, notices et traités particuliers relatifs à l'histoire de France* (Paris, 1838), vii, 400–2. Examples of books in France dedicated and/or presented on New Year's Day: Laurent Joubert, *Traité du Ris* (Paris, 1579), dedicated by Joubert to Princess Marguerite de France, Jan. 1, 1579; Jean Vostet, *Almanach, ou Prognostication des Laboureurs reduite selon le Kalendrier Gregorien* (Paris, 1588), dedicated by Vostet to the Prior of Flammerécourt Jan. 1, 1588; Pierre de L'Estoile, *Mémoires-Journaux*, ed. G. Brunet et al. (Paris, 1888–96), X, 107. Books may have continued to have a more important place in New Year's gifts in England than in France: H. S. Bennett, *English Books and Readers, 1475–1577* (Cambridge, 1952) 48–9; L. A. Montrose, 'Gifts and Reasons: The Contexts of Peele's *Araygnement of Paris*,' *ELH* 47 (1980), 451–2. J. Veyrin-Forrer, 'Un collectionneur peu connu, François Rasse Des Neux, chirurgien parisien', in *Studia Bibliographica in Honorem Herman de la Fontaine-Verwey*, ed. S. vander Woude (Amsterdam, 1968), 393, 402.

[31] N. R. Ker, *Medieval Manuscripts in British Libraries* (Oxford, 1969), I: London, 67–9, 154–5 and *passim*.

Who finds me should return me
To the one written below, for I am his ('je suis sien')
Reason wishes it, God command it
In the goods of others, you have nothing ('vous n'avez rien')
Jean de Beaujeu, architect
and his friends.[32]

There are also indications among these informal gifts of the broader social purposes already noted with dedicated books. People sometimes gave books away to strangers with no expectations of personal return. There was no counter-gift, no eventual reciprocity; it can just be called 'gratuitious', in the Stoic or Christian language of the sixteenth century. Most of the examples are religious ones. In 1560, the Jesuit Possevino came to a Lyon swarming with heretics; he had catechisms printed up at his expense and distributed them in the streets. In 1574, satirical books attacking Catherine de Medici, the king and his council were published by Protestants and in the words of one observer, 'were strewn about as far as the wine cellars of Avignon, where the chambermaids and valets going to draw wine for their masters often found them at their feet. So great was the fervour of those who escaped the [St Bartholomew's Day] Massacre to make known the innocence of the slain, the cruelty and perfidy of the killers and the injustice of the councillors.'[33]

Finally, schemes were worked out by publishers to combine the selling and giving of God's gifts: the profits would go to the poor. The ordinances of the Aumône-Générale of Lyon were published on that basis in 1539, as was a Geneva Bible of 1588. The latter was subsidised by '*gens de bien*, who wanted only to serve God', and other merchant-publishers and printers were advised that it would be especially dishonest and uncharitable to pirate the book. In fact, selling seems often to have dominated over giving: the Aumône-Générale of Lyon found it strange in 1562 that Antoine Vincent had not yet turned over his profits from the Reformed Psalter—surely he had met expenses after two or three years—and the deacons of the Bourse de Pauvres Etrangers in Geneva had to remind certain French publishers in 1567 of their promise to pass on their profits from Calvin's *Sermons*. 'It is

[32] *Horae beate Marie Virginis ad usum ecclesie romane* (Paris, 1491), copy at Cambridge University Library, Inc. 5. D. 1. 19 [2530] (I am grateful to Virginia Reinburg for this reference). Jean de Coras, *De Impuberum* (Toulouse, 1541), copy at the Bibliothèque municipale de Toulouse, Rés. C xvi 60. A. J. V. Le Roux de Lincy, *Recherches sur Jean Grolier, sur sa vie et sa bibliothèque* (Paris, 1866), 87–8. G. D. Hobson, 'Et Amicorum', *The Library*, 5th ser., iv (Sept. 1949), 87–99.

[33] *La Chronique lyonnaise de Jean Guéraud, 1536–1562*, ed. J. Tricou (Lyon, 1929), 150. Pierre de L'Estoile, *Journal pour la règne d'Henri III (1574–1589)*, ed. Louis-Raymond Lefèbvre (Paris, 1943), 56–7.

shameful that those who profess the Gospel, who ... receive the Holy Supper of Our Lord Jesus ... care so little about paying what they owe.'[34]

IV

The giving away of booklets in the streets was an unlikely event during the centuries before printing, but in our last example of books as gifts—the bequest—the pattern was firmly in place during the Middle Ages. Bequests of books are found in Anglo-Norman wills of the eleventh and twelfth century; the library of the Sorbonne was constructed from them in the thirteenth century; legacies of religious books, service books and grammars by chaplains and lay commoners in the city of York in the fourteenth and fifteenth centuries were very numerous indeed. A recent study of the wills of some 978 English peers and peeresses in the late Middle Ages found that forty-two per cent of the men and fifty-eight per cent of the women made gifts of books. The beneficiaries of the peers were mostly their kinfolk; those of the commoners were divided among clercial institutions, schools, family and friends.[35] Since books were movables and not part of the legal patrimony, heirs could then decide whether to keep them or sell them. In fact, sometimes they did sell their gifts, while presumably holding back Books of Hours and the like as special family property. An instructive example is found in the library of more than two dozen manuscripts, most of them legal books, belonging to a local judge in the County of Foix in the late fifteenth century. Seven books came from bequests, including a Bible from an uncle; thirteen manuscripts he had purchased, six of them from heirs selling them after their parents' death; three manuscripts the judge had ordered copied himself; and one set of books on grammar and logic had been given to him by a friend. When he died he divided them equally between his two sons.[36]

[34] *La Police de l'Aulmosne de Lyon* (Lyon: Sébastien Gryphius, 1539); H. de Boissieu, 'L'aumône-générale de 1539 à 1562', *Revue d'histoire de Lyon*, viii (1909), 267. *La Bible, qui est toute la saincte escriture* (Geneva: Jérémie des Planches, 1588), Advertissement aux Marchands libraires et Imprimeurs. Archives de la Charité de Lyon, E10, p. 443. *Sermons de M. Iean Calvin sur le V. livre de Moyse, nommé Deuteronome* (Geneva: Thomas Courteau, 1567), ff. * v^{v}–* vi^{v}.

[35] M. Sheehan, *The Will in Medieval England* (Toronto, 1963), p. 284. R. Rouse, 'The Early Library of the Sorbonne', *Scriptorium*, 21, no. 1 (1967), 42–51. J. H. Moran, *Education and Learning in the City of York, 1300–1560* (Borthwick Papers, no. 55; University of York, 1979), 14–38. J. Rosenthal, 'Aristocratic Cultural Patronage and Book Bequests, 1350–1500', *Bulletin of the John Rylands University Library of Manchester*, 64 (Spring 1982), 522–48.

[36] C. Barrière-Flavy, 'Jean de Roquefort, juge-mage du Comté de Foix, 14 ...– 1474', *Bulletin périodique de la Société Ariégoise des sciences, lettres et arts*, xiv (1914–16), 11, 26–9.

Bequests of books continue, of course, all through the sixteenth century, with the changes introduced by the economy and culture of printing resembling those we have discussed above. To begin with, a wider social circle could now make such gifts as the library of the single book—the printed Hours, the printed Bible, the Psalms, the craft manual—appeared in the families of tradesmen. The beneficiaries still included relatives, religious institutions and schools, but legacies were made to friends as well. A missal printed in Lyon in 1510 passed down from one priest to another, all associated with the same chapter or parish, over 167 years. A more unusual set of Protestant bequests was made in 1556 by Demoiselle Jacqueline de Duaizie, a refugee in Geneva from Anjou. She disposed of 108 books, but they represented only three titles, a Bible and other religious works from the presses of the pastor, Philibert Hamelin. Presumably she had bought them in the first place to assist him in his godly work. Her recipients were the Bourse de Pauvres Etrangers and four neighbours—a shoemaker, a pursemaker, a ribbonmaker, and 'a poor girl from Anjou'—and she said explicitly that the books could be sold and the money used in a suitable way.[37]

Demoiselle Jacqueline's bequest is an example of a new flexibility in the use of the book as gift and also of a gift without immediate hope for return, that is, without expectation of prayers for the repose of her soul. It also expresses insouciance about the border between giving and selling even in the case of religious books. It seems likely (though only extensive research could establish it) that the willingness of heirs to sell books they had received increased with the expanded book market and calculating family strategies of the sixteenth century. On the one hand, Montaigne bequeathed his library to his daughter, who in turn bequeathed it to the vicar-general of Auch, and the jurist Claude Dupuy bequeathed his to his sons, who added to it and then bequeathed it to the Royal Library, of which they had been guardians. On the other hand, the many books so lovingly collected by the surgeon François Rasse Des Neux were sold by his son and heir to a Parisian bookseller, and the library of 700 volumes put together by a young Lyon pastor in the late sixteenth century was sold by his heirs to the Reformed Church of Lyon and not bequeathed to it[38]. And to

[37] On the size of libraries at death, see A. Labarre, *Le Livre dans la vie amiénoise du seizième siècle* (Paris, 1971), Part II. *Missale ad usum lugdunensis ecclesie* (Lyon: Claude Davost dit de Troyes for Jean Huguetan, 1510), signatures in copy at the Bibliothèque Nationale, Rés. B2665. Archives d'Etat de Genève, Notaires, J. Rageau, II. 65^{r-v}; on the printer-pastor Philibert Hamelin, see P. Chaix, *Recherches sur l'imprimerie à Genève de 1550 à 1564* (Geneva, 1954), 194.

[38] J. R. Marboutin, 'La librairie de Michel de Montaigne leguée à un vicaire général d'Auch', *Revue de Gascogne*, xxi, n.s. (1926), 60–6. A. Franklin, *Précis de l'histoire de la bibliothèque du Roi, aujourd'hui Bibliothèque Nationale* (Paris, 1875), 127–37. Veyrin-Forrer,

move back to 1525, Erasmus in his old age did not follow the example of his Godly Feast and give away his books to his friends. Instead he sold his library to the admiring Polish humanist John à Lasco for a good price, while keeping the use rights over it till he died ten years later.[39]

With Erasmus's gifts and sales, let us stop and see what conclusions we can draw about books beyond the market. First, in a century in which the book was being produced by one of the most capitalistic industries in Europe, it continued to be perceived as an object of mixed not absolute property, of collective not private enterprise, despite the unequal distribution of monetary rewards. This happened not only because the facts of collaboration were displayed upon the title page, but because of the persistence of a powerful tradition for understanding what a book was and what it embodied: something not just created by us, but inherited, given by God, given by others. The book was a privileged object that resisted permanent appropriation and which it was especially wrong to view only as a source of profit.

Buying and selling did not, then, automatically obliterate God's share as strict evolutionary schemes would have us expect, nor did markets in books simply replace gifts. If anything, the number of gifts increased and the kinds of donors and recipients multiplied. The spirit and practice of the gift did change, however. At one end of the spectrum, there was a great porousness between the world of commerce and the world of gifts, as publishers used gifts to entice authors, get privileges and enhance sales and as they presented themselves as both givers and sellers. Buying and giving jostled each other in charity projects and authors savoured both presents and sales.

At the other end of the spectrum, the world of gifts expanded as an alternative to the market and market values. Relations between donor and patrons were represented in a wide variety of ways, and books were dedicated or given for broad social purposes that went beyond strict reciprocity. The Olivétan Bible challenged not only those who were preoccupied with profits, but those who wanted return from their gifts. Meanwhile for persons with only a few books on their shelf or living in remote areas, the given book may have loomed larger in their lives than the purchased one.

The philosophy of the gift survived beyond the distinctive circumstances of the sixteenth century. It affected concepts of how the great

---

'François Rasse Des Neux', 414–5. 'Inventaire des Livres de feu Mr de Brunes faict en Decembre 1603 ... Depuis acheptez par l'Eglise reformee de Lyon', Bibliothèque de l'Académie des Sciences de Lyon.

[39] F. Husner, 'Die Bibliothek des Erasmus', in *Gedenkschrift zum 400 Todestage des Erasmus von Rotterdam* (Basel, 1936), 228–59.

private libraries of the seventeenth century were to be used. Symbols of status or power though they were, these collections of books were not be hoarded. In his *Advice on Establishing a Library* of 1627, Gabriel Naudé said that the collection was to be built up by gifts enticed from friends and by purchases, but then was 'not to remain hidden under a bush, but rather be consecrated to the usage of the public and so far as practicable, be accessible to the least of men'. Even John Locke, who went quite far in questioning God's share in individual property and who during his lifetime seems to have made presents of no more than fifty books in his library of 3000—each one carefully registered in his catalogue—affectionately bequeathed the library to his cousin and dearest friends. To jump to our own century, Walter Benjamin talked of his own library in the language of gifts. Unpacking his books, he comes upon some picture albums which had been made by his mother and inherited by him, the start of his library. 'Actually, inheritance is the soundest way of acquiring a collection. For a collector's attitude toward his possessions stems from an owner's feeling of responsibility toward his property. Thus it is in the highest sense the attitude of an heir, and the most distinguished trait of a collection will always be its transmissibility.'[40]

The interesting question, however, may not be the persistence of the idea, but the strength of its critical function. The wings of the Prince beat fast; the engine of the 'block-buster book' smokes. Can the spirit of the gift generate change or is it just infinitely adaptable?

[40] Gabriel Naudé, *Advis pour dresser une bibliothèque. Presenté à Monseigneur le President de Mesme* (Paris, 1627), 98–115, 151–61. K. Pomian, 'Entre l'invisible et le visible: la collection', *Libre*, 3 (1978), 3–56. J. Harrison and P. Laslett, *The Library of John Locke* (2nd edn., Oxford, 1971), 7–8, 44–5. W. Benjamin, *Illuminations*, tr. H. Zohn (New York, 1978), 59–67, 'Unpacking My Library, A Talk about Book Collecting.'

THE ORIGINS OF THE CRIME OF CONSPIRACY

By Professor Alan Harding, M.A., B.Litt., F.R.Hist.S.

READ 16 SEPTEMBER 1982

'THE criminal law', said Sir James Fitzjames Stephen with his usual trenchancy, 'stands to the passion of revenge in much the same relation as marriage to the sexual appetite'.[1] The basic reason for the existence of the criminal law is not to punish 'offences against society' (whatever they might be) but to allow the private passion for revenge to be released in a controlled way.

The English criminal law began where the bloodfeud left off. The machinery set up by Henry II in the Assize of Clarendon is irrelevant here, for jury-presentment before justices in eyre identified the notorious criminal rather than punished the particular crime. This was left for the victim or his kinsmen and friends to avenge by means of the appeal of felony, which was supposed to culminate in a duel between accuser and accused. Towards the end of the thirteenth century, bills complaining of trespasses against the king's peace and asking simultaneously for the punishment of the criminals and compensation to the complainants provided a safer method of avenging lesser injuries, which as misdemeanours, and with the element of civil compensation removed, came to constitute a second tier of crimes, below the felonies. The procedures of the criminal law, like civil actions, have been created in response to the demands of private litigants, not of the crown. Naturally the king could pardon a trespass against his peace, but he could not remit the right of a victim of felony to his revenge, and a royal pardon for homicide stipulated that the beneficiary must independently 'make peace with the kin'. Even accusations of treason were normally made by the appeal of an individual accuser, and tried by battle; and the definition of treason was extended only a little and with difficulty beyond attacks on the persons of the king and his family.[2]

The fact that the criminal law, even the law of treason, was founded on the grievances of individuals heightens the interest of conspiracy,

[1] Quoted by P. Stein and J. Shand, *Legal Values in Western Society* (Edinburgh, 1974), 131, from J. F. Stephen, *General View of the Criminal Law of England* (2nd edn., 1890).

[2] J. F. Stephen, *A History of the Criminal Law of England* (1883), i. 244–250; *The Roll of the Shropshire Eyre of 1256*, ed. A. Harding (Selden Soc., 96, 1981), xlii–xlvii, 307; J. G. Bellamy, *The law of treason in England in the later middle ages* (Cambridge, 1970).

the one crime which must be collective in its commission and has often, it will be argued, been seen as having a collective victim—as being a 'public' crime against the community at large.

The first of the three parts of the lengthy Criminal Law Act of 1977 was entirely devoted to a comprehensive definition of conspiracy. It had been judicially defined as an agreement to effect not only acknowledged crime, but any 'unlawful object', this itself being a matter for judicial interpretation. That the mere agreeing was a crime in itself seemed to be implied by the fact that penalties had been awarded on charges of conspiracy which were sometimes greater than the statutory maximum for the crime which was conspired. The 1977 act created a new statutory offence of conspiracy defined as conduct necessarily leading to the commission of a substantive crime, and attached maximum penalties identical with those for the underlying offences. The common law offence, that is conspiracy as it had been defined by the judges in particular cases, was abolished—except in two areas in which it seems that the mere combination of a number of people to effect an undesirable but not (at least so far) identifiably criminal object is still to be regarded as in itself dangerous to society, the areas of commercial and sexual morality. The assumption of a danger to society is suggested by the repetition of the word 'public' in the descriptions of the two surviving forms of 'independent' conspiracy. One of them is 'conspiracy to corrupt public morals'. The other is conspiracy to defraud, which covers not only an agreement to cause a private individual 'economic loss by depriving him of some property or right ... to which he is or would or might have become entitled', but also one to cause 'a person performing public duties ... to act contrary to his public duty' even if no individual loses by it.[3]

The great modern case on 'the corruption of public morals', the *Ladies' Directory Case*, which ended in the House of Lords in 1961, led the judges to speculate on the whole purpose and history of the criminal law. Frederick Shaw was convicted in the Central Criminal Court of conspiracy to corrupt public morals in that he had arranged for the publication of a prostitutes' directory in which the ladies themselves had advertised. In the Court of Criminal Appeal, Shaw contended that there could be no such offence as conspiracy to corrupt public morals, since there was no crime or civil wrong of corrupting an individual's morals, but the court accepted the Crown's argument that 'at common law any act calculated and intended to corrupt public morals (as opposed to the morals of a particular individual) is an indictable misdemeanour'. The House of Lords entertained no doubt that there remained in the courts of law 'a residual power to enforce the supreme and fundamental purpose of the law, to conserve

[3] Criminal Law Act, 1977; *Annotated Legislation Service*, 249, esp. paras. 11–14, 56–8.

not only the safety and order but also the moral welfare of the State'; and considered that criminal conspiracy was a necessary concept to deal with combinations the purposes of which, 'though not perhaps specifically illegal ... would undermine principles of commercial and moral conduct'. The only dissenting voice was Lord Reid's, who nevertheless accepted the view of criminal conspiracy as the invention of Star Chamber, 'which recognised its possibilities as an engine of government', and as the development (after the fall of Star Chamber) of the common law judges, who had gone on making new crimes 'because Parliament played a comparatively small part, and there was no reception of any foreign system'.[4]

It will be argued here that, on the contrary, the crime of conspiracy was not made by Star Chamber and the seventeenth-century courts, or by the courts at all: it took shape in the late thirteenth and early fourteenth centuries, and Parliament was concerned with it almost from its own beginning as an institution, because it was always an offence against the public authority of the state. It has long been known that there was a civil wrong of conspiracy from the thirteenth century, for an ordinance which can be assigned to 1293 gives a remedy by writ for an injury so named.[5] But the view has been that in the middle ages, both as a tort and as a crime, conspiracy meant only the concerted abuse of legal procedure—the organised prosecution of false accusations out of spite or for gain. In the *Poulterers' Case* of 1611, which is supposed to mark the transition to the modern law of conspiracy, the complainant alleged in Star Chamber that he had been the victim of a conspiracy 'to procure him to be indicted, arraigned, adjudged and hanged' for robbery. Fortunately, at the assizes the grand jury had refused to indict him, which allowed the defendants in Star Chamber to move that no action lay for their admitted 'combination, confederacy and agreement', because it was settled law that a writ of conspiracy was not good unless the aggrieved party had been tried and acquitted of the false charge. But a case in Star Chamber was begun by a bill, not a writ, and according to Coke's report of the case, the judges ruled that 'a false conspiracy betwixt divers persons shall be punished, although nothing be put in execution'.[6]

Holdsworth regards the *Poulterers' Case* as decisive in breaking the medieval restrictions of conspiracy to agreements to corrupt legal proceedings because (as reported by Coke) it gave authority to a quite

[4] *Shaw v D.P.P.*, [1961] 2 W.L.R., 897 ff.

[5] P. H. Winfield, *The History of Conspiracy and Abuse of Legal Procedure* (Cambridge, 1921), 26; the definitive discussion of the early writ of conspiracy is in *Select Cases in the Court of King's Bench*, ed. G. O. Sayles, iii (Selden Soc., 58, 1939), liv–lxxi.

[6] D. Harrison, *Conspiracy as a Crime and as a Tort in English Law* (1924), 12–16; the *Poulterers' Case* is in 9 Rep. 55b, Moore 814.

recent assimilation by Star Chamber of conspiracies to attempts. The Court had taken to punishing attempts to commit a wide variety of unlawful acts, and conspiracies were attempts: if it punished conspiracies to do acts which were neither crimes nor torts (such as to fight duels) it was simply because, as 'the arm of sovereignty', it had discovered new acts which were 'contrary to public policy' so that 'conspiracy to effect them must be treated as a crime'. But what then was the use of the idea of conspiracy? Why were these acts not simply made crimes in themselves; and how could conspiracy turn them into crimes, if it did not have its own unlawfulness? Holdsworth seems to be carrying back a modern lawyer's understanding of conspiracy into an age with a quite different outlook, and indeed introducing technical complications into an area of the law still ridden with crude ideas of what is required for the 'safety and order of the State'.[7] Coke did not think that the rule in the *Poulterers' Case* was of recent origin: it was 'full and manifest in our books', such as in the 'usual commission of oyer and terminer' which gave power to punish every 'coadunation, confederacy or false alliance' *before* the unlawful acts proposed could be executed.[8]

Coke was expressing the law's suspicion of private associations, united by 'bond or promise', in terms which were older than the Common Law itself. The idea of conspiracy may not have been borrowed from what Lord Reid called a 'foreign system', but it was used in English statutes in senses which had been evolving in European laws since Roman times. Eight hundred years before Coke, Charlemagne laid down the punishment for conspirators, including *ubi vero nihil mali perpetratum fuit*—where 'nothing be put in execution'.[9] 'Conspiracy' had been used by the Romans of plots against the state (*contra rem publicam* or *populum Romanum*) and to kill persons in authority, and it had already become virtually synonymous with *conjuratio* (association by oath).[10] Oath-taking was the central element of conspiracy in the middle ages, when social order depended on oaths of loyalty to lords and rulers which could be easily transformed into communal oaths of solidarity against the authorities. The idea of conspiracy derived its scope and power from its yoking with conjuration. On the one hand, the oath-taking gave an objective form to political dissent,

[7] W. S. Holdsworth, *A history of English law* (1922–38), iii. 402–3, v. 203–5, viii. 382; [1961] 2 W.L.R., p. 915.

[8] 9 Rep. 55b.

[9] *Capitularia Regum Francorum*, ed. A. Boretius (Monumenta Germaniae Historica, Legum Sectio II: Hanover, 1883), i. 124 (805).

[10] See *A Latin Dictionary*, ed. C.T. Lewis and C. Short, s.vv. *conjuro*, *conspiro*; the Corpus Iuris Civilis, D. 1.2.2.24 (*proditionis conjurationem ... detexerat*) and D. 48.19.16 (*puniuntur consilia, ut coniurationes et latronum conscientia*). Cf. the Vulgate's description of a *conjuratio* of forty or more jews not to eat or drink till they had killed Paul (Acts 23:13).

making it distinguishable from the overt attacks on rulers in which it might be expressed. On the other hand, identification with collective oath-swearing gave the notion of conspiracy particular power in the area of legal procedures and relationships, for these relied much on the oaths of witnesses and jurymen. After Charlemagne's edict on conspirators comes a chapter on who shall be admitted as oath-helpers in courts of law, which also prescribes the loss of a hand for perjury.[11]

The Carolingian legislation against conspiracy derives from that of the Church, which for many centuries after the fall of Rome had the only developed apparatus of government for private associations to challenge. An often-repeated canon of the Council of Chalcedon in 451 ordered the degradation of clerks *coniurantes aut conspirantes* against their bishops or fellows. In 847, the Council of Mainz decreed 'concerning conspiracy' that excommunication should be pronounced on all who made rebellious conjurations and conspiracies (*coniurationes et conspirationes rebellionis et repugnantiae*) against the king and the one legitimate hierarchy of authority in Church and State.[12] Sworn conspiracies presented a special danger to the legal and administrative procedures of the Church, since the ecclesiastical courts relied even more than lay courts on the collective swearing of oath-helpers and witnesses.[13] But the statutes drawn up for the Cistercian order in 1237 and 1257 show that 'conspiracy' signified a much wider threat by private associations to the 'public laws' of an institution. Conspirators and rebels were to be solemnly excommunicated on Palm Sunday and exiled from their convents 'without hope of return', and they included any who took a dispute to an outside court or appealed against the

[11] *Capitularia Regum Francorum*, i. 124 (805). For Coke's 'coadunation' see *ibid.* 318 (822–3): Volumus de obligationibus, ut nullus homo per sacramentum nec per aliam obligationem adunationem faciat; et si hoc facere praesumpserit, tunc de illis qui prius ipsum consilium incoaverit aut qui hoc factum habet in exilio ab ipso comite in Corsica mittatur ...' For further examples of the fear of collective oaths, and the identification of conjuration with conspiracy, see ibid., ii. 299, 309 (prohibition by Charles the Bald and the bishops in 862 of *infractiones immunitatum et incendia et assalituras in domos et coniurationes et conspirationes et seditiones et raptus feminarum* ...); and J. F. Niermeyer, *Mediae Latinitatis lexicon minus* (Leiden, 1954–76), s.vv. *conjurare, conjuratio, conjurator, conjuratus. Adunatio* appears in British sources from *c.*800: *Revised Medieval Latin Word-List*, prepared by R. E. Latham (1965), s.v. For the use of *conspiratio* and *conjuratio* together in a political context in the twelfth century, see Orderic Vitalis, *Ecclesiastical History*, ed. M. Chibnall (Oxford, 1969–80), i. 274, 277, ii. 212, 216, 307, 314, iv. 82, 268, 278, 280, 284, vi. 32, 334, 448.

[12] *Capitularia Regum Francorum*, i. 56, 77, ii. 177, 309.

[13] In Anglo-Saxon law, an accused priest was only put to the ordeal if he was destitute of friends to act as *consacramentales*, and then but to the mild ordeal of *panem conjuratam*, the morsel of bread conjured to choke the guilty man. The ordeals were themselves brought within the concept of conjuration, which acquired the secondary meaning of the solemn invocation of the instruments of the ordeal to show God's judgment: F. Liebermann, *Die Gesetze der Angelsachsen* (Halle, 1898–1916), i. 281, 286, 405, 424, ii. 39.

authority of their superiors, since this could 'work the subversion and ruin of the whole order'. In the election of abbots, statements like 'we will not have anyone who is not of our own house and country' were forbidden as smacking of conspiracy; and none of the four senior abbots of the order should call sectional meetings at general chapters, since they too made for schism and conspiracy.[14]

English lawyers were therefore applying a wide concept of conspiracy to disrupt public administration, when in 1293 they devised a writ of conspiracy as a remedy for the concerting of false accusations in the courts. The earliest known case of conspiracy in England, the arraignment of Robert of Oxford in King's Bench at Michaelmas 1253 for making a conspiracy at Woodstock so that the abbot of Pershore was unable to carry out the official duties on which he had been sent by the king, contains no suggestion that the obstruction was of judicial administration.[15] But Bracton was certainly aware of the canon disqualifying known conspirators from making accusations.[16] What brought this particular concept of conspiracy to vigorous life in the Common Law was a transformation of English legal procedure in the second half of the thirteenth century. The king had begun to encourage the submission of oral complaints or *querelae* against his officials, without the formality of civil writs or criminal presentments. In this way the courts first took cognisance of the personal injuries which were the stock-in-trade of officials, and which made up a vast new legal category of 'torts' between pleas of land and accusations of felony: forcible eviction, seizure of goods and crops, unjust imprisonment, defamation and extortion. From 1278 onwards, the writ of summons to the eyre announced that the justices would hear trespasses and plaints concerning the king's ministers or anyone else. For many of these grievances writs to begin civil actions for damages were provided; but since they came before the king's justices as trespasses against his peace they could also be treated as indictments of a new second tier of crimes. Now generally written down as bills (in attor-

[14] B. Lucet, *Les Codifications Cisterciennes de 1237 et de 1257* (Centre National de la Recherche Scientifique, Paris, 1977), D. IV. 2–3, V. 18, VI. 5, 11, VII. 12, X. 7, 9, XV. 10. Gratian's canon excluding proved conspirators from acting as accusers in the church courts must stem from an awareness of the corruption which a judicial system dependent on collective oaths was liable to; but in the *Decretum* also the *conjurationum et conspirationum crimen* prohibited by all 'public laws' is a wider political factionalism amongst the clergy (Causae III, q.4, c.5; XI, q.1, c.21).

[15] *King's Bench*, ed. Sayles, iii, p. cxxiii.

[16] Decretum, Causa III, q. 4, c. 5; *Bracton on the Laws and Customs of England*, f. 118b, tr. S. E. Thorne, ii (Cambridge, Mass., 1968), 335. Bracton also takes from the Digest D. 48.19.16) a list of crimes which includes *consilia, ut coniurationes* (f. 105; tr. Thorne, ii, 299; cf. Winfield, *The History of Conspiracy*, 93). He might also have known the passage in the Digest (D. 42.1.33) concerning witnesses bribed by the 'conspiracy' of the opposing parties.

ney's French rather than the Chancery clerk's Latin of the writs), complaints were the source of a new form of criminal prosecution. When the judges were put on trial in 1289 for a variety of sins, it was alleged against Solomon of Rochester that as justice in the Suffolk eyre of 1286 he maliciously arranged for bills to be presented against one Henry of St Edmunds. Solomon answered that it was customary in the eyre that anyone might take a bill to a justice, who was bound to pass it on to the presenting jurors, so that if they found it true they might include it among their indictments. The first original bills in eyre to survive are in fact from 1286, and one of them is endorsed *ista billa est vera* ('the bill is true'). This was the origin of indictment in the strict sense (that is, a jury's endorsement of a bill of accusation), which in the fourteenth century became the method of public prosecution of crimes (felonies as well as trespasses) in all the royal courts, from King's Bench down to the justices of the peace.[17]

The temptation to invent or embellish the bill of complaint,[18] and to corrupt the jury which had to pronounce on its worth, was irresistible. And a jury persuaded to swear falsely in a private interest fitted the concept of an illicit conjuration exactly. King and parliament, which could not remain indifferent to the wholesale corruption of indicting jurors, first instructed the justices in eyre, within a few months of the order of 1278 to hear *querelae* of trespass from all-comers, to inquire further of 'confederates and conspirators' who bound themselves by oath to support their friends in assizes, jury-trials and recognitions, and confound their enemies.[19] Two years later a Herefordshire man sued for trespass twelve men whom he described as 'conspirators and confederates together for saving and condemning whom they willed in assizes, juries and inquisitions': they had indicted him of homicide because he would not pay blackmail, but he had been acquitted at gaol delivery.[20] The government's next attempt to curb malicious prosecution was by the parliamentary ordinance of 1293 which provided a specific writ of 'conspiracy and trespass' returnable in King's Bench for anyone who wished to complain of 'conspirators, inventors and maintainers of false *querelae*'.[21] With this ordinance

[17] A. Harding, 'Plaints and Bills in the History of English Law, mainly in the period 1250–1350', *Legal History Studies 1972*, ed. D. Jenkins (Cardiff, 1975), esp. 75–6.

[18] *King's Bench*, ed. Sayles, vii (Selden Soc., 88, 1971), 191.

[19] *Conjuratus* could mean conspirator, fellow-monk or fellow-juror (Latham, *Revised Medieval Latin Word-List*, 107). As *De Mutuis sacramentis*, the order to the justices became a permanent new chapter of the eyre: H. M. Cam, *Studies in the hundred rolls* (Oxf. Stud. in Soc. and Legal Hist., ed. P. Vinogradoff, vi, 1921), 56–9.

[20] *King's Bench*, ed. Sayles, i (Selden Soc., 55, 1936), 76. For conspiracy in a civil plea in 1290, see *Rotuli Parliamentorum*, i. 58–9.

[21] *Rot. Parl.*, i. 96a; Winfield, *History of Conspiracy*, chap. II; *King's Bench*, ed. Sayles, iii, pp. liv–lxxi.

began a stream of conspiracy cases in King's Bench, and also the case-law on which legal historians have tended to concentrate, rather at the expense of the statutes. The element of jury-corruption is clear in the majority of the early cases, and it was possible, as it would not be later, for there to be a lone defendant to a writ of conspiracy—the suborner of the jury. (His usual answer was that notoriety, 'wild rumour', brought about the indictment, not his contrivance.)[22] But the action was not limited in its early days to indictments or appeals of felony. Conspiracy to corrupt civil process was quite often alleged. The jury in an assize of novel disseisin was said to have recited a verdict drafted by the defendant, by 'arrangement and conspiracy'; and an Oxfordshire parson was alleged to have persuaded people to bring writs of novel disseisin and mort d'ancestor in order to share the winnings, promising one of them 'a jury of the country which would be to his liking' (*inquisicionem patrie pro voluntate sua*).[23] The idea of conspiracy covered the whole spectrum of ways in which the legal process was corrupted, by maintenance, embracery and champerty. Yet this was joined to conspiracy in its political sense, for the developing processes of law and government were turned into a medium for the harassment of one's enemies. So, in 1301, a prior who had been the collector of a clerical subsidy in the diocese of Lincoln five years before alleged conspiracy against a rector who clearly thought too much had been taken from his church: the rector and others, 'for the purpose of altogether destroying the prior and his aforesaid house, falsely and maliciously leagued themselves together', and agreed to inform the treasurer and barons of the exchequer that the prior had levied the subsidy by a roll 'containing a great sum of money' and

[22] *King's Bench*, ed. Sayles iii, pp. 61–2, 81–2, 84–6; cf. *The Eyre of London, 1321*, ed. H.M. Cam, ii (Selden Soc., 86, 1969), 357.

[23] *King's Bench*, ed. Sayles, ii, 168; iii, 18, 22–3, 34, 49–50, 84–6. Some of the early cases did not allege corruption of juries at all: ibid., 61–2, 73–4, 80–1. The conspiracy of lone defendants seems to have consisted in the way they corrupted the proceedings of a court, whether by pleading forged documents or subverting juries. As counsel said in a plea of 1312, 'conspiracy supposeth that false allegations and deceit were employed to the detriment of the other party contrary to the form of law': *Year Book of 5 Edward II*, ed. W. C. Bolland (Selden Soc., 33, 1916), 215. The connection with court proceedings is borne out by the fact that the writ of conspiracy was originally regarded as a judicial writ: *King's Bench*, ed. Sayles, iii, 22–3; but cf. *Early Registers of Writs*, ed. Elsa de Haas and G. D. G. Hall (Selden Soc., 87, 1970), cxxiii, cxxvii, lxxxv, cxxiv-cxxxv). The church courts suffered in the same way: in King's Bench, a Nottinghamshire vicar was accused of conspiracy to present and defame a woman before the visitor of the archbishop of York for adultery with a monk; and the Prior of St Neot's complained of a conspiracy which included getting a woman to appeal him of rape, accusing him to the bishop of Lincoln of incontinence with the same woman, and declaring that he had raised the standard of the king of France on his church and was expelling all the monks who spoke English (*King's Bench*, ed. Sayles, iii, 50–2, 95–6).

rendered his account at the exchequer 'by a certain other roll, containing in it five marks fewer'.[24]

The corruption of legal and administrative procedures had grown, as the procedures grew, to be a new public scourge: in 1305, the Ordinance of Conspirators recognised it as such. It had been countered in 1293 by the provision of a civil writ of 'conspiracy and trespass', only because there was as yet no realisation that new crimes could be invented by statute. But in the articles added to the charters in 1300, the king ordered his justices to award inquests without writ to complainants of 'conspirators, false informers, and evil procurers of dozens, assizes, inquests and juries', and anyone was invited to sue for the king against royal ministers guilty of maintaining pleas for a share of the winnings—in this case, forfeiture to the king being the only result envisaged.[25] The establishment of a class of criminal trespasses from bills prosecuted for the king was completed by the first trailbaston commissions of 1305. *The Ordinatio de trailbastons* issued in the February parliament of that year ordered that those indicted before these special justices of oyer and terminer of the 'enormous trespasses' of maltreating jurors for telling the truth and abusing their power and lordship to retain gangs of malefactors should be tried at the king's suit if no private accuser appeared, outlawed if they did not answer the charge, and if convicted gaoled till they redeemed themselves. The party of trailbaston justices that visited York found their powers insufficient: all 'great matters' were concealed from them 'par procurement e aliaunces des genz du pais', and their commission, of which they sent the king a transcript, did not cover the problem. Almost certainly in response to this letter, another ordinance, 'of conspirators', was added to the one 'of trailbastons', and copies sent to all the parties of justices. In order to take in all the ways in which the law was being manipulated for private ends, this *finalis diffinicio conspiratorum*—the first statutory definition of a crime in English law—was wide: conspirators were not only those who allied with each other by oath, covenant or other bond, falsely to indict and acquit; but also those who retained men of their country by livery (*a lour robes*) or fees to maintain their evil enterprises and stifle truth, the takers as well as the givers; and the stewards and bailiffs of great men who used lordship, office or power to maintain private law-suits or accusations, other than concerned themselves or their masters.[26]

[24] Ibid., 106–8. In another case, a parson complained that, because he would not supply them with corn, eight men conspired to denounce him to the receiver of *querelae* against the clergy as having excommunicated a royal bailiff, a charge it was exceedingly difficult to disprove (ibid., 82–3).

[25] *Statutes of the Realm*, i. 139. Cf. *Britton*, ed. F. M. Nichols (Oxford, 1865), bk. 1, chap. 22, sect. 19, and *King's Bench*, ed. Sayles, iii, pp. liv–lv, lxx.

[26] A. Harding, 'Early trailbaston proceedings from the Lincoln roll of 1305', in

To understand the full significance of conspiracy in the growth of English law and administration we need to shift attention from the civil writ provided in 1293 to the crime defined by the ordinances of 1305. The proceedings in the Eyre of London in 1321 show that the king was concerned with 'leagues and confederacies, by agreements, oaths and other unlawful means' going far beyond agreements to procure false indictments. At the opening of the eyre, those who had been previously attainted 'of any false alliance or maintenance of any false party by which common right was hindered or any manner of conspiracy' were told to stay away from the court; and the justices spent whole days sitting 'within a certain chamber to take inquests both of confederates and conspirators and other matters touching the lord King's Crown'. In one case five leading citizens were indicted of an alliance 'by mutual oaths to maintain false plaints'; to control 'by their confederation and enterprise' all elections of mayors, sheriffs and other officials of the lord King; and to assess royal aids 'so that their confederates should be spared and others of the City oppressed.' The London proceedings also show judges and counsel trying to sort out legitimate alliances 'by parentage and affinity' from illegitimate ones, by oath and covenant—and also how hard it was to eradicate the disease without killing the law itself, which relied so much on conjuration.[27]

Parliament, which itself received complaints of conspiracy and was suspicious of bills advanced by lawyers amongst the commons, vacillated between condemnation of conspirators and anxiety lest honest men trying to do their duty as indicting jurors should be mistaken as such. It urged that conspirators who 'by false imagination, scheming and conspiracy', indicted honest men in every borough and hundred in the land, corrupted trial jurors to give the verdicts they wanted,

---

Medieval Legal Records edited in memory of C. A. F. Meekings, ed. R. F. Hunnisett and J. B. Post (1978), 144–9; Sayles prints the letters between the king and the justices at York in *King's Bench*, ii, pp. cxlix-cli; for the Ordinance of Conspirators, see *Rot. Parl.*, i, 183, and *Statutes of the Realm*, i, 145. The procuring of false indictments and assize-verdicts from packed juries remained the unifying thread of the offence in the trailbaston proceedings: Harding, 'Early trailbaston proceedings', nos. 46, 47, 50, 51, 52; *Wiltshire Gaol Delivery and Trailbaston Rolls, 1275–1306*, ed. R. B. Pugh (Wilts. Rec. Soc., 23: Devizes 1978), nos. 935, 947, 963–5, 1009; *Law and Order in Fourteenth Century Cheshire: The Trailbaston Roll of 1353*, ed. P. H. W. Booth (University of Liverpool Institute of Extension Studies: Dec. 1975), nos. 43, 46–51. But the ordinance of 1305 shifted the focus to the bands of retainers by whom the administration of justice was being perverted: the phrase 'such as maintain Men in the Country with Liveries or fees for to maintain their malicious Enterprises' cannot be dismissed as a vague appendage, as it is by Winfield (*History of Conspiracy*, 2).

[27] *Eyre of London*, ed. Cam, i (Selden Soc., 85, 1968), xxv, cxi-cxiii, 16, 27, 40–2, 44–53.

and even threatened 'les Aturnez de la Court le Roi' acting for their opponents, should be solemnly excommunicated by the bishops (as in 1433 it was still remembered had been done in Edward II's reign), and have their covenants and oaths annulled.[28] Lords were sworn in Parliament not to harbour any felon, nor retain any man by indenture or oath, nor give any livery contrary to law, nor be guilty of maintenance or assent thereto, nor stay the execution of the King's writ.[29] But it was quickly realised that the threat of a charge of conspiracy was itself the best way of coercing jurors. As he launched the trailbaston inquests, Edward I found it necessary to forbid the granting of writs of conspiracy against juries of indictment, for 'if this were suffered many people would fear to be put on inquests and indict no man however guilty'.[30] It soon became settled law that the writ did not lie against indictors. Nevertheless, by the time of the parliament of the summer of 1306, petitions were arriving from 'those who served the king before the justices of trailbaston' complaining that men convicted of conspiracy subsequently bought themselves on to inquests 'to confound those who had faithfully indicted them', and the king was compelled to suspend the law that no-one should be taken and imprisoned unless indicted by the oath of twelve jurymen. The parliament of 1393 was still complaining of evil-doers indicted by honest men and then acquitted by corrupt juries, who promptly brought writs of conspiracy against their indictors in foreign counties: if jurymen were frightened from telling the truth, it would be to the 'very great destruction of the enforcement of the law of the realm'.[31]

The obstruction of law and government by conspiracies amounted, it seems to me, to a crisis of public morals far more real than the organisation of sexual vice so called by the judges in 1961. Conspiracy was the first crime to be defined in parliament because it threatened the whole system of justice on which the state was being erected, and perverted the great new means of political communication between the king and his subjects by bills of complaint. The threat was not from ephemeral agreements, but (to use Coke's words in the *Poulterers' Case*) from 'coadunations, confederacies and false alliances' given a semi-permanent existence by oaths and liveries. Conspiracy in the sense of private alliances, not treason narrowly defined as attacks on royal persons, was the real crime against the state in the fourteenth

[28] *Rot. Parl.*, i. 201a, 289a, 299a, 330b; ii. 60a, 137a, 142b, 165a, 407b; iii. 627b; iv. 120, 127a, 147a, 421a; v. 28. See iii. 288b for an allegation of conspiracy to give false information to the king's council which was discussed in Parliament.

[29] *Rot. Parl.*, vi. 287b, 288a.

[30] *Calendar of Chancery Warrants*, i. 241–2.

[31] *Year Books of 5 Edward II* (1311–12), ed. W. C. Bolland (Selden Soc., 31, 1915), 114–16; *Eyre of London, 1321*, ed. Cam, ii, 356–7; *Rot. Parl.*, i. 201a (no. 63), ii. 259b, 265b; iii. 306a, 318a; *Calendar of Close Rolls*, 1302–7, 397.

century. Royal councillors and judges were required by their oath, as it was laid down in 1306, to reveal to the king any alliances they had made amongst the baronage which would impede them in their duties.[32] Piers Gaveston was accused of 'accroaching to himself Royal power and Royal dignity' by 'making alliance of people by oath to live and die with him against all others'.[33] That conspiracy was not assimilated to treason but remained a separate crime was because sworn alliances were too much a part of the artistocratic way of life for the king to be permitted to bring them within the scope of the penalties meted out to traitors. The expressed intention of the great Statute of 1352 was to exclude from the definition of treason the activity of riding about the country in bands to kill, rob and hold to ransom.[34] Yet this concerted defiance of public order by the gentry, and the 'conspiracy and false covin' of powerful townsmen such as in 1340 disrupted the sale of the produce of a subsidy of wheat, fleeces and lambs, and required 'great treaty and parlance' between Lords and Commons to defeat it,[35] constituted the real threat to royal power, which the idea of conspiracy was needed to identify.

After the medieval period, the idea of conspiracy was displaced from the areas of its original importance by statutes which punished directly the oath-taking which had given conspiracies substance. The Unlawful Oaths Act of 1797, for example, made it a felony punishable by seven years transportation to administer or take an oath to be of any association or confederacy with the purpose of disturbing the public peace; or to obey the orders of leaders not having lawful

[32] *Rot. Parl.*, i. 219.

[33] Ibid., 283b.

[34] Bellamy, *Law of Treason*, chap. 4, esp. 90–1. 'Conspiring' is very often joined with 'compassing and imagining' in the description of late medieval treasons, but only to emphasise the length of the preparation of the attack on the king. The association did not in itself constitute treason, and Coke insists that the 'compassing, intent or imagination, though secret' must be proved by an overt act, such as the obtaining of weapons, powder or poison, for the execution of the conspiracy: *Fifty-Third Report of the Deputy Keeper of the Public Records* (1892), 28–33; *Rot. Parl.*, vi. 436b; Holdsworth, *History of English Law*, iii. 291, viii. 311.

[35] *Rot. Parl.*, ii. 117. See *King's Bench*, ed. Sayles, vi, 94–7, for an example of a sworn confederacy at Guildford in 1354, which succeeded in gaining control of the commission of the peace. Indictments before the justices of the peace reveal the same types of activity at a lower level: confederacies and unlawful agreements by local officials and tax-collectors to extort money for their own use, intertwined with conspiracies to maintain false quarrels and procure false indictments. Even the confederacy and conspiracy of two men to alter the date on a notarial instrument pleaded in a case in a church court between a parson and his parishioners was the subject of an indictment before the J.P.s, because this was held to undermine the procedures of church law *and* the peace of the lord king and the tranquillity of his people in the said parish: *Proceedings before the Justices of the Peace in the Fourteenth and Fifteenth Centuries*, ed. B. H. Putnam (The Ames Foundation: Cambridge, Mass., and London, 1938), 69, 71, 72, 221, 362, 385–6, 408.

authority; or not to discover an unlawful combination or confederacy.[36] Long before that, the law of perjury had displaced the law of conspiracy as the chief sanction against the corruption of the legal process out of which had come the original perception of the threat to public authority from sworn associations. Perjury and subornation of perjury were defined in the sixteenth century because only then were witnesses being regularly heard in the secular courts, but they overlapped much of conspiracy's former province. They too were thought to grow 'by unlawful retainers, maintenance, embracing, champerty and corruption of good, as well of the Sheriffs as of other officers. . . .' The dangers of using the law of perjury and the law of conspiracy against the abuse of legal procedure were also similar: false oaths were almost impossible to separate from true ones, and widespread perjury charges, it was feared, would make men reluctant to inform or testify.[37]

But despite the wide scope of perjury, and the definition of a tort of malicious prosecution in place of the civil injury remedied by the writ of conspiracy, a crime of conspiracy to pervert the course of justice survived on slightly shifted ground. Crises in public morality like those caused by the manipulation of juries in the early fourteenth century and the suborning of witnesses in the sixteenth were bound to recur as the judicial system developed. There was another in the late eighteenth and early nineteenth centuries, when the initiative in criminal prosecution fell into the hands of a more organised and professional police, who yet remained dependent on piecemeal rewards. For a time 'blood-money conspiracies' between the police and their criminal contacts endangered the whole system of prosecution.[38]

What happened to conspiracy as its foundation in collective oaths crumbled away was not extension by the judges from abuse of legal procedure to agreements for any unlawful purpose, but the definition of a number of substantive offences out of the multifarious criminal activities of sworn associations. Conspiracy to pervert the course of justice was one. Another was conspiracy to corrupt public morals (in the sexual sense), which the judges in the *Ladies' Directory Case* were right in thinking had long existed in English law, though they still did

[36] 37 Geo. 3, c. 123; cf. 52 Geo. 3, c. 104.

[37] *Statutes of the Realm*, ii. 589–90; M. D. Gordon, 'The Perjury Statute of 1563; A Case History of Confusion', *Proceedings of the American Philosophical Society*, 124 (1980), 446–8; idem, 'The Invention of a Common Law Crime: Perjury and the Elizabethan Courts', *American Journal of Legal History*, 24 (1980), 152, 165–6.

[38] Holdsworth, *History of English Law*, viii. 386–7; L. Radzinowicz, *A History of English Criminal Law* (1948–68), ii. 326 ff. In 1816, three London policemen were sentenced to death for aiding and abetting the crime of counterfeiting which they had inveigled some Irishmen into committing: they almost got away with their plot because they swore their victims to secrecy and the Irishmen, as Catholics, would not break their oaths even when they realised they had been duped (ibid., 336).

not go far enough back for its origins. They made much of *Rex v. Delaval*, the case from 1763 in which Lord Mansfield proclaimed King's Bench to be 'the *custos morum* of the people'. Sir Francis Delaval, William Bates (a musician) and John Fraine (an attorney) had been charged with an unlawful combination and conspiracy to remove a girl of eighteen from her apprenticeship to Bates and place her in the hands of Sir Francis for the purposes of prostitution. In the court's opinion this was a conspiracy 'contrary to decency and morality', and quite properly the subject of an information by the girl's father, 'an innocent and injured man'. This case is important because it shifts the essence of the crime of seduction from the injury to father or husband to the lascivious purpose, and gives public immorality the narrowly sexual connotation perpetuated by the modern judges.[39] There are fourteenth-century cases to show that schemes to seize and marry women against the will of their families (though quite often with the woman's own approval) were recognised as a distinctive form of conspiracy from the beginning. In 1377 there was a general complaint to the king in parliament that men from Wales, Lancashire, Cheshire and other 'franchised places' were riding through the marcher counties in sworn confederacies, and carrying off women marriageable and already married into strange country;[40] and a few years later, two brothers were indicted before justices of the peace in Wiltshire of many confederacies and conspiracies, and in particular of conspiring with unnamed associates to carry off a married woman, procure her a divorce, and marry her to the younger of the two.[41] These cases anticipate seventeenth- and eighteenth-century indictments for conspiracy to commit adultery, to secure a marriage to the prejudice of others, and to procure wards of court to marry.[42]

This is now one of the only two independent forms of criminal conspiracy—that is, one for which there is no underlying offence which would be criminal on the part of an individual—yet it was originally just a minor aspect of the threat of private confederacies to public order. For most of its history the chief concern of the law of conspiracy has been the other member of the pair discerned by the judges in 1961: the corruption of commercial, not sexual, behaviour. Again the outlawry of trade conspiracies did not start with the

[39] *Shaw v. D.P.P.* [1961] 2 W.L.R., 909, 915, 923; *Rex v. Delaval* [1763] 3 Burr. 1434. The moralising may have been necessary because, as Lord Tucker pointed out in *Shaw v. D.P.P.* (930), 'the girl's master was willing and she was not in the custody of her father'.

[40] *Rot. Parl.*, iii. 42–3, 81; *Statutes of the Realm*, ii. 9–10; cf. P.R.O., Just. 1/437, m. 11 for a Lancashire case of 1357 which seems to fit the description; *raptus feminarum* was associated with Carolingian conspiracies (footnote 12 above).

[41] *Proceedings before the Justices of the Peace*, ed. Putnam, 386.

[42] Harrison, *Conspiracy as a Crime and as a Tort*, 16–17, 29, 110, 120.

eighteenth-century recognition of ephemeral schemes to cheat or defraud,[43] for they too were a familiar type of medieval sworn association. The statute of 1824 which first exempted combinations of workmen from the law of conspiracy and substituted other provisions 'for protecting the free employment of capital and labour', swept away thirty-three English, Irish and Scottish acts, the list of which is an extraordinary monument to the idea of conspiracy in restraint of trade. Fourth in the list stands 'The Bill of Conspiracies of Victuallers and Craftsmen' of 1548, which was directed against those who 'conspired and covenanted together to sell their victuals at unreasonable prices: And likewise artificers, handicraftsmen, and labourers' who made 'confederacies and promises, and have sworn mutual oaths not only that they should not meddle with another's work, and perform and finish that another hath begun, but also to constitute and appoint how much work they shall do in a day, and what hours and times they shall work.' Third in the list is an Irish 'Act for Servants' Wages' of Henry VIII's reign; second a statute of 1425 entitled 'Masons shall not confederate themselves in chapters and assemblies'. And at the head of the list stands 'so much of a certain act passed in the thirty-third year of King Edward the First, entitled *Who be conspirators and who be champertors*, as relates to combinations or conspiracies of workmen or other persons to obtain an advance or to fix the rate of wages ... and as relates to combinations or conspiracies of masters, manufacturers or other persons, to lower or fix the rate of wages ...'[44]

There is, of course, nothing about workmen or manufacturers in the ordinance of conspirators of 1305, but there very well could have been. A fear of popular conjurations is evident in Carolingian capitularies, and from the twelfth century the threat to public peace was seen to arise in particular from the communes of merchants and artisans, formed by oaths of solidarity against the aristocratic feudal world.[45] The tightening of royal control over the towns meant that the urban conspiracies which came to the notice of the king's courts were often of sections of the townspeople against the town officials and royal administration. Philippe de Beaumanoir, writing his *Coutumes de*

[43] Harrison, ibid., 21–2, 82 ff.

[44] 5 Geo. 4, c. 95.

[45] *Capitularia Regum Francorum*, i. 51 (c. 16), 64 (c. 26), 301 (c. 7); *Annales Bertiniani*, ed. G. Waitz (MGH Scriptores, 1883), 51; Niermeyer, *Lexicon Minus*, s.v. conjurare; G. Duby, *The Three Orders: Feudal Society Imagined*, tr. A. Goldhammer (Chicago and London, 1980), 28–30, 186, 216; *Constitutiones et acta publica imperatorum et regum*, i (911–1197), ed. L. Weiland (MGH Legum Sectio IV, 1893), 246; cf. T. N. Bisson. 'The Organized Peace in Southern France and Catalonia, ca. 1140–ca. 1233', *Amer. Hist. Rev.*, 82 (1977), 305, for the institution of peace at Montpellier, followed immediately by a prohibition of 'conjurations and conspiracies', and all confraternities except those approved by lords or bishops 'for urgent necessity or evident utility'.

Beauvaisis about the year 1280, includes 'alliances made against one's lord or against the common profit' amongst the crimes which call for special vengeance. Barbarossa had shown how to deal with the former by his destruction of the rebellious Lombard communes. The latter—alliances against the common profit—exist when people 'make agreements that they will not work at so low a fee as before, and raise it on their own authority and resolve that they will not work for less, bullying and threatening fellow-workmen who will not join the union.' For Beaumanoir they are against common right because they inflate the cost to the community of essential services.[46]

The crime of conspiracy was first defined in English law to comprehend the threat from bands of gentry and liveried retainers, fostered by the war-crisis at the end of the thirteenth century, but the age-old fear of popular conspiracy was only waiting to be given preeminence by economic crisis. The first type of popular conjuration to be recognised in England was that of serfs who banded together to win their freedom. This fitted very well into an idea of conspiracy as corruption of the legal process by false oath-swearing, because legal proof of free or unfree status and procedures for reclaiming fugitive villeins had relied since Merovingian times on the collective oaths of family and neighbours.[47] Within a few months of the ordinance of 1305, an indictment was made before the Wiltshire trailbaston justices against the 'conspirators' who had 'falsely and maliciously abetted and maintained' the Prior of Ogbourne's villeins in their plea against the prior in the king's court: thirty years later, these villeins were themselves accused of conspiracy when they contributed to a common purse in order to fight for ancient demesne status.[48] In its thirteenth-century statutes, the Cistercian order had shown itself particularly fearful of conspiracies among lay-brothers. In the 1330s the Ledger-Book of Vale Royal Abbey, a recently-founded Cistercian house in Cheshire, describes a long drawn out 'conspiracy to obtain their liberty' by the

[46] Philippe de Beaumanoir, *Coutumes de Beauvaisis*, ed. A. Salmon (Paris, 1899–1900), 446–9; for the conspiracies or *takehans* of Flemish towns in the late thirteenth century, see *Les Olim ou Registres des Arrêts rendus par la Cour du Roi*, ed. Comte Beugnot (Paris, 1842), ii. 64 (no. xi), 116 (xxvi), 326–7.

[47] *Lex Ribuaria*, ed. F. Beyerle and R. Buchner (MGH Legum Sectio i, 1954), 114 (1.6), 110 (1.11), 119 (1.14); *Formulae Merowingici et Karolini Aevi*, ed. K. Zeumer (MGH Legum Sectio v, 1882–6), 213–14; *Capitularia Regum Francorum*, i. 191 (c. 9), 268 (c. 2), 315 (c. 2); P. R. Hyams, 'The proof of villein status in the common law', *Engl. Hist. Rev.*, 89 (1974), 721–49. For the lords' perennial fear of conspiracies by their serfs, *ministeriales* and freedmen, see D. 1.12.1.10 of the Corpus Juris Civilis; the Bamberg Dientstrecht (1057–64) in *Monumenta Bambergensia*, ed. P. Jaffe (Berlin, 1869), 50 ff; Lucet, *Les Codifications Cisterciennes*, D. x. 9.

[48] *Wiltshire Gaol Delivery and Trailbaston Rolls*, ed. Pugh, no. 1009; R. H. Hilton, 'Peasant movements in England before 1381', *Econ. Hist. Rev.*, 2nd ser. II (1949), reprinted in *Essays in Economic History*, ed. E. M. Carus-Wilson, ii. 83–4.

villeins of Darnhall, a manor with which the monks had been endowed by Edward I and plausibly ancient demesne: the villeins' campaign involved nocturnal assemblies in the woods, a complaint to the justiciar of Chester, a petition to parliament, and setting out 'like mad dogs' to demand justice of the king in person at Windsor.[49] By the time of the Peasants' Revolt in 1381 there were regular commissions of oyer and terminer concerning bondmen who had 'rebelliously withdrawn the customary services due' to their lords, and had 'in divers assemblies mutually confederated and bound themselves by oath' to resist their lords.[50] In the sixteenth century and into the seventeenth, villein conspiracy survived in the confederacies of copyholders to deprive landlords of their manorial rights which were punished in Star Chamber.[51]

Commercial conspiracy in a stricter sense was brought under the law by the labour legislation after the Black Death, which froze workmen's wages and the prices charged by carriers and sellers of victuals.[52] The government tried to make servants swear to observe these laws,[53] and sworn associations of artisans were formed to resist them. A statute of 1361 annulled the 'alliances and covins of masons and carpenters, and the congregations, chapters, ordinances and oaths made amongst them or to be made in the future.'[54] In 1395, it was the turn of the tanners to be accused of conspiracy, confederacy and covin to bring down the price of the hides they purchased, and to raise the price at which they sold them after tanning.[55] Merchants who made 'conspiracy, confederacy, covin, machination or murmur or wicked device' to circumvent the regulations of the Staple became liable to forefeit their goods by a statute of 1353;[56] and in 1376 there was a complaint in parliament against Lombard merchants who, 'by their false compassing and fraud, and conspiracy between them', purchased wool and other goods on credit, posing as agents of reputable com-

[49] *The Ledger-Book of Vale Royal Abbey*, ed. J. Brownbill (Lancs. and Ches. Rec. Soc., lxviii, 1914), 31–2, 37–42.

[50] *Calendar of Patent Rolls*, 1377–81, 204; Putnam, *Proceedings before the Justices of the Peace*, 11.

[51] Holdsworth, *History of English Law*, v. 204, n. 4; *Select Cases before the King's Council in the Star Chamber*, ii (1509–44), ed. I. S. Leadam (Selden Soc., 25, 1910), 38 ff, 184 ff: in the first case it was complained that 'the inhabitants of the said whole town of Thingden contrary to your peace laws and statutes ... doth assemble themselves and do confederate and combinate themselves ... and call common councils ... and make a common purse', and in the second there was talk of 'alliances', 'confederates' and 'false conspiracy and covin'.

[52] B. H. Putnam, *The Enforcement of the Statutes of Labourers* (New York, 1908), Appx. 8–11.

[53] *Rot. Parl.*, ii. 234a.

[54] *Statutes of the Realm*, i. 367 (34 Edw. 3, c. 9).

[55] *Rot. Parl.*, iii. 330–1.

[56] Ibid., ii. 251.

panies which denied all knowledge of them when they failed to pay.[57]

The terms in which the rebels of 1381 and 1450 were prosecuted suggest that economic crisis had moved the target of the 'final definition of conspirators' in 1305 from aristocratic retinues to urban and peasant conventicles, and begun to create a new image of social subversion by the lower orders. In a conspiracy at Beverley, which was said to threaten 'the annihilation of the whole community', the *communes conspiratores* were the official collectors of a local customs duty who sought to pocket the money, using the old conspirators' weapon of false appeals as part of their armoury of extortion.[58] But artisans and peasants were also said to have been *ad invicem confederati, interligati et jurati* or *invicem confederati et conspirantes*, and allegations of secret councils in the woods and forced oaths were widespread. At Scarborough, rioters bound themselves 'with one assent', by oaths as well as liveries, to support each other's quarrels and forced people to swear loyalty to them and to the commons of all England.[59] The followers of Jack Cade in 1450—yeomen, husbandmen and labourers—were accused of 'conspiring in unlawful conventicles'.[60] For Thomas Marowe, when he gave his reading on the commission of the peace in 1503, the term 'conventicles' embraced not only illicit assemblies of the people but also agreements to bring false appeals and indeed every conversation between two or more persons with a view to committing an unlawful act: which were punishable even if all the parties to the plot were never together at the same time and nothing was carried through.[61] The primary meaning of criminal conspiracies had become the subversive associations of the common people.

I conclude firstly that the law of conspiracy *is* an exception to Fitzjames Stephen's generalisation that the criminal law exists to legitimise revenge for injuries to individuals. Conspiracy was originally the crime against the whole community represented by the mere existence of sworn confederacies working in the private interest. That is why it was the first crime to be defined in parliament, and why over

[57] Ibid., 350b.

[58] A. Réville and C. Petit-Dutaillis, *Le soulèvement des travailleurs d'Angleterre en 1381* (Paris, 1898), 190–7, 260 ff.

[59] Ibid., 177, 180, 184, 186, 187, 192, 199, 206, 253–4, 256, 267. Cf. P.R.O., KB 9/166/2, where an Essex leader is indicted of assembling the men of a township and swearing them to revolt. In the summer of 1381 the villeins of the abbot of Chester were said to have 'gathered in secret confederacies within the woods and hidden places'.

[60] KB 9/42/1, mm. 16–17, for example.

[61] B. H. Putnam, *Early Treatises on the Practice of the Justices of the Peace in the Fifteenth and Sixteenth Centuries* (Oxf. Stud. in Soc. and Legal Hist., ed. P. Vinogradoff, vii, 1924), 372–3. Marowe says nothing of oaths; common purses and strike funds were already more important at the level of popular conspiracies.

the course of the centuries parliament has often redefined it by statute. Along with the basic concepts of injury to the individual, by homicide or robbery, the threat of private associations to the civil order of the State is one of an ancient set of ideas on which the criminal law rests. The sort of legal history which traces the evolution of modern doctrines teleologically through a series of cases does not work very well for concepts of crime, which tend to be based on a simple morality which is appealed to by the judges as occasion demands.

But, secondly, this morality is not unchanging, and the suspicion of private associations which was deep-rooted in medieval society derived a special complexion from the mode and timing of the introduction of conspiracy into English law. It came in to identify the evil of false conjurations within the legal process itself, at a time when the bill of complaint was giving new opportunities for the profitable abuse of court procedures. Like political liberty,[62] conspiracy developed its meaning within the context of the judicial system, because the administration of justice was the first area in which the State asserted its exclusive authority. But as well as changing the face of the law, bills were demanding from king and council in the new institution of parliament consistent policies towards other general problems of English society, which were exacerbated by the Black Death; and in order to combat the obstruction of royal administration by private associations in these new areas, other old senses of conspiracy needed to be incorporated into English law.

Thirdly, and finally, the shifting application of the idea of conspiracy actually extended awareness of the public authority which private associations challenged. A crime must have a victim, whether a person or an institution, and the definition of a new crime defines a new sort of victim. The main victim of conspiracy was quickly seen to be not a set of individuals but the system of public administration which we call the State: the sworn associations which so troubled late medieval society made their contribution to the growth of public authority nonetheless. The very fact that conspiracy was treated in law both as a private injury and as a crime gave it the image of a widely-diffused social evil, threatening (like the Beverley conspiracy in 1381) 'the annihilation of the whole community' as simply plotting against the persons of its rulers never could. The difficulty of rooting out conspiracies without further damaging a system of justice reliant upon the conjurations of jurymen also showed that what was at stake was a true public morality which would sustain rather than subvert lawful authority.

The watershed between a concept of crime as serious personal injury, revenge for which the king merely sanctioned and controlled,

[62] A. Harding, 'Political Liberty in the Middle Ages', *Speculum*, 55 (1980), 423–43.

and the punishment of some activities as criminal because they seemed to undermine the very system of justice, was passed by 1305 with the Ordinance of Trailbastons, which made 'enormous trespasses' punishable at the king's suit alone, and the Ordinance of Conspirators, which began the statutory definition of the new category of crime. These 'misdemeanours' were distinguished by the obvious inappropriateness to them of the extreme penalties which were automatically incurred by convicted traitors and felons. The statutes which developed the criminal law now had the task of prescribing what sort of recompense was owed society by (for instance) conspirators who might have done no harm to specific individuals. They experimented with fines, the pillory and imprisonment, in doses increased for the second and third offence; the forfeiture by the conspiratorial tanners of their hides; and in the act of 1548 against the conspiracies of victuallers and craftsmen, the dissolution of an offending corporation and the holding of the individual offender 'as a man infamous, and his saying, depositions or oath not to be credited at any time in any matters of judgment'.[63]

[63] *Rot. Parl.*, iii. 331; 2 & 3 Edw. 6, c. 15.

RIOT PREVENTION AND CONTROL IN EARLY STUART LONDON

By K. J. Lindley, M.A., Ph.D.

READ AT THE SOCIETY'S CONFERENCE 17 SEPTEMBER 1982

THE notion that London conforms to an urban crisis model in the seventeenth century has recently been challenged in a bold reassessment of how the City adapted to change and coped with its problems at a grass-roots level.[1] Too much stress, it is argued, has been placed upon disorder in the capital, wrongly depicted as constantly prone to rioting and criminality, to the neglect of its ordered and stable features which enabled London to weather a period of unprecedented political upheaval without a popular uprising. Yet has disorder in seventeenth-century London received too much emphasis, and just how effective were the endeavours of municipal and other authorities to maintain peace on the streets? This paper will attempt to gauge the seriousness of the problem posed by periodic rioting in the capital, and the efficacy of measures of riot prevention and control, in the period from James I's accession to Charles I's departure from London, allegedly driven out by uncontrollable tumult and sedition, in January 1642. No answer to these questions would be complete, however, if the investigation were simply confined to the area under the lord mayor's jurisdiction, for disturbances which began in the suburbs could soon cross over the City's limits or the citizens themselves could participate in disorders outside those limits.

Few years passed without at least one disturbance on the streets of early Stuart London and its suburbs serious enough to merit official concern. Traditional holidays and festivals, and especially Shrove Tuesdays, were a regular source of anxiety as apprentices, and sometimes other unruly elements, engaged in acts of ritualised yet very real violence. Shrove Tuesday riots occurred on at least twenty-four of the thirty-nine years under discussion, normally in the suburbs and especially the northern suburbs within easy reach of traditional recreational areas.[2] Some years witnessed simultaneous outbreaks of violence

[1] Valerie Pearl, 'Change and stability in seventeenth-century London' in *The London Journal*, v, no. 1 (1979), *passim*; id., 'Social policy in early modern London' in *History and Imagination: essays in honour of H. R. Trevor-Roper* ed. H. Lloyd-Jones, V. Pearl and B. Worden (1981), *passim.*

[2] P. Burke, 'Popular culture in seventeenth-century London' in *The London Journal*,

in more than one neighbourhood, like Shrove Tuesday 1617 when there were riots in Lincoln's Inn Fields and Drury Lane, Finsbury Fields and Wapping. The numbers involved were often substantial, varying from one or two hundred rioters in the more modest incident to crowds numbered in their thousands in the most spectacular, and they were drawn from a much wider area than the immediate vicinity of the riot. Three of the five apprentices arrested during the Norton Folgate disturbance of 1608, for example, came from intramural parishes and the other two were from St Giles without Cripplegate and Southwark.[3] Violence was generally directed at specific targets, particularly brothels and playhouses. Windows were smashed, houses were invaded and their occupants assaulted, or, in the worst cases, properties were actually demolished, and constables and other officers who stood in the way were also assaulted. The repeated attacks upon a Shoreditch brothel presided over by Joan Leake, widow, on Shrove Tuesday 1612, 1613 and 1614, which culminated in the demolition of the property, provide a prime example of the ritualised nature of much of the violence, and the rioters could not fail to have derived a sense of legitimacy from Joan Leake's being dismissed from keeping an alehouse at the same sessions which saw the commitment of a handful of her 1612 assailants.[4] The blackest Shrove Tuesday was undoubtedly that of 1617 when large-scale rioting broke out in three separate centres. In the gravest incident, thousands of apprentices and other unruly subjects (some of the victims, perhaps, of the current dislocation of trade) forced their way into a new playhouse in Drury Lane, destroyed its contents and had entered upon its demolition when they were finally dispersed. On the same day, rioters broke into Finsbury prison, released the prisoners, smashed its windows and untiled the roof, while at Wapping several houses were demolished, and many others damaged, by rioters who hurled brickbats at a sheriff and a justice of the peace trying to restore order.[5]

None of the other traditional festivals approached Shrove Tuesday in the persistence and magnitude of its disorder, despite the great vigilance believed essential as they fell due. May Day aroused suf-

iii, no. 2 (1977), 144–6. There is documentary evidence of Shrove Tuesday disturbances on the following inclusive dates: 1606–9, 1611–14, 1616–21, 1623–4, 1628–9, 1632–6, and 1641. The evidence is to be found in the Middlesex sessions records, the repertories of the court of aldermen, privy council registers and state papers domestic.

[3] Greater London Record Office (henceforth G.L.R.O.), MJ/SR. 457/58–62, 76–7.

[4] Ibid., 517/140; 519/20, 65–6, 73; 529/6–9, 20, 78, 98; ibid., MJ/SBR. 1/490–1, 586–90; 2/50, 56; ibid., MJ/GBR. 1/214, 216–7; 2/16.

[5] *Acts of the Privy Council, James I* (henceforth *A.P.C.*) iii. 175, 193–4; P.R.O., SP 14/90/105–6, 135, 143; A. M. Dingle, 'The role of the householder in early Stuart London, *c.* 1603–*c.* 1630' (M.Phil. thesis, University of London, 1974), 51.

ficient anxiety in 1606 to cause the postponement of Garnet's execution from the 1 May 'for fear of disorder amongst prentices and others in a day of such misrule'. Yet in actual fact there were only eight possible May Day disturbances in the period 1603 to 1642, six of which occurred in the suburbs and the other two within the City's limits.[6] Both the numbers involved and the scale of violence were also correspondingly less; there was only one instance of a cottage being demolished and most of the action took the form of hurling stones through windows, assaults on constables and other officers and a threatening assembly around a maypole. The festivals of Midsummer Eve, the Vigil of St Peter, St Bartholomew's Day and Christmas excited official concern with even less genuine reason than May Day: revellers caused some minor trouble on Midsummer Day 1622; there was a riot at Bartholomew Fair in 1605; and the antics of a lord of misrule and his lieutenants from the Temple disturbed the peace of Ram Alley and Fleet Street around Christmas 1628.[7] The 'December days' of 1641 did witness exceptional disorder but this had very different origins and direction than the violence associated with traditional festivals. However, even within the tense political climate of May 1640, Whit Tuesday ostensibly provided the opportunity for the more customary besieging of a brothel.[8]

Popular xenophobia, and especially hatred of Spain, combined in most cases with a virulent anti-catholicism, made foreign ambassadors and their servants liable to abuse and affronts as they passed along London streets[9] and occasionally full-scale riots ensued. Ambassadors could feel particularly vulnerable when the traditional festivals came round; the Spanish ambassador retired to Nonsuch prior to Shrove Tuesday 1621 and the Venetian ambassador was feared to be the intended victim on May Day 1626.[10] The accidental knocking over of

[6] G.L.R.O., MJ/SR. 418/132; 575/142; 649/59; 808/437; 809/33-6, 39-41; 893/50; 912/312, 315; Corporation of London Records Office (henceforth C.L.R.O.), Rep. 44, f. 229; ibid., sessions of gaol delivery, 25 May 1615.

[7] C.L.R.O., Jor. 26, f. 218; 28, ff. 18, 84; 29, f. 375; 30, f. 228; 33, f. 129; 36, f. 286; 39, f. 95; ibid., Rep. 27, ff. 64, 66; 36, f. 185; 42, ff. 57–8; *The court and times of Charles I*, ed. R. F. Williams (1848), i. 311–14.

[8] P.R.O., SP 16/455/7–8.

[9] There were relatively minor affronts offered to the Imperial ambassador in 1605, the Spanish ambassador in 1612, the Venetian ambassador and two of his servants in 1635 and servants of the Persian ambassador in 1636 (C.L.R.O., Rep. 27, f. 51; 50, ff. 14, 294; *The court and times of James I*, ed. R. F. Williams (1848), i. 191–2; *Cal. State Papers Venetian*, xxiii, 437). Foreign nationals working in London were also subjected to abuse—for example, Spanish subjects and their servants in 1608, 1615 and 1618, and French factors in 1642 (C.L.R.O., Rep. 28, f. 279; 32, f. 118; *Analytical index to the series of records known as the Remembrancia*, ed. W. H. Overall (1878), 260; P.R.O., SP 16/488/81).

[10] P.R.O., SP 14/119/90; *A.P.C., Charles I*, i. 451.

a child by one of the Spanish ambassador's servants as he rode down Chancery Lane, on the evening of 13 July 1618, caused a major riot. Believing the child to have been killed, an angry crowd pursued the servant to his master's residence at the Barbican where perhaps as many as four or five thousand people laid siege to the house and smashed its windows, cursing the Spaniards and demanding the surrender of the servant. Only with the greatest of difficulty, and a judicious amount of appeasement, were the rioters eventually dispersed.[11] A fracas involving some of the French ambassador's servants on 28 October 1619 brought about two hundred people to the embassy gates and windows, who became extremely agitated when a local constable was rumoured to have been murdered within the embassy, and only dispersed when the same constable appeared to placate them.[12] Hatred of Spain and the projected match made heroes out of three apprentices sentenced to be whipped at the cart's tail for verbally abusing the Spanish ambassador in 1621. About three hundred people rescued the apprentices from custody on the 4 April and apparently would have had the assistance of a thousand others had they been required.[13] Two years later, the same ambassador complained that he and his household were virtually under siege and the termination of negotiations with Spain was celebrated by stoning the embassy.[14] The Venetian embassy also came under attack in 1631 and 1635,[15] and the resort of English catholics to mass at catholic embassies provoked rioting around the French embassy in 1626 and further outrages outside the same embassy, and the Spanish and Portuguese embassies, during the anti-popery hysteria of 1641. The Spanish ambassador, appalled at the rioters' threats to kill him and level the embassy, questioned whether England was a civilised nation to tolerate such behaviour against a foreign embassy.[16]

Demoralised and unpaid sailors and soldiers, returning from the campaigns against Spain and France, brought commotion to the capital in the years 1626 to 1628 as they defied proclamations forbidding their resort to the City or the Court and clamoured for their pay.[17] One of the sailors who rioted at the Fortune playhouse in May 1626 dismissed the charge to keep the peace in the King's name with the words, 'he cared not for the King, for the King paid them no

[11] *C.S.P. Ven.*, xv. 281–2; *Court . . . of James I*, ii. 81–2; P.R.O., SP 14/98/18.

[12] P.R.O., SP 14/111/22.

[13] *Court . . . of James I*, ii. 247–9.

[14] P.R.O., SP 14/152/4; C.L.R.O., Jor. 32, ff. 256–7; *C.S.P. Ven.*, xviii, 262.

[15] P.R.O., PC 2/41/119; ibid., SP 16/295/37; *C.S.P. Ven.*, xxiii, 437–8.

[16] *C.S.P. Ven.*, xix, 350; xxv, 145–6, 148–9, 203, 214; P.R.O., SP 16/485/50; C.L.R.O., Jor. 39, f. 193.

[17] C.L.R.O., Jor. 33, f. 319; 34, ff. 52, 227.

wages', and another boasted that those arrested would be rescued from prison before the morning.[18] The Duke of Buckingham's coach was brought to a halt by needy sailors in the following August, and in October it was smashed into pieces by one hundred and fifty sailors as the duke attended a meeting of the privy council. Meetings of the navy committee became hazardous occasions as unpaid sailors threatened retribution; in November about three hundred sailors forced open the gate of the treasurer of the navy, Sir William Russell, in Tower Street; and Buckingham's dinner was interrupted by six desperate captains from the Irish service who invaded his chambers at Whitehall.[19] At the beginning of 1627, Sir William Russell's windows were smashed by a crowd of five hundred sailors who vowed to join up with the apprentices on Shrove Tuesday and make it a day to remember. Hundreds of sailors pressed before the palace gates at Whitehall on 1 February, and during the year supposed dependents of the favourite risked being stopped in their coaches to have money extracted from them.[20] Bands of mutinous sailors, three to four hundred strong, were reported to be snatching food and committing other outrages throughout the capital at the start of 1628, and one of these bands attacked Buckingham's residence. There were incidents in the vicinity of Clerkenwell in March and April, and sailors flocked to the White Lion prison, in Southwark, to demand with threats the release of arrested comrades.[21] Sailors and soldiers were later participants in some of the dramatic disturbances of 1640–2 in the capital. A Rochester sailor suffered a traitor's death after the Lambeth and Southwark riots of May 1640, and the Southwark glover who had beaten the drum at the head of the rioters was apparently a drummer in a company due for service in the north. A thousand sailors, casualties of the slump in trade, marched towards the Tower on 10 May 1641 beneath a flag from one of their ships and pulled down two houses, and, in a more familiar role, over a hundred sailors in January 1642 attacked houses in St Martin-in-the-Fields upon the malicious information that they were bawdy houses.[22]

Gentlemen of the Inns of Court contributed to disorder in the capital, mainly by an over-zealous defence of the privileges and immunities of their Inns. Officers trying to carry out their duties near, or within, Lincoln's Inn were violently mishandled in 1614, 1619 and 1629, and some gentlemen of the Temple ducked other officers in the

[18] G.L.R.O., MJ/SR. 649/53-8.

[19] *Court . . . of Charles I*, i. 141–2, 175–7; *C.S.P. Ven.*, xix, 587; P.R.O., SP 16/35/44; ibid., 39/78; C.L.R.O., Jor. 34, f. 27.

[20] *Court . . . of Charles I*, i. 189, 191, 194; *C.S.P. Ven.*, xx, 119.

[21] *C.S.P. Ven.*, xx, 606–7; G.L.R.O., MJ/SBR. 4/626, 649; *A.P.C.*, *Charles I*, iv. 354.

[22] B.L., Sloane MS. 1467, ff. 114–15; *Commons Journals*, ii, 143; G.L.R.O., MJ/SR. 891/2.

nearby Thames in 1618 and 1629.[23] However, the most notorious incident involved gentlemen from Gray's Inn who were believed to have played a major role in the invasion of the Middlesex sheriff's office in Holborn in June 1638 and the assault upon an undersheriff.[24]

Royal households and servants also enjoyed something of a privileged status where arrests were concerned, as a Middlesex undersheriff was sharply reminded when he pursued a debtor into St James's palace on 7 December 1618. The resultant confrontation with the comptroller of the prince's household was revived a week later when he and his footmen were set upon as they emerged by coach from Gray's Inn.[25] An affray at the Royal Exchange involving some of Charles I's Italian musicians in February 1629 threatened to escalate into more widespread violence when the musicians rejected a constable's plea for order and proceeded into Cornhill brandishing drawn swords. When local people began hurling stones, the constable preserved the peace by securing the musicians' arrest, an action that resulted in a rebuke to the lord mayor for not observing the customary procedures demanded by their status.[26] But the Court had much more reason for offence in March 1638 when a major riot at Charing Cross threatened to spill over into the palace grounds at Whitehall.[27]

The Charing Cross riot may have had its origins in a riotous rescue from custody, apparently a growing problem in the 1630s. An arrest made in Chancery Lane in January 1639 led to serious rioting close to Temple Bar, and in another incident near Charing Cross in the following November a constable was mobbed by over sixty rioters and a watchman was fatally injured in Covent Garden.[28] However, the two most celebrated London riots prior to the 1640s were the pursuit and murder of Dr John Lambe, Buckingham's reputed magician, in 1628 and an exceptionally violent outrage in Fleet Street in 1629.

Lambe was jostled and reviled as 'the duke's devil' by a crowd of apprentices and boys in Moorfields, on 13 June, as he made his way home from the Fortune playhouse. The crowd grew in size as it pursued Lambe, and a hastily hired guard of sailors, through Moorgate and down Coleman Street to the Windmill Tavern at the end of Old Jewry. With five hundred rioters swarming around his tavern, the vintner had no option but to hand Lambe over to the crowd who so

[23] P.R.O., STAC 8/49/6; ibid., SP 16/148/9, 18, 20, 35; B.L., Hargrave MS. 283, f. 8; *Remembrancia index*, 452; C.L.R.O., Rep. 41, ff. 8, 30, 171–2.

[24] P.R.O., PC 2/49/265, 292, 313, 331, 337, 346, 358, 372, 380; ibid., 50/184.

[25] Ibid., SP 14/104/37–8, 38I; *A.P.C., James I*, iv. 333; *Court ... of James I*, ii. 114.

[26] *Remembrancia index*, 455–6; P.R.O., SP 16/136/40, 40I; *A.P.C., Charles I*, v. 333–4.

[27] P.R.O., SP 16/386/74, 93; ibid., PC 2/49/46–7.

[28] Ibid., PC 2/50/19; G.L.R.O., MJ/SR. 866/32; 864/70, 166; 960/153; ibid., MJ/GBR. 4/330, 332, 334.

badly mauled him that he died shortly afterwards. An outraged government commenced an action in King's Bench against the City for the negligence of its officers in failing to come to Lambe's assistance during the three-hour duration of the incident (until it was too late), or to arrest any of his assailants. The whole episode was essentially a demonstration against the hated favourite, whose own murder was predicted in a seditious rhyme which gained currency immediately afterwards. It left a lasting impression and was ominously recalled in May 1640 in the lines 'that Charles and Marie do what they will, We will kill the Archbishop of Canterbury like Doctor Lambe'.[29]

The Fleet Street riot, on the night of 10 July 1629, had its origins in the violent opposition of some army officers to an arrest being attempted by sheriff's officers. At its height, rioting engulfed a considerable area, along Fleet Street and the Strand and up St Martin's Lane and Drury Lane, as the taverns emptied and gentlemen from the Temple were drawn in. The use of swords and firearms resulted in two or three deaths, and there were several persons seriously wounded on both sides as local officers struggled to contain the violence. When the lord mayor and sheriffs eventually arrived on the scene with some of the trained band, the rioters threw up barricades as the whole affair began to degenerate into an open rebellion against authority. Two rioters were subsequently executed for murder but the ostentatious burial they received caused further scandal.[30]

Grave disorder was not confined to the streets and recreational areas of London and its suburbs; the prisons too occasionally erupted into tumult. Inmates of the King's Bench and Marshalsea prisons in Southwark, for example, revolted against corruption and ill-treatment. King's Bench prisoners mutinied in July 1620 and again in March 1640, and those in the Marshalsea rioted in May 1639, and the trained bands were needed to restore order.[31]

The period from the dissolution of the Short Parliament to Charles's final departure from London witnessed disorder on an unprecedented scale as an explosive combination of political crisis, trade depression and plague, and a resurfaced and newly confident religious radicalism, was ignited by rumour and panic fears, and the population of the cities of London and Westminster, the suburbs and the south bank of the Thames took to the streets in their thousands to demonstrate or

[29] *Court ... of Charles I*, i. 364–5, 367–8; *D.N.B.*, xi. 442–3; J. Rushworth, *Historical Collections* (1721), i. 618, and ii. 145–6; *C.S.P. Ven.*, xxi, 157; P.R.O., SP 16/528/78; ibid., 107/78; ibid., Baschet's transcripts, 31/3/72, f. 151.

[30] *Court ... of Charles I*, ii. 24–5; P.R.O., SP 45/10/113; ibid., 16/146/62; ibid., 147/74; ibid., 148/20; C.L.R.O., Rep. 43, ff. 281–2, 302, 328; 44, ff. 37, 74, 115, 200, 296.

[31] *A.P.C., James I*, v. 239–40, 243, 259; P.R.O., PC 2/50/382, 422, 697–8; ibid., 51/360; ibid., SP 16/421/162; ibid., 422/39, 39I; ibid., 424/65.

take direct action. These disturbances have been described elsewhere,[32] but their significance in exposing the deficiencies and severe limitations of the traditional means of maintaining order in London will emerge later.

Ultimate responsibility for the policing of the City of London rested with the lord mayor who, when disorder threatened, issued precepts to the aldermen in their respective wards demanding action from them or other officers. As head of the City's trained bands, the lord mayor also directed precepts to relevant captains when military help was needed. And behind the lord mayor stood the King and privy council ready to intervene and call the municipal authorities to account for reported negligence or inefficiency. The existence of liberties and privileged places about the City, which shared the suburbs' notoriety as places of refuge for social and religious dissidents, hampered efficient policing.[33] The suburbs themselves were the responsibility of the justices of the peace and, if military aid was called for, the lords lieutenant of Middlesex and Surrey. Law enforcement was very much more difficult in Middlesex than in the City given the far larger parishes and the presence of some of the poorest and most radical elements of society. There was a distinct tendency on the part of the City magistrates to exaggerate the size of the suburbs' population (which remained below that of the City throughout this period) and shuffle off responsibility for serious and persistent disorder onto areas where their jurisdiction did not stretch.[34] Yet even disturbances like Shrove Tuesday riots that regularly occurred in the suburbs drew their participants from a wide urban compass, including areas well within the City's jurisdiction.

The prevention of disorder could result from more positive steps than plain repression and, in this context, the absence of food riots in London (if one excludes the desperate actions of hungry sailors in 1628) demands an explanation. The answer is to be found in the existence of a system of poor relief in the City, far in advance of the rest of England, which paid careful attention to the provision

[32] V. Pearl, *London and the outbreak of the Puritan Revolution* (Oxford, 1964), chap. 4; B.S. Manning, *The English People and the English Revolution* (1976), chaps. 1–5.

[33] The extension of the lord mayor's jurisdiction over Whitefriars, Blackfriars, Coldharbour and other liberties in 1608 did not entirely eradicate this problem. The bailiff of Whitefriars apparently remained a powerful figure who might delay taking action without instructions from his patron, and a tenant in Blackfriars who refused to pay his rent in 1614 believed that no constable would dare come to distrain, or a sheriff to effect an arrest, for nonpayment where he lived (Pearl, *London*, 38; A. M. Dingle, 'The role of the householder', 20–1; P.R.O., STAC 8/112/4; ibid., 295/2).

[34] N. G. Brett-James, *The growth of Stuart London* (1935), 215–16, 223; Pearl, *London*, 17, 40–3; id., 'Change and stability' 7; *Harleian Miscellany*, vii. 505–6.

of food and fuel to meet the needs of the poor.[35] Provocative public events which might lead to disorder were postponed or cancelled. Garnet's execution was adjourned so as not to coincide with May Day, and the state funeral originally intended for Buckingham was replaced with a private burial at night.[36] Contemporary authorities were sometimes acutely aware, therefore, of the existence of definable limits to their ability to preserve order in the capital.

Civil authorities from the lord mayor to the local watch and ward had allotted roles to play in the prevention or suppression of riots. Apart from sanctioning action, the lord mayor occasionally intervened directly to check upon the state of the watch, or to send a guard (albeit tardily) to rescue Dr Lambe, or to tackle the rioters himself with a guard of halberdiers or some of the trained bands. The London sheriffs often assisted the lord mayor on these occasions in addition to performing separate duties in quelling disorder.[37] On at least one occasion aid was forthcoming from an eminent authority; in 1618 the lord chief justice personally intervened to appease the tumult outside the Spanish ambassador's house.[38]

The officer who bore one of the most onerous and immediate responsibilities in maintaining order was the constable who was often one of the first to come into contact with rioters. The little work that has been done on the conduct of the office, and quality of its occupants, in the City of London points to an increasing unwillingness to assume the constableship as the burdens associated with it increased. The court of common council, concerned at the evasion of service by some of the better qualified citizens, by paying a fine or appointing less competent deputies, tried to remedy the worst abuses in 1619 and 1621, probably without much success. One major responsibility of the constable, with a particular relevance to riot prevention, was to supervise the watch, and negligence could result in a short spell of imprisonment, yet during the turmoil of 1640 and 1641, when effective

[35] For all its relative sophistication, the system could sometimes break down when livery companies failed to furnish the market with their set proportion of wheat meal, and the poor did occasionally die of starvation in the City's streets and lanes. Professor Pearl's discovery of a relatively humane social policy in operation in seventeenth-century London has acknowledged limits—vagrants received the same harsh treatment in London as elsewhere (Pearl, 'Social policy', *passim*; C.L.R.O., Jor. 33, ff. 144, 304; 34, ff. 165, 311; 35, f. 262; 37, f. 172; 39, f. 14; ibid., Rep. 43, ff. 9, 160–2.

[36] Above pp. 110–11; *C.S.P. Ven.*, xxi, 337.

[37] C.L.R.O., Rep. 31 part I, ff. 38, 94; ibid., sessions of gaol delivery, 18 Mar. 1612; Rushworth, *Historical Collections*, i. 618; *Court . . . of Charles I*, i. 311–14; *C.S.P. Ven.*, xxv, 97, 145–6; P.R.O., SP 16/485/50; B.L., Add. MS. 11,045, ff. 122–3.

[38] *Court . . . of James I*, ii. 81–2.

policing was of paramount importance, constables were accused of failing to fulfil that duty.[39]

Constables in both London and the suburbs could sometimes show courage and skill in dealing with a riot but they were probably most effective in removing the smaller scale disorder. They endured physical and verbal abuse and open defiance, yet attention to duty was not always recognised and applauded by higher authorities. The privy council rebuked a constable who had helped defuse a potential riot near the Royal Exchange in 1629 by arresting some disorderly royal musicians—although the court of aldermen acknowledged his service and ordered that his costs be met.[40] A constable of St Martin-in-the-Fields found himself indicted as a rioter when he attempted to appease a crowd of angry apprentices in December 1641. The apprentices had laid siege to the Mermaid Tavern where some of their fellows were being held prisoner for hurrying down to parliament with arms after Colonel Lunsford's attack on the London citizens. The constable adopted a conciliatory approach, 'there being no other way', as he later stressed, 'to deal with such a multitude', and secured their agreement to disperse if the prisoners were released, but the violent response of those within the tavern led to its being stormed. The constable's mildness was taken for complicity and he was accused by the keeper of the tavern of being the instigator of the rescue, and was only saved from trial by the intervention of the House of Commons.[41]

Counterbalancing this attention to duty were the instances when constables failed, or even refused, to take action against rioters. A constable of St Sepulchre was overwhelmed by the size and disposition of the crowd that surrounded him in 1604; a constable of St Botolph by Aldgate was fined £2 for refusing to help the sheriff's officers arrest the rescuers of their prisoner in 1628 (although the fine was halved upon a pledge of future compliance); and, in the same year, constables and other officers in Southwark were criticised for not making arrests among the sailors threatening the White Lion prison.[42] But far greater official dismay was felt at the inactivity of constables and other officers at the time of Dr Lambe's murder, and some paid for their negligence with a short period of imprisonment.[43] Far from helping to suppress the Fleet Street riot of 1628, a constable of St Dunstan in the West

[39] A. M. Dingle, 'The role of the householder', 65–6, 93–4, 132, 236; C.L.R.O., Jor. 31, ff. 73, 317–18, 353–4; 39, ff. 140, 262; ibid., Rep. 31 part I, ff. 38, 94, 111; 31 part II, f. 317.

[40] *A.P.C., Charles I*, v. 333–4; C.L.R.O., Rep. 43, ff. 120–1.

[41] Manning, *The English people*, 77–8; House of Lords Records Office, main papers, 15 Jan. 1642 petition of Peter Scott, one of the constables of St Martin-in-the-Fields; *C.J.*, ii. 382.

[42] P.R.O., STAC 8/160/16; C.L.R.O., Rep. 42, f. 306; *A.P.C., Charles I*, iv. 354.

[43] *A.P.C., Charles I*, iv. 492, 505.

apparently tried to rescue one drunken offender from custody as officers were conveying him to prison.[44]

The original obligation of householders to serve their turn at the duty of watch and ward had been largely replaced, in London at least, by the payment of assessments to hire men to perform those duties. In theory, watchmen and warders served at set hours, protected by corslets and armed with halberds, and could be summoned at double or, in rare instances, treble strength during periods of actual or anticipated disorder. But, in practice, these duties were all too often carried out by unsuitable persons, the correct hours of watches in particular were not observed and they did not always possess halberds,[45] and there is every reason to believe that these deficiencies were even more marked in the suburbs. Occasionally men refused to obey the summons to watch, like the seven inhabitants of St Andrew's, Holborn, in May 1620, or some of those summoned on Shrove Tuesday 1634 and 1636,[46] and in 1640–2 this reluctance to serve may have been more pronounced, especially when some of those summoned sympathised with the aims of the rioters and demonstrators. Shortly after the disturbances of May 1640, for example, an apprentice of Whitefriars threatened: 'If I be forced to watch I will turn Rebel with the rest of my fellow Apprentices'.[47]

Watchmen and warders reportedly served a useful function in preventing or controlling disorder on Shrove Tuesday 1618 and Christmas 1628, or in disturbances in Bucklersbury in March, and near Temple Bar in August, 1615.[48] The watchman killed in Covent Garden in 1639, the warders wounded in Moorfields on Shrove Tuesday 1606 and the watchmen injured in the Fleet Street riot of 1629 were all presumably endeavouring to carry out their duties.[49] Special duties were assigned to them during periods of serious unrest: a strong watch was maintained in each precinct following the riotous rescue of apprentices in 1621; they mounted a guard around the clock to prevent further attacks upon Spaniards in the vicinity of the Strand and Covent Garden in 1623; and they helped control mutinous sailors in

[44] C.L.R.O., Rep. 42, ff. 57–8.

[45] A. M. Dingle, 'The role of the householder', 151, 158, 217–21; C.L.R.O., Jor. 27, ff. 19, 168; 28, f. 18; 29, f. 14; 33, f. 267; 35, f. 438; ibid., Rep. 31 part I, ff. 33, 38; 31 part II, f. 317; 51, f. 354.

[46] C.L.R.O., recognisance 11 May 1620; G.L.R.O., MJ/SBR. 6/6; ibid., MJ/SR. 807/10–12, 14. Cf., C.L.R.O., Rep. 33, f. 165.

[47] G.L.R.O., MJ/SR. 877/2. A local watchman had also been one of the besiegers of the French embassy in 1619 and had assaulted one of the ambassador's coachmen with his watchman's bill (P.R.O., SP 14/111/22).

[48] P.R.O., SP 14/96/23; ibid., STAC 8/215/23; ibid., 62/13; *Court ... of Charles I*, i. 313–14.

[49] G.L.R.O., MJ/SR. 960/153; C.L.R.O., Rep. 27, f. 169; 46, ff. 44–5.

1626–8.[50] But the most onerous duties were repeatedly placed upon the watch and ward in 1640–2 as, for example, after the attack upon Lambeth palace in May 1640 when double watches were ordered in London, Westminster and Southwark, and a nightly guard of twenty or thirty men was set at the foot of London bridge to restrict the movement of potential trouble-makers.[51] The scale of the problem of maintaining order during the 'December days' is reflected in the ordering of a treble watch and ward throughout the City to prevent tumults, one-third of whom were to be armed with muskets (which were to be used only in circumstances of dire necessity). However, such exceptional disorder exhausted the limited resources of the watch and ward, and new regulations approved by common council on 4 January 1642 had little real impact on the problem.[52]

Every London householder was under a special obligation to render assistance in maintaining order and, when trouble was expected, he could be required to equip himself with a halberd and remain ready for action either within his home or on alert outside the door. The City compensated those householders and their servants who were wounded in 1629 coming to the assistance of the authorities during the Fleet Street riot, while those who refused to aid officers, or even encouraged the rioters, were severely censured.[53] Householders were also expected to exercise control over members of their household and prevent them from disturbing the peace, and when Shrove Tuesday or other festivals approached they were warned to keep a tight rein upon their apprentices, servants and children or they would be held personally responsible for their offences. After the apprentices' involvement in the attack upon Lambeth palace in May 1640, all householders within a five-mile radius of the City were ordered to exercise a special vigilance over their servants and apprentices, and similar instructions were issued during the turbulent days of December 1641.[54] Nevertheless, judging by the regularity of Shrove Tuesday

[50] *Court . . . of James I*, ii. 248; *Court . . . of Charles I*, i. 186; P.R.O., SP 14/152/26.

[51] P.R.O., PC 2/52/482–3, 493–4.

[52] Ibid., SP 16/488/17; C.L.R.O., Jor. 39, ff. 262, 264.

[53] C.L.R.O., Rep. 43, ff. 281–2, 302, 328; 44, ff. 37, 74, 115, 200; *Court . . . of Charles I*, ii. 25.

[54] A. M. Dingle, 'The role of the householder', 58, 233; C.L.R.O., Jor. 30, ff. 48, 192; 31, f. 317; 32, f. 221; 33, ff. 52, 129; 39, ff. 79, 84, 253, 262; ibid., Rep. 35, f. 146; P.R.O., SP 14/120/97; ibid., 16/453/16; ibid., PC 2/52/482–3.

Threats to call masters to account for the unruly behaviour of their apprentices were sometimes carried out. A number of masters were bound over for allowing their apprentices liberty to commit riots on Shrove Tuesday 1611, and fines were imposed on masters upon other occasions for breaches of the peace by their apprentices and servants (G.L.R.O., MJ/SR. 498/55–63; C.L.R.O., book of fines 1517–1628, ff. 246, 259). But occasionally they themselves were culpable, as in 1616 when a Shoreditch apprentice,

riots, and the continued involvement of apprentices in some of the disturbances of 1640–2, these directives were not universally obeyed.

In the fight against disorder, there was one officer whose prime function was to keep in check those very members of society deemed most riot-prone—the provost marshal.[55] Yet provost marshals do not appear to have had much of a role in subduing rioters in early Stuart London before May 1640, when they were mobilised to help restore order. Far from according assistance earlier, two of the marshal's men were imprisoned in Newgate for turning a blind eye to the mobbing of Dr Lambe.[56]

The City's magistrates and individual officers were taken to task by the King and privy council when they appeared remiss in dealing with rioters. James I was said to have been furious with the City for adopting a low-key approach to the assault upon the Spanish ambassador's house in 1618, and the rescue of the apprentices who had insulted the ambassador in 1621 brought James hurrying to the Guildhall from Theobalds to harangue the City and threaten to station a garrison in their midst and revoke their charter if they did not maintain better order.[57] Charles I was appalled at the inactivity of the City's magistrates during Dr Lambe's long pursuit and the City was fined £1,000 in King's Bench for failing to attach any of the murderers.[58] However, some accusations of negligence may have arisen from a misinterpretation of the measured approach sometimes adopted by the authorities in defusing a riot. A vigorous attempt to retain custody of the apprentices in 1621, for example, would have produced an immediate escalation of violence, as a further one thousand people had been about to join the rescuers.[59] Furthermore, the tactic of appeasing rioters, and ostensibly removing the cause of grievance, had a vital role to play in crowd control, as the lord chief justice himself demonstrated in 1618 when he dispersed the huge crowd outside the Spanish ambassador's by taking into custody the servant who had knocked over the child.[60]

---

arrested as a suspected instigator of a Shrove Tuesday riot, was rescued from the headborough by his mistress (G.L.R.O., MJ/SR. 547/87).

[55] The office had originally been a military post for maintaining discipline within the army but became a peace-time appointment towards the end of the sixteenth century, with a special responsibility to deal with vagrants and establish control over riotous London apprentices and servants (by martial law executions if necessary) in the 1590s (P. Williams, *The Tudor Regime* (Oxford, 1979), 202–3, 204, 229, 388; B.L., Lansdowne MS. 66, ff. 241–2).

[56] P.R.O., SP 16/455/7–8, 102; ibid., PC 2/52/483; C.L.R.O., Jor. 39, f. 141; ibid., Rep. 42, f. 213; *A.P.C., Charles I*, iv. 505.

[57] *Court . . . of James I*, ii. 85, 248.

[58] C.L.R.O., Jor. 36, ff. 37, 50; Rushworth, *Historical Collections*, ii. 145–6.

[59] *Court . . . of James I*, ii. 247–8.

[60] Ibid., pp. 81–2. Riotous sailors in 1626 were beguiled by promises of wages (*Court . . . of Charles I*, i. 141–2, 175, 189; *C.S.P. Ven.*, xix, 468, 587). A provost marshal calmed

When the civil powers failed to restore order, or required a show of force, military assistance was enlisted from the trained bands of London and, where necessary, of Middlesex and Surrey as well. The London trained bands, composed of 6,000 men under twenty captains, were reorganised in 1616 into four regiments commanded by colonels and under the generalship of the lord mayor. The neglect of the early years of James I had produced worrying deficiences in arms and equipment, training and men and, despite regular privy council exhortations, the borrowing of arms and other abuses continued, with the alleged connivance of those responsible for the annual inspection.[61] The poor state of the City's munitions was starkly revealed in 1629 when the trained bands went into action against the Fleet Street rioters 'unfurnished of shot and powder to perform the service wherein they were employed'.[62]

The trained bands came to be regularly called upon to help preserve the peace on Shrove Tuesdays and May Days as, for example, on Shrove Tuesday 1623 when eight hundred men were required to muster and train under eight City captains—four hundred in Moorfields, two hundred in Smithfield and two hundred on or near Tower Hill. Although the Middlesex trained bands contributed to these efforts, the expense involved caused resentment.[63] Absenteeism marred the trained bands' efficiency,[64] and the frequency of Shrove Tuesday riots at least must raise doubts about the efficacy of such assistance. Apart from this regular service, companies were mobilised to mount guards about the City in 1627 against tumultuous sailors; to help disperse the Fleet Street rioters in 1629; and to suppress riots in the Marshalsea and King's Bench prisons in 1639 and 1640 respectively.[65] From May 1640, the trained bands shared the increasingly heavy burden of maintaining order in the City and suburbs. Southwark trained bands were ordered to muster in St George's Fields on 11

---

rioters intent on demolishing a brothel on Whit Tuesday 1640 by feigning cooperation with them and eventually managed to arrest a prime offender (P.R.O., SP 16/455/7).

[61] L. Boynton, *The Elizabethan militia 1558–1638* (1967), 210, 216, 217, 255; C.L.R.O., Jor. 29, ff. 296, 342; 30, ff. 47–8, 60; 31, f. 293; 33, f. 162; 34, f. 269; 37, ff. 73, 79, 92; 38, f. 212; ibid., Rep. 35, f. 120; B.L., Egerton MS. 2541, f. 400; *C.S.P. Ven.*, xvii, 433.

[62] *A.P.C., Charles I*, vi. 126.

[63] C.L.R.O., Jor. 30, f. 128; ibid., Rep. 37, ff. 105–6; *A.P.C., James I*, v. 377–8; ibid., vi. 152–3; *A.P.C., Charles I*, i. 346–7, 451; *C.S.P. Dom., 1635–36*, 196.

[64] There were periodic complaints of absenteeism. Large numbers of men absented themselves from the 1615 muster and fines were levied upon absentees from the 1618 muster and Shrove Tuesday service in 1623 and 1632. But the deterrent effect of fining in the case of the 1618 and 1623 absentees must have been weakened by the subsequent return of the fines (C.L.R.O., Rep. 32, f. 183; 33, f. 418; 34, f. 68; 37, ff. 108–9, 114, 145, 233; 46, f. 126; 51, f. 210).

[65] P.R.O., SP 16/53/10; ibid., PC 2/50/382; ibid., 51/360; C.L.R.O., Rep. 41, f. 102.

May 1640 after a clear warning of trouble, but scarcely had the men returned home that evening when about five hundred rioters assembled there and marched on Lambeth palace.[66] During the nights that followed, the trained bands of Southwark and Surrey mounted an exacting routine of watches until contingents of the London and Middlesex trained bands were drafted in to give some relief. At the same time, the lord mayor was instructed to place one thousand to one thousand five hundred of the more reliable of the trained bands on alert, and six thousand foot recruited out of the trained bands of Essex, Kent, Hertfordshire and Surrey were ordered to be billeted near London.[67] Contingents of the London and Middlesex trained bands were regularly mustered and trained throughout Strafford's trial, and they opposed the large crowd of sailors who were advancing towards the Tower in May 1641. Between 8 March and early July 1641, the City companies alone accumulated a total of fifty-five days and ten nights of service and that help continued to be required, especially during the 'December days'.[68]

A crucial question in 1640–2 was the degree of reliability that could be placed upon the trained bands as a bulwark against disorder. The King apparently had only limited confidence in the City's trained bands in May 1640 when he felt it necesary to recruit additional military support in adjacent counties, and the political and religious sympathies of some of the men, combined with a general reluctance to proceed against their own neighbours, certainly detracted from their effectiveness as a force for order.[69] The French ambassador speculated that they may have turned a deaf ear to the noise accompanying the attacks on the Southwark prisons on 14 May 1640 when they finally appeared on the scene as the rioters were dispersing and detained one man (who was later acquitted). It was rumoured, moreover, that the trained bands 'would fall upon them that took the bishops' part' rather than suppress the rioters.[70] The commander of one of the two contingents of horse that neglected to serve in Southwark after 14 May 'gave the man the provost marshal sent to warn him ill language'.[71] Tumultuous apprentices in December 1641 were unimpressed by the calling in of the trained bands, according to the Venetian ambassador,

[66] P.R.O., PC 2/52/483–4; ibid., Baschet's transcripts, 31/3/72, f. 150; Rushworth, *Historical Collections*, iii. 1085.

[67] P.R.O., PC 2/52/491–2; B.L., Add. MS. 11,045, f. 117.

[68] P.R.O., PC 2/53/108–9; ibid., SP 16/486/99; C.L.R.O., Jor. 39, f. 185; ibid., Rep. 55, ff. 162, 368; *C.J.*, ii. 143.

[69] Pearl, *London*, 104–5, 108, 119–20.

[70] P.R.O., Baschet's transcripts, 31/3/72, f. 156; ibid., SP 16/468/139.

[71] Ibid., SP 16/454/12. Some of the one hundred Middlesex musketeers sent to guard the Queen Mother also expressed great reluctance to perform that service (Rushworth, *Historical Collections*, iv. 267).

'as these troops are for the most part the masters of these very apprentices'.[72] By the end of 1641, however, significant numbers of the City's trained bands were not responding to the call for service and Charles was on the verge of finally losing control over them to his political opponents, and with it any hope of reasserting his authority over rioters and demonstrators. Similarly, in Middlesex, the trained band of St Martin-in-the-Fields revolted against the control of men ill-affected to parliament and secured parliamentary approval of a new captain with wholly different sympathies. Charles left a capital whose streets he believed he could no longer control on 10 January, and the very next day contingents of the trained bands provided part of the guard at the triumphal restoration of Lord Kimbolton and the five members to their seats in parliament.[73]

Any role that punishment might serve in riot prevention was vitiated by the difficulty of tracking down offenders who could so readily melt into the vastness of the City and its suburbs.[74] Most of those successfully apprehended were proceeded against at sessions of the peace or gaol delivery, except in the case of particularly grave unrest when special sessions of oyer and terminer were deemed appropriate, and a few were brought into Star Chamber. Sessions of oyer and terminer were convened upon six occasions: after Shrove Tuesday 1617, the attack on the Spanish ambassador's house in 1618, the Fleet Street riot of 1629, the Holborn riot of 1638 (to deal with the 'meaner sort' of offender), the Lambeth and Southwark riots of May 1640 and the invasion of the court of high commission in 1640. However, in the three latter cases, it proved difficult to apprehend and secure the conviction of offenders.[75]

Only in exceptional instances were the fines imposed upon rioters heavy and even then they could be mitigated by the court. Although a period of imprisonment might also be imposed until fines were paid, or sureties found, it was again only in exceptional cases that it formed an integral part of the punishment. Seven men convicted for besieging

[72] *C.S.P. Ven.*, xxv, 272.

[73] C.L.R.O., Jor. 40, f. 10; Pearl, *London*, 173; B.L., Add. MS. 14827, ff. 10–11; Rushworth, *Historical Collections*, iv. 484.

[74] Seven or eight months of effort by messengers, for example, resulted in the arrest of only eight of the twenty persons sent for by privy council warrant for their part in the 1638 Holborn incident (P.R.O., PC 2/50/184). In an attempt to overcome this problem, surgeons were sometimes enjoined to inform the authorities about any suspects they might have treated, and information gained in this way led to the arrest of one of the Lambeth palace assailants (P.R.O., SP 45/10/113; ibid., Baschet's transcripts, 31/3/72, f. 168).

[75] *A.P.C., James I*, iii. 175; *Court . . . of Charles I*, ii. 23–4; P.R.O., PC 2/49/292, 372; ibid., 53/47; ibid., SP 16/453/81I; B.L., Add. MS. 11,045, ff. 130–1; ibid., Sloane MS. 1467, ff. 114–15, 123–4; C.L.R.O., proceedings on a commission of oyer and terminer, Aug. 1618.

the Spanish ambassador's in 1618 faced one of the heaviest penalties, with fines of £500 each and imprisonment in Newgate for a year or more until they were paid. Three of the 1617 Shrove Tuesday rioters were fined £6 13s. 4d. and imprisoned in irons for a year, and another six faced fines of £2 each and three months' imprisonment in irons. Close interrogation, or even torture in the case of a Lambeth palace assailant, could also be added to the harrowing experience of confinement in a disease-ridden gaol.[76] Ten self-confessed Shrove Tuesday rioters in 1607 were sentenced to be whipped through the streets at the cart's tail,[77] but this form of punishment had the obvious drawback of inviting a riotous rescue, as the authorities were reminded in 1621, and hence was rarely imposed upon rioters.

Death sentences were threatened upon one or two occasions,[78] but the threat could be implemented only when the incident itself had been judged felonious, or where individual rioters were found to have committed a felony in the course of a riot. Two of the 1629 Fleet Street rioters were executed for murder (while, in contrast, nobody paid for Dr Lambe's murder), and after the riots of May 1640 had been classified as rebellious a Rochester sailor was hanged, drawn and quartered at dawn in Southwark with an expedition suggestive of an anxiety to avoid the execution becoming the signal for further disorder.[79] Other rioters were killed in the course of incidents, especially when the authorities were licensed to open fire on them.[80] Yet it is indeed a remarkable fact that so little blood was actually spilt on the streets of London in the turbulent days that led up to the outbreak of the Civil War. Part of the explanation is to be found in the restrained and self-disciplined behaviour of the London crowd, and the way in which its energies were channelled by a good measure of political

[76] C.L.R.O., session of oyer and terminer, Aug. 1618; G.L.R.O., MJ/GBR. 2/114–15; P.R.O., SP 16/454/39.

[77] G.L.R.O., MJ/SR. 444/98–100.

[78] James I was said to have wanted the execution of arrested Shrove Tuesday rioters in 1617 to set an example, but had to rest content with fines and imprisonment in irons, and after the attack upon the Spanish ambassador in the following year summary execution by martial law was threatened against future offenders (P.R.O., SP 14/90/106; ibid., 187/59).

[79] The Southwark glover racked to extract information was rumoured to have been shown mercy. Those who had invaded the court of high commission also risked execution for it was judged a capital crime to attack a court of justice (B.L., Sloane MS. 1467, ff. 114–15; ibid., Add. MS. 11,045, f. 130).

[80] Three or more Shrove Tuesday rioters died in the storming of a playhouse in 1617; watchmen were reported to have killed two sailors in 1627 and another two were shot down by the trained bands as they advanced on the Tower in May 1641; a besieger of the White Lion prison in May 1640 was killed; and Sir Richard Wiseman died of wounds sustained in Dec. 1641 (P.R.O., SP 14/90/105; B.L., Sloane MS. 1467, f. 111; *Court ... of Charles I*, i. 186; Manning, *The English people*, 80).

direction,[81] but some role must also be accorded to the inadequacies or indifference, restraint or partisanship, of those upon whom the duty of maintaining order rested.

Even when due allowance has been made for the exaggerated fears of contemporary authorities, the rioting which intermittently disturbed the peace of early Stuart London and its suburbs constituted a problem of serious proportions. However, given the severe limitations of the civil and military resources available for riot prevention and control, it is perhaps remarkable that the problem did not assume even greater urgency. When those resources were rigorously put to the test in 1640–2 they were found to be largely inadequate and unreliable; they left the King without any effective control over events in the streets of his capital.

[81] Pearl, 'Change and stability', 5–6.

SIR JOHN FIELDING AND THE PROBLEM OF CRIMINAL INVESTIGATION IN EIGHTEENTH-CENTURY ENGLAND

By John Styles, M.A.

READ AT THE SOCIETY'S CONFERENCE 17 SEPTEMBER 1982*

EIGHTEENTH-CENTURY England witnessed an extraordinary transformation in the capacity to disseminate information. Improvements in communications, particularly the turnpike roads and the postal service, together with the multiplication of printing presses and newspapers, underpinned what has been described as an 'information explosion'.[1] The changes which these developments wrought in the political and commercial life of the nation are increasingly familiar to historians.[2] Their impact on eighteenth-century crime and policing is less so.

That impact was twofold. First, the new methods of disseminating information provided an important supplement to available techniques for the investigation of criminal offences. Advertisements of rewards for information concerning stolen property or offenders fled from justice became a familiar characteristic of almost all eighteenth-century newspapers. The newspaper offered an unrivalled vehicle for distributing such intelligence to a large public across a wide area. Handbills containing similar information, run off by most printers at an hour's notice, provided the same facility with less delay, but over a more restricted geographical span. Hardly surprisingly, these new techniques almost entirely superseded the principal pre-existing vehicle for the far-flung dissemination of criminal intelligence, the cumbersome hue and cry.[3]

Second, improvements in the capacity to disseminate information brought about a vast expansion in public access to news and interpretations of criminal activity. Criminal offenders, their offences, their

*I should like to thank John Brewer, Joanna Innes and John Langbein for their comments on earlier versions of this paper.

[1] J. Brewer, *Party, Ideology and Popular Politics at the accession of George III* (Cambridge, 1976), 158.

[2] See in particular N. McKendrick, J. Brewer and J. H. Plumb, *The Birth of a Consumer Society* (1982), *passim.*

[3] For an analysis of the impact of newspaper advertising, see my forthcoming article on crime advertising in the eighteenth-century provincial newspaper.

trials and their punishments had long been objects of fascination in both polite and plebeian circles. Indeed they were the subject matter of a great deal of sixteenth- and seventeenth-century pamphlet literature and printed ephemera. The eighteenth century, however, saw not only an enormous expansion in the availability and dissemination of literature concerning crimes and offenders, but also changes in its character. Thus, at the same time as the volume of such literature expanded, by means of the newspapers and the more extensive printing of broadsheets and chapbooks, information about crimes and offenders of a more systematic character became available on an unprecedented scale. The appearance in the press of reports and advertisements about offences, the reporting there of assize and quarter sessions trials, and the printing of calendars of prisoners provided both officialdom and a broad public with an accessible (though not necessarily accurate) measure of fluctuations in the incidence and character of offences. At the same time an expanded pamphlet literature, often reprinted in the newspapers alongside essays, correspondence and editorials on the subject of crime, provided a running commentary on these burgeoning inventories of crimes, prisoners, and executions. By such means those entrepreneurs of criminal prophylaxis who so flourished in the later eighteenth century were supplied not only with vehicles to distribute their remedies, but with much of their empirical raw material and with an audience which, though still obsessed with the particularities of offences and offenders, was learning to envisage crime as an impersonal, statistical problem.

No-one during the eighteenth century exploited these developments in communications more energetically than John (after 1761 Sir John) Fielding. Throughout his twenty-six years as the government-financed principal magistrate for Westminster, from 1754 to 1780, this blind man managed a criminal investigation apparatus which centred on the use of his office at Bow Street, Covent Garden, as a clearing house for information about offences and offenders, in its early years mainly from within the metropolis and its immediate vicinity.[4] At Bow Street, information about unsolved crimes and offenders fled from justice was recorded and then disseminated to the public in the form of advertisements in selected newspapers asking for further information. To encourage law officers and the public to make reports to Bow Street, either in person or by post, Fielding publicised the facilities available at his office in broadsheets and pamphlets, as well as in the newspapers. He also encouraged the press to report his work as an examining magistrate at Bow Street. Such reports were one element in a wider

[4] For general surveys of Fielding's activities see R. Leslie-Melville, *The Life and Work of Sir John Fielding* (1934) and L. Radzinowicz, *A History of English Criminal Law* (4 vols., 1948–68), iii (1956), 11–62.

educational effort that Fielding conducted by such methods to alert the public to the character and techniques of offenders and to promote his ideas for crime prevention.

The originator of this system of criminal information management was not John Fielding himself, but his half-brother and immediate (though short-serving) predecessor as principal magistrate for Westminster, Henry Fielding the novelist. John Fielding, however, considerably extended these techniques. He applied them most ambitiously in his General Preventative Plan of 1772, designed to collect, collate and circulate criminal information on a national scale for the first time. It is with the origins and significance of the General Preventative Plan that this paper is principally concerned.

In order to understand the form taken by Fielding's General Preventative Plan, its author's extremely sanguine expectations of it, and the highly favourable reception it enjoyed among those who administered the criminal law, it is necessary to consider the enormous obstacles which still existed in the mid-eighteenth century, despite improvements in communication facilities, to the apprehension of offenders who had secreted themselves in parts of the country distant from the scene of their crime. An examination of a particularly well-documented episode in 1756 will serve to illustrate those obstacles.

On Monday, 19 January 1756, a man calling himself William Wilkins appeared before Samuel Lister, an exceptionally active justice of the peace for the West Riding of Yorkshire.[5] Wilkins claimed to be a clothier from a place he called Lodgemoor, near Painswick, in the county of Somerset. He came before Justice Lister, at the latter's house near Bradford, as a consequence of his failure to pay his reckoning at various inns. Although he had virtually no cash, among the items found in his possession were a pocket book containing two bills of exchange (for £20 and £80 respectively), made payable to William Wilkins, and a promissory note for the enormous sum of £1100. These Lister suspected to be forged, because two letters, one postmarked Gloucester, found in Wilkins's pocket indicated that he and his wife had been associated with others in the forgery of bills of exchange and other commercial paper. They suggested that he had fled from his home to Yorkshire in order to escape prosecution.

In fact the so-called William Wilkins was one Edward Wilson, a woollen clothier from Painswick in Gloucestershire (there was no such

[5] The following discussion is based on Bradford City Library (henceforth B.C.L.), Deeds Collection, 16/11/10, Samuel Lister's letters and undated drafts on the case. For a fuller account of Lister's career as a magistrate and the contribution to it of this case, see J. Styles, 'An eighteenth-century magistrate as detective: Samuel Lister of Little Horton', *Bradford Antiquary*, New Ser., 47 (1982) 98–117.

place in Somerset), over 140 miles from Bradford. During 1754 and 1755 he had been involved in the forgery and circulation in the West Country of commercial paper to the value of £4000 or £5000. It appears that some time before August 1755 Wilson fled from Gloucestershire, for during that month he appeared in Leeds in Yorkshire. His choice of the town as a refuge was probably determined by his occupation, Leeds being the marketing centre for the West Riding woollen textile industry. On his arrival there he was able to make himself readily accepted by offering to instruct manufacturers in the production of thin cloth for the Turkey trade, a Gloucestershire speciality. He was shown considerable respect and was said to have behaved with 'modesty and decency'.[6] But his manufacturing scheme failed, leaving him destitute (apart from the forged note and bills in his possession). It was in these circumstances that he took off on a round of inns in various West Riding textile towns that culminated in his appearance before Justice Lister.

Lister was convinced that Wilson was guilty of forgery—a capital offence—and determined that he should not escape justice. Having committed his suspect to prison on the grounds of failure to find sureties for his good behaviour, the Yorkshire magistrate was faced with the problem of how to obtain more information about him. He was not without clues as to Wilson's origins. The fugitive's statement and the letters found in his possession suggested he came from either Somerset or Gloucestershire. Lister, however, had very little knowledge of or connection with the West Country. Despite the fact that Painswick was, like Bradford, a cloth-producing centre, neither he nor his friend the Recorder of Leeds, a prominent barrister whom Lister consulted, were sure whether the town was in Gloucestershire or Somerset. Nor were they acquainted with even the names of any magistrates in those two counties. Time was short. The letters suggested that Wilson's associates were to appear at the forthcoming Lent Assizes in one of the western counties. If they were acquitted in Wilson's absence, they could not be tried again on the same change.[7] Moreover, it was uncertain how long Wilson could be held in custody merely for want of sureties. He might secure a rapid release if friends came to stand bail for him.

Confronted with these difficulties, Lister was obliged to resort to speculative expedients to establish the validity of his suspicions. By securing the names and addresses of individuals of some standing in the western counties with whom people he knew in Yorkshire were acquainted, he attempted to send particulars of the affair by post into the vicinity of Wilson's crimes. His friend the Recorder of Leeds

[6] B.C.L., Deeds, 16/14/10, Richard Wilson to Lister, 19 Jan. 1756.

[7] They would have been able to plead 'autrefois acquit'.

provided the name and address of his former landlord at Bath, whom he believed (mistakenly) to be an *ex officio* magistrate for that borough. Some time later the Recorder recalled the name of a major Gloucestershire gentleman clothier of his acquaintance. At the same time Lister spread the word in the Bradford area that he required contacts in the West Country. His Bradford mercer and a Gloucestershire man travelling in Yorkshire were able to supply him with the names and addresses of two Gloucestershire gentlemen, both of whom were probably large-scale clothiers.

Lister wrote to all four with a description of the suspect, copies of the bills, note and letter, and a request that all these items be made public. He asked his correspondents to undertake inquiries themselves, or, if the 'places mentioned should be at too great a distance from you, you will please to transmit the papers to any magistrate or gentleman of your acquaintance that can make inquiry more conveniently'.[8]

There was no certainty that any of the people to whom the Yorkshire justice had written (none of whom were acting magistrates) would either be able or prepared to assist him. The same weakness applied to his other detective strategy—the newspaper advertisement. On the advice of the Recorder of Leeds, Lister drew up an advertisement describing Wilson and giving an outline of the case. This he arranged to have inserted in a London newspaper by a Gray's Inn barrister who regularly corresponded with a Bradford attorney. The London barrister chose *The General Evening Post*. This was one of a number of thrice-weekly London evening newspapers which circulated more widely in the provinces than other metropolitan papers. However, Lister could not be certain that anyone in the West Country acquainted with the affair would see it. After all he was advertising in a London, not a local paper.

In the event, the newspaper advertisement proved successful. The Yorkshire magistrate received four letters in reply to it from parties with an interest in the case. Some of them came to Yorkshire to identify Wilson, who was removed by habeas corpus to Gloucester, where he stood trial for forgery at the 1756 Lent Assizes. He was convicted and sentenced to death.

This did not mark the end of Lister's involvement. Wilson's execution was respited, which suggested that he was likely to receive a commuted sentence or a pardon. The forger proceeded to send Lister an extremely cheeky letter, demanding the return of the papers which the magistrate had taken from him in January. Lister received other requests for some of the same documents, in particular one on behalf of the man who had acted as prosecutor in Wilson's trial at Gloucester, but who was himself charged after the assizes with forgery by the other

[8] B.C.L., Deeds, 16/14/10, draft of Lister to anon., n.d. (about 1 Feb. 1756).

interested parties. Confronted with these various requests and not at all sure what was going on, Lister turned to another London barrister. The latter consulted a judge on his behalf about the propriety of returning the forgeries to the convicted man and arranged the final disposal of the various papers after the judge refused to assist. That was the end of the affair as far as Lister was concerned, but it was an ending that left him confused and exasperated. At the end of May 1756 he commented that 'there has been a great scene of villainy amongst these people, and ... I do not know which of them is the greatest'.[9]

The obstacles to the transmission of criminal intelligence over long distances which are revealed by the 1756 Gloucestershire forgery case were regularly met with by those attempting to bring serious offenders to justice under such circumstances in the mid-eighteenth century. The 1756 affair provides a particularly striking illustration of these obstacles because the problems associated with acquiring and disseminating information were especially acute in this instance. Those in Yorkshire who became involved were third parties in the affair, ignorant of the precise circumstances, and great urgency attached to their efforts. The particular problems of criminal intelligence which the case illustrates can be grouped under four headings.

First, the very ease with which an offender could escape discovery by flight to a part of the country remote from the scene of his offence. Edward Wilson was not advertised in the Gloucester newspaper by those he had defrauded, but considerable efforts were made in his native county to apprehend him. Yet even when he was taken up in Yorkshire it is doubtful whether his secret would have been discovered, had he not had the misfortune to appear before Lister, who was an exceptionally assiduous justice and considered himself unusual in his practice of searching those accused of trivial offences.[10] Admittedly Wilson's expertise in the woollen industry provided him with a plausible front in Yorkshire, but the experience of much more notorious fugitives suggests that an innocuous cover was not essential to escape detection in a distant locality.[11] Nevertheless, it helped. Offenders of a professional character, like the renowned John Poulter and his

[9] B.C.L., Deeds, 16/14/10, draft of Lister to Mr Rookes, 26 May 1756.

[10] B.C.L., Deeds, 16/14/10, draft of Lister to 'Dear Alan', n.d.

[11] Take, for example, Thomas Rowden, with Dick Turpin and Samuel Gregory one of a group of men who achieved extraordinary notoriety as a result of their robberies in the London area in 1734 and 1735. They were advertised in the official *London Gazette* and much reported in other London newspapers. Rowden, having fled to Gloucestershire and adopted an alias, was apprehended there in 1736 for putting off counterfeit coin and convicted. Neither at his trial nor during nine months he subsequently spent in Gloucester gaol was his true identity discovered. See D. Barlow, *Dick Turpin and the Gregory Gang* (Chichester, 1973), 123, 231–2, 241–4, 301–3.

associates in the early 1750s, or the Coventry gang in the early 1760s, used networks of safe houses, were possessed of a multiplicity of well-established aliases and were often adept at disguise. These offenders appear to have been able to move with considerable security to and fro across provincial England, between the provinces and London, and even across the Atlantic, often returning from transportation almost as soon as they arrived in America. The risk of apprehension for such people appears to have been largely confined to the period during and immediately after the commission of their offences. These included burglary, horse stealing and pickpocketing, as well as the infliction on the public of a variety of frauds at fairs, races and other gatherings.[12]

Second, the profound ignorance displayed by a leading county magistrate and a prominent provincial barrister of places and people, particularly justices of the peace, in a distant part of the country. It is important to bear in mind, however, that it was only after 1790, with the publication of national directories which carried (incomplete) information on the identity and addresses of acting magistrates in any particular locality, that information of this kind became readily available in print.[13]

Third, the expense and inconvenience which the dissemination of criminal intelligence could entail. Lister's advertisement in *The General Evening Post* cost him approximately seven shillings.[14] In addition he incurred considerable postal charges. The affair illustrates how unpredictable the cost and inconvenience of involvement in such a case might be. The complications that followed Wilson's conviction not only perplexed Lister, but put him to the expense of additional letters and of engaging a London barrister. He appears to have received no

[12] For Poulter see J. Poulter alias Baxter, *The Discoveries of John Poulter alias Baxter* (6th edn., Sherborne, 1753), 3–27. For the Coventry gang see J. Hewitt, *A Journal of the Proceedings of J. Hewitt, Senior Alderman of the City of Coventry and one of His Majesty's Justices of the Peace for the said City and County, in his Duty as a Magistrate* (2nd edn., 2 vols., Birmingham, 1790), i, 117–220.

[13] See P. Barfoot and J. Wilkes (compilers), *The Universal British Directory of Trade, Commerce and Manufacture* (2nd edn., 5 vols., 1793), *passim.* It is curious that Lister did not attempt to write to the mayors of Gloucester, Bath or Bristol, who were magistrates *ex officio* and could be located without knowledge of their names. However, it is also striking that the surviving documents suggest he wrote only to people to whom he had a formal introduction from someone in Yorkshire. Perhaps he considered such connections were more to be depended on in such a case than the sometimes questionable enthusiasm of anonymous magistrates for upholding the law.

[14] The editions of *The General Evening Post* that carried Lister's advertisement (which appeared twice) do not appear to have survived. It is possible to establish the approximate cost to Lister by comparing a draft of the advertisement among his papers with the run of *The General Evening Post* for 1736 held at the Guildhall Library, London, which carries the prices charged for different lengths of advertisement.

offer of reimbursement from the aggrieved parties. A single episode of this nature was hardly a difficult financial burden for a provincial gentleman to bear, but the inconvenience alone was enough to discourage many lesser magistrates from following Lister's example, let alone poorer victims of crime. If a number of offenders were involved, the cost, in both time and money, could become prohibitive for even the most zealous justice of the peace.[15]

Fourth, the absence of any official facility for distributing information about suspected offenders between counties and regions, other than the traditional hue and cry, which had (with certain exceptions) already fallen into desuetude. The 1756 affair demonstrates that the newspaper advertisement could serve as an effective substitute for such a facility, but it was a substitute that suffered from serious shortcomings. Resort to a newspaper advertisement was far from universal in such cases. As we have seen, those in Gloucestershire attempting to apprehend Edward Wilson did not choose to advertise him in *The Gloucester Journal*. Newspaper advertisements, and more particuarly, the rewards customarily offered for information in advertisements placed by victims of offences, could be expensive. Moreover, the pattern of mid-eighteenth century newspaper circulation did not lend itself to the dissemination of information over very long distances.

The thirty-five provincial newspapers in existence in the mid-1750s were geographically restricted in their circulations.[16] England was divided into a patchwork of newspaper territories, each based on a particular printing town. A potential advertiser who was ignorant of the precise destination or provenance of a fugitive, having advertised in his local paper or made local enquiries, had little to gain by advertising in other provincial papers, unless he went to the trouble of advertising in all of them. For most potential advertisers this was an entirely impractical undertaking, given the difficulty of locating the other papers, delivering the advertisement and paying for it. Crime advertisements originating well outside the established territory of a particular provincial newspaper were extremely rare during the 1750s.[17]

The thrice-weekly London evening papers were distributed much

[15] This was the predicament of which John Hewitt, the extraordinarily active Coventry magistrate, complained to the Treasury in 1766. See P.R.O., T 1/449, Treasury In-letters, 1766, Memorial of John Hewitt, 20 March 1766.

[16] G. A. Cranfield, *The Development of the Provincial Newspaper, 1700–1760* (Oxford, 1960), 21, 202–6.

[17] Take, for example, *The Gloucester Journal* in the years 1754 and 1755. Although crime advertisements came from quite distant parts of south and mid Wales, which evidently fell within the paper's territory, all those originating in England came either from Gloucestershire itself, or from immediately adjacent counties, with the sole exception of one from a place in Shropshire barely fifty miles from Gloucester.

more extensively and regularly carried crime advertisements originating in distant parts of the country.[18] Yet despite the evidence of the 1756 forgery affair, there are grounds for caution as to the effectiveness of the London press in this regard. The London evening papers enjoyed an extensive provincial circulation, but they were distributed relatively thinly. One of Samuel Lister's correspondents pointed out that 'the General Evening Post is not, you know, universally received', and urged him to place his advertisement in every London paper and in *The Gloucester Journal*.[19] Moreover, it was probably not easy for people in the provinces to place such advertisements in the London papers if they had no-one to act on their behalf in the capital.

The obstacles to long distance detection illustrated by the 1756 Gloucestershire forgery case were precisely those that Sir John Fielding addressed in his General Preventative Plan of 1772. The Plan has been described in several histories of eighteenth-century policing.[20] A brief outline is necessary here to demonstrate exactly how it was tailored to confront those obstacles and to point out a number of features that have gone unrecognised.

Between September 1772 and September 1773 Fielding sent out five printed circular letters to the clerks of the peace of all the English and Welsh counties for submission to the county magistrates in sessions and to the mayors and other chief magistrates of corporate towns. These outlined his Plan and solicited support.[21] The scheme he proposed had two elements. First, he asked the provincial magistrates, borough and county, to supply detailed descriptions to his office in Bow Street of felons or cheats escaped from justice and of people apprehended on suspicion of such offences. He requested that gaolers should be required to keep descriptions of those committed to their custody and to enter them in the assize calendars, which were already being sent to Bow Street. He also asked officials and the public to supply descriptions of horses stolen or stopped.[22]

[18] *The General Evening Post* in 1736 carried crime advertisements from as far away as Yorkshire, Bristol and Norfolk, and *The London Evening Post* in 1756 as far as Flintshire and Lancashire, although in both cases the vast majority of their crime advertisements originated in the metropolis or adjacent counties.

[19] B.C.L., Deeds, 16/14/10, A.B. to Lister, n.d. (about 3 Feb. 1756).

[20] For example, Radzinowicz, *History*, iii. 47–54; P. Pringle, *Hue and Cry: The Birth of the British Police* (1965), 183–194; T. A. Critchley, *A History of Police in England and Wales, 900–1966* (1967), 32–5.

[21] Radzinowicz, *History*, iii. Appendix i, 479–485, reprints four of the circulars, and some of the covering letters. For the fifth circular (that dated Bow Street, 11 Sept. 1773) and other covering letters, see Surrey Record Office, Kingston, Q5 2/6, Surrey Quarter Sessions bundles, Mich. 1772 to Mich. 1773. The following outline of the Plan is, unless otherwise stated, based on these circular letters.

[22] *Manchester Mercury*, 22 and 29 Dec. 1772.

This element of the Plan was hardly original. The Bow Street office had served as a central clearing house for criminal information within the metropolis and its immediate vicinity since Henry Fielding's day. Moreover, John Fielding had already enormously extended the very limited provincial connections of his half-brother and the latter's prededessor as principal magistrate for Westminster, Sir Thomas De Veil.[23] As early as 1756 John Fielding was inserting advertisements in the London papers about provincial fugitives on behalf of the victims of their crimes, although there is no evidence that Samuel Lister knew of or made any attempt to use his services in that year.[24] By the 1760s, Fielding regularly placed advertisements in the London evening and many provincial papers, some about specific offences and others asking magistrates to correspond with him about unsolved crimes, suspects taken into custody and offenders fled from justice.[25]

It was the integration of these procedures into a national system for collating and circulating the information thus obtained that was the second and truly innovatory element of the 1772 Plan. Fielding proposed to redistribute this information throughout the country in a printed format suitable for public display. He and his half-brother had both operated an equivalent system within the London area, after 1752 by arrangement with daily newspapers, initially *The Public Advertiser,* but later also *The Gazetteer.* Prior to 1772, however, Fielding had not attempted systematically to provide such a facility on a national scale.[26]

The pattern of newspaper circulation in the provinces made it impossible for advertisements in a couple of commercially-circulated newspapers (London or provincial) to offer the combination of national coverage and local penetration that Fielding required for his criminal intelligence. His solution was a twofold one. First, he had all the information he received from the provinces regarding offences, stolen property, fugitive offenders and those committed to prison, as

[23] For Henry Fielding see *Covent Garden Journal*, 30 June 1752; for De Veil see Pringle, *Hue and Cry*, 68–9. A clearing house for criminal information, operating mainly within the London area, but with provincial connections, had been the lynchpin of Jonathan Wild's activities in the 1710s and 1720s: see G. Howson, *Thief-Taker General* (1970), 66–9 and 125–6.

[24] *London Evening Post*, 5 Feb. 1756.

[25] See *York Courant*, 8 Nov. 1763; *London Evening Post*, 7 Aug. 1766; *Salisbury Journal*, 1 Sept. 1766; *Cambridge Chronicle*, 3 Aug. 1771. By the 1760s Fielding was already experienced in the use of such advertisements in provincial papers, having employed them to promote his Universal Register Office during the previous decade. See, for example, *Gloucester Journal*, 16 July 1754.

[26] His advertisements about offenders and offences in the London evening and provincial newspapers before 1772 were essentially sporadic. He continued after that year to place advertisements in the provincial press on the same basis. See *Manchester Mercury*, 14 Sept. 1773 and *Norwich Mercury*, 24 Dec. 1773.

well as information of the same kind from the metropolis, entered in a newspaper. This was sent *gratis* to mayors, acting county magistrates and gaolers throughout the country and was available on sale to the public at large. It also included advice about criminal matters, news of improvements in the General Preventative Plan and reminders to law officers to promote it.

During the first year of the Plan's operation (October 1772 to October 1773) this purpose was achieved by an arrangement with a London thrice-weekly newspaper, *The London Packet or New Lloyd's Evening Post*. Every Monday the paper transformed all or part of its front page into 'The General Hue and Cry', printed in large type with a distinctive border to facilitiate cutting out for public display. Fielding asked that the section be stuck up by mayors in the market places of their towns and by county magistrates at some conspicuous place on a public road. From the autumn of 1773, when the Plan secured long-term government finance to the tune of £400 per annum, Fielding dispensed with the arrangement with *The London Packet* and published his own newspaper entitled *The Hue and Cry*, which he circulated in the same way. Its contents were similar to its predecessor's. At first it was published on a weekly basis, though it soon became fortnightly and by the end of the 1770s appeared monthly.[27]

Second, Fielding supplemented *The Hue and Cry* by circulating cumulative, printed lists of those offenders who remained at large despite the appearance of their descriptions in his newspaper. The lists were originally intended to be produced quarterly, but from the start Fielding omitted printing a quarter's list if he felt sufficient names were not available. By the later 1770s they were appearing half yearly or yearly. Initially Fielding sent a copy to all mayors and clerks of the peace, with the request that enough should be reprinted at the expense of each corporation or county to be distributed to constables for stricking up on the church door or in another prominent place in every parish. After the Plan acquired government funding, he was able to have sufficient printed himself to send to every magistrate, high and petty constable, gaoler and house of correction keeper in the country, most of whom he supplied via the county clerks of the peace.

Yet however effective the machinery Fielding devised for circulating his criminal intelligence, the success of the Plan ultimately depended on the ability and willingness of those whom it reached to act

[27] Some, but not all, of the copies of *The London Packet or New Lloyd's Evening Post* for the period Fielding used it survive in the Bodleian Library. I have been unable to discover any copies earlier than 1786 of *The Hue and Cry* that Fielding and his successors published from Oct. 1773. However, a virtually continuous run of much of the information Fielding and his successors inserted in these publications is available from Dec. 1772 in *The Newcastle Courant*, which reprinted most of it on its front page.

appropriately. Fielding was, of course, supplying a public that was already responsive enough to information of this kind to make local crime advertising in newspapers and handbills a much-used detective technique. Nevertheless, all the literature associated with the Plan carried exhortations to greater responsiveness from the public and local officials alike. To stimulate the participation of the latter, Fielding also made more concrete proposals. He suggested that after each list was issued, magistrates should instruct all parish constables to make searches under the terms of the 1744 Vagrant Act (17 Geo. II, c. 5), in order to flush out the offenders named therein. He also requested that he should be supplied by the county clerks of the peace and gaolers with the names and addresses of all acting magistrates and high constables. These were important not simply for the purpose of his general correspondence. Fielding insisted that a warrant should accompany descriptions of fugitive offenders sent to Bow Street. Knowledge of the names and addresses of local officials enabled him, on a discovery being made, to send the warrant direct to the appropriate locality, thereby avoiding delay, inconvenience and the expense of moving the prisoner by habeas corpus.

Thus the General Preventative Plan provided specific remedies for each of those obstacles to the dissemination of criminal intelligence that were evidenced in the 1756 Gloucestershire forgery affair. It put regular, detailed descriptions of fugitives and unidentified suspects in custody, including their occupations, their customary aliases and disguises, and their *modus operandi*, into the hands of local officials throughout the country and made them widely accessible to the public. In addition, it provided both a central repository for criminal intelligence and a machinery for transferring information rapidly between officials in different parts of the country. This facility was provided at minimal expense, Fielding paying for correspondence, as well as for distributing *The Hue and Cry*.[28]

Fielding promoted his 1772 and 1773 proposals with enormous zeal—he was nothing if not an inspired self-publicist. His enthusiasm was reciprocated by county benches and corporation authorities throughout provincial England. It is impossible to provide a definitive list of their responses, but it is clear that Fielding did not greatly exaggerate when he claimed his proposals had received 'their unanimous approbation'.[29] Out of forty-six English counties or divisions of counties with their own quarter sessions for which sessions records survive and have been surveyed, evidence of a positive response from the magistrates in sessions to Fielding's proposals is found in twenty-

[28] Although it should be noted that the vast majority of entries in *The Hue and Cry* carried rewards.

[29] P.R.O., SP 37/10, Sir J. Fielding to Earl of Suffolk, n.d. (January 1773).

six. Newspaper reports reveal a positive response in another four of that forty-six. In only one county—Surrey—is there any evidence of opposition. This appears to have arisen from an unwillingness to pay for reprinting Fielding's lists.[30] By contrast, in twenty-five of the counties or divisions surveyed there is evidence of a decision to reprint the lists and have them circulated for display, the expenses to be met out of the county or divisional rate. Because county sessions documents and newspaper reports were not compiled in a uniform manner, it is probable that many of the counties for which no response is recorded did in fact support the plan, as Fielding claimed. Borough records for the period are, unfortunately, very uninformative about such matters. Nevertheless, the newspapers indicate positive responses in large corporate towns like Worcester and Newcastle, while no record of opposition has been discovered.[31] Subsequently Fielding was to assert that *The Hue and Cry* was 'stuck up in the market place of every corporation town from Cornwall to Edinburgh, by order of the Mayors and chief officers of such corporations'.[32]

In some places the authorities did much more than Fielding had requested in his circular letters. In 1772 the magistrates of Northumberland, Durham and Cumberland, in conjunction with those of the borough of Newcastle, paid for Fielding's 'General Hue and Cry' (later his *Hue and Cry*), together with a compilation of local crime information along the same lines, to be inserted weekly in *The Newcastle Courant.* This was to continue into the 1790s. At Manchester in the same year a meeting of the principal inhabitants, at the suggestion of T. B. Bayley, the active local magistrate, set up their own 'Bow Street' office for criminal intelligence. For almost a year, they too had Fielding's 'General Hue and Cry' reprinted in the two Manchester newspapers, in conjunction with local crime information. The proprietors of *Jackson's Oxford Journal* and *The Stamford Mercury* also reprinted "The General Hue and Cry' for approximately the same period.

The co-operation that Fielding received from the localities was not restricted to disseminating his criminal intelligence. An analysis of the provenance of the 187 entries in *The Hue and Cry* (as reprinted in *The Newcastle Courant*) for the year 1774 reveals that although there was a bias towards London, Middlesex and the home counties, which accounted for forty-three per cent of the 168 entries whose origin is known, only five English counties were not represented.[33] A similar

[30] Surrey Record Office, Kingston, Q5 2/6, Surrey quarter sessions bundles, Mich. 1772, Sir J. Fielding to T. Lawson, 17 Oct. 1772.

[31] Fifteen borough quarter sessions records were surveyed.

[32] *Newcastle Courant*, 20 July 1776.

[33] The counties of Northumberland, Cumberland and Durham are not included in this calculation because entries from those counties went in the local crime section.

pattern and diversity of origin characterises the entries in the lists that survive. The numbers of cases that appeared in *The Hue and Cry* may appear to be small, but the numbers of offenders moving between regions was probably not very large. However, almost all the entries concerned those serious offences—murder, aggravated theft and horse theft—that were the occasion of disproportionate public and official anxiety.

How successful was the General Preventative Plan? An example from 1773 and 1774 will serve to illustrate the Plan in operation. In July 1773 Richard alias John Myett, alias Early, alias Dart, alias Mason, described by Fielding as 'a very extraordinary offender', broke into a silversmith's shop at Wallingford in Berkshire and stole a large quantity of silver. Particulars of the theft and a description were promptly inserted in 'The General Hue and Cry'. Within a fortnight Myett was apprehended at Lawton in Cheshire, 130 miles from Wallingford. There he succeeded in escaping, though without his booty. He was advertised again in 'The General Hue and Cry', but evaded capture. During the ensuing autumn and winter he undertook various burglaries in the Salisbury area, where he had worked some two years previously. When his former employer at Salisbury was burgled in February 1774, Myett was suspected. He was therefore advertised once again in Fielding's paper and two weeks later was apprehended as a consequence at Darlington, 260 miles from Salisbury. He was subsequently convicted and hanged.[34]

This and the other available examples of the Plan's successes derive principally from reports in the provincial press.[35] It is impossible to provide a systematic assessment of its success rate, because such reporting was sporadic and Fielding's own Bow Street records have not survived. We do know that, by March 1773, at least ten of the thirty-six offenders in Fielding's September 1772 list had been apprehended.[36] However, there is no certainty that they were apprehended because they were in the list and the representativeness of these figures is questionable given that the 1772 list had been compiled before the Plan took effect. Even if a satisfactory clear-up rate could be established, its significance for an evaluation of the scheme's impact would

[34] *Newcastle Courant*, 31 July, 21 Aug. 1773; 5 and 12 Mar., 23 July 1774. *Salisbury Journal*, 14 Feb. 1774.

[35] For other successful cases see *Chelmsford Chronicle*, 23 July 1773; *Leeds Intelligencer*, 19 Oct. 1784; *Manchester Mercury*, 9 Feb. 1773; *Newcastle Courant*, 11 Sept. 1773; *Nottingham and Newark Journal*, 1 May 1773; *Norwich Mercury*, 9 Nov. 1776; *Reading Mercury*, 12 Sept. 1774.

[36] The Sept. 1772 and Mar. 1773 lists (the second included a list of those in the first who had been apprehended) survive in several quarter sessions collections, for example Essex Record Office, Q/SB b272/58 and 64, Essex quarter sessions bundles, Easter 1773.

be difficult to gauge, because there is no available data for equivalent cases before 1772. Moreover, it is important to bear in mind that Fielding's objectives were as much preventative as detective.

Perhaps the best judgment one can offer is that the Plan could hardly have failed to be an improvement on pre-existing long-distance detection techniques, given their inadequacies. That this was widely believed to be the case is indicated by the praise that the 1772 and 1773 innovations continued to receive after some years in operation. For example, in 1775 a Coventry correspondent to *The London Evening Post* referred to the Plan's 'multitude of admirers'. The next year the printer of *The Norwich Mercury*, a paper with no special links with Bow Street, described *The Hue and Cry* as a 'useful paper'. After 1776, successive editions of Burn's *Justice of the Peace* carried a paragraph commending the Plan as an established success.[37]

Although the General Preventative Plan was widely regarded as a success, it was also subject to limitations, which became increasingly obvious when Fielding attempted to intensify its operation in 1775. In order to understand these limitations it is first necessary to explain why his 1772 and 1773 proposals were, from the start, so favourably received. The shortcomings of the existing facilities for long-distance dissemination of criminal intelligence, Fielding's enormous national reputation and his established links with influential provincial magistrates all played a part here.[38] The visibility of the problem of inter-regional offenders during the 1760s, in particular the publicity given to the Coventry gang, combined with the increase in indictments for serious offences after the Seven Years War, may have predisposed local officials to favour the Plan.[39]

Another key element in the Plan's favourable reception was the particular form Fielding chose for it. The 1772 and 1773 proposals offered the benefits of a police apparatus that was integrated and centralised, without demanding a wholesale reconstitution along uniform lines of the administration of criminal justice. What Fielding described as his 'favourite preventative machine' was not a bureaucratic engine that necessitated new personnel performing a novel set

[37] *London Evening Post*, 14 Jan. 1775; *Norwich Mercury*, 9 Nov. 1776; R. Burn, *The Justice of the Peace and Parish Officer* (16th edn., 4 vols., 1788), ii. 655–6.

[38] Fielding's provincial reputation was such by 1762 that in that year a Penrith bailiff who operated a horse theft and retrieval operation along the lines of Jonathan Wild could refer to himself as 'Justice Fielding': P.R.O., ASSI 45/26/6/50 P: Assizes Northern Circuit Depositions, examination of J. Winter, 10 Aug. 1762.

[39] For public familiarity with the Coventry Gang, see *York Courant*, 30 Oct. 1764; for indictments see D. Hay, 'War, Dearth and Theft in the Eighteenth Century: The Record of the English Courts', *Past & Present*, no. 95 (1982), 123–6, 135–46.

of duties.[40] As he was at pains to emphasise, it was entirely consistent with the existing character of the English civil power. Indeed he cleverly argued that it constituted a form of police superior to that of foreigners for this very reason.

Such an argument was not, however, entirely consistent with the underlying thrust of Fielding's proposals. In part, the scheme represented an extension of the voluntary principle on which the established success of the newspaper crime advertisement was founded. Fielding's Plan provided a more extensive and systematic facility than any newspaper, but it exploited the same willingness among the general public and officials to respond to such a facility. From the start, however, it was distinguished from newspaper crime advertising by a disproportionate emphasis on the role of officials—especially magistrates—in channelling information and taking appropriate follow-up action. Fielding's subsequent efforts to intensify the operation of the scheme concentrated almost entirely on the activity of officials. This is hardly surprising, given that once the Plan was widely known the capacity of his promotion techniques further to increase public responsiveness was probably limited. But in order to secure the sort of action from local officials that he believed the Plan required, he was eventually obliged to propose far-reaching changes in the character of the existing local government apparatus.

Initially many county and borough magistrates proved eager to respond to Fielding's requests for intensified activity by local officials. As we have seen, a large number of counties and boroughs paid to reprint his lists. In those counties, orders were given to the high constables of the various hundreds to undertake the dispersal of the lists among the petty constables. The response to Fielding's other requests for official action in 1772 and 1773 is more difficult to establish. In making these requests, he did not ask for a specific reply from the magistrates in sessions. A note of their decision is, therefore, much less likely to have been entered in the sessions records than in the case of reprinting the lists, where a reply was requested. The sessions records surveyed do reveal six counties that in 1772 and 1773 ordered gaolers to compile descriptions of prisoners, five that provided the names and addresses of chief constables, and three that began to order searches under the Vagrant Act of 1744, but it is probable that there were many others.

These were not, however, forms of official action that were new in principle, or that implied a major transformation of the roles of the officials involved. Payments out of the county rates for advertising offenders, especially those escaped from houses of correction, were not uncommon. High constables had long been the principal intermedi-

[40] Fielding circular dated 19 Oct. 1772.

aries between the county quarter sessions and the petty constables, in particular superintending the enforcement of various types of warrant. In some counties (though not all) quarterly searches under the Vagrant Act were regularly enforced. Gaolers already kept records of their charges. The compilation by county officials of register books of offenders' descriptions was not unknown.[41]

The proposals Fielding circulated to the county benches in February 1775 were more radical. He had already expressed concern about the problem the lack of justices in many districts posed for a Plan that relied so heavily on the magistracy for its execution. In his 1775 circular he expressed doubts about the capacity of even the most enthusiastic magistrate to operate the Plan to best effect. 'Magistrates in the country, however public-spirited they may be, can only back our warrants, recommend peace officers to execute them, and examine offenders when taken, and such like; but ... in general, much more is required, in cases of these pursuits, than is proper to ask a magistrate, or possible for his superior station to admit of'.[42]

His recommended solution was to have the high constables pursue and apprehend fugitives. Indeed he proposed that for at least one hundred miles from London, high constables for those Hundreds through which ran the principal roads from the capital should be resident on those roads, that their expenses in pursuits should be paid by the county, or that they should be paid a salary to enable them to keep a horse for that purpose. This expenditure was to be financed out of a tax on places of public entertainment, in itself a preventative measure. He also suggested that the high constables' houses should display a board with the words 'HIGH CONSTABLE', so that travellers could give notice of robbers. In addition, he called for the number of petty constables in each parish to be increased.

The reaction of the county benches to these proposals was cool. Although Fielding asked for a reply, evidence of any kind of response is limited to eight counties or divisions out of forty-five surveyed, in marked contrast to the reception of his earlier proposals. Of that eight, five expressed hostility at least some of the proposals, or did no more than send Fielding the names of the existing high constables (which several counties had been doing since 1772). The only response of the

[41] The Clerk of the Peace for Cumberland was ordered early in 1772 thereafter to make out lists of the names and descriptions of vagrants passed; Cumbria Record Office, Carlisle, Q 7/3, Cumberland quarter sessions Public Order Book, 1767–78, Easter 1772.

[42] Undated printed circular from J. Fielding headed 'To the Acting Magistrates of the Counties at large throughout ENGLAND, in their Quarter Sessions assembled'. This circular and its covering letter, dated 28 Feb. 1775, survive in several quarter sessions collections, for example Kent Record Office, Q/SB 1775, Kent quarter sessions papers, 1775.

Westmorland magistrates was to order Fielding's circular to be filed. In Suffolk, the Beccles bench informed Fielding that the high constables were already resident in parishes on the great road to London, but they 'being persons of very considerable property would not approve of having such boards over their doors as Sir John desires'. The Lincolnshire Lindsey bench informed him that, although his proposal 'would very much contribute to the end proposed', their division was not on any of the great roads, was over one hundred miles from London and few of the offenders escaping from the capital came there. 'Therefore the justices do not think it necessary to appoint an additional number of petty constables within this division.' Their only practical measure was to send the names of the existing high constables. This course of action was also the sole recorded response of the Staffordshire and Devon benches, and one that, in the case of Devon, was associated with reservations about Fielding's 1775 proposals as a whole.[43]

For one of the three remaining counties—the East Riding of Yorkshire—there is no record of a specific quarter sessions response to Fielding's 1775 circular, but each high constable was provided in that and the next year with four pairs of handcuffs to be kept for the use of their Wapentake. This suggests a move to employ the high constables as thief-takers in the way Fielding had proposed. The other two counties—Derbyshire and Lincolnshire Holland—both recorded their approval for the scheme.[44] In Holland, which, unlike Derbyshire, was within one hundred miles of London, the high constables were ordered to put up boards on their houses. None of these three counties appears, however, to have taken any further practical steps to carry out Fielding's proposals. There is no record of a salary being paid to high constables after 1775, nor were extra petty constables appointed in each parish or township. This also appears to be true of those counties for which there is no direct evidence of any response to the 1775 circular, or at least of those among them for which it has been possible to make some assessment of the appointment

[43] Cumbria Record Office, Kendal, WQO/9, Westmorland quarter sessions Order Book, 1770–80, Easter 1775; Suffolk Record Office, Ipswich, B 105/2/44, Suffolk quarter sessions Order Book, 1770–1776, Beccles, Easter 1775; Lincolnshire Record Office, Lindsey quarter sessions Minute Book, 1774–7, Gainsborough, Easter 1775; Staffordshire Record Office, Q/SO 17, Staffordshire quarter sessions Order Book, 1775–81, Easter 1775; Devon Record Office, Exeter, Q/S 1/2, Devon quarter sessions Order Book, 1759–1776, Easter and Summer 1775.

[44] Humberside Record Office, Beverley, QSV 1/6, East Riding quarter sessions Order Book, Michaelmas 1775 and Easter 1776; Derbyshire Record Office, Derbyshire quarter sessions Order Book, 1774–80, Easter 1775; Lincolnshire Record Office, Holland quarter sessions Minute Book, 1771–84, Spalding and Boston, Easter 1775.

and payment of high and petty constables.[45] For example, even in the Liberty of St Albans, immediately adjacent to Middlesex, the bench did not see fit after 1775 to appoint high constables resident on either the Great North Road or the London–Manchester road.[46]

At first sight it is curious that Fielding's 1775 circular received such limited support. In themselves, many of its proposals were neither new in principle or in practice. High constables were, like petty constables, peace officers, with an obligation to make pursuit in cases of felonies reported to them. In many counties they were paid at least some of their expenses. In a number they received a salary—£12 per annum in Cumberland after 1772. Elsewhere they were allowed to deduct 'poundage' from the county rate which they collected.[47] Nor was it uncommon for a quarter sessions or a vestry to appoint an additional petty constable for a parish, or a beadle or watchman to assist the petty constable.[48]

Viewed as a package, however, Fielding's 1775 proposals implied remodelling the customary roles of the officials concerned. The most important task of the county high constables was to collect the county rate. In addition they had a wide range of administrative duties. Their activities as peace officers were almost entirely confined to superintending the petty constables. To transform them into active pursuers of fugitives from justice and of highway robbers was to add a new dimension to their office, and one that was in some respects at odds with their existing duties. It is hardly surprising that county benches were unenthusiastic, when Fielding's proposal would have restricted their choice of candidates for a vital revenue-raising office to those resident on the principal highways. Even if magistrates had wanted to put Fielding's scheme into operation, the fact that in perhaps half the counties high constables held office for life made any rapid shift towards roadside locations impossible. Moreover, high constables in many counties were men of some standing—wealthy yeomen or lesser gentry. Such status reinforced their authority in their superintending and revenue-raising duties, but it meant that for them to be put on

[45] Given the difficulty of proving a negative this cannot be a definite conclusion. It is based on a survey of quarter sessions collections and, in the case of the East Riding, Derbyshire and Holland, of parish (particularly contables') records.

[46] Hertfordshire Record Office, LSMB/1: St Albans Liberty quarter sessions, Draft Minute Book, 1776–86, Epiphany Sessions 1777.

[47] S. and B. Webb, *The Parish and the County* (1963), 501; Cumbria Record Office, Carlisle, Q/7/3: Cumberland quarter sessions Public Order Book, 1767–78, Easter Sessions, 1772.

[48] For example see Gloucestershire Record Office, Q/SO/5, Gloucestershire quarter sessions Order Book, 1724–34, Summer Session 1724.

public call as pursuers of criminals was probably no more acceptable socially than it was for magistrates.[49]

To interfere with the established mix of duties undertaken by the high constables must have appeared all the more unnecessary in view of the relatively small numbers of inter-regional fugitives or highway robberies in most provincial Hundreds. As the comments of the Lincolnshire Lindsey bench indicate, this was certainly a powerful argument against appointing extra petty constables in every parish. After all, in many places where the weight of business necessitated them, supplementary constables or ancillary officers were already provided. This was the case in a large number of non-incorporated urban areas, including Horncastle in Lindsey itself.[50]

Fielding's 1775 proposals are best understood as a further step in what amounted to a programme to extend to the nation as a whole the essentials of the Bow Street system as it operated within the metropolitan area. There, the collection and dissemination of criminal intelligence were combined with systematic follow-up action by officials under Fielding's direction. But such official action was possible precisely because this was an urban area with a distinctive institutional framework, where the pressure of criminal business was on a scale that was without parallel in provincial England. London, Westminster and urban Middlesex, though smaller in total area than many provincial Hundreds, contained perhaps a tenth of the nation's population and a disproportionate share of its serious criminal offences. To confront such offences throughout the metropolis, Fielding was in receipt of government finance, which enabled him to devote all his energies to crime fighting and to employ a small team of full-time thief-takers. He was also able to call upon the services of large forces of constables and watchmen, including some exceptionally diligent high constables, such as Saunders Welch, high constable of Holborn from 1747 to 1755. The latter were probably the inspiration for the new role he envisaged for their provincial counterparts.[51] In the provinces the pressure of criminal business and the numbers and character of the local peace

[49] For the character and duties of high constables see S. and B. Webb, *The Parish and the County*, 489–502 and Cumbria Record Office, Kendal, Browne of Troutbeck *Mss.*, vol. XV, Accounts of Benjamin Browne's disbursements as high constable of Kendal Ward, 1711–31.

[50] J. N. Clarke, *Watch and Ward in the Countryside* (Horncastle, 1982), 8.

[51] For Fielding's activities in London see the sources cited in note 4. From the 1750s Fielding used his London thief-takers on provincial pursuits and enquiries, sometimes at the request of magistrates or others in the provinces. However, their use in this way appears to have been limited and sporadic, partly because of the pressure of metropolitan business and partly because Fielding could afford to employ only a small number of thief-takers: see for examples P.R.O., T 1/449, Treasury in-letters, 1766, Fielding's account for 1765–6.

officers were very different. Indeed, the only places in provincial England that provided the density of local peace officers that Fielding felt his Plan required were the corporate towns. It is significant that, unlike his earlier circulars, that of 1775 was not directed to the mayors of those towns.

Yet the lack of enthusiasm in the counties for the 1775 proposals did not undermine the operation of the established components of the General Preventative Plan. It continued to flourish after Fielding's death in 1780 and under the 1792 reforms of the police of the metropolis. It was the object of much interest from later police reformers and eventually developed into the modern *Police Gazette.*

For most historians of police, the endeavours of Henry and John Fielding mark the beginning of that process of police reform which culminated, after 1856, in a national system of semi-autonomous, uniformed police forces. They have identified as the stimulus to reform the contradiction between a manifestly inefficient eighteenth-century criminal justice system and the growing problems of crime and control associated with the socio-economic changes of the era of the industrial revolution. The character of the eventual outcome and the time taken to reach it are explained as the consequences of tension between on the one hand a widely-recognised need for an efficient police system and on the other a combination of constitutional scruple, official parsimony and general inertia.[52]

This paper has focused on a single episode of police reform, but it serves, nevertheless, to draw attention to some objections to the broad thrust of this historiography. These objections centre on the notion of police 'efficiency'.[53] Insofar as the efficiency of eighteenth-century policing has been analysed by historians, it has been either by drawing on the works of eighteenth-century commentators on the subject, such as the Fieldings or Patrick Colquhoun, or by counting the numbers of law officers. The danger of over-reliance on the evidence of commentators who were in the main advocates of police reform, with an interest in blackening the reputation of the existing law enforcement apparatus, is clear enough. It is also important to emphasise the drawbacks of attempts to gauge efficiency by counting officials. More did not necessarily mean better, and, as this paper has indicated, changes in the performance by law officers of their responsibilities under the criminal law might owe as much to changes in the facilities available to them—in other words in the manner in which they were

[52] See, for example, Radzinowicz, *History*, iii, *passim*, iv (1968), p. v, and Critchley, *A History of Police*, 18–50.

[53] For the use of 'efficiency' see, for example, ibid., 69 and 71, and Radzinowicz, *History*, iii. 324.

able to discharge those responsibilities—as to changes in their numbers.[54]

Nevertheless, there were limits to the willingness and ability of those who manned the existing law enforcement apparatus to exploit opportunities that became available to them. This was Fielding's experience in 1775. But did the unwillingness of many county magistrates in that year to reconstitute the role of the high constables or to appoint extra petty constables as Fielding requested, perpetuate 'inefficiency'? It probably did in the narrow, technical sense that an opportunity to apprehend and perhaps deter some additional offenders was thereby lost. But the significance of that lost opportunity for policing in a wider sense depends on whether controlling such offenders was a policing priority important enough to outweigh any costs their apprehension would have imposed on the law enforcement apparatus as a whole. It was over precisely this issue that Fielding and the county magistrates were in disagreement, a state of affairs that itself reflected differences in their conceptions of policing.

Fielding, sitting in Bow Street at the controls of his preventative machine, viewed the problem of the inter-regional criminal in its totality. His experience of managing the Bow Street system in the London area and the success of his provincial criminal intelligence-gathering made him peculiarly aware of the problem of the serious offender. He was especially concerned at the ability of those offenders he frightened out of London to find refuge in the provinces. Effective prevention demanded that the machine operate throughout the nation on as uniform a plan as possible, irrespective of local need. He saw a vast pool of fugitives from justice waiting to be trawled. Only by denying them any haven could they be eliminated and, more particularly, others deterred from following in their footsteps.

The county magistracy had other priorities. This is not to suggest that they were hostile to the idea of a general, preventative police system, designed to increase the proportion of offenders apprehended. On the contrary, such systematisation had considerable attractions, especially to those exceptionally active magistrates who were key figures on the county benches and who increasingly conceived of their role in terms of a notion of disinterested public service.[55] The reaction

[54] See, for an example of the use of numbers of officials as a measure of their efficiency, J. M. Beattie, 'Towards a Study of Crime in Eighteenth-Century England: A Note on Indictments', in *The Triumph of Culture: Eighteenth-Century Perspectives*, ed. P. Fritz and D. Williams (Toronto, 1972), 309. For modern research which suggests that increases in police manpower do not necessarily lead to significant improvements in detection, see J. Burrows and R. Tarling, *Clearing up Crime* (1982).

[55] I think there is a danger in some recent studies of underestimating the concern of many provincial magistrates to see serious offenders apprehended; for example, D.

of the county benches to the 1772 and 1773 circulars demonstrates that they were willing to respond with enthusiasm, flexibility and some expenditure to proposals of this kind, if they were based on the existing law enforcement apparatus. The attractions of Fielding's preventative machine only began to pall when, for the sake of a national uniformity that bore no relation to local needs, it threatened to unbalance what was a multi-purpose local administrative apparatus. Thus what appears from one perspective as a characteristically eighteenth-century failure to adopt sensible reforms offering efficient policing, emerges from another as a concern to ensure what is best described as policing appropriate to local circumstances. As so often, to adopt a narrow criterion of technical efficiency is to embrace the standards and perceptions of the reformers.

Philips, '"A New Engine of Power and Authority": The Institutionalization of Law Enforcement in England, 1780–1830', in *Crime and the Law*, ed. V. A. C. Gatrell, B. Lenman and G. Parker (1980), 160–1.

THE NEW POLICE, CRIME AND PEOPLE IN ENGLAND AND WALES, 1829–1888

By D. J. V. Jones, B.A., Ph.D., F.R.Hist.S.

READ AT THE SOCIETY'S CONFERENCE 18 SEPTEMBER, 1982

MY subject is the new police of the nineteenth century. It was said of policemen in Mid-Wales in the later part of that century that, after five years of looking at sheep, their minds turned to emigration, drink and suicide. Writing this paper has been a comparable travail. My initial enthusiasm for the topic has been somewhat crushed by the weight of evidence and the models of police historians.[1] The evidence is vast and problematical. This is not the world of the historian of the seventeenth or eighteenth centuries. Great parliamentary and government papers, an ever-widening range of local and national statistics, countless newspaper files, court records and police books await the historian of the nineteenth century. Much material is still being catalogued, and a great deal of police evidence has yet to be collected.

The problems in using this evidence are fairly obvious. Let me give just three examples. First, the historian has to be aware of the degrees of bias and control in government information. The much-used reports on the police of 1828, 1839 and 1852–3 have to be seen in the context of government policy; members and witnesses were chosen with great care, and unfavourable evidence was sometimes put aside. In parliamentary debates, too, ministers showed considerable skill in their use of evidence, and took full, if not unfair, advantage of the information on deviance that had been flowing into the Home Office since 1805. Statistics, claimed the opposition to the Police Bills, were being treated as facts, and some of the best historians and prophets at Westminster found themselves out-manoeuvred and swept along.[2]

Secondly, the records of the police themselves also have their share of difficulties. Much of the front-line information on crime and policing has gone for ever. I am thinking here of the occurrence books, the

[1] For two surveys of the records in existence, see D. J. V. Jones and A. Bainbridge, *Crime in Nineteenth-Century Wales* (Social Science Research Council Report, Swansea, 1975) and D. T. Brett, *The Police of England and Wales: a Bibliography, 1829–1979* (3rd edn., Bramshill, 1979). I should like to thank Mr Brett for his assistance in obtaining some of the publications used in this lecture.

[2] See, for instance, the complaints of Forster, Sobell and Henley. Hansard, cxl, 1856, cols. 2145–2152 and 2165–2172.

charge sheets, the daily station registers and some of the personal police diaries which were often destroyed or lost. What we are left with for the decades before the 1880s are the tidied records of bureaucracy: the annual reports of chief constables, inspectors and commissioners, the national police statistics, and the early memoirs of an increasingly self-conscious profession.[3] This evidence has, in fact, been deeply mined in the twentieth century by writers of over two hundred books and pamphlets on the British police. Significantly, many of these writers were, or are, policemen, and their publications can now be found in the Police Staff College Library, at Bramshill in Hampshire.

Of all the police material the annual chief constables' reports are the most used and abused. With their coded messages, selected statistics, bland assertions and epilogues of self-praise, they are the classic products of a new and wary profession. The best of them, such as those housed in the Manchester Local History Library, only highlight the deficiencies of the rest.[4] When in the 1860s the Watch Committee of that town complained of the level of delinquency recorded in the annual reports, the chief constable replied that information-gathering was simply more thorough and honest in his town than anywhere else.

The third problem of evidence concerns the relationship between the police and people.[5] Richard Mayne, one of the first Metropolitan commissioners, collected information on people's attitudes towards the 'Peelers', filing away praise and criticism and combing newspapers for relevant letters and material. But this early obsession with public opinion was partly a reflection of anxiety and ignorance. It was, and remains, difficult to establish the reception which the new police received in the first decades of their existence. What, for example, were the views of the agricultural population, which supplied so many of the police recruits? And how did small businessmen, shopkeepers, ministers of religion, independent master craftsmen and others regard the man in blue uniform? Evidence does exist on their relationship with the police, but much of it has been ignored by writers intent on reinforcing stereotype images.

By way of explanation, let me turn to those models of police history which I mentioned at the start of the lecture. There are two dominant

[3] For comments of criminologists and sociologists on the difficulties of such records, see, for instance, J. Ditton, *Contrology: Beyond the New Criminology* (1979), and N. Walker, *Crime, Courts and Figures: An Introduction to Criminal Statistics* (Harmondsworth, 1971).

[4] The reports are in the Manchester Central Library, Local History Section, 352.2.M.1, 1843–92.

[5] Probably the best historical work to date in this area is W. R. Miller, *Cops and Bobbies: Police Authority in New York and London 1830–1870* (Chicago, 1973). Sociologists have been more interested in the subject. See, for example, M. Banton, *The Policeman in the Community* (Tavistock, 1964).

images or interpretations. The first is closely associated with Charles Reith.[6] Writing at the time of the horrors of the Second World War, he set the emergence of the new police in the context of a comparable world of anarchy and mob disorder. The fabric of society in the late eighteenth and early nineteenth centuries was, in Reith's opinion, torn asunder. The machinery of law and order was both inefficient and corrupt, and the population as a whole stood firmly against the introduction of a state police, believing it to be inimical to freedom. Yet, in a remarkably short time—actually from 1829–56—Britain established the most effective and professional police force in the world, subject to the common law and set on the path of impartiality and independence. This new police quickly won control over the mob, held crime within acceptable limits, and won the confidence and lasting admiration of the British people.

In recent years, however, this dominant view of police and police history has been challenged by another. Historians of the left, with their belief in modern community policing, find much to admire in the tolerance and policing of pre-industrial Britain. They relate the emergence of the new police to the rise of capitalism, the demands of industry and a growing concern over social control. Mr Robert Storch, for instance, quotes with approval Engels' comment that the bourgeoisie love the soothing power of a policeman's truncheon.[7] In the opinion of such historians, the function of the new police was simple: to destroy the existing working-class culture and to impose 'alien values and an increasingly alien law' on the urban poor. The response was predictable: permanent working-class hostility and a high level of anti-police violence, leading in a fairly direct line to Toxteth and the riots of 1981.

We have, therefore, two models of police history, the one involving consensus and the other conflict. Both are interesting interpretations, and both are very influential in terms of modern politics and sociology. But, if my view of 1829–1888 is correct, the historian cannot be truly satisfied with either model.

I want, in this paper, to consider three controversial questions. Why were the new police established? What contribution did they make to the so-called peace and equipoise of Mid-Victorian Britain? How did

[6] There are of course many books by Reith, but the classic interpretation can be found in *British Police and the Democratic Ideal* (Oxford, 1943). His ideas have influenced many subsequent writers. Compare D. Ascoli, *The Queen's Peace* (1979).

[7] The two important articles by R. D. Storch are, 'The Plague of Blue Locusts. Police Reform and Popular Resistance in Northern England, 1840–57', *International Review of Social History*, xx (1975), and 'The Policeman as Domestic Missionary: Urban Discipline and Popular Culture in Northern England, 1850–80', *Journal of Social History*, ix (1976).

society respond to the men in blue? None of these questions, however, can be answered without introducing a much-neglected area of study. It is sometimes forgotten, in the celebrations and denigrations of the Police Acts, that the emergence of professional policing was a gradual process in many parts of Britain. There were rural areas where the appointment of paid constables, London policemen and regular patrols in the late eighteenth and early nineteenth centuries matched the creation of hundreds of protection societies, the development of a massive gamekeeping service and the building of new prisons.[8] In Gloucestershire, for example, one of the keenest supporters of the County Police Act of 1839, the machinery of law and order had been overhauled by the 1830s.[9]

In the largest urban districts more striking advances had been made in policing, and I believe that historians should pay rather more attention to them. From at least the mid-eighteenth century, anxious ratepayers and improvement commissioners had done much to establish salaried police forces, and the second decade of the nineteenth century witnessed a great expansion of night as well as day patrols. Much to his regret, William Cobbett returned from America in 1820 to a land where poverty and policemen walked hand in hand. Like other contemporaries he knew that the division between the old and new police was not always a distinct one. In Worcester, Walsall, Portsmouth, Leeds, Bradford and certain other towns men who were to become the new police under Act of Parliament were already in office during the 1820s and 1830s. And, of course, the Reform Crisis and the Municipal Corporations Act of 1835 pushed these reforms further.[10] By 1842 one estimate put the number of embodied policemen in England and Wales at 10,000, more than half the number of 1857 and almost a third of the figure of 1881.[11]

But there were regions of Britain where the rate of change was slow, throughout the nineteenth century. Though technically under the Police Act of 1856, some districts retained older or alternative notions of policing and efficiency.[12] Certain counties continued, until the 1870s, to use parish constables alongside their new policemen, and

[8] Some of the vast amount of primary material in this area has been collected in *Policing and Punishment in Nineteenth-Century Britain*, ed. V. Bailey (1981), S. McConville, *A History of English Prison Administration 1750–1877*, i (1981), and D. J. V. Jones, *Crime, Protest, Community and Police in Nineteenth-Century Britain* (1982).

[9] B. C. Jerrard, 'The Gloucestershire Police in the Nineteenth Century', M.Litt. thesis, Bristol University, 1977, chaps. 1 and 2.

[10] The standard work on these early developments is T. A. Critchley, *A History of Police in England and Wales, 900–1966* (1967).

[11] *Parliamentary Papers* (*henceforth P.P.*), 1852, xxx, i. Number of Police, England and Wales, 1835–52, and J. M. Hart, *The British Police* (1951), 34.

[12] As exemplified by Mr Henley, M.P. See Hansard, cxl, 1856, col. 2171.

some communities refused to accept a government police grant or to appoint the required minimum of police officers.[13] Oldham, Ashton-under-Lyne and Stockport, cauldrons of the industrial revolution, where three examples, though more typical perhaps was Pwllheli, one of the smaller rebel towns. For two decades, this north Wales town angered the government inspector by claiming that it needed only one watchman and had no serious crime. Pwllheli's amalgamation with the county police force in 1879 was one of the many signs at this time that the old order was finally passing away.[14]

The pressures and ideas that culminated in the Police Acts of 1829–56 were many. The traditional view is that these Acts were simply a response to increased crime and disorder, especially in the big cities and industrial centres. This was the gist of Peel's case in 1829 and of Russell's ten years later. Certainly, there was, over the first four decades of the century, a great rise in the number of trials for indictable offences and in summary committals to gaol. By the mid-century, when prisons were full of juveniles, vagrants, suspected thieves and the like, Henry Mayhew remarked that 'it is almost impossible for a poor man to escape jail'.[15] Engels likened the rising crime figures to social warfare, but there were some who took a more jaundiced view.[16] They knew that recent legislation, both national and local, greater financial assistance for prosecutors, reduced sentences, and more courts, gaols and police had all helped to swell the tide of recorded delinquency. People inside and outside Westminster testified that the real situation has been worse in the eighteenth century. 'That crime has proportionately decreased is undeniable, ...' wrote Dr W. C. Taylor in 1839; 'Who now sleeps with pistols beneath his pillow or hangs a blunderbuss within reach of his bolster.'[17] Disraeli, in the debates on the County Police Bill of that year, made the same point, and asked his colleagues if they shared Russell's vision of civil war in Britain. Even Chadwick, the greatest advocate of a national police force, noted in 1828 that public habits had improved, and, a quarter of a century later,

[13] C. Pilling, 'The Police in the English Local Community, 1856-80', M.Litt. thesis, Cambridge University, 1973, and H. Parris, 'The Home Office and the Provincial Police in England and Wales, 1856–70,' *Public Law*, autumn 1961, chap. 3.

[14] J. O. Jones, 'The History of the Caernarvonshire Police Force, 1856–1900,' M.A. thesis, University of Wales, 1956, chap. 5.

[15] H. Mayhew, *The Criminal Prisons of London* (1861), 341, cited in M. Ignatieff, *A Just Measure of Pain. The Penitentiary in the Industrial Revolution, 1750–1850* (1978), 186.

[16] F. Engels, *The Condition of the Working Class in England, 1844*, ed. W. O. Henderson and W. H. Chalenor (Oxford, 1958), 149.

[17] W. C. Taylor, 'The Moral Economy of Large Towns', *Bentley's Miscellany*, vi (1839), 481. Compare *P.P* 1818, VIII, Third Report on the State of the Police of the Metropolis, 32, and *P.P.*, 1828, VI, Report on the Police of the Metropolis, 9.

he had the difficult task of pleading for a compulsory Act in the face of declining statistics of crime and riot.[18]

But, of course, the debate was not just about statistics and the physical threat to the state, important though the latter undoubtedly was. In their more private moments reformers knew that a successful revolution in policing was also dependent on a change in attitudes. The purpose of the government reports of 1828 and 1839, and of a host of social novels and surveys, was to lower society's tolerance of crime and protest. Joseph Fletcher, lecturing to the British Academy in the mid-century, pleaded with landowners and industrialists to take seriously the threat to the country's prosperity and progress.[19] The dangers were clear: Liverpool, through which almost half our overseas trade passed, was the home of the Irish, the juvenile delinquent and the prostitute; the South Wales coalfield, the centre of the iron industry, lay open to the marauding Scotch Cattle; and the great corn fields and game preserves of East Anglia, the granary of London, were at the mercy of the incendiary and the poacher. Only in the well-policed regions, argued Chadwick, was the danger being contained.

For most police reformers there were three related dangers—the criminal class, the vagrant and 'the unreformed working classes'.[20] Although historians now doubt whether there was any such thing as a criminal class outside London, contemporaries believed that it existed.[21] Much of the work of the Royal Commission of 1839, and of the early police forces was documenting the numbers, abode, attitudes and income of this class. The tables and analyses that were published owed much to the pioneering schemes of John Fielding and Patrick Colquhoun. It appeared that each large town had its own colony of outcasts. One police officer compared St Giles, for example, to a game preserve; at least he knew where to find his offenders.

Vagrancy was a related problem. In the aftermath of the Napoleonic Wars, and again in the twenty years from 1829 to 1849, much of Britain experienced exceptional levels of vagrancy, and Chadwick's commissions on the Poor Law and Constabulary spelt out its physical, moral and financial dangers. Vagrants were widely regarded as incipient, if not actual, criminals. During the early years of Victoria's

[18] On this, see for instance, Hansard, xlix, 1839, cols. 731–2, L, 1839, cols. 116–17, *P.P.*, 1852–3, XXXVI, Second Report on the Police, 81–8, and L. Radzinowicz, *A History of English Criminal Law*, iv (1968) 67–78.

[19] J. Fletcher, *Summary of the Moral Statistics of England and Wales* (n.p., 1847–9), 84–5. In their efforts to reduce society's tolerance of crime and riot, Fletcher, Chadwick and others could be bitterly over-critical of older methods of policing.

[20] The best source for Chadwick's views of capitalism under threat is *P.P.*, 1839, XIX, Report of the Royal Commission on the Constabulary Force.

[21] For a regional study, see D. Philips, *Crime and Authority in Victorian England* (1977), 287.

reign new poor-law policies and the Irish famine greatly increased the numbers on the road. 'God protect us from these people' was the cry from Cumberland to Kent, and some districts unquestionably appointed their new policemen as a direct challenge to the threat.[22]

The threat of the 'unreformed working classes' was more controversial. Edwin Chadwick, and his disciples amongst the clerical magistrates of the countryside and the nouveau riche of the towns, were highly critical of the insobriety, indiscipline and attitudes of a large section of working people. Estimates put the loss through pilfering at work, absenteeism and violent strikes at several hundred thousand pounds a year. The Royal Commission of 1839, which gave much attention to work practices and picketing, promised that a state police would provide the social oil to keep the wheels of capitalism turning.

Undoubtedly these warnings by police reformers brought a response from those who had gained most from the Reform Act of 1832. Yet it would be wrong to assume that the urban bourgeoisie was solidly in favour of a state police. Chadwick knew as well as anyone that there were employers who were happy to live with, although perhaps at some distance from, the tensions of capitalist society. They preferred to deal with workmen on their own terms. Riot was, after all, an old adversary, and as for Chartism, the new danger, some even regarded that as a passing upset. In small country towns, and even in industrial Oldham and Bradford, there were people who put their trust, and money, in private policing, insurance policies and the reassurance of an occasional military presence.[23]

It is clear, therefore, that neither rising crime rates and disorder, nor the attitudes of the urban middle class, can fully explain why a nationwide and statutory police force came into being during the mid-century. In the 1830s and 1840s there were still several ways in which the machinery of law and order could have developed. Chadwick and his friends were concerned about the great expansion of private and company policing, and about the attempts by magistrates to improve existing systems of control.[24] Historians, with the benefit of hindsight, have rather ignored these alternative developments but they had considerable popularity. Between 1840 and 1855 the county of Kent, under the vigorous leadership of T. L. Hodges and William

[22] Bradford, Shropshire and Merioneth were examples of this. The threat of vagrancy and 'vagrancy crime' has been neglected in the story of the police. But see W. L. Burn, *The Age of Equipoise* (1964), 168–9, and D. J. V. Jones, *Crime, Protest*, chap. 7.

[23] For interesting studies of Bradford and Oldham policing, see G. Smith, *Bradford's Police* (Bradford, n.d.), and D. Taylor, *999 and all that* (Oldham, 1968).

[24] See for instance, *P.P.*, 1839, XIX, Report of the Royal Commission on the Constabulary Force, 54–5, 82 and 169–170.

Deedes, brought forward six Bills to inject new life into the ancient constabulary.

The fact that a new police system was eventually established owes much to two other influences on the direction and pace of change. The first of these was the partial erosion of the county bench's natural opposition to preventive policing and intervention from Westminster. A great deal is rightly made of county resistance to the most ambitious schemes of Russell and Graham, but it is sometimes forgotten that twenty-four shires adopted the permissive Police Act of 1839 within two years of its passing, and that the support of county members of Parliament was essential, especially to the success of the Bill of 1856.[25]

The leaders of county society, especially those who had both landed and industrial interests, were often the decisive voice in the local debates over the new police. Some lords lieutenant and magistrates had become alarmed at the incidence of crime, poaching, vagrancy and violence in the countryside as well as the towns. Incendiarism, the destruction of machinery, the killing of animals and other forms of criminal protest highlighted the deficiencies of traditional methods of control and detection. I have examined the correspondence between the East Anglian counties and the Home Office in the years from 1816 to 1851, and this reveals a growing awareness, notably in the 1830s, of the value of a professional and patrolling body of policemen. The final debates before the adoption of a new police structure for West Suffolk and Cambridgeshire were set in the context of widespread arson, vagrancy and Poor Law offences.[26] Lord Euston, of the former county, together with great landowners such as Lord Ellenborough in Gloucestershire, the Marquis of Bute in Glamorgan and Sir Baldwin Leighton in Shropshire, made valiant efforts to convince doubting and money-hugging farmers, and some industrialists, that the interests of the wide community were in the end their own.

The other instrument of change was the government. Modern social historians too often ignore the state, but in this case pressure from government was important. Peel, Russell, Graham and Grey were committed to establishing a country-wide police force. Not only was it, in their eyes, a crucial part of general reforming policy, but it was also one which was being strongly recommended by professionals in

[25] A new study of the County Act is D. Foster, *The Rural Constabulary Act 1839* (1982).

[26] P. Muskett, 'Agrarian Protest in East Anglia in 1822', *Agricultural History Review*, forthcoming; J. P. D. Dunbabin, *Rural Discontent in Nineteenth-Century Britain* (1974) 51–7; D. J. V. Jones, 'Thomas Campbell Foster and the Rural Labourer', *Social History*, I, i (1976), 18–19; and *P.P.*, 1852–3, XXXVI, First Report on the Police, 107, and Second Report, 14–15. The prevalence of this rural crime did not always lead to such police reforms, and some leaders of country society came out against them. Ibid., 26–7, and 58–9.

the peace-keeping business.[27] The Duke of Wellington, Sir Richard Jackson and Sir Charles James Napier drew ministers' attention to the dangers of relying too heavily on a thin and dispersed military force. From Luddite days onwards, and certainly after 1819, the question of a police force began to figure more prominently in government memoranda, and, of course, the Home Office was constantly drawing on the experience of the police which it supervised in London and Ireland. By the late 1830s and early 1840s, as the New Poor Law was imposed, and the Chartist threat grew, the necessity for better policing became clearer to governments. Several hundred Metropolitan Police were sent on the orders of the Home Secretary to the trouble spots.

Miss Hart is obviously correct in emphasising the importance of the Chartist crisis in police history, but it was only after the threat had passed that ministers were able to carry out effectively the policy that Peel had wanted to pursue since 1822. Very briefly, that meant giving military help to strife-torn communities on the understanding that they establish a regular police force. Some years later, during the election and industrial troubles of 1852–3, the message was repeated and again in 1855. This time threats of invasion, the coming of war, and, of course, the ending of transportation, increased the determination of government.[28] It needs to be stressed that in the mid-1850s ministers were giving a lead, at a time when some communities, which had sailed through the storm of 1848, were happy with the *status quo*. Indeed, it says much for the skill of governments that they piloted the Metropolitan Police Act of 1829 through Parliament without opposition, and in 1839 and 1856 obtained very comfortable Commons majorities for their major police proposals.

The significance of these Acts in British political and social history has become a matter of considerable debate amongst historians. Opinions vary enormously: some writers, including Charles Reith, argue that the new police were chiefly responsible for the comparative peace and declining crime rates of later Victorian society, whilst others believe that the impact of the police has been exaggerated. Other factors were, in the opinion of the latter school, more important. Contemporaries were also divided in their judgements, though in the field of public order most of them claimed that the influence of the police was vital. The first annual reports of chief constables praised the manner

[27] A new and useful addition to the secondary sources on government policy is E. M. Spiers, *The Army and Society 1815–1914* (1980), chap. 3. The classic work on government and the police is still Radzinowicz, *History*.

[28] J. M. Hart, 'Reform of the Borough Police, 1835–56', *Eng. Hist. Rev.*, lxx (1955), 427; F. C. Mather, *Public Order in the Age of the Chartists* (Manchester, 1959), chap. 4; and H. I. Dutton and J. E. King, *Ten Per Cent and No Surrender; the Preston Strike 1853–4* (Cambridge, 1981), 161.

in which their men controlled riot and violence. Certainly, where police numbers were greatest—London, Liverpool and Manchester, for example—there was considerable evidence to support this view. David Goodway, in his recent study, confirms that the London police did control popular disturbances remarkably well in the 1830s and 1840s.[29] Many of the earliest 'Peelers', or 'crushers'—as they were also called—were especially chosen and trained for crowd control, and their comparative success over the next twenty years enabled governments to come out strongly against using the military as a preventive force. In some of the later troubles, like the female strike against meat prices in 1872 and the Tithe riots in Wales, the police even put aside their more aggressive role and played a sensitive part in calming tempers. But, of course, they did not stop demonstrations or riots. In the scores of protests of the 1870s and 1880s their presence was sometimes inadequate and occasionally counter-productive. During the industrial and political demonstrations of these years, both in London and elsewhere, the task of the police was a particularly unenviable one, and they became, all too easily, the object of popular violence. Soldiers had to be called to their assistance, and bitter criticisms from the middle class rained on the heads of chief constables and Home Secretaries.[30]

In fact, it has been claimed, most recently by Mr Donald Richter, that the nineteenth-century crowd largely tamed itself independently of police reforms. 'It seems clear,' he writes, 'that whatever order did prevail was due as much to crowd restraint as to police effectiveness'.[31] There is some truth in this, but it would be wrong to minimise the police contribution to the general decline in all the statistics of violence after the mid-1860s and early 1870s. In a rapidly expanding world the police diaries show how much of every day was devoted to establishing new standards of public order. Where, as in London or Cardiff, the urban population was growing at a truly exceptional rate, the first task of the men in blue was to control the streets and eradicate lingering tolerance of personal and public violence. The criminal statistics reflect this priority; considerable police influence was undoubtedly brought to bear on vagrants, drunkards, prostitutes, street traders and noisy teenagers.[32] By the mid-1870s police reformers registered a marked improvement in city life; respectable residents now rested more comfortably in close proximity to those three great 'moral teachers': the gaol, the workhouse and the police station.

Historians of social control are about to become hooked on the

[29] D. Goodway, *London Chartism*, 1838–48 (Cambridge, 1982), 12.
[30] Some of this story is told in D. C. Richter, *Riotous Victorians* (1981).
[31] Ibid., 167.
[32] See the graphs of police arrests in D. J. V. Jones, *Crime, Protest*, 129, 163, 167.

moral or cultural aspects of policing. The reasons for this are many. The new police, in the pursuit of order, attacked the more open and violent forms of popular recreation in the mid-century, and kept a close watch on the public house, brothel and fair.[33] In small country and urban districts, often where a reforming clerical magistrate sat on the Bench, there were even claims that the character of the working class was being transformed by preventive policing. To Chadwick's delight, the number of 'idle and dissolute' people seemed on the decline. But it is also true that in many areas the police had not the numbers, support nor inclination to be genuine 'moral missionaries'. The first head constables of Oldham and Liverpool spent much of their time controlling drunken police constables and dragging them away from the arms of ladies of the street.

Real and consistent intervention, in the shape of reforming legislation, vigilance committees, and special police units, came to most large cities during the last years of our period. At the great ports the moral battle was fought with a particular intensity, though the actual outcome was frequently less successful than Puritans stated. In Cardiff, for example, where impressive campaigns were launched against prostitution and Sunday drinking, policemen emerged from brothels and clubs with egg, and sometimes worse, on their faces. Superintendents even sabotaged the moral endeavour of some watch committees, complaining that such work lost their men popular sympathy and reduced time spent on proper policing—the prevention and detection of crime.[34]

The role of policemen as defenders of property has always been open to debate. My own and Mr Gatrell's researches confirm Disraeli's view that the long-term patterns of criminal behaviour are not due simply to more or better policemen.[35] The downward turn of the crime rate after the peaks of the mid-century can be explained only by a complex variety of factors. Those closest to the realities of working-class crime had, for example, few doubts of the general relationship between the economy and delinquency.[36] What they believed, how-

[33] The police were, of coure, only one of a number of influences here. See R. W. Malcolmson, *Popular Recreations in English Society 1700–1850* (Cambridge, 1973), H. Cunningham, *Leisure in the Industrial Revolution, 1780–1880* (1980) and A. Howkins, *Whitsun in Nineteenth-Century Oxfordshire*, History Workshop Pamphlet, No. 8, 1972.

[34] D. J. V. Jones and A. Bainbridge, *Crime in Wales*, section V. 'At best the police can only make clean the outside of the platter', admitted the commissioner of the Metropolitan Police in 1870: *P.P.*, 1870, xxxvi, 468.

[35] The debate is set out in V. A. C. Gatrell, 'The Decline of Theft and Violence in Victorian and Edwardian England' in *Crime and the Law: The Social History of Crime in Western Europe since 1500*, ed. V. A. C. Gatrell, B. Lenman and G. Parker (1980).

[36] This is confirmed by a reading of the police records and analysis of the criminal statistics. See ibid., D. J. V. Jones, *Crime, Protest*, and Fletcher, op. cit., 82.

ever, was that the changing structure of industry, the developments in education, and improved policing were all evening out the natural relationship between crime and the economy. Thus Manchester police chiefs in the crisis of 1847–8 and the cotton famine of the early 1860s, insisted that crime rates were not as high as could be expected. To paraphrase several reports, the criminal class was being contained and the starving poor were showing remarkable patience.[37]

The crucial question for us is: what part did the new police play in that process of containment? They made three particular contributions. Firstly, street crimes such as pickpocketing and mugging declined with the help of a regular police presence in the streets. Indeed any rise in these statistics, as in London during the 1860s, produced a panic amongst the well-to-do Victorians. Secondly, the new police, as they became a more numerous and professional body, placed the 'criminal classes' under greater surveillance. In the mid-century some of the toughest urban areas were invaded for the first time, as authority set up its new stations and fifteen-minute patrols. And over the next quarter of a century the police gradually took the initiative over those who lived regularly on the proceeds of crime. In these years the police in town and country gained much greater powers over suspected and known criminals, and new methods of identification and communication were introduced into the force. 'How complete the power of the police!' exclaimed one observer. 'The strong arm of the law has bent their [offenders'] strong and obstinate wills ...'[38] Thirdly, the police claimed a deterrent effect on ordinary people who committed the occasional crime. A large number of known criminals in the nineteenth century were men, women and children out of work or in casual employment. During the last four decades of the century these people also came under closer police surveillance. The Poaching Prevention Act, the Industrial Schools Acts, the Vagrancy Act and many other national and local laws were used to warn and control people on the margins of respectable society.

It is now impossible to measure the precise influence of the new police on property-crime levels. We know, from the many requests for police patrols, that tradesmen, farmers and suburban householders valued their assistance. Although the main influences on the rate of serious rural crime during the 1830s and 1840s appear to have been economic ones, the optimism and rising property values in those districts which adopted the County Police Act of 1839 deserves to be

[37] See, for example, Manchester Central Library, Local History Section, 352.2. M1, reports of 1846–8, and 1863. For the rural story in which the 1860s seem to have been a turning-point, see D. J. V. Jones, 'Rural Crime and Protest', in *The Victorian Countryside*, ed. G. E. Mingay (1981).

[38] Junius Junior (Johnson), *Life in the Lower Parts of Manchester* (Heywood, n.d.) 8.

mentioned. Similarly, one should record the general support given to the new police by those two great institutions, the Church of England and the Norwich Union insurance company. Many people believed, probably with good reason, that after an initial stutter, the detection and conviction rates of the men in blue did improve. My own work on the Metropolitan Police indicates a rise in the detection rate of known felonies of some 20% between 1840 and 1892; and an increase in the proportion of stolen property recovered. In fact, it was usually only a dramatic outbreak of burglary, house-breaking and robbery which seriously called into question police efficiency.[39] And even here the dialogue of criticism is an interesting one. It reminds us that increasingly the business of defending one's property and of pursuing offenders was being taken over by the police constable. In 1873 Superintendent James Dunlop of the St James Police Division, London, reported that owner-occupiers no longer bothered to lock all their doors and shutters.[40] And sleepy victims of burglary, when reprimanded by the police for their lack of precautions, were likely to reply, in typically modern style, 'crime is your business'.

This brings me to the last section of the paper—on the people's response to the New Police. Can I remind you of the two prominent historical interpretations? According to Reith there was almost universal opposition to the schemes of Chadwick, Peel, Russell and Grey, but once the new police were established they gradually won the affection of all the British people. The other view, held by Robert Storch, sees the new police as the welcome child of the urban bourgeoisie but as the enemy of the working class. The 'English working class ...' he writes, 'was not ... easily reconciled to the advent of a policed society.'[41] Would it be cowardly to suggest that there is a degree of truth in both interpretations?

Amongst the propertied classes there was, from at least the 1830s, a general appreciation of the idea and value of a reformed police force. The vital questions were these: who was to control it, and who was to finance it? These were the twin pillars of the London vestries' opposition to Peel's Act of 1829, and of any borough and county opposition to the subsequent Police Acts of 1839 and 1856. The economic argument was simple. In 1844, for example, the remodelled Manchester police cost well over £23,000, three times, as one wag noted, the amount of stolen property, and the adoption of county forces some-

[39] For this, and for much of the background to these paragraphs, see Gatrell, op. cit., and D. J. V. Jones, *Crime, Protest.*

[40] *P.P.*, 1874, XXVIII, Report of the Commissioner of Police for the Metropolis, Appendix 3.

[41] R. D. Storch, in *Jnl. Soc. Hist.*, ix (1976), 494.

times doubled the county rate. Asked in 1850 to explain why the West Riding, with all its industrial problems, had refused to adopt the County Police Act of 1839, Edward Denison M.P. replied that it was simply 'a question of pounds, shillings and pence'.[42] In some districts it was only the 25% government grant offer of 1856 and of 50% in 1874, which brought a significant improvement in police numbers.

The second pillar of opposition was more profound but perhaps less important. There was suspicion, amongst a wide range of people, of any central government control over the police. When, in the mid-century, government threatened to impose its own standards of police efficiency and police regulations, the cry was 'local sovereignty in danger'. 'No amount of cooking would make it palatable to the public', said Captain Sobell, M.P. for Bath, of the Police Bill of 1856. 'It was the most un-English measure he had ever read.' But when compromises and assurances were made by ministers, as was done in the early 1830s with the London vestries, and again in 1856 with the boroughs, some of the most ardent defenders of local rights, including Sobell, fell into line. In the opinion of an angry J. A. Roebuck, they had sold the future for the immediate prospect of government finance and promises of limited state interference.[43]

During our period the propertied classes still retained considerable control over the nature of policing in their communities. There was, notably in the boroughs, still much of the master-servant mentality in the relationship between the police committees and the new constables appointed under Act of Parliament. Despite the slowly growing influence of the inspectorate and the Home Office, the new police were widely regarded as the particular servants of the ratepayers.[44] In some towns the central police station was placed in or near the town hall, and for twenty years the 'Peelers' were required to perform all manner of local services—dealing with fires, reporting broken sewers, relieving vagrants and the like. And the notion of service went even deeper than that. The policemen were warned, although in St James' or rural Gloucestershire they hardly needed the lesson, that they had to be especially conscientious and discreet when dealing with the most

[42] Cited in D. Foster, op. cit., 21. Some districts, including those in Lancashire and Gloucestershire, did seek to abolish or reduce the forces set up under the Act of 1839.

[43] R. O. Sopenoff, 'The Police of London: the Early History of the Metropolitan Police, 1829–56', Ph.D. thesis, Temple University, 1978, chaps. 4, 5, and the comments of Sobell, Roebuck and Walmsley in Hansard, cxl, 1856, col. 2152, and cxlii, 1856, cols. 305 and 611. Sobell and Muntz accepted the 'inevitable', but wanted central government to pay half the cost of police pay and clothing. Ibid., cols. 305 and 306.

[44] The lack of direction of consistent interest in police policy on the part of Home Secretaries for a generation after the Police Act of 1856 is perhaps exaggerated somewhat in Parris, op. cit., 235. J. Pellow, *The Home Office 1848–1914* (1982), 39 and 136, claims that decisions were taken at the level of inspectors and heads of department.

influential members of the public. My own work, on rural and urban Wales, indicates that, with a few exceptions, the men in blue followed this advice.

Sadly, the relationship between the new police and the lesser propertied groups—the artisan homeowner, the small shopkeeper and the peasant farmer—has been virtually ignored by historians. But the Metropolitan commissioners, provincial police chiefs and newspaper editors were sometimes delighted, and even surprised, by the assistance which the small ratepayers offered the new police.[45] In many places, an initial suspicion of the powers and cost of the 'Peelers' turned rapidly into appreciation. Breakdowns of property crime in nineteenth-century Manchester indicate one of the reasons for this.[46] They showed that it was the petty landlord, the corner shopman and the skilled workman of the poorer districts who suffered as much as anyone from the ravages of crime. It was these little people of town and country, and not the great factory owners or aristocrats, who felt the most benefit from a regular police presence and their services as prosecutors in court. Certainly, the surviving police diaries of the time reveal that the small property owners provided the beer, company and information that made a lonely policeman's lot bearable.

What was the response, finally, of the non-propertied to the new police? We have, I believe, to move carefully between two striking historical images of the late nineteenth century: that of the lazy, bumbling and even friendly target of some popular jokes, and that of the repressive agent encountering resistance and violence. There was considerable opposition to the new police at the outset, as can still be seen in London's *Weekly Dispatch* and *True Sun*, and in many provincial papers. Much of the hostility was directed towards the Metropolitan Police under the control of the Home Secretary, and towards such as the Gloucestershire county force of 1840 with its barracks and Irish officers. When these men were armed with cutlasses and sent across county into urban districts to impose unpopular edicts like the Poor Law Amendment Act or to prevent the holding of mass meetings, as in 1839 and 1842, the 'Peelers' were much resented. At such times, in the view of the Chartists, these 'blue spies' were almost as bad as the military, that old and trusted arm of the aristocracy.[47]

[45] From the start reformers believed that these people were a vital element in the success or failure of police reforms. *P.P.*, 1839, XIX, 40–1, 104 and 154–5, *P.P.*, 1852–3, XXXVI, first report, 25–7 and 64–7, and Hansard, cxl, 1856, cols. 2176–9.

[46] On the thefts from houses with the poorest rentals, see, for example, the Manchester Central Library, Local History Section, 352.2 M1, report of 1849.

[47] Sopenoff, op. cit., chap. 5, and *The Early Chartists*, ed. D. Thompson (1971), 73–81. See the interesting and varied response of the Chartists to professional policing in *Northern Star*, 23 Mar. 1839.

It would be wrong, however, to leave the matter there. Many of the urban population, and that includes some Chartists and working-class leaders, accepted local professional policemen as a fact of life, welcomed the standards of public order and security which they helped to set, and made considerable use of them. There have been several claims recently that the working class used the men in blue less than the old parish constables, but I do not find much evidence of this. Working people soon provided a lot of the complaints and information that led to the police summonses and prosecutions.[48] People sometimes dealt with problems outside the courts during the nineteenth century, but this was true of areas with and without a new police presence.

What ordinary people resented was the class bias in certain aspects of policing and, to a lesser extent, their lack of control over the constabulary. This is borne out, for example, by the comments of Joseph Arch, and the reminiscences of people living as the turn of the century. In the countryside the Poaching Prevention Act of 1862 brought upon the police some of the opprobrium usually reserved for gamekeepers.[49] In the large towns, too, there was some concern at the use or abuse of increased powers of arrest, search and move-on; in mid-century London and Manchester thousands of ordinary people were taken into custody and then quickly discharged without a case being brought against them. Indeed, it is generally true that police discretion continued to be used against the very poor offender: the tramp, the street folk, the unemployed, the marginal people and the outsiders.[50] Working-class reactions to this aspect of policing deserve proper study.

Some members of the working class tried, in the second quarter of the nineteenth century, to gain a degree of control over the emerging police forces, and there was a return to this theme in the 1880s and again at the time of the industrial troubles prior to the first World War.[51] There was a strong feeling on occasions such as London's 'Bloody Sunday' (13 November 1887) and throughout the long North Wales quarrymen's strike some years later, that the police did not act in a neutral fashion. It has been suggested that the lack of working-class control of the police was one reason why there was so much violence against these officers. A small number of anti-police riots

[48] Claims in D. Philips, op. cit., 124, and V. Bailey, op. cit., 71–2. Compare this, however, with B. Weinberger, 'Crime and Police in the late nineteenth century', M.A. thesis, Warwick University, 1976, 55–8.

[49] See, for example, *Nottingham Journal*, July-Oct. 1862; *P.P.*, 1872, X, report on the Game Laws, evidence of Arch; and *P.P.*, 1873, XIII, report on the Game Laws, evidence of Walpole and Haward.

[50] Miller is illuminating here. See, for instance, op. cit., 62–3, and 123.

[51] J. Foster, *Class Struggle and the Industrial Revolution* (1974), 56–61, and V. Bailey, op. cit., 105 and 113–14.

heralded the appointment of outsiders as new policemen and the use of Metropolitan constables to enforce unpopular legislation.[52] There were also, as Robert Storch tells us, many attacks on constables throughout the nineteenth century, though the national statistics of indictable and summary committals indicate a fairly consistent decline in their number, at least after the 1850s.[53] The last run of high figures, in the 1860s and early 1870s, partly coincided with stricter enforcement of Licensing, Poor Law and Vagrancy Acts. The urban police baiter of this period was young, unemployed and drunk, and often of Irish extraction. In the last three decades of the century, however, fewer and fewer such people appeared before the courts, mirroring closely the decline in recorded violence generally in society.

In conclusion, the Victorians had grounds for the optimism that characterised the 1870s. In a world of staggering urban expansion and major social problems the apparent decline in criminal behaviour, serious disorder, and revolutionary feeling was a matter of some surprise and much satisfaction. But what part the police had played in this great social transformation of the nineteenth century was by no means clear, even to the most perceptive of contemporaries. Historians need to be similarly cautious. It seems most probable that the new police made a significant contribution to the defence of property and order, but the extent of that contribution has yet to be fully analysed. Despite the many books on police history, we are still on the perimeters of the subject. All I feel certain about is that the introduction, role and reception of the police in the years from 1829 to 1888 was more complex and intriguing than the models of police history allow.

After the 1870s the story of policing changes considerably. Only late in the century did the numbers of constables outside London rise dramatically, to anything approaching the modern level.[54] About this time too, the government began to display a keener interest in the control, functions and facilities of the British police. And the police forces at last began to develop a national perspective and a special

[52] These riots were often more complex than they first appear. There were not many of them. For evidence on some, perhaps grudging, acceptance of the police by groups of people in the poorer districts, see D. Taylor, op. cit., 122–3, D. Goodway, op. cit., 102, and Miller, op. cit., 108–9.

[53] The most recent studies of attacks on the police are by R. D. Storch, in *Inter. Rev. Soc. Hist.*, xx (1975), and in V. Bailey, op. cit., 66–76. At least 12–13,000 policemen were attacked every year, though the regional patterns do show interesting variations. The story of the battles between the police and the Irish has yet to be told.

[54] There were 15,860 provincial police in 1871 and 10,350 in London. By 1901 the comparative figures were 27,360 and 16,900. J. M. Hart, *The British Police* (1951), 34. Gatrell, op. cit., 275, gives somewhat different figures.

esprit de corps.[55] One illustration of this was a new interest in their own records and history. Policemen began to write the first of those histories that now fill the Staff College Library at Bramshill. History had become the stuff of policing and, incidentally, a popular alternative to drink and self-destruction.

[55] Useful studies on the developing ethos and values of the police are Pilling, op. cit., chaps. 4, 5, and K. Birch, 'The Merioneth Police 1856–1950', M.A. thesis, University of Wales, 1980, chaps. 3 and 4.

HISTORY AND THE IRISH QUESTION

By R. F. Foster, M.A., Ph.D., F.R.Hist.S

READ 15 OCTOBER 1982

'HISTORY is more backward in Ireland than in any other country', wrote J. R. Green's Anglo-Irish widow fiercely in 1912.

> Here alone there is a public opinion which resents its being freely written, and there is an opinion, public or official, I scarcely know which to call it, which prevents its being freely taught. And between the two, history has a hard fight for life. Take the question of writing. History may conceivably be treated as a science. Or it may be interpreted as a majestic natural drama or poem. Either way has much to be said for it. Both ways have been nobly attempted in other countries. But neither of these courses has been thought of in Ireland. Here history has a peculiar doom. It is enslaved in the chains of the Moral Tale—the good man (English) who prospered, and the bad man (Irish) who came to a shocking end.[1]

Through her own works on early Irish society, Mrs Green had set herself, not to produce a scientific or a poetic history, but simply to reverse the moral of the story; and with the establishment of the Irish Free State ten years after this outburst, events seemed gratifyingly to show that the good had come into their kingdom. The re-writing of history after this consummation, following the practice of most irredentist states, is part of the subject of this paper; but more important, perhaps, is the intention to establish such a process in a wider framework, stretching back over a longer period.

If the connections seem at times tenuous, and the omissions glaring, they may charitably be accounted for by the relief of abandoning the microscopic detail of high politics in favour of drawing a more general picture. Nonetheless, the use of history by politicians and intellectuals provides a theme which will recur: the frequent personification of 'Ireland' in nationalist writing is matched by the personal identification, on the part of a long line of Irish activists, of their country's history with their own identity. 'The general history of a nation may fitly preface the personal memoranda of a solitary captive,' wrote John Mitchel in his *Jail Journal*; 'for it was strictly and logically a *consequence*

[1] Alice Stopford Green, *The Old Irish World* (Dublin and London, 1912), 9.

of the dreary story here epitomized, that I came to be a prisoner.'[2] Time and again national history is presented as an actor in personal autobiography; by the same token, Irish leaders emphasised the apostolic succession of nationalism by identifying themselves with specific evangelists from the country's past.[3]

This was just one way in which past history was made to serve a legitimising function for present commitment. In a wider sense, moral attitudes could be inferred from ideas of 'Gaelic' or even 'Celtic' practice and traditions, overlaid and corrupted by conquest. In late nineteenth-century Ireland, egalitarianism was held to have flowered in the Celtic mists, much as in England democracy was supposed to have flourished in the Teutonic forests. As professional historians, we can ignore both myths; as revisionists, Irish scholars have gone so far as to dismiss most of the canon of Irish history as conceived by the generation of 1916. However, mid-twentieth-century revisionism can itself be seen as part of the pattern whereby the study of Irish history reacts in a Pavlovian way to the dictates of politics; and the whole process can only be elucidated by considering the roots of the Irish discovery of their past, and the resulting interpretations of that past, on both sides of St George's Channel. It must also involve, at the conclusion, some consideration of very recent history, trenching upon politics. In so doing, this paper exposes itself to most of the criticisms it levels at history's treatment of the Irish question; and thus becomes part of the process.

The concept of nationalism has been defined and analysed with increasing rigour in recent years; the history of the Irish case, for obvious and pressing reasons, has been the subject of a spate of recent enquiry.[4] Fortunately, this is no part of my brief; but it is relevant to examine the point when the writing of Irish history came to have an effective political function in the public domain. The background to this is *not* to be found in the series of explanatory 'histories' from the time of Giraldus Cambrensis, and including Fynes Moryson, Edmund Spenser, Edmund Campion, Sir John Davies and company.[5] The didactic

[2] John Mitchel, *Jail Journal* (Dublin, 1918 edn.), xlvi. All the Young Irelanders adopted this approach; see also Sir Charles Gavan Duffy's 'A Birdseye view of Irish History', interposed as chapter 4 of *Young Ireland: a fragment of Irish History* (1880).

[3] Parnell with Grattan, for instance, and Pearse with Emmet; see D. Ryan, *Remembering Sion* (1934), 119.

[4] S. Cronin, *Irish Nationalism: a history of its roots and ideolgy* (Dublin, 1980); T. Garvin, *The Evolution of Irish nationalist politics* (Dublin, 1981); D. G. Boyce, *Nationalism in Ireland* (1982).

[5] Giraldus Cambrensis (Gerald de Barry), *The Irish Historie composed and written by Giraldus Cambrensis* (completed in 1185), in Raphael Holinshed, *The First Volume of the Chronicles of England, Scotlande and Irelande* (1577); Edmund Spenser, *A view of the State of*

nature of their work was self-confessed, and obvious to contemporaries; their function can only be understood in terms of their time. In some quarters, much emphasis is put on the fact that these works represent English manipulation of early Irish history in order to excuse the Conquest.[6] So, indeed, they do; but to expect otherwise is to require a detached historical sense exercised on behalf of Irish history, at a time when it was not applied to English history, or any other. The more sophisticated tradition which concerns us begins with antiquarian explorations in the late eighteenth century, compounded with the various senses of nationalism—colonial, Gaelic and revolutionary—stirring in Ireland at the time.

The coherent effort to establish an Irish past did, of course, rely on some of the material in the earlier histories just mentioned; but the work of the Royal Irish Academy (founded in 1786) and other learned institutions of the time was far more directly inspired by the exploration of bardic tradition, the archaeological evidence scattered profusely throughout the island, and the exploration of indigenous folk culture.[7] As elsewhere in Europe, those most enthused by the process were rarely themselves of the 'indigenous folk'; as so often in Irish history, they were largely the Anglo-Irish middle classes, and the sociological explanations for this (especially in the age of surviving, if largely ignored, penal legislation against Catholics) are obvious. But antiquarianism reacted with the discovery of folk tradition and the Ossianic cult to produce history-writing which attempted to use evidence in place of hearsay, and to present a history of the land and its various peoples, rather than a rationalisation of administrative or religious policy in the guise of history.[8] Liberal nationalism both used and was reinforced by the antiquarian and romantic view of early Irish history; the capacity of the land to assimilate its invaders, a matter for censure in earlier commentaries, was implicitly now approved of.

A number of caveats should be established early on. For one thing,

---

Ireland (completed 1596); Edmund Campion, *A Historie of Ireland: written in the yeare 1571*; Richard Stanihurst, *The Historie of Ireland* (1577; Stanihurst edited Campion and Cambrensis); Sir John Davies, *A discovery of the true causes why Ireland was never entirely subdued* ... (1612); Fynes Moryson, *An history of Ireland from the year 1599 to 1603* (written *c.* 1617).

[6] See for instance N. Lebow, 'British Historians and Irish history' in *Eire-Ireland*, viii, no. 4 (1973), 3–38.

[7] See Norman Vance's pioneering article 'Celts, Carthaginians and constitutions: Anglo-Irish literary relations, 1780–1820' in *Irish Historical Studies*, xxii, no. 87 (1981), esp. 220 ff.

[8] Especially Charles O'Conor, *Dissertations on the ancient history of Ireland* (1780) and Sylvester O'Halloran, *Introduction to the study of the history and antiquities of Ireland* (1772).

the scholarship of these polite enthusiasts was far from impeccable, and remained prone to wishful thinking; the seductive spirit of Ossian beckoned them down false trails like a will-o'-the-wisp. The real importance of the Royal Irish Academy in collecting Irish antiquities did not come until later, with George Petrie's advent to the Council in the 1830s. And a certain amount of hokum was inseparable from the fashion: the philology of Charles Vallancey, obsessed with the Punic root of the Gaelic language and culture, is one example;[9] the later controversy over the origins of the Round Towers another;[10] the work of Thomas Comerford, who attempted to relate Gaelic culture to that of ancient Greece, might also be instanced.[11] Nor should 'liberal nationalism' be anachronistically defined; Petrie, Caesar Otway, Frederic Burton and other enthusiasts could still be of Unionist beliefs as well as of Protestant stock;[12] and while it is always remembered that the 'Patriot' politician Henry Flood left a celebrated bequest to encourage study of the Irish language, it is often forgotten that he did so for antiquarian, not revivalist, purposes.[13] But artistic and literary evidence shows that it was from this time that the currency of thought, running on antiquarian and historiographical lines, familiarised the Irish mind with shamrocks, wolf hounds, round towers, the cult of Brian Boru, and the image of an ecumenical St Patrick. And the historical work of Thomas Leland and John Curry combined a repudiation of the old propagandists with the discoveries of the new antiquarians, to produce detailed and fairly scholarly interpretations of Irish history.[14]

By 1800, political developments in America and France as well as in Ireland itself infused a new direction into the current of historical thought; but even after the trauma of rebellion and Union, the political uses of antiquarianism and of early Irish history continued. An improving Ascendancy landlord like William Parnell produced amateur histories with titles like *Enquiry into the causes of popular discontent in Ireland* (1805) and *Historical Apology for the Irish Catholics* (1807), in

[9] Charles Vallancey, *An essay on the antiquity of the Irish language, being a collation of the Irish with the Punic languages* (1772): see Vance, op. cit., 226–7.

[10] See J. Sheehy, *The rediscovery of Ireland's past: the Celtic Revival 1830–1930* (1980), 62. An antiquarian priest, Father Horgan of Blarney, finally in desperation built one himself, 'to puzzle posterity as antiquity has puzzled me'. See W. R. Le Fanu, *Seventy years of Irish Life* (1893), 175–6.

[11] Thomas Comerford, *History of Ireland from the earliest accounts of time to the invasion of the English under King Henry II* (1751).

[12] See F. Grannell, 'Early Irish ecclesiastical studies' in *Irish Anglicanism 1869–1969* (ed. Fr. M. Hurley, S.J.) (Dublin, 1970), 39–50.

[13] See Sir Laurence Parsons, Bt, *Observations on the bequest of Henry Flood* (Dublin, 1795).

[14] Thomas Leland, *The history of Ireland from the invasion of Henry II* (London, 1773); John Curry, *An historical and critical review of the civil wars in Ireland* (1775).

between prospecting for antiquities and restoring a seventh-century church at Glendalough.[15] The Gaelic Society of Dublin was founded in 1807, declaring that 'an opportunity is now, at length, offered to the learned of Ireland, to retrieve their character among the Nations of Europe, and shew that their History and Antiquities are not fitted to be consigned to eternal oblivion'; others followed.[16] In fact, the heyday of patriotic antiquarianism was nearly past; but the heyday of patriotic historiography was at hand.

The nature of the 'patriotism', however, was not yet exclusive. From the 1830s, Church of Ireland scholars devoted themselves to research into early Irish ecclesiastical history; their findings had a forum in Petrie's *Irish Penny Journal*, founded in 1840 to explore 'the history, biography, poetry, antiquities, natural history, legends and traditions of the country'. Of course, Irish Anglicans had an apologetic and propagandist motivation, besides a 'patriotic' one; their preoccupation, then and later, was to establish their church as the true 'Ancient, Catholick and Apostolic Church of Ireland', the uncorrupted continuation of early Irish Christianity rather than the offshoot of Tudor statecraft.[17] This aim vitiated much of their research. Nonetheless, a tradition of restoration, fieldwork, and the recording of antiquities helped towards the understanding of the past. This was greatly reinforced by editions of early Irish texts prepared by the Irish Record Commission (1810–30) and the Irish Historical Manuscripts Commission (founded in 1869), and by the facsimile edition of medieval codices issued by the Royal Irish Academy; if commentaries tended to apologetics, texts remained relatively uncorrupt. And some Irish historians at least had already been impressed by the sceptical spirit of Henri Bayle, and were determined to doubt all testimony and tradition; notably Edward Ledwich, whose *Antiquities of Ireland* consciously attempted to demolish 'bardic fictions'.[18]

These developments were accompanied by a new wave of predictable but sound histories of Ireland, too long to detail here, but vitally important in considering the early nineteenth-century background to intellectual patriotism in the age of Young Ireland. Many used ori-

[15] See my *Charles Stewart Parnell: the man and his family* (Brighton, 1976), chap. 3. Parnell used illustrations from early Gaelic customs and history which show familiarity with the historiographical developments of the day.

[16] See *Transactions of the Gaelic Society of Ireland*, i (1808). Other societies included the Iberno-Celtic Society (1818), the Irish Archaeological Society (1848), the Celtic Society (1848), and the Irish Archaeological and Celtic Society (1853).

[17] See Grannell, op. cit., for a consideration of this.

[18] Rev. Edward Ledwich, *The antiquities of Ireland* (1790). For a full critique see D. Macartney, 'The writing of history in Ireland 1800–1830', *Irish Hist. Stud.*, x, no. 40 (1957), 347–63.

ginal records, critically analysed; many attempted to distance themselves from contemporary political preoccupations. But the overall impression was to show early Ireland as bright with culture, not dark with barbarism; the Celt was no longer considered congenitally addicted to massacre; the methods of conquest employed by England in Ireland were generally deprecated. Such reassessments did not, of course, percolate through to the English public;[19] but, aided by Thomas Moore and the fashion for Irish ballads, they helped reinforce the sense of Irishness which the ideologues of Young Ireland exploited so astutely in the 1830s and 1840s.[20] 'On the neutral ground of ancient history and native art', wrote Sir Charles Gavan Duffy long afterwards, 'Unionist and nationalist could meet without alarm.'[21] This was not, however, the case; and it is a disingenuous statement, reflecting the position of Gavan Duffy the federalist and ex-colonial governor in 1880, not of Gavan Duffy the ardent Young Irelander in 1840. Ancient history and native art could be easily manipulated; for instance, those who wrote slightingly of the reliability of annalistic evidence were often consciously criticising the strain which identified with the Gaelic polity and thus implicitly attacked the Union. And even the membership cards of Young Ireland made their own statement, being embossed with images from Irish history establishing the iconography of sustained struggle which was to characterise the nationalist version of Irish history. The figures of Brian Boru, Owen Roe O'Neill, Patrick Sarsfield and Henry Grattan were posed against harps, sunbursts, and the Parliament House in College Green, wreathed by shamrock.[22] Young Ireland politicians like Thomas Davis graduated into politics by writing historical studies—in Davis's case a vigorous but tendentious rehabilitation of the 'Patriot Parliament' of James II.[23] And though Davis combined this with a belief in 'learning history to forget quarrels',[24] his successors took a directly contrary approach.

For, even as the materials for studying Irish history were slowly being collected and arranged in a way that might facilitate dispassion-

[19] See Lebow, op. cit., 33–5.

[20] On ballads see G. D. Zimmerman, *Irish political street ballads and rebel songs 1780–1900* (Geneva, 1966) and M. Murphy, 'The Ballad singer and the role of the seditious ballad in nineteenth-century Ireland: Dublin Castle's view', *Ulster Folklife*, xxv (1979), 79–102.

[21] Gavan Duffy, *Young Ireland*, 280.

[22] Sheehy, op. cit., 37. Also see ibid. on subjects of Irish historical painting at this time.

[23] *The Patriot Parliament of 1689, with its statutes, votes and proceedings*, edited with an introduction by Sir Charles Gavan Duffy (New Irish Library, Dublin, London and New York, 1893).

[24] See B. Farrell, 'The paradox of Irish politics' in *The Irish Parliamentary Tradition* (Dublin, 1973), 19–20.

ate analysis, a tendentious and political priority was taking over. It is doubtful if the great antiquarians John O'Donovan, Eugene O'Curry and George Petrie would have recognised themselves under the title given by the Reverend Patrick McSweeney to his study of their historical work in 1913: *A Group of Nation-Builders*. But that is what constituted their importance to retrospective opinion. And history-writing after the Union, even under titles which trumpeted themselves as 'impartial', very often directed itself at a political moral.[25] In the campaign for Catholic Emancipation both sides used 'history' to prove and disprove massacres and disloyalty over the centuries; during parliamentary debates 1641 and the Treaty of Limerick were as bitterly contested as the actual issue of Catholic rights in 1829, rather to the bewilderment of English Members.[26] This was emblematic of what was to come.

Ironically, in the early nineteenth century, a composite—one might almost dare to say interdisciplinary—approach to the Irish past was just becoming possible; it was represented by the epic effort put into the early work of the Ordnance Survey, which was contemporarily described as associating geography with 'the history, the statistics, and the structure, physical and social, of the country'.[27] Thomas Larcom recruited scholars of the quality of O'Donovan, Petrie and O'Curry, and furnished his researchers with demanding and densely written instructions about discovering the traditions of their designated areas.[28] To explore the history of place-names alone meant embarking on something very like the history of a locality. But the finished result of this magnificent conception stopped at one parish study, finally produced in November 1837, and so loaded with accretions and detail that the original idea of accompanying every map with a similar study

[25] See Rev. Denis Taaffe, *An impartial history of Ireland, from the time of the English invasion to the present time, from authentic sources* (4 vols., Dublin, 1809–11); cf. Francis Plowden, *An historical review of the state of Ireland, from the invasion of that country under Henry II, to its union with Great Britain on the first of January 1801* (2 vols., London, 1803).

[26] Macartney, op. cit., 359.

[27] *Dublin Evening Mail*, 27 Mar. 1844.

[28] 'Habits of the people. Note the general style of the cottages, as stone, mud, slated, glass windows, one story or two, number of rooms, comfort and cleanliness. Food; fuel; dress; longevity; usual number in a family; early marriages; any remarkable instances on either of these heads? What are their amusements and recreations? Patrons and patrons' days; and traditions respecting them? What local customs prevail, as Beal Tinne, or fire on St John's Eve? Driving the cattle through fire, and through water? Peculiar games? Any legendary tales or poems recited around the fireside? Any ancient music, as clan marches or funeral cries? They differ in different districts, collect them if you can. Any peculiarity of costume? Nothing more indicates the state of civilisation and intercourse.' J. H. Andrews, *A paper landscape: the Ordnance Survey in nineteenth-century Ireland* (Oxford, 1975), 148.

was abandoned.[29] The controversy over this has been long-lived and need not be disinterred here; Alice Stopford Green, who grandiloquently interpreted the Ordnance Survey team as 'a kind of peripatetic university, in the very spirit of the older Irish life', believed that their work magically 'revealed the soul of Irish Nationality and the might of its repression', and was accordingly suppressed by the Government.[30] The Survey's most recent historian, in a classic study, points out the injudiciousness and impracticality of the original concept, and the shapelessness attendant upon interpreting 'modern topography' as 'ancient history'.[31] The politics of the Report irrepressibly assert themselves; but its historiographical background is of at least equal significance, for here can be seen archaeology, geography and a cautious sense of historical enquiry working together.

However, as Gavan Duffy cheerfully admitted, that 'cautious and sober strain' of learning was chiefly the province of middle-class scholars, some of the gentry, and dilettante Protestant clergy;[32] and the future was with Young Ireland's *Library of Ireland* series of pocket histories, the street ballad, the pious cliché, and the historical novel (to write one of which was Davis's great unfulfilled ambition).[33] The revival of Irish historiography which was built upon by Young Ireland, by Celtic Revivalism, and even by an impeccable Unionist like W. E. H. Lecky, was dominated by this consciousness—as evident in the assumptions of learned pamphlets as in those of hedge schools. A history lesson delivered by a teacher in a Munster hedge school in the early nineteenth century was described by a contemporary:

> He praises the Milesians, he curses 'the betrayer Dermod'—abuses 'the Saxon stranger'—lauds Brian Boru—utters one sweeping invective against the Danes, Henry VIII, Elizabeth, Cromwell, 'the Bloody' William of the Boyne, and Anne; he denies the legality of the criminal code, deprecates and disclaims the Union; dwells with enthusiasm on the memories of Curran, Grattan, 'Lord Edward', and young Emmet; insists on Catholic Emancipation; attacks the

[29] T. F. Colby, *Ordnance Survey of the county of Londonderry, volume the first: memoirs of the city and north-western liberties of Londonderry, parish of Templemore.* See Andrews, op. cit., 157 ff.

[30] A. S. Green, op. cit., 56–61. Also see M. Tierney, 'Eugene O'Curry and the Irish tradition' in *Studies*, li (1962), 449–62.

[31] Andrews, op. cit., 173–7.

[32] *Young Ireland*, 75, n.

[33] Ibid., 289. See also John Banim, *The Boyne Water* (1826), reprinted in 1976 by the Université de Lille with an introduction by Bernard Escarbelt. On the *Library of Ireland* see also M. Buckley, 'John Mitchel, Ulster, and Irish nationality, 1842–1848', in *Studies* lxv (1976), 30–44, which analyses Mitchel's contribution to the series, and Boyce, op. cit., 161–2. Gavan Duffy remarked that Irish history was 'ransacked' for suitable examples and arguments; *Young Ireland*, 104.

> Peelers, horse and foot; protests against tithes, and threatens a separation of the United Kingdom ...[34]

This vividly depicts history being elided into politics, and into the sense of national identity built upon a powerfully articulated consciousness of past grievances as much as present discontents.

And this was the historical consciousness displayed at popular levels by the Irish to countless Victorian travellers, who on their fact-finding missions were constantly exposed—half fascinated and half appalled—to the rhetoric of Irish nationalist history. Sometimes, indeed, they seem to have been unconsciously subjected to the Irish taste for guying their own image; the experiences of innocents like Mr and Mrs S. C. Hall, as well as those of the hard-headed Thackeray and Carlyle, record many ironies enjoyed at their unwitting expense by the cynical natives.[35] Travellers from the Continent, like de Tocqueville and de Beaumont, may not have been exempt either.[36] But de Beaumont, if he did not originate it, popularised the genocidal theory of England's historical policy towards Ireland; and the same note of vehement moralising enters the history of his compatriot Thierry, warmly praised by Gavan Duffy.[37] Other foreign publicists entered the field, including Karl Marx.[38] And, finally, the demotic view of Irish history found its way by unlikely channels into the English consciousness.

This was not always acknowledged, at the time or since; and some of those responsible tried later to cover their tracks. Macaulay's *History* is notable for its scathing remarks on Irish barbarianism,[39], Robert Southey's Toryism was notoriously unreconstructed, and Lord Lytton

[34] P. J. Dowling, *The Hedge Schools of Ireland* (1935), 111–12.

[35] See Mr and Mrs S. C. Hall, *Ireland, its scenery, character etc.* (3 vols., 1841–3); Thomas Carlyle, 'Reminiscences of my Irish Journey' in *Century Illustrated Monthly Magazine* xxiv (1882), May–July; William Thackeray, *The Irish Sketch Book* (1843). On this Irish tendency see my article 'Parnell and his people: the Ascendancy and Home Rule', *Canadian Jnl. of Irish Studies* vi, no. 1 (1980), 110–11.

[36] Alexis de Tocqueville, *Journeys to England and Ireland*, ed. J. P. Mayer (1958); Gustave de Beaumont, *L'Irlande sociàle, politique et religieuse* (Paris, 1839).

[37] *Young Ireland*, 167; Augustin Thierry, *Histoire de la Conquête de l'Angleterre par les Normands* (Paris, 1825).

[38] Marx notably in his articles in the *New York Tribune*: 'A small *caste* of robber landlords dictate to the Irish people the conditions in which they are allowed to hold the land and live on it' (11 July 1853); 'the Irish landlords are confederated for a fiendish war of extermination against the cottiers' (11 Jan. 1859), etc. Engels's view was that 'Irish history shows one what a misfortune it is for a nation to have subjugated another nation; all the abominations of the English have their origin in the Irish Pale': Engels to Marx, 24 Oct. 1869, in *Ireland and the Irish Question* (Moscow, Progress Publishers, 1971), 274. Both Marx and Engels laid heavy emphasis on Irish 'national character' as a motive force in Irish history; see I. Cummins, *Marx, Engels and National Movements* (1980), 109.

[39] See especially *History of England from the Accession of James II*, ii. 128.

became the rabidly anti-Irish hymnologist of the Primrose League. But in youth Macaulay wrote epic poetry about the Gaelic resistance to Strongbow, Southey eulogised Robert Emmet, and Lytton produced verses commemorating Hugh O'Neill's war against Elizabeth.[40] Even as unlikely a figure as Samuel Smiles was inspired to write the history of a people whom one would have expected him to condemn as more opposed to self-help than any in the world. 'It is necessary that Irish history should be known and studied for we are persuaded that *there* only is the true key to the present situation to be found—*there* only are the secret springs of Irish discontent to be traced.'[41]

Most Victorian intellectuals felt that this was so; though the argument is not, in fact, self-evidently true, and in terms of economic policy at least it may be strongly contested.[42] But every Victorian pundit dipped into Irish history and whatever panacea he was manufacturing emerged subtly altered.[43] 'I know tolerably well what Ireland was,' confessed John Stuart Mill to an Irish economist, 'but have a very imperfect idea of what Ireland *is*.'[44] This could stand as an epigraph for the ruminations of others as well as himself; and it was reflected in the lacunae and contradictions so evident in Mill's own writings on

[40] In May 1885 Lytton sent Churchill, as commissioned, 'The Lay of the Primrose', of which the last verse ran:

> When, O say, shall the Celt put his blunderbuss down,
> Cease to bully the Commons, and menace the Crown?
> When shall Erin be loyal, and Britain repose,
> Neither fawning to rebels, nor flying from foes?
> That shall be, saith the Primrose, nor ever till then,
> When the country is honestly governed again,
> When the realm is redeemed from the Radical's hand
> And the Primrose comes blossoming back to the land.

(Lytton to Churchill, 18 May 1885; Churchill MSS., Churchill College, RCHL v/601.) It does not appear to have found its way into print.

[41] Samuel Smiles, *History of Ireland and the Irish people, under the government of England* (1844), iv. Cf. Gavan Duffy, *Young Ireland*, 81: 'Many men refrain from reading Irish history as sensitive and selfish persons refrain from witnessing human suffering. But it is a branch of knowledge as indispensable to the British statesman or politician as morbid anatomy to the surgeon.'

[42] See especially B. Solow, *The land question and the Irish economy 1870–1903* (Cambridge, Mass., 1973).

[43] Carlyle, predictably, was the exception. Towards the end of his Irish tour he concluded: 'Remedy for Ireland? To cease generally from following the devil ... no other remedy that I know of ...' ('Reminiscences of my Irish Journey', iii, 440). Earlier he had, however, been impressed by the Royal Irish Academy museum: 'really an interesting museum, for everything has a certain *authenticity*, as well as national or other significance, too often wanting in such places'. Ibid, 27.

[44] J. S. Mill to J. E. Cairnes, 29 July 1864, quoted in E. D. Steele, 'J. S. Mill and the Irish Question: *The Principles of Political Economy* 1848–1865' in *Hist. Jnl.* xiii, no. 2 (1970), 231.

Ireland.[45] It has been shown how untypical was his pamphlet *England and Ireland*, when viewed in the canon of his work; but it is with this strident piece, subjecting economics to a moral and political approach to landholding, that his views on Ireland are identified. And though the pamphlet argued—as he himself reiterated afterwards—*for* the Union, its effect was to reinforce the nationalist opposition to the measure. On a different level but in a similar manner, Matthew Arnold's belief in Celtic qualities, though part of an argument for bringing Celtic culture fully into the Anglo-Saxon cultural and political system, reinforced a view of early Irish history and an interpretation of Celticism which strengthened irreconcilable ideas of separatism.[46] The most influentially misinterpreted authority, however, in this unintentional *trahison des clercs*, was the historian W. E. H. Lecky.

Sitting down to write his *History of England in the Eighteenth Century*, Lecky was increasingly preoccupied by the history of Ireland: both as an Anglo-Irishman and as a rather troubled liberal. He knew the dangers, seeing Irish history as 'so steeped in party and sectarian animosity that a writer who has done his utmost to clear his mind from prejudice, and bring together with impartiality the conflicting statements of partisans, will still, if he is a wise man, always doubt whether he has succeeded in painting with perfect fidelity the delicate gradations of provocation, palliation and guilt'.[47] His *History of Ireland*, extracted from the original production for a special edition in 1892, remains a classic of liberal historiography; but despite his commitment to rationality and cool scepticism, it was dictated as much by topical preoccupations as guided by the pure light of research.[48] For one thing, he was writing *contra* James Anthony Froude, whose study of *The English in Ireland*[49] had maligned and belaboured the native Irish in a manner not to be seen again for a hundred years.[50] Lecky wrote against Froude, not for nationalist reasons, but because, as an Anglo-Irish Unionist, he feared that Froude's distortions by their very exaggeration would support the case being made by the nationalists for Home Rule. (He also worried deeply about the unintended effect of

[45] As incisively demonstrated in ibid., and in 'J. S. Mill and the Irish question: reform and the integrity of the Empire, 1865–1870', *Hist. Jnl.*, xiii, no. 3 (1970), 419–450.

[46] See J. V. Kelleher, 'Matthew Arnold and the Celtic Revival' in *Perspectives of Criticism*, ed. H. Levin (Cambridge, Mass., 1950), 197–221.

[47] His preface to the separate edition of the *History of Ireland* considers at some length the problems of writing Irish history and the steps he had taken to obviate them.

[48] See A. Wyatt, 'Froude, Lecky and the humblest Irishman', *Irish Hist. Stud.*, xix, no. 75 (1975), 267–85.

[49] J. A. Froude, *The English in Ireland in the Eighteenth Century* (1872–4). There is a large secondary literature of refutation by Thomas Burke, W. H. Flood, John Mitchel, J. E. McGee, and others.

[50] Until, that is, E. R. Norman's *History of Modern Ireland* (Harmondsworth, 1971).

his own early *Leaders of Public Opinion in Ireland*, and opposed what would have been a very profitable reprint.) Both Froude and Lecky, in the context of the 1880s, saw their histories as relevant to the contemporary struggle for Home Rule. Froude argued, in Salisburian terms, the 'Hottentot' case of Celtic incapacity for self-government. Irish criminality 'originated out of' Irish Catholicism; Protestant virtues were commercial and social as much as religious. (This is not an anticipation of Weber and Tawney, but reflects the more exotic fact that Froude had regained his lost faith through a sojourn in a Wicklow rectory.) Culture as well as worship could be defined in religious terms, and 'Irish ideas' were a debased set of beliefs which should have been socialised out of the natives. Moreover, Anglo-Irish colonial nationalism was equally corrupt; Irish declarations that they would fight for nationhood should, then and now, be seen as bluff.

In contradicting the former statements, Lecky came near to implicitly refuting the latter: notably in his use of Grattan's parliament of 1782 to rehabilitate the Ascendancy class under siege in his own lifetime. He treated Orangeism and Protestant evangelicalism with faint distaste; not only a reaction against Froude, but a reflection of the fact that he was also the historian of the rise of rationalism. The exclusion of the Catholic gentry from political rights, and the ensuing development of the priest in politics, distressed him; he believed 'the secularization of politics is the chief measure and condition of political progress',[51] by which criterion Irish politics were regressing back to infinity. But this was precisely the lesson which many of his readers did *not* learn from his book; they came away from it imbued with ideas of Irish nobility, English pusillanimity, the missed chance of Grattan's Parliament, and the perfidiousness of the Act of Union. Lecky himself, by this stage of his life, did not want to see Grattan's Parliament restored; an opinion in which he believed Henry Grattan would concur.[52] But the immorality of Union seemed to many the moral of his book.

It was, moreover, a moral drawn by politicians. 'I read for the History School at Oxford in the 'seventies', recalled Herbert Gladstone, 'and subsequently lectured on history. Froude, Lecky, Matthew Arnold, Goldwin Smith and John Bright brought me to conviction on Irish affairs. Four of my guides lived to be distinguished Unionists. Nevertheless their facts and arguments led me to an opposite conclusion.'[53] Politicians of all colours had this nodding familiarity with

[51] H. Montgomery Hyde (ed.), *A Victorian historian: private letters of W. E. H. Lecky, 1859–1878* (1947), 41–2.

[52] Letter to *The Times*, 9 June 1886.

[53] 'The trouble with Ireland was not only social and racial. It could not be explained by unjust land laws or the sway of an alien established church. These were superadded embroilments. The root cause was English autocracy.' H. Gladstone, *After Thirty Years* (1928), 263–4.

Irish history (the most dangerous kind of acquaintance); and in private correspondence as well as public exchanges they wrangled good-naturedly about recondite issues. Thus Sir William Harcourt and Lord Randolph Churchill beguiled their time in 1889 with letters detailing the arguments for and against the honesty of Irish politicians in the eighteenth century.[54] The effect on W. E. Gladstone of his readings in Irish history was more cataclysmic. He had Gavan Duffy's word for it that Carew's campaign in sixteenth-century Munster was the closest historical parallel to the Bulgarian atrocities;[55] he had Lecky's authority for the iniquity of the Act of Union. 'He talked of the Union—' recorded Lord Derby:

> called it a frightful and absurd mistake, thought Pitt had been persuaded into it by the King, who believed it would act as a check upon the Catholics, said that every Irishman 'who was worth a farthing' had opposed it, and if he had been an Irishman he would have done so to the utmost ... quoted as I have heard him do before, a saying of Grattan about 'the Channel forbidding Union, the Ocean forbidding separation'—which he considered as one of the wisest sayings ever uttered by man—then dwelt on the length of time during which Ireland had possessed an independent, or even a separate legislature.[56]

Gladstone, as so many others, was dazzled by the historians' notions of Grattan's parliament: the acceptable face of Irish nationalism. The Irish pamphlet literature of the 1860s and 1870s, much of it written by insecure or improving landlords, adverted constantly to this; it had been much in the minds of those who initially supported Isaac Butt.[57] Samuel Ferguson, despite Ulster and Tory associations, had once called for the restoration of Grattan's Parliament (though the 'plebeianizing' nature of the Home Rule movement, and the Phoenix Park Murders, later moderated his ardour); it was a reaction shared by an important element of the gentry before the political polarisation

[54] See Churchill to Harcourt, 29 Nov. 1889, Harcourt MSS. 217/63, writing 'in support of a plea of "not guilty" to your charge of "bumptious ignorance"', and enclosing a pamphlet based on a speech at Perth (5 Oct. 1889) which involved a lengthy historical exegesis on the Union. Harcourt, who had earlier stated that not 'one honest man' in Ireland approved of the measure, replied at great length, with much historical reference to back up his case (Churchill MSS., RCHL xiv/3340).

[55] *Young Ireland*, 93.

[56] Derby's diary, quoted in J. R. Vincent, 'Gladstone and Ireland', *Proc. Br. Academy*, lxiii (1977), 223.

[57] A good example is H. M. D'Arcy Irvine's *Letters to the rt. hon. W. E. Gladstone on the Irish Land Bill* (1870), which speaks on behalf of 'the descendants of the Irish patriots of 1800, and the great body of the middle classes of all creeds', invoking the hallowed date of 1782.

of the 1880s. The idealisation of the late eighteenth century, a direct result of the way history had been written, remained; wandering in Wicklow in 1911 John Synge, no admirer of the class whence he sprang, mused that 'the broken greenhouses and moth-eaten libraries, that were designed and collected by men who voted with Grattan, are perhaps as mournful in the end as the four mud walls that are so often left in Wicklow as the only remnants of a farmhouse'.[58]

Among those politicians who idealised 1782, of course, the prime example was a Wicklow gentleman whose ancestors included both a famous anti-Union patriot, and the improving pamphleteer quoted earlier: Charles Stewart Parnell. He was not, in fact, a reader of the literature discussed above; his strength as an Irish politician lay in his *not* knowing Irish history.[59] But his preoccupation with Grattan's Parliament, as invented by popular history, irritated those of his followers who had thought Home Rule through. 'There is no subject about which Mr Parnell is so ignorant as that of Irish history,' wrote James O'Connor Power,

> and his contempt for books is strikingly shown in his reference to Grattan's Parliament. Mr Parnell deceives himself, through sheer indifference to history and a dislike of the trouble of inquiry into facts, when he tells us he wants Grattan's Parliament. Does Mr Parnell want a parliament in Dublin controlled by a few nominees of the British Cabinet who, under the Viceroy, constitute an Irish government in no way responsible to the Irish House of Commons? If not, then it is not Grattan's Parliament he wants, and it is not Grattan's Parliament he should ask for.[60]

But Grattan's Parliament, as legitimised by historians, remained the objective to be cited, for most of Parnell's audience. The idealisation was based on Sir Jonah Barrington's account of an Irish 'nation' that never was,[61] on Thomas Newenham's erroneous ideas of Irish prosperity as created by the parliament of 1782,[62] on Lecky's misplaced

[58] *In Wicklow and West Kerry* (Dublin, 1912), 17.

[59] For Parnell's knowledge of Irish history see F. S. L. Lyons, *Charles Stewart Parnell* (1977), 37–8, and 'The political ideas of Parnell', *Hist. Jnl.*, xvi, no. 4 (1973), 749–75.

[60] *The Anglo-Irish quarrel: a plea for peace* (1880).

[61] *The Rise and Fall of the Irish Nation* (Paris, 1933).

[62] T. Newenham, *A series of suggestions and observations relative to Ireland submitted to the consideration of the Lord President and Council* (Gloucester, 1825); for Newenham's ideas and influence see H. D. Gribbon, 'Thomas Newnham 1762–1831' in *Irish population, economy and society: essays in honour of the late K. H. Connell*, ed. J. M. Goldstrom and L. A. Clarkson (Oxford, 1982), 231–47. His ideas were repeated in Alice Murray's influential *Commercial and financial relations between England and Ireland from the period of the Restoration* (London, 1903).

faith in the influence of Foster's Corn Law,[63] and in the general prescription of nationalist historians that prosperity was automatically induced by native government and poverty by alien rule.

By the end of the nineteenth century, given that many such assumptions had become articles of faith for the English intelligentsia as well as the Irish people, it need not surprise us to find them governing the popular mind. What Lecky did for readers of the journals, A. M. Sullivan's *Story of Ireland* did for the general reader.[64] While Irish literacy seems to have been remarkably high in the late nineteenth century, the Irish literature which preoccupied the populace still awaits its historian; but a pioneering impressionist survey carried out in 1884 is of some interest in showing the hegemony enjoyed by Davisite poetry and history in one Cork parish. The list of histories most often borrowed from the Catholic Young Men's Society Reading-room told its own tale.[65] A popular conception of history facilitated the general view that saw the Home Rule movement as 'the heirs of all the ages that have fought the good fight after their several ways':[66] a notion which, while enabling Parnell to walk the political tightrope, was very far from the truth. And when Parnellism collapsed, the popular conception of history instantly located the catastrophe in the context of a long succession of Saxon (rather than Anglo-Irish) betrayals.

Sinn Fein was to prove the successor movement to the Irish Parliamentary Party, but in everyday ways which were strategically underplayed at the time;[67] its emphasis was rather upon a specific reading

[63] 'One of the capital acts in Irish history; in a few years it changed the face of the land and made Ireland to a great extent an arable instead of a pastoral country.' The case against this and other misconceptions is trenchantly summarised by Joseph Lee, 'Grattan's Parliament', in Farrell, op. cit., 149–50. 'Foster's Corn Law did not reverse an existing trend; at the very most it slightly accentuated it.'

[64] First published 1867; acutely analysed in Boyce, op. cit., 247 ff.

[65] J. Pope Hennessy, 'What do the Irish read?', *Nineteenth Century*, xv (Jan.–June 1884), 920 ff. 'Abbé MacGeohegan's *History of Ireland from the earliest times to the Treaty of Limerick*, with John Mitchel's continuation; D'Arcy McGees's *History of Ireland to the Emancipation of the Catholics*; Duffy's *Four Years of Irish History*, with the preceding fragment, *Young Ireland*; A. M. Sullivan's *Story of Ireland*; Justin H. McCarthy's *Outline of Irish History*; Lecky's *History of the Eighteenth Century*; Walpole's *History of Ireland to the Union*; O'Callaghan's *History of the Irish Brigade in France;* Justin McCarthy's *History of our own Times*—, these are the most read; but the works of Macaulay, Hallam, Froude, with Father Tom Burke's *Refutation of Froude*, are read also. In biography Madden's *Lives of the United Irishmen*, *The Life and Times of Henry Grattan*, Moore's *Life of Lord Edward Fitzgerald*, Wolfe Tone's *Memoirs*, Mitchel's *Jail Journal*, Maguire's *Father Mathew*, seem to be favourites.' Ibid., 926.

[66] *United Ireland*, 13 Aug. 1881.

[67] See D. Fitzpatrick, *Politics and Irish Life 1913–1921: Provincial experience of War and Revolution* (Dublin, 1977).

of history. The founder Arthur Griffith's ideas of autarky in economics and racial purity in politics fused an idealisation of Grattan's Parliament with a belief in Celticism which brought together the teachings of nineteenth-century historians, ancient and modern: the very name of his first weekly, *United Irishman*, was a reference to Mitchel and Tone, and the politics of Sinn Fein synthesised constitutionalism with implicit violence.[68] Griffith's 'Hungarian policy' of boycotting institutions in order to win separate but equal status under the crown was itself based upon misapplied historical 'parallels': as George Birmingham acidly pointed out, if Griffith was really following the Hungarian model he should have seen that the equivalent of the Magyars were the Anglo-Irish.[69] But Griffith, and still more his contemporaries among nationalist ideologues, defined 'Irish' in a way that implied, or even stated, its congruence with 'Gaelic' and 'Catholic'. And this sectional reading, the result of sectional history, set the tone of twentieth-century nationalism.

It was an identification which contradicted the official spirit of Young Ireland, but which had achieved dominance in the late nineteenth century, for political and educational as well as intellectual reasons.[70] Its articulation by the Gaelic Revival has been too much, and too ably, analysed to be worth pursuing here.[71] Shaw remarked that 'there is no Irish race any more than there is an English race or a Yankee race [but] there *is* an Irish climate which will stamp an immigrant more deeply and durably in two years, apparently, than

[68] See D. Macartney, 'The political use of history in the work of Arthur Griffith', in *Jnl. of Contemporary Hist.*, 8 (1973), 67. It is worth, however, quoting Griffith's utilitarian view of the ends of education: 'The secondary system of education in Ireland ... was designed to prevent the higher intelligence of the country performing its duty to the Irish State. In other countries secondary education gives to each its leaders in industry and commerce, its great middle class which as society is constructed forms the equalizing and harmonizing element in the population. In Ireland secondary education causes aversion and contempt for industry and "trade" in the heads of young Irishmen, and fixes their eyes, like the fool's, on the ends of the earth. The secondary system in Ireland draws away from industrial pursuits those who are best fitted to them and sends them to be civil servants in England, or to swell the ranks of struggling clerkdom in Ireland.' *The Sinn Fein Policy* (Dublin, n.d., but delivered as a speech to the first annual conference of the National Council, 28 Nov. 1905).

[69] George Birmingham, *An Irishman looks at his world* (London, 1919), 12–13.

[70] In 1868 Gerald FitzGibbon's pamphlet *Ireland in 1868* (noted by Marx as the distillation of the Ascendancy case) emphasised the complete lack of tension between Protestant and Catholic at university, on the Bench, and in professional life; but the same author's *Roman Catholic priests and national schools* (1871) held that the denominational nature of national schools had bred the idea of the true Irishman as Catholic and Celtic, and driven a wedge between those whose interests were objectively identical. The polarisation of politics in the 1880s saw the solidifying of this process.

[71] See especially F. S. L. Lyons, *Culture and Anarchy in Ireland 1890–1939* (Oxford, 1979).

the English climate will in two hundred';[72] but this reading of Irish history went as unheard as the expostulations of John Eglinton, George Russell, W. B. Yeats and others who saw themselves as no less Irish for being of identifiably settler descent. What happened instead was that the period of nationalist irredentism saw the culmination of historical writing which mined the past for political continuities and extrapolations.

Patrick Pearse is of course the prime mover in this process, and in recent years much has been done to clarify the misinterpretations and elisions upon which he built his view of history: a visionary world of early Celtic traditions where racial identification was automatic, a national sense was the paramount priority, and the sacrificial image of the ancient hero Cuchulainn was inextricably tangled with that of Christ.[73] Not only Pearse's youthful *Three Lectures on Gaelic Topics* (1897–8), but all he wrote and taught up to his execution in 1916, owed everything to John Mitchel and the *Library of Ireland*, and nothing to the researches of Eoin MacNeill, whose path-breaking lectures on early Irish society were delivered in 1904 and published two years later.[74] Pearse's use of Irish history was that of a calculatedly disingenuous propagandist; it was this that enabled him, for instance, so thoroughly to misinterpret Thomas Davis.[75] But if it is argued—as it might be—that the importance of Pearse's distortions is diminished by the fact that he was very far from being an accepted historian, it is instructive to turn to Alice Stopford Green, with whom this paper began.

Daughter of an archdeacon in County Meath, and wife of the greatest popular historian of the age, Mrs Green moved from revising her husband's works to writing medieval history on her own account, and ended as a formidable and virulently partisan advocate of Irish nationalism. This identification was reflected in works like *The Making of Ireland and its undoing* (1908), *Irish Nationality* (1912) and *The Irish State to 1014* (1925). A Freudian, or a seeker after symbols, might note that from the age of seventeen she spent seven years in semi-blindness, and during the ordeal relied upon an already well-stocked mind and

[72] G. B. Shaw, *Prefaces* (1938), 443–4. Cf. E. E. Evans, *The Personality of Ireland: habit, heritage and history* (revised edn., Belfast, 1981), 43–4, where an elegant demonstration is given of the 'mongrel' nature of the Irish 'race'.

[73] See Fr. Francis Shaw, 'The Canon of Irish History: a challenge' in *Studies*, lxi (1972), 113–52; R. Dudley Edwards, *Patrick Pearse: the triumph of failure* (1977); J. V. Kelleher, 'Early Irish history and pseudo-history', *Studia Hibernica*, 3 (1963), 113–27.

[74] On MacNeill see Michael Tierney, *Eoin MacNeill: scholar and man of action*, ed. F. X. Martin (Oxford, 1980), esp. 90–6.

[75] He identifies Davis with a commitment to physical force (*Political Writings and Speeches* (Dublin, 1924), 323–4); but Davis, especially in a celebrated essay on 'Moral Force', specifically denied that this was an answer. See B. Farrell, op. cit., 19.

a remarkable memory; for her view of Irish history represented a similarly restricted vision, and an ability to feed omniverously on preconceptions. The concept of 'the Irish national memory', indeed, recurs obsessively in her works;[76] she may be seen as a representative of those Ascendancy Irish whose insecurity drove them to extremes of identification,[77] much as the urban nationalist intellectuals of the era embarked upon a narodnik search for 'the West'.[78] Mrs Green's pre-invasion Ireland was a classless, egalitarian 'Commonwealth', where 'the earliest and the most passionate conception of "nationality"' flourished;[79] 'democratic' continuities were asserted, the purity of 'Gaelic' culture emphasised, and the moral as well as aesthetic superiority of 'Gaelic civilization' trumpeted.[80] Despite her declarations in introductions and footnotes of indebtedness to Eoin MacNeill, the scholarly subtlety and tentativeness of his approach to the early Irish past had no part in Mrs Green's productions; and probably for that reason they entered the mainstream of Free State culture.

Here they remained, despite the accumulated findings of historians who showed that land patterns in early Christian Ireland argue for a landholding system very far from her idealised version of Gaelic society,[81] that the so-called High-Kingship of Ireland did not exist before the middle of the ninth century,[82] and that—as MacNeill indicated in 1904—the received framework of early Irish history was an invention of chroniclers from the ninth century and later, working assiduously for the glorification of their patrons. If, however, Mrs Green was fooled by what a later historian has crisply called 'the concoctions of the Annals',[83] she had a real and immediate reason for being thus fooled: the desire to establish a legitimate continuity for Irish separatism. George Russell, on the other hand, knew and

[76] See for instance *A history of the Irish State to 1014*, ix, 85, etc.

[77] Cf. George Moore on Douglas Hyde: 'By standing well with ... MPs, priests, farmers, shopkeepers ... Hyde has become the archetype of the Catholic Protestant, cunning, subtle, cajoling, superficial and affable.' *Vale* (1914), 249.

[78] This was, however, a process of some antiquity; see J. Sheehy, op. cit., 26–7, for a delightful description of Sir William Wilde's journey to the Aran islands in 1857 with a 'freight of Ethnologists and Antiquarians'.

[79] *History of the Irish State*, chap. 6.

[80] See especially *Irish Nationality*, 13, 14, 20–1, 28, 76, 95, 165.

[81] Notably the work of Kathleen Hughes; for a summary see Evans, op. cit., 58–9.

[82] See especially D. A. Binchy, 'The origins of the so-called High Kingship', Statutory Lecture, Dublin Institute of Advanced Studies, 1959.

[83] Kelleher, 'Irish History and pseudo-history', 120–2, for the case against the 'Book of Rights' and other sources as twelfth-century creations. 'So extensive was the revision of historical evidence that we have, I would say, about as much chance of recovering the truth about early Christian Ireland as a historian five hundred years from now would have if he were trying to reconstruct the history of Russia in the twentieth century from broken sets of different editions of the Soviet encyclopaedia.'

accepted that his view of early Ireland was legendary and symbolic, and thus 'more potent than history'.[84] But the spirit of the Free State was more in accord with Mrs Green's literalism. Thus the *Catholic Bulletin*, bemoaning modern times in 1925, reflected Mrs Green's vision when it remarked 'it is very different in Ireland now to those old days when the poorest Catholic family would, on assembling in the evenings, discuss scholastic philosophy and such subjects'. And in the same year the same journal recommended Daniel Corkery's *Hidden Ireland* to 'G. W. Russell and his clique . . . they will there see how the Gael, the one Irish nation with the Irish literature, regards and dealt with and will deal with that mongrel upstart called Anglo-Irish tradition and culture'.[85]

What followed was the institutionalisation of a certain view of history in the Free State, as instructed by the Department of Education from 1922, and memorialised in textbooks that did duty for the next forty years. Teachers were informed that 'the continuity of the separatist idea from Tone to Pearse should be stressed'; pupils should be 'imbued with the ideals and aspirations of such men as Thomas Davis and Patrick Pearse'.[86] Thus history was debased into a two-dimensional, linear development, and the function of its teaching interpreted as 'undoing the conquest'; even the architecture of the Irish eighteenth century was stigmatised as ideologically degenerate. One must be wary of falling into the same trap as those who, by condemning the sixteenth- and seventeenth-century historians, imply that scientific objectivity was possible at that time; textbooks in English schools in the 1920s and 1930s were hardly models of fairminded detachment. Moreover, in the new state of Northern Ireland, the recommendations of the Lynn Committee (established in 1921) reflect an equally strong sense of history as a tool, or weapon, to be manipulated through the schools.[87] But the popularisation of synthetically invented traditions in the Free State and the Republic served a directly political function important enough to bear analysis; and it came about as the result of a longer process than is sometimes assumed, a development which I have attempted to sketch in this paper.

[84] Æ (G. W. Russell), 'Nationality and Cosmopolitanism in Art', 1899, printed in *Some Irish Essays* (Dublin, 1906), 18.

[85] *Catholic Bulletin*, Feb. and June 1925, quoted in M. O'Callaghan, 'Language and religion: the quest for identity in the Irish Free State' (M.A. thesis, University College, Dublin, 1981).

[86] Ruth Dudley Edwards, op. cit., 341.

[87] 'We think that the powers of the Ministry to regulate and to supervise the books used in schools should be very strictly exercised in the matter of historical textbooks. No books bearing on the subject of history should, without previous official sanction, be permitted to be used in any schools under the Ministry.' Quoted in John Magee, 'The teaching of Irish history in Irish schools', *The Northern Teacher*, x, no. 1 (1970).

Moreover, the process itself created some contradictions and paradoxes which bring me to my conclusion. One is that the exclusive glorification of one strain in Ireland's complex history caused as a reaction the equally tendentious glorification of another, and led to an idealisation in some quarters of the 'Anglo-Irish': a sentimentalisation of the Bourbon spirit which distinguished a class notable in the main for their philistinism and bigotry, who, when the testing time came, failed in everything—social duty, political imagination, and nerve.[88] More important for my purpose is the major paradox: the fact that the institutionalised debasement of popular history was accompanied from the 1940s by a historiographical revolution in academic circles which, within twenty-five years, reversed nearly every assumption still being made by the textbooks. The foundation under Eoin MacNeill of the Irish Manuscripts Commission in 1929 had something to do with this; so did the formation of the Ulster Society for Irish Historical Studies, and the Irish Historical Society, a few years later. Bureaucratic philistinism, and an idiosyncratic attitude to the availability of government records, provided obstacles in North and South—as they still do. But a school of Irish history evolved, at the research level, which transcended traditional divides within Southern society and culture, as well as across the new border.[89]

By the 1960s, the work of a whole generation of scholars had exploded the basis for popular assumptions about early Irish society, the conquest, the plantations, the eighteenth-century parliament, the record of landlordism, and most of all the continuities between the various manifestations of 'nationalism': in some cases, reverting to ideas held in the past by minority opinion, but contemptuously dismissed.[90] By the mid-1960s, coinciding with signs of realism and adaptation in Irish politics, a number of indications presaged the establishment of a new interpretation of Irish history as a complex and

[88] This is reflected by the adoption among historians of George Russell's *Irish Statesman* as the agreed source for quotations showing the sanity and cosmopolitanism of the Anglo-Irish in the Free State; but as O'Callaghan (loc. cit., note 85) reminds us, it spoke for far fewer of them at the time than did the less liberal *Church of Ireland Gazette* or *Irish Times*.

[89] For a retrospect and a commentary see R. Dudley Edwards, 'Irish History: an agenda' in *Irish Hist. Stud.*, xxi, no 81 (1978), 3–19.

[90] The case for interpreting the Land War of 1879–82 as a revolution of rising expectations has been established by Solow, op. cit.; P. Bew, *Land and the national question in Ireland 1858–82* (Dublin 1978); W. E. Vaughan, 'An assessment of the economic performance of Irish landlords 1851–81' in *Ireland under the Union: varieties of tension* (Oxford, 1980), ed. F. S. L. Lyons and R. B. Hawkins, 173–200; J. Donnelly, *The land and the people of nineteenth-century Cork* (1974), and others. But it is also to be found in Anna Parnell's astringent 'Tale of a Great Sham' (N.L.I. MS. 12,144) and in Terence McGrath's *Pictures from Ireland* (1880) which described the Land War in terms of an adroit takeover by the middling tenantry, manipulating a credit squeeze.

ambivalent process rather than a morality tale. The Institute of Irish Studies was founded in Belfast in 1965, with the object of co-ordinating research in different disciplines. An important Report on the teaching of history in Irish schools appeared in 1966.[91] In the same year, a new Irish history school textbook was launched which at last replaced the didactic tracts that had done duty for decades.[92] Most symbolically, the commemoration of the 1916 Rising produced some unexpected historiographical results. One was a work by an Old Republican scholar which portrayed Dublin Castle in 1916 as characterised by well-meaning muddle and a vague acceptance of the desirability of Home Rule.[93] More strikingly, a Jesuit historian, commissioned to write an article on Patrick Pearse to celebrate the anniversary, produced an intemperate and violent attack on Pearse's preference for striking a rhetorical blow against an England that had put Home Rule on the statute book, instead of taking on the Ulster Volunteers who had prevented its implementation; and went on to denounce Pearse's falsification of past history in the interests of present politics.[94]

Not the least significant thing about this outburst, however, was the fact that the article was deemed unsuitable for publication in 1966, and saw the light of day six years later, only after its author's death. And this points up the paradox mentioned earlier. Revisionism in Irish history-writing has reached the point where a great deal which the nationalist historians tried to overturn has been dispassionately re-established.[95] It would be tedious as well as time-consuming to detail the areas of Irish history where the stereotypes have been upset.[96] This has been done with the aid of sociology, geography,

[91] See report on 'The Teaching of History in Irish Schools', 1966, in *Administration* (Journal of the Institute of Public Administration, Dublin), Winter, 1967, 268–85. This committee included historians who were influential in the new school of history-writing, and emphasised throughout the need for impartiality and an international perspective. Also see John Magee, *op. cit.*

[92] T. W. Moody and F. X. Martin, *The course of Irish History* (Dublin, 1966). Previously the field had been held by M. Hayden and G. A. Moonan, *A short history of the Irish people from the earliest times to 1920* (Dublin, 1921), and J. Carty, *A junior history of Ireland* (Dublin, 1932).

[93] L. Ó Broin, *Dublin Castle and the Easter Rising* (1966).

[94] See Fr. Francis Shaw, op. cit.; and for comments, F. S. L. Lyons, 'The dilemma of the Irish contemporary historian', *Hermathena*, cxv (1973), 53; Ruth Dudley Edwards, op. cit., 341–2; T. Brown, *Ireland: a social and cultural history* (1979), 287–9.

[95] See A. S. Green, *The old Irish World*, 38–9, which attacks as unhistorical the propositions that there was no national sense in early Ireland; that early Irish society had no parliament; and that the Celtic 'race' in Ireland was inextricably mixed with immigrant stock.

[96] A useful commentary is to be found in T. W. Moody, 'Irish history and Irish mythology', *Hermathena*, cxxiv (1978), 7–24; and a guide to recent research in *Irish historiography 1970–79*, ed. J. Lee (Cork University Press, for the Irish Committee of

economics, and most of all a new approach to statistics. Mentalities, Presbyterian as well as Catholic, have been examined.[97] In the early period the Irish Sea has been reinterpreted as the centre, not the frontier, of a cultural area. In the plantation era, patterns of settlement and the very framework of dispossession have been revised. Divergent local socio-economic and political cultures have been analysed; our sheer ignorance about—for instance—the effects of the Famine have been stringently exposed. In recent years Irish historians have presented their readers with a version of ancient Ireland where some estates were worked by slaves,[98] and of early Christian Ireland where much of the damage to churches was done, not by invaders, but by marauding rival abbots;[99] we have even been shown a Dermot McMurrough who is not the villain of the piece.[100] To take another period, the Fenians have been presented as 'easily recognisable and fairly typical mid-Victorians', using the movement as a vehicle for leisure activities and not particularly committed to Republicanism;[101] Sinn Fein has appeared as a similarly utilitarian and ideologically uncommitted machine for the brokerage of local power politics;[102] the Land War has been seen as 'sacrificing economic progress on the altar of Irish nationalism';[103] and 'traditional Ireland', so far from a frugal rural community exempt from the taint of materialism and modernisation, has been explosively derided by an Irish economic historian as 'full of rats who just did not know how to race'.[104]

It might be assumed that the point had been reached for which Shaw hoped in the 1920s, when he wrote of the national history:

> There are formidable vested interests in our huge national stock of junk and bilge, glowing with the phosphorescence of romance. Heroes and heroines have risked their lives to force England to drop

Historical Sciences, 1979). Also see M. J. Waters, 'Irish history without villains: some recent work on the nineteenth century', *Victorian Studies*, xvi, no. 2 (1972), 223–4.

[97] See for instance D. W. Miller, *Queen's Rebels: Ulster Loyalism in Historical Perspective* (1979) and 'Irish Catholicism and the Great Famine' in *Jnl. of Soc. Hist.*, 9 (1975), 81–98; E. Larkin, 'The devotional revolution in Ireland, 1850–75', in *Amer. Hist. Rev.*, 77 (1972), 625–52; and the work of the late K. H. Connell, in *Irish peasant society: four historical essays* (Oxford, 1968).

[98] Evans, op. cit., 59.

[99] A. T. Lucas, 'Plundering of churches in Ireland' in *North Munster Studies*, ed. E. Rynne (Limerick, 1967), 172–229.

[100] F. X. Martin's 1975 O'Donnell lecture presented this unexpected picture.

[101] See R. V. Comerford, 'Patriotism as pastime: the appeal of Fenianism in the mid-1860s' in *Irish Hist. Stud.*, xxii, no. 87 (1981), 239–50.

[102] D. Fitzpatrick, op cit.

[103] B. Solow, op. cit., 204, and R. D. Crotty, *Irish agricultural production: its volume and structure* (Cork, 1966).

[104] J. Lee, 'Continuity and change in Ireland, 1945–70' in *Ireland 1945–70* (Dublin, 1979), 177.

> Ireland like a hot potato. England, after a final paroxysm of doing her worst, has dropped Ireland accordingly. But in doing so she has destroyed the whole stock-in-trade of the heroes and heroines ... We are now citizens of the world; and the man who divides the race into elect Irishmen and reprobate foreign devils (especially Englishmen) had better live on the Blaskets where he can admire himself without disturbance. Perhaps, after all, our late troubles were not so purposeless as they seemed. They were probably ordained to prove to us that we are no better than other people; and when Ireland is once forced to accept this stupendous new idea, goodbye to the old patriotism.[105]

But what has happened is a contrary process: academic revisionism has coincided with popular revivalism. The version of Irish history presented in P. S. O'Hegarty's influential *Ireland under the Union* persists: 'the story of a people coming out of captivity, out of the underground, finding every artery of national life occupied by the enemy, recovering them one by one, and coming out at last into the full blaze of the sun ...'.[106] This is true not only among politicians, but also among popular historians (and *a fortiori* television historians).[107] The simplified notions have their own resilience: they are buried deep in the core of popular consciousness, as recent analysis of folk attitudes in rural Ireland has shown.[108] The point should also be made that the triumph of revisionism in Irish academic historiography is a particularly exact instance of the owl of Minerva flying only in the shades of nightfall: events in the island since 1969 have both emphasised the power of ideas of history, and the irrelevance of scholarly revolutions to everyday attitudes.[109] (Nor have Irish readers, at any level, been particularly anxious to explore the historical analysis offered by scho-

[105] G. B. S[haw], 'On Throwing out Dirty Water', in *Irish Statesman*, 15 Sept. 1923; quoted in Lyons, *Culture and Anarchy*, 165.

[106] Dedicatory Preface to *A history of Ireland under the Union* (Dublin, 1952). It might be added that this is a work of wide reading and dense texture, in which original documentation and personal reminiscence is used to powerful effect; but it is nonetheless pervaded with an obsession.

[107] See for instance S. Cronin, op. cit., and R. Kee, 'Ireland: a television history'.

[108] See H. Glassie, *Passing the time: folklore and history of an Ulster community* (Dublin, 1982), 83, which records the 'education' transmitted in rural Fermanagh. '"It took the boys in Fenian days to carry it on until the Men Behind the Wire came ... The old fight had to be fought, and it had to be fought from the days of eighteen and sixty-seven, and indeed it went back further. Seventeen and ninety-eight, that was the first Rising. That's what you want to know: the background to everything."' Also see ibid., 639 ff., for observations about the keeping of 'alternative history' in local communities. In a similar manner, the memory of dispossession lasted on at atavistic levels, noted by Arthur Young, and often since (see for instance T. Garvin, op. cit., 16).

[109] Cf. however, P. M. Kennedy, 'The decline of nationalistic history in the West, 1900–1970' in *Jnl. of Contemporary Hist.*, 8 (1973), 77–100.

lars from other countries.)[110] But the discrepancy between beliefs in the university and outside it raises some questions. The transition from piety to iconoclasm may have been too abrupt for the change to percolate through. But the depressing lesson is probably that 'history' as conceived by scholars is a different concept to 'history' as understood at large, where 'myth' is probably the correct, if over-used, anthropological term. And historians may overrate their own importance in considering that their work is in any way relevant to these popular conceptions: especially in Ireland. The habit of mind which preferred a visionary Republic to any number of birds in the hand is reflected in a disposition to search for an Irish past in theories of historical descent as bizarre as that of 'the Cruithin people' today,[111] the Eskimo settlement of Ireland postulated by Pokorny in the 1920s,[112] the Hiberno-Carthaginians of Vallancey, or the Gaelic Greeks of Comerford.

Such an attitude goes with the disposition to legitimise, to praise and to blame, conspicuously evinced by the traditions of Irish history-writing as surveyed in this paper. Recent scholarship has, however, inclined towards the line of Goldwin Smith, articulated by his study of *Irish History and Irish Character* in 1861: 'There is no part of all this which may not be numbered with the general calamities of Europe during the last two centuries, and with the rest of these calamities buried in oblivion.' Elsewhere in his rather weary and acerbic, but essentially sympathetic study, the same author remarked that the 'popular writer on Irish history' should 'pay more attention than writers on that subject have generally paid to general causes, [should] cultivate the charities of history, and in the case of the rulers as well as the people, [should] take fair account of misfortunes as well as crimes'.[113] Professional Irish historiography has turned this corner; but the question which should interest future historians is why the 'popular Irish history' is taking so long to follow.

[110] The work of M. W. Heslinga, *The Irish border as a cultural divide* (Assen, Netherlands, 1962) has received less attention than might be expected; and Erhard Rumpf's pioneering *Nationalism and socialism in twentieth-century Ireland*, published in German in 1959, had to wait until 1977 for an English translation (under the imprint of Liverpool University Press). When carrying out research, Dr Rumpf was told 'by an authority on Irish politics' that he could not hope to analyse the dynamic of Irish nationalism: 'There was no sociological, sectarian or class problem or angle in the Sinn Fein movement, or any part of it, from beginning to end' (xv).

[111] I. Adamson's book *Cruithin: the ancient kindred* (Newtownards, 1974) is interpreted by Unionist ideologies as arguing for an indigenous 'British' people settled in Ulster before the plantations.

[112] Elegantly mocked by E. Curtis in the *Irish Statesman*, 7 Nov. 1925: 'We must beat our harps into harpoons and our wolfdogs into walruses.'

[113] Goldwin Smith, *Irish History and Irish Character*—'an expansion of a lecture delivered before the Oxford Architectural and Historical Society at their Annual Meeting in June 1861'—(1861), preface, and 193.

PRESIDENTIAL ADDRESS

By Professor J. C. Holt, M.A., D.Phil., F.B.A., F.S.A.

FEUDAL SOCIETY AND THE FAMILY IN EARLY MEDIEVAL ENGLAND: II. NOTIONS OF PATRIMONY

READ 26 NOVEMBER 1982

NOTIONS are potent but nebulous, often direct and determining in their effect but themselves indeterminate in origin and structure. My title is designed to circumvent two lines of thought which have largely circumscribed the study of inheritance in the eleventh and twelfth centuries hitherto. First, I shall say something here and there about succession, but it will be only a subsidiary part of the argument. Heritable title was not diminished by unsettled rules of succession. On the contrary, in the eleventh century as in the thirteenth, it was emphasised and nourished by the claims and counter-claims of competitors. In such disputes the opposing arguments were couched in a common language; it is the language, therefore, that will be my first concern. Second, for this same reason I shall also pay scant attention to the jurisdictional aspects of inheritance. To be sure, in post-Conquest England inheritance amounted not to a title but to a claim upon a lord; heritable title was realised when the lord admitted it; no concession by a tenant was as secure as it could be made until his lord had confirmed it. But lord and vassal also shared the same language. Each inherited; each knew that a vassal might be disinherited. *Hereditas*, *jus hereditarium*, *exheredare*: these and similar terms expressed and informed their attitudes, no matter whether, on a particular occasion, they were for or against hereditary practice. It is reasonable therefore to enquire what assumptions and imagery lay behind the words.

It is best to begin on relatively firm ground with a case-history from the late twelfth century. At the end of April 1201 an assize of *mort d'ancestor* was held before King John's justices at Tewkesbury to determine whether Adam of Cockfield, father of Margaret, was seised in demesne as of fee-farm of the manors of Cockfield, Semer and Groton in Suffolk on the day he died and whether Margaret was his nearest heir.[1] The case was brought against the abbot and prior of Bury St

[1] *Curia Regis Rolls*, i. 430.

Edmunds and was terminated in Margaret's favour. She was no more than an infant. The real victor was her guardian, Thomas de Burgh, tenant of the abbey and brother of Hubert de Burgh, the King's Chamberlain.[2] Powerful men were involved in the action. The justices proceeded with despatch. Thomas de Burgh apparently ensured that the jury was made up of knights, tenants like him of the abbey.[3] Their verdict was very much in their own general interest.

The case was reported in the rolls of the court, and also in two separate passages in the chronicle of Jocelin of Brakelond.[4] It is therefore possible to supplement the pleadings and the verdict with Jocelin's own account and with an appendix to the chronicle by William of Diss, monk of Bury, which reads very much like a deposition of the abbey's case for the action held at Tewkesbury. These three distinct sources, supplemented by charters in which the Bury archive was rich, allow an almost complete account, in which the views of both lord and tenant are fully represented, of the development of heritable tenure in the Cockfield fee.

The first point to grasp is that this particular inheritance was a variegated accumulation made up of terms of tenure laid down over a long period punctuated by disputes and settlements. Two of the manors, Semer and Groton, were acquired by Adam's grandfather, also called Adam, in the reign of Stephen and had been held at farm ever since for three generations. But the tenure had never been strictly hereditary. The rents were increased at the first succession;[5] the second Cockfield, Robert, apparently conceded in 1188 that he had no hereditary title;[6] and in *c.* 1191 Adam of Cockfield, the decedent of 1201, was party to an agreement with the abbot and convent which laid down that at his death the manors were to revert to the convent without any claim from his heirs who would have no hereditary right therein.[7] All this proved in vain. The jurors of 1201 overrode or ignored Adam's charter, which was read in court. They reviewed the long and continuous tenure, noting that both Adam and his grandfather had died seised and that Robert, Adam's father, had held throughout his life. They concluded that such long tenure constituted a fee-farm.[8] Thereby they converted *de facto*

[2] Thomas de Burgh bought the wardship for 500m. from Hubert, archbishop of Canterbury, who, in turn, had paid £100 for it to the abbot of Bury (*The Chronicle of Jocelin of Brakelond*, ed. H. E. Butler (1949), 123).

[3] Ibid., 123–4.

[4] Ibid., 123–4, 138–9.

[5] Ibid., 138.

[6] *Curia Regis Rolls*, i. 430.

[7] *The Kalendar of Abbot Samson of Bury St Edmunds and related documents*, ed. R. H. C. Davis (Camden 3rd ser., lxxxiv, 1954), 127–8.

[8] *Curia Regis Rolls*, i. 430; *Jocelin of Brakelond*, 124.

succession into *de jure* inheritance. Their line of thought was by no means novel.[9]

The descent of the third manor, Cockfield, was a different story, for in 1201 the abbot (none other than Abbot Samson) conceded in court that Robert of Cockfield on his death-bed had said that Cockfield was his right and inheritance. The court took the abbot's statement as an admission. Cockfield was not referred to the jury, but adjudged at once to Margaret, Robert's grand-daughter.[10] The abbot's uncertainty was shared by others of the convent. Jocelin of Brakelond felt that Cockfield may have been different in this respect because it had not been included with the other manors in the concession of hereditary title by Robert and Adam of Cockfield.[11] William of Diss's more detailed account is of great interest: the Cockfield family, he stated, had no charter entitling them to the manor of Cockfield, only a writ of seisin of King Henry I, incorrectly sealed, charging Abbot Anselm to allow Adam I of Cockfield to hold it as long as he paid his rent in full; but William allowed that Robert of Cockfield had avowed in the abbot's presence that he believed Cockfield to be his hereditary right on account of long tenure, in that his grandfather, Lemmer, held the manor long before his death, and Adam his son throughout his life and Robert himself throughout his life, in all nearly sixty years.[12] Robert's death-bed statement was closely similar to the knights' verdict in 1201: long tenure and uninterrupted succession established hereditary title.

Cockfield was divided into two manors. The portion still in dispute in 1201 was that assigned to the sustenance of the monks.[13] The other portion of the township, according to William of Diss, had been held by Lemmer, Robert's grandfather, by hereditary right and, with the assent of Abbot Anselm, had been converted from socage tenure to half a knight's fee in the reign of King Stephen.[14] Moreover this second portion was but one of several tenements held by hereditary right, for which Robert of Cockfield had the abbey's charters, which indeed William of Diss read aloud in the presence of Abbot Samson and many others. These amounted to at least one knight's fee in the time of

[9] Compare the claim of Robert de Valognes, 1158–9, that he held Northaw wood by hereditary tenure of the abbey of St Albans. In this case, too, the wood had been held by successive generations of the Valognes family, and men equated such tenure with hereditary title despite the contrary evidence of the abbey's charters (*Gesta Abbatum Monasterii Sancti Albani*, ed. H. T. Riley (Rolls ser., 1867–9), i. 160–2).

[10] *Curie Regis Rolls*, i. 430.

[11] *Jocelin of Brakelond*, 123.

[12] Ibid., 139.

[13] For land assigned *ad victum monachorum* see V. H. Galbraith, 'An Episcopal Land-Grant of 1085', *Engl. Hist. Rev.*, xliv (1929), 363–8.

[14] *Jocelin of Brakelond*, 138–9.

Abbot Anselm 1121–48, to one and a half fees in 1166 and to at least two fees by 1200.[15] Some of these charters survive in the Bury records. In the earliest Abbot Anselm confirmed to Adam of Cockfield and his heirs tenure *jure hereditario* in return for one knight's service of the lands which his father had held in Lindsey and Cockfield.[16] But none of these charters indicates that Adam's father, Lemmer, held Cockfield *jure hereditario* as William of Diss states. The only hint that this was so lies in a distinction which William does not mention: Adam was to hold *jure hereditario* in Lindsey and Cockfield, but Abbot Anselm made no mention of hereditary right when he confirmed Adam in all his father's and his own purchases and acquisitions.[17]

There is yet another complication. So far the story has been concerned with land, inherited or acquired, held on varying terms for diverse renders and services. Throughout, the tide ran in the tenant's favour towards heritable succession. But at one point Abbot Samson was able to stem it. When Robert of Cockfield died *c.* 1191 Adam laid claim to the half hundred of Cosford as his hereditary right on the ground that his father and grandfather had held it for eighty years or more. The claim was rejected, despite the fact that Adam had strong supporters including Roger Bigod, earl of Norfolk; for Abbot Samson pointed out that such hereditary tenure would make room for royal intrusion into the liberty of the abbey, if by chance Adam or his heir fell into the mercy of the king or was subject the Crown's prerogative wardship.[18] So while land might become hereditary, office might not. But the abbot's victory was won at a cost. This dispute too went to the king's court in an action of *mort d'ancestor*. It was settled by final concord in which the abbot confirmed numerous socage lands to Adam to be held hereditarily and in perpetuity in return for the renunciation of his claim to the half hundred.[19]

This evidence allows an almost complete reconstruction of the development of heritable tenure in the Cockfield fee. It is a little hazy at the beginning of the story. We cannot be certain on what terms Lemmer held Cockfield unless we accept William of Diss's statement of his heritable title from roughly eighty years later. But it is certain that by the 1130s Lemmer's son, Adam, held this manor, from which the family came to take its name, *jure hereditario*. The fee was augmented by purchase and acquisition. Descent by primogeniture was

[15] *Feudal Documents from the Abbey of Bury St Edmunds*, ed. D. C. Douglas (British Academy Records of Social and Economic History, viii, 1932), 120–1; *Liber Rubeus de Scaccario*, ed. H. Hall (Rolls ser., 1896), 393; *Jocelin of Brakelond*, 123.

[16] *Feudal Documents*, 120–1.

[17] Ibid., 118–19.

[18] *Jocelin of Brakelond*, 123.

[19] *Feet of Fines, Henry II and Richard I* (Pipe Roll Soc., xvii), 9–11; *Kalendar of Abbot Samson*, 71–2.

reinforced by the conversion of socage tenements, which might be partible, into knight's fees, which were not.[20] Yet heritable tenure in some estates held at farm was not secured until the third generation after Adam, in the interest of the infant Margaret, and then only after action in the king's court in 1201. Moreover, the claim to heritable title in office had to be abandoned in 1191. It is plain that inheritance was a complex matter. It varied in strength and was established over different periods from one form of property to another. The lord was readier to admit some heritable tenures than others, the tenant readier to sustain claims here and abandon others there.

It is worth remembering that this complex evolution, covering eighty years or more and involving at least two legal actions in the king's court, took place without any open breach between the Cockfields and their monastic lords. The family was not dissident. The first Adam of Cockfield acquired Semer and Groton in the reign of Stephen because of his ability to defend them in the abbot's interest against neighbouring castellans;[21] Robert of Cockfield was one of the custodians of the abbey during the vacancy of 1180–2;[22] in succeeding generations their advancing fortunes were confirmed by the abbots. Only perhaps in 1201, in the verdict at Tewkesbury, does the issue of inheritance appear as one of principle, with the abbot and convent ranged on one side and the knightly tenants on the other. For the rest the picture is one of men of business fashioning a *modus vivendi* which both resolved differences and satisfied mutual interests.

The objections to accepting this as a definitive case history are obvious. Even for Bury it may be misleading. For William of Diss hereditary tenure was synonymous with tenure by charter. 'He had good charters', he wrote of Robert of Cockfield, 'for all the tenements which he held of St Edmund by hereditary right'; William even talked of 'hereditary charters', and his final word was that neither Adam nor Robert had any charters for the land in dispute in 1201 in Cockfield.[23] Such coincidence of hereditary and written title belonged to the early thirteenth rather than the early twelfth century. For Lemmer, as we have seen, the charters mentioned by William of Diss have not survived. The earliest Bury deed conveying hereditary title seems to be a charter of Abbot Anselm for Maurice of Windsor, the abbey's steward, of 1114–19.[24] Going back further still the well known notification of the acceptance of King William's knight, Peter, as Abbot Baldwin's feudal man suggests that the documentation of enfeoffment in the

[20] Glanvill, *De Legibus*, vii. 1, 3; ed. G. D. G. Hall (1965), 71, 75.

[21] *Jocelin of Brakelond*, 123.

[22] Ibid., 8, 10.

[23] Ibid., 138–9.

[24] *Feudal Documents*, 111.

years immediately following the Conquest was quite inchoate, if indeed any weight at all can be placed on so corrupt a text.[25] It has some value, however, in at least one respect. It was produced in unusual circumstances to solve a particular problem—what to do about the services of a tenant who also owed service to the King? Some of the charters mentioned by William of Diss were also produced in special circumstances; they marked the termination of disputes, for example. Yet William assumed that charters were the norm, the necessary evidence of settled undisputed tenure. He was not the last to do so. Such charters are our main source of information on the development of hereditary tenure. These sources are reduced to a trickle and then run almost dry as we follow them back from the twelfth to the eleventh century. We tend to think that this is also true of the ideas they embodied, that hereditary notions were fresh sprung in the dawn of the Norman settlement. That this was not so, that the Normans came to England with well developed notions about inheritance, will be one of my main arguments.

In another respect the history of the Cockfield family is a sure guide. Throughout a period covering roughly eighty years the several different facets of their tenure were described in the same terminology: *feodum*, *jus*, *heres*, *hereditas*, *jus hereditarium*, *in feodo et hereditate*. Only once throughout the varied record of the family's tenure does the word *patrimonium* appear and only then as a means of distinguishing heritable land which had been inherited from heritable land which had been acquired.[26] Yet it was a patrimonial system and one strongly rooted in primogeniture to which these terms were applied.[27] Institutions had become far more precise than the words used to describe them. One reason for this is that, with one obvious exception, the vocabulary was ancient. The exception was *feodum* which was engendered by the development of hereditary military tenures in the late eleventh century. The rest had a long history in which the major source was the *Corpus Juris Civilis*,[28] and such a venerable pedigree, however dimly perceived and understood, gave to the Cockfields and to all others who used them a sense of security. What better vehicle could there be for the establishment of heritable fiefs than those terms which in antiquity had sprung from heritable title? But the consequences for the historian are important and daunting. The language may have remained the same but the notions which it expressed did not.

[25] D. C. Douglas, 'A Charter of Enfeoffment under William the Conqueror', *E.H.R.*, xlii (1927), 245–7. For further comment see below, 219–20.

[26] *The Kalendar of Abbot Samson*, 17–19. My reading of this evidence is a little different from that suggested by Professor Davis, ibid., 17, n. 2.

[27] For further comment see below, 211–13.

[28] See especially Institutes, II, xiv, xix.

How did the terms acquire the relatively precise usage of the second half of the twelfth century? The jurisdictional answer is that they were defined by the interplay of lord and tenant in seignorial and royal courts.[29] But the words were not confined to these arenas. Nor could they be divorced from their history. In deploying them lords, tenants, justices and jurors were resorting to a language which might seem to be very restricted and very simple. Beneath the surface, however, it was rich in imagery and associations.

To trace this language back into pre-Conquest Normandy is to enter a different world. In twelfth-century England inheritance has been viewed as a seignorial concession.[30] In eleventh-century Normandy it was more like a primordial right over which, in time, the dukes came to exercise superiority. Inherited land and alodial land were treated as one and the same, *alodum* sometimes appearing simply as a colloquialism for *hereditas*.[31] These equations were first expressed, and indeed in Normandy the whole language of inheritance was first generated, in the records of ecclesiastical and monastic endowment. Here, at first sight, they seem oddly out of place, for the language of inheritance and generation ill became the church in an age of reform which laid such emphasis on celibacy. But the convenience of terms which had a legal connotation outweighed such considerations. Hence the monks of Fécamp obtained a lordship to be held *jure hereditario in alodum* and *in alodum et hereditatem perpetuam*.[32] At Le Mont St Michel the monks received a benefaction to be held *in omni successura generatione*.[33] An estate was conferred on St Ouen *perpetua hereditate*; this house enjoyed its superiority over the daughter house of Sigy *jure hereditario*.[34] Some of the charters of the founder of La Trinité du Mont also provided that the monks were to hold *jure hereditario*. They received further concessions *in perpetua hereditate* or *in perpetuam hereditatem*.[35] Such words were part of the common jargon of conveyancing. They

[29] S. E. Thorne, 'English Feudalism and Estates in land', *Cambridge Law Journal*, new ser., vi. (1959), 193–209; S. F. C. Milsom, *The Legal Framework of English Feudalism* (Cambridge, 1976), esp. 154–86.

[30] Space restricts me to the baldest of summaries of the contributions of Professor Milsom and Professor Thorne.

[31] See the charter 1035–*c.* 1040 of John, abbot of Fécamp—'Odo . . . totam hereditatem suam, quam communi voce alodum dicimus, contulit . . .' *Recueil des Actes des Ducs de Normandie (911–1066)*, (hereafter *R.A.D.N.*) ed. Marie Fauroux (Mémoires de la Société des Antiquaires de Normandie, xxxvi, 1961), no. 93. Compare the less direct analogy drawn by Albert, one-time abbot of Jumièges in *Chartes de l'abbaye de Jumièges*, ed. J.-J. Vernier (Société de l'histoire de Normandie, (1916), i. 57.

[32] *R.A.D.N.*, no. 71 (1034).

[33] Ibid., no. 132 (1054–5).

[34] Ibid., nos. 43 (1015–26), 103 (1037–*c.* 1045).

[35] Ibid., nos. 83 (1030–5), 84 (1030–5), 101 (1043), 123 (1051), 201 (1051–66), 202 (1051–66), 233 (1066).

were shared with the Anglo-Saxon *landbocs* and Carolingian *diplomata*.[36]

It may be that these words were used in order to express monastic title in a language which the layman could grasp and understand. But this is scarcely a sufficient explanation. A monastery received gifts in hereditary right from donors who enjoyed hereditary title. The emphasis on ecclesiastical tenure *jure hereditario* was surely aimed at transferring to the beneficiary such right as the donor had in the benefaction. In extreme cases God or Christ or the saints intruded into the family succession. Land became the *legitima hereditas* of St Wandrille.[37] Odo son of Geoffrey granted land *in perpetuam hereditatem* to Fécamp because he made 'no other person but God his heir of all his land in the whole of Normandy'.[38] A certain Heloise, on becoming an anchorite, made Christ the heir of her patrimony which she conceded to the abbey of Coulombs.[39]

This bond between inheritance and monastic endowment is equally obvious on the side of the benefactors. In one of the earliest recorded grants to St Wandrille, 996–1006, the donor granted 'a certain estate conceded to me by hereditary right by my ancestors'.[40] Other benefactors of the abbey during the next fifty years granted 'land of my hereditary right' or land 'pertaining to me by hereditary right from my relatives to be held by the monks forever'.[41] It was a similar story at Fécamp where in 1006 Duke Richard II supplemented his father's endowment with further concessions from his 'hereditary right'.[42] At St Ouen the monks received 'part of his inheritance' from Roger son

[36] F. M. Stenton, *The Latin Charters of the Anglo-Saxon Period* (Oxford, 1955), 87–8; E. John, *Land Tenure in early England* (Leicester, 1964), 39–63.

[37] *R.A.D.N.*, no. 95 (1037–*c.* 1040).

[38] Ibid., no. 93 (1035–*c.* 1040).

[39] Ibid., no. 230 (1066). Subsequent genealogical accident sometimes upset such arrangements. Some time after 1035 a certain knight Gilbert, 'lacking an heir', conceded all his inheritance in Condé and elsewhere to St Peter of Préaux, the grant being agreed by Robert son of Humphrey, i.e. Robert de Beaumont. Gilbert's wife subsequently gave birth to a daughter who married Roger de Croixmarez. That the initial grant was a *post obitum* gift is revealed by the fact that the charter was only produced long afterwards when Gilbert died as a monk of Préaux 1078–*c.* 1090. Eventually, after much discussion, Roger de Croixmarez asked Abbot William to pay the relief on (*relevaret*) Gilbert's 'honour' to Roger de Beaumont *de quo beneficium erat.* This was agreed. Roger de Beaumont then conceded the estate to the abbey on the understanding that the monks were to have only half of Condé during Roger de Croixmarez's life, with the reversion of all he had there at his death except for 30 acres with a house, court and orchard and two knights. These, along with the other properties conceded in the original grant, were to be held by Roger's heir who would pay relief (*relevaret*) to the abbot and monks for them *sicuti mos est terre.* The effect was to confirm the original grant, but with sitting tenants, including the donor's heir (Archives de L'Eure, H.711. Cartulaire de S. Pierre de Préaux, f. 100).

[40] 'Tradidi quemdam fundum, mihi ab antecessoribus meis jure hereditario concessum' (ibid., no. 7).

[41] Ibid., nos. 134 (1037–55), 125 (1051).

[42] Ibid., no. 9.

of Hilbert.[43] Viscount Erchembald, on entering La Trinité du Mont, gave the house his meadow in Sahurs and all that he held by hereditary right in Celloville.[44] Such terms were not restricted to the acts of the greatest men. *Milites* might hold alodial property.[45] Freemen might be called *alodarii*.[46] Before 1050 William fitz Osbern confirmed to his foundation at Lyre the land of Theodoric Tirel, presumably his vassal, 'which was left to him from the inheritance of his father'.[47] At almost the same time Robert de Beaumont confirmed to St Wandrille Foucarville with its church and nine manorial tenants, *hospites*, with 'whatever belonged to him by hereditary right'.[48]

The language of inheritance was shared. The same words could be used to describe both the capacity of the donor and the title of the beneficiary. They expressed the fact that there was a cohesive bond between inheritance and endowment. You cannot give what you have not got. To give is to hold the wherewithal to give. To give in perpetuity is to assert or imply that in some way you have had more than a life interest in what you give. That tight logical knot bound together not only donor and beneficiary, but also both to their lord. Much of the evidence used above is drawn from charters in which the dukes of Normandy confirmed or attested the grants of their men. Many reasons have been advanced in the past for the great wave of monastic endowment and benefaction set in motion by the dukes and accelerated and enlarged by their vassals in the course of the eleventh century. The donor's desire to atone or repent, on occasion in retirement in the house which he or his family had founded; the prestige which the new foundation brought to the founding family; the convenience of a house under family patronage as a receptacle for sons, daughters and sundry relatives; all these have been rightly emphasised. None of these motives, however, comes so close to explaining the close coincidence of monastic endowment and an emergent aristocracy as the simple point that a grant in perpetuity and inherited tenure were logically inseparable. To give emphasised that. To record the gift in a document confirmed or attested by the duke at one and the same time recognised his superiority and embodied his approval both of grant and hereditary tenure.

Any man of sufficient substance to hold or acquire land in free tenure might profit from this mutual security of benefactor and beneficiary. Against his doing so there was no social barrier short of the ever steepening slopes which led to the great divide between free and

[43] Ibid., no. 42 (1015–26). [44] Ibid., no. 82 (1030–5).
[45] Confirmation of Duke William for Fécamp, 1035–40 (ibid., no. 94).
[46] Confirmation of Duke William for Jumièges, 1060–6 (ibid., no. 220).
[47] Ibid., no. 120 (*c.* 1050). [48] Ibid., no. 129 (1046–53).

unfree. But there were obstacles, ranging from procedural complications to serious jurisdictional and tenurial doubts about the donor's capacity. The many surviving charters in which lords confirmed specific grants by individual tenants, the Norman *pancartes* and the Anglo-Norman charters of confirmation in which tenants-in-chief enumerated the grants of their men, all attest that the service with which the land was burdened gave the superior lord so great a say that a grant made without his approval was infirm. The lord's charter of confirmation, his attendance at the ceremony where the grant was made, or the promulgation of the tenant's grant in the lord's court, were an important, often the essential, element in the emerging notions of warranty.

But here too the logic of benefactions which were to be enjoyed in perpetuity began to seep in. Some lords, taking regard perhaps of their own administrative ease in the face of the importunities of potential benefactors and beneficiaries, began to shift ground, from confirming the particular grants of each of their tenants to enunciating general rules governing such alienations. Such licences became commonplace after the Norman conquest. In a charter of 1080, conveying revenues and tithes in Normandy and England to St Florent-lès-Saumur, William de Briouze conceded: 'And if any of my men shall give or sell anything (to the monks) I approve.'[49] If Hugh earl of Shropshire's confirmation of the lands and privileges of his father's foundation at Shrewsbury is to be trusted, he or his father conceded that any of his barons, burgesses or knights whosoever wished, might give to the abbey any of their lands and rights without any licence from him or his heirs so that neither donors nor recipients of such alms would perform any further service to him.[50] There was yet another pattern at Chester. There Earl Hugh and his wife granted that their barons might grant to St Werburgh 100 shillings worth of land during life and a third of their goods with their bodies at death.[51] A generation later Henry count of Eu, lord of Hastings, in a grant which foreshadowed later mortmain legislation, was even more meticulous. 'I Henry count of Eu concede to the church of St Martin of Battle whatever my men in England and Normandy have given or shall give to the same church in alms for the sake of their souls excepting the

[49] *Chartes normandes de l'abbaye de Saint-Florent près Saumur*, ed. M. P. Marchegay (Mémoires de la Société des Antiquaires de Normandie, 3rd ser., x, 1880), 678–81. The passage occurs in a variant reading of a duplicate original. There is another text with a correct dating clause in Bouhier's transcripts, 'Cartulare comitum pictaviensium et engolisme', B.N., MS. Lat. 17089, ff. 910v–11.

[50] *The Cartulary of Shrewsbury Abbey*, ed. Una Rees (Aberystwyth, 1975), i. 9.

[51] *The Chartulary or Register of the Abbey of St Werburgh, Chester*, ed. J. Tait (Chetham Soc., lxxix, 1920), 17.

caput of their manors and the knight service.'[52] By the middle of the twelfth century such facilities were being extended well down the social scale. In a charter of 1148–55, Hugh son of Richard of Hatton, tenant of ten fees of the earldom of Warwick, founder of Wroxall Priory, granted the church of Claverdon to St Mary of Monmouth, a priory of St Florent-lès-Saumur, with the provision that if any of his men wished to give to that church and the brethren there keeping watch in worship of God an acre or two, saving his service, the gift should remain firm and undisturbed.[53]

In all these cases the tenant's power to alienate was limited not only by the particular restrictions which his lord might apply but also very frequently by the nomination of the beneficiary. Moreover blanket approval of alienation was not free from ambivalence. The concession of Henry count of Eu was one of two such charters. One was a general licence to alienate. The other differed in certain respects: it made no reservation of knight service, it included sale as well as gift, and, after giving general permission to alienate, it went on to confirm particular alienations.[54] Count Henry's concession was confirmed by his successor, John, sometime before 1170[55] and was elaborated by his great grand-daughter Alice, countess of Eu, between 1219 and 1246.[56] She too confirmed whatever her men had given or sold in alms to Battle. In her day the reservation of military service which her ancestors had sometimes made no longer held good, but she also enumerated the

[52] Huntington Library, San Marino, BA 42/1526. Henry succeeded in 1096 and died in 1140. The charter probably comes from earlier rather than later in this period. It is of antique script, has no seal and no indication that it ever carried one, and bears the *signa* of Count Henry and others.

[53] Livre noir de St Florent-lès-Saumur, B.N., Nouv. Acq. Lat. 1930, f. 34; J. H. Round, *Calendar of Documents preserved in France* (1899), no. 1146. Round's date of 1151–7 seems to depend entirely on the date of the confirmation of John, bishop of Worcester (ibid., no. 1147). The attestation of Robert, prior of Monmouth, indicates 1148 × 1155. For Hugh son of Richard see *Red Book of the Exchequer*, i. 325 and V. C. H., *Warwickshire*, iii. 116–17.

[54] Cartulary of Battle Abbey, Lincoln's Inn, Hale MS. 87, ff. 52v–3.

[55] London University Library, Fuller Collection, I/28/1. Count John, like Henry, concedes 'whatever my men in England and Normandy have given or shall give ... excepting their capital manor and knight service'.

[56] Fuller Collection, I/28/3. Alice's grant is not derived directly from the earlier concessions. She confirmed past grants and sales without reference to those which might be made in the future, and her enumeration of the grants belongs to the more usual pattern of seignorial confirmations rather than to the general licences conceded by Counts Henry and John. Her confirmation included 8½ m. charged on a half knight's fee in Whatlington 'by distraint on the same half fee if necessary'. All the grants were confirmed 'cum omnibus pertinencis necnon et warda castri cum omnibus que de predictis terris sive redditibus ad me vel ad heredes meos pertinent'. Even so the series indicates that seignorial control was stricter and more specific in the thirteenth century than it had been earlier.

grants which her tenants had made. The general licence to alienate was still not so strong that detailed confirmation would not strengthen it.

The arguments so far has been aimed at establishing that monastic endowment strengthened inherited capacity. This was true whenever and wherever land and rights were granted in perpetuity or, as later, in free and perpetual alms. It was given its sharpest emphasis when land held in hereditary right was granted as a perpetual inheritance. However, the use of a common language had a further effect of even greater import. It not only strengthened and spread the notion of inheritance. It also contributed powerfully to transforming it. It converted inherited right into heritable claim. Donors were envisaged as giving from their inherited land because that strengthened their capacity to give. But once they were envisaged as endowing a monastery by hereditary right they were dealing not with the past but with the future, not with ancestors but with heirs, not simply with inheritance but with heritability.

This too was injected into the language by logical necessity. There is no doubt that the primary sense of the hereditary right of the donor, as it figures in the Norman charters of the early eleventh century, was simply that he had inherited the land or rights in question. They were held *paterno jure*[57] or *ab antecessoribus*.[58] As Baldwin Filleul put it in 1051, in conferring his alod of Glicourt on St Wandrille, he could be seen to have possessed it 'in full ownership and freely from his father and forefathers'.[59] But the act of transfer to a beneficiary added something new. Inheritance in the past underlay the donor's capacity to give. But if the land was to remain with the recipient for good the hereditary descent had to be broken, the recipient himself taking the place of the heir. Every act of perpetual endowment in short involved the claims which the donor's heir might bring. Indeed endowment was probably the main instrument whereby such heritable claim was aired and refined. So between 1035 and 1040 Duke William confirmed to Fécamp the land of Richard fitz Goscelin de Bardouville in four villages in the Pays de Caux which were to become the property of the monastery on Richard's death *nullo herede calumniante vel reclamante*.[60] At about the same time in rather different circumstances the Duke persuaded Abbot John of Fécamp to give to Hugh son of the Viscount Hugh a life interest in one of the monastery's alodial lands *sine ulla calumnia sui heredis aut proheredis*.[61] In some documents the inheritance was allowed

[57] *R.A.D.N.*, no. 34 (1025).

[58] Ibid., no. 7 (996–1006).

[59] 'Quod a patribus et proavis solidum et quietum hactenus possedisse videor' (ibid., no. 124).

[60] Ibid., no. 94.

[61] Ibid., no. 93.

to run to the death of the sons of the donor. In 1015–17 Roscelin, canon of the cathedral of Rouen, bequeathed to St Ouen all the inheritance which he possessed to go to the church 'after his death and the death of his two sons ... who were heirs to the inheritance', the monks meanwhile to enjoy the tithe of the property. His nephew, Gonduin, made similar provisions for the inheritance of him and his son, and Roscelin ended by calling down the wrath of God on any of his heirs or any 'extraneous' person who interfered with his benefaction.[62] In other documents the heir's claim had a negotiable quality to be expressed in guarantees or cash. Between 1037 and 1048 William count of Arques and Mauger archbishop of Rouen gave Perriers-sur-Andelles to the monks of St Ouen in memory of their father, Duke Richard II, and accepted 300l. so that 'none of their heirs, relatives or men, giving themselves to the Devil, should contradict or challenge the gift'.[63] Such arrangements did not always work. In 1066 it was recorded that the gift of Heloise who had become an anchorite, made Christ her heir and ceded her lands in Autieux to the abbey of Coulombs, had been overridden by her nephew who seized the property by force. Only God's mercy and the persuasion of Duke William and his wife Matilda brought him in penitence to restore the gift.[64]

By the time they invaded England the Normans' notion of inheritance was expressed in terms which were both complex and sophisticated. The inheritance might descend to the holder not just from his father or from vaguely defined ancestors but also from the maternal line.[65] Women might inherit and make benefactions on their own.[66] Wives might give endowments from their hereditary right with the approval of their husbands.[67] A husband might give land which he held by right of his wife, with her consent.[68] Inheritance from collaterals, brothers and uncles, was common. And just as the inheritance could be derived from varied sources, so it might be subject to varied claims, not just from sons but from brothers and nephews.[69] Even an

[62] Ibid., no. 21. Compare ibid., no. 19 (1006–17) in which a certain Drogo released the land of his brother and vineyards which he had acquired in Bailleul to St Ouen after his and his wife's death, conceding the land to the monks *sine ullo herede* so that they were to succeed him in eternity without any claim of heirs. He also gave two mills which he had constructed at the gate of Le Goulet with his two sons and heirs who were to pay an annual rent for them. After their death no-one was to be heir or successor on their part to make claim against the monks.

[63] Ibid., no. 112.

[64] Ibid., no. 230.

[65] Ibid., no. 51 (1023–6).

[66] Ibid., nos. 55, 95 (1025–6, 1037–*c.* 1040).

[67] Ibid., no. 173 (1035–66).

[68] Ibid., no. 167 (1035–66).

[69] Ibid., nos. 147 (1060), 230 (1066). Such claims could lie hidden behind a grant of an inheritance. Sometime between 1044 and 1078, probably before 1066, the knight

heir still unborn might be included. Hence in the decade before the Conquest Herfred, brother of Genscelin, bequeathed his part of the land in Daubeuf to St Martin du Bosc 'in hereditary right after his death if he did not have an heir'.[70] Indeed the claim of heirs could already be envisaged as extending into the future as long as the accompanying endowment lasted. In 1063 Odo, steward of Duke William, died at the age of twenty-six. His father Stigand, 'who loved him dearly in his life and even more dearly after his death', commemorated his death with endowments to the cathedral church of Rouen and the abbey of St Ouen, stipulating that 'no abbot nor any man that might ever be should alienate his gifts' and, if he did, then Stigand's heir might intervene and obtain them on the same terms as the intruder.[71]

The inheritance was often sharply distinguished from the benefice and from precarious tenure. 'I have a certain alod', announced Albert, abbot of St Mesmin de Micy, 'from my maternal inheritance not of the benefice of any one' in 1023–6.[72] At about the same time documents in which Duke Richard confirmed grants to Fécamp, Jumièges and St Ouen, indicated that they were made both from the various grantors' paternal inheritance and from the benefices which were ducal rights.[73] Inheritances and alodial possession could be bought and sold, with transfer of full title, both by churches and laymen.[74] Other forms of tenure could be converted into alodial, perpetual or hereditary right. In 1047–63 Robert, abbot of St Wandrille, paid 25l. for a twelve-year lease of land in Lébecourt, purchased from Nicholas son of Baldric. Subsequently, at Nicholas's request, he paid a further 12l. and acquired the land in perpetual possession as the alod of St Wandrille.[75] When Emma granted land to St Ouen 1015–26 she distinguished between her alods and the vill of Meslay which she held

---

Ansketil son of Turulph made a *post obitum* gift, with the consent of his wife and sons, to the abbey of St Peter of Préaux of whatever came to him by right from paternal inheritance in Tourville and Campin. At his death the inheritance was divided among his surviving brothers. The abbey's portion amounted to three tenant-holdings (*hospites*) and two of the brothers, Gilbert and Geoffrey, persuaded Abbot Ansfrid to grant them to them *in beneficio*, with Geoffrey rendering the service. It was noted that this was done without the advice and agreement of the monks (Archives de l'Eure, H. 711, ff. cviii, cxii).

[70] *R.A.D.N.*, no. 218.

[71] Ibid., no. 158.

[72] Ibid., no. 51.

[73] Ibid., nos. 34, 36, 53.

[74] For purchases by La Trinité du Mont, ibid., nos. 130 (1053), 143 (1059), by St Wandrille, ibid., no. 154 (1047–63) and by Boscherville, ibid., no. 197 (1050–66). See ibid., no. 83, for a purchase by Goscelin viscount of Rouen from Helto son of Gilbert, 1030–5.

[75] Ibid., no. 153.

as a benefice of Duke Richard. It was Richard himself and he alone who could and did convert the grant of this benefice into a perpetual inheritance of the abbey.[76] In one remarkable case an inheritance figured as a realty even when the tenant had been driven out by his feudal superior. A document of 1059 records that Adam de St Brice, ejected by Duke William, was received in the city of Tours by the monks of St Julien. He was honourably entertained and provided with a horse worth 12l. In return he gave the monks Roncheville 'which was his right' in Normandy, if they could obtain it from Duke William. They promptly did so. Ultimately Adam was restored and his gift was confirmed by the Duke.[77] This tenement was described as a 'right' and not directly as an inheritance. That it was in fact such is clear from the statement that Adam had been disinherited.

This brings us face to face with the interplay between inheritance and lordship. This was a rich confusion of individual encounters any one of which might impose its own legal requirements on the common language. One such set of circumstances is revealed at an early date, 1011–33, and at a middling social level, by a charter of Henry abbot of St Ouen which records the purchase of fifty acres of arable land in Auzouville from Gunduin, 'our knight'. The agreement laid down that none of Gunduin's successors should claim any hereditary right therein. However, to that straightforward alienation of hereditary land Gunduin added a further ten acres of his better land, as a gift, not a sale, on the understanding that 'we should agree that the *beneficium* which he held from us should go to his sons after his death on the same terms of service whereby he served'. Gunduin's son, Hugh, attested and signed the charter and received a penny to buy a bow.[78] That provided for at least one succession to a *beneficium*. The arrangement is not too far removed from the arguments which took place over the Cockfield fee more than a century later. In the long run hereditary right came to reside both in lord and tenant. Between 1088 and 1096 Ralph fitz Ernest, vassal of Robert de Beaufour, who was in turn vassal of William count of Évreux, conveyed the church of St Germain de Varaville to the abbey of Troarn. His grant was confirmed by William count of Évreux *sicut rem que ad hereditatem meam pertinet* and was attested by Robert de Beaufour who also confirmed *ex toto in fine hereditabiliter in elemosina* the grant which Ralph fitz Ernest had made *hereditabiliter*.[79]

[76] Ibid., no. 43.

[77] Ibid., no. 142.

[78] Archives départementales, Seine-Maritime, 14H, 255.

[79] B.N., MS. Lat, 10086, f. xlv–xlvb; R. N. Sauvage, *L'abbaye de Saint-Martin de Troarn* (Mémoires de la Société des Antiquaires de Normandie, 4th ser., iv, 1911), 145–6. For another charter, 1020–30, recording the hereditary title of the lord, Hugh bishop of Bayeux, in benefaction of a tenant see *Chartes de l'abbaye de Jumièges*, i. 21–2.

There might be analogous ambiguities in ducal acts. Service was due to the duke from alods and inherited lands as well as from *beneficia*. The alod was distinguished from the *beneficium* not by absence of service but by the long possession derived from family succession, by relative security of tenure and by easier alienability.[80] Any ducal confirmation of the grant of alodial or inherited property acknowledged the duke's superiority and some degree of tenurial dependence. Richard II confirmed grants both of inheritances and *beneficia*,[81] and Duke Robert confirmed to la Trinité du Mont the grants which his faithful men had made 'from their hereditary property with our agreement'.[82] On occasion ducal confirmation was expressed so strongly that the act of confirmation almost had the quality of a conveyance willy-nilly of a vassal's property. The knight Ascelin sold the land which belonged to him in Grosfy, but Duke William's confirmation was a simple conveyance of his vassal's land; only the chance survival of the deeds of sale makes clear that the land was Ascelin's 'right' to which his heirs might lay claim.[83] Duke William also confirmed lands to St Wandrille, at the request of three of his knights, in terms which did not specify whether the land was theirs or his, whether it was alodial property in which the services gave the duke an interest or *beneficia* in which the knights had only a life estate.[84] The duke's lordship could even be used as a defence against the importunities of heirs. In 1066 itself a dispute occurred in the family of John bishop of Avranches. The bishop wished to give half the land of Vièvre, which was his inheritance, to his cathedral church. His nephew Robert, son of Richard de Beaufour, challenged this, claiming that he had received the land from his uncle, as a hereditary gift. He was bought off with the gift of 10l. and the commendation for his lifetime of five of the bishop's knights. He was probably doing no more than assert a hereditary claim. But the bishop could call on the advice of great men including Roger de Beaumont, and he secured the transaction by surrendering the land to Duke William 'so that it should be free and quit of all claims from relatives'. The Duke then conveyed the land to the cathedral church.[85] In that example lordship and inheritance were in direct antithesis.

[80] R. Carabie, *La propriété foncière dans le très ancien droit normand* (*xie–xiiie siècles*), I. *La propriété domaniale* (Caen, 1943), 230–43; L. Musset 'Réflexions sur *alodium* et sa signification dans les textes normands', *Revue historique de droit français et étranger*, 4th ser., xlvii (1969), 606.

[81] *R.A.D.N.*, no. 53 (1025–6).

[82] 'Memorati fideles ex rebus hereditariis suis et ex nostra cessione . . . deputaverant' (ibid., no. 61, 1030).

[83] Ibid., no. 109; F. Lot, *Études critiques sur l'abbaye de St Wandrille* (Paris, 1913), no. 26.

[84] *R.A.D.N.*, no. 126.

[85] Ibid., no. 229.

Ducal power could be applied brutally. On occasion ducal superiority was asserted in sovereign terms. One of the very few occurrences of the word *patrimonium* is in Duke William's confirmation in 1050 of the foundation of St Evroul wherein he threatened that those who violated his charter would be guilty of *lèse-majesté* (*nostre reum esse majestatis*) and would merit the ascription of all their patrimony to the ducal demesne.[86] There patrimony and majesty were placed in sharp contrast, the most secure inheritance against the supreme secular authority. But in other documents the dukes seem at one with their men. Duke Robert founded Cérisy from the lands which belonged to him by hereditary right.[87] His endowment of Le Mont St Michel speaks of the land he possessed 'for his own use by hereditary right'.[88] Duke William also granted judicial rights which he possessed 'as his hereditary share',[89] and precluded his successors from overturning his grants in perpetuity.[90] The Duchy itself was acknowledged to descend by right of inheritance.[91] On the face of things, therefore, there is little ground for thinking that the dukes' view of inheritance was different from that of their vassals.

The underlying reality was that the notion of inherited or heritable right was not dependent on ducal authority. To be sure, Duke William especially made grants of land which became hereditary in famous families which, like the Beaumonts, took their names from these new properties. But it would be hazardous to assume that in so doing he conveyed hereditary title in enfeoffment as his youngest son did for his vassals half a century later as king of England. It is more probable that he conveyed possession, which was then inherited, at which point all the notions of hereditary right which I have described came into play to reinforce title in the second generation. There are some examples where a duke created perpetual title. Duke William for example conferred on St Wandrille five churches in the Cotentin which he had previously granted to Robert de Beaumont, to be held *jure perpetuo*.[92] The grant to St Wandrille was made with Robert's agreement, for the salvation of both him and the duke, and the whole

[86] Ibid., no. 122.

[87] Ibid., no. 64 (1032).

[88] Ibid., no. 73.

[89] 'Per sortem hereditariam' (ibid., no. 146).

[90] Ibid., no. 148.

[91] See the charter of Duke Robert (1027–35) which reviews the descent of the Duchy on the death of Richard II—'Eo denique celestia, ut credimus, scandente regna, principatum ejusdem nominis Richardus filius illius obtinuit. Sed cita morte preventus, jure hereditario fratri suo Rodberto eundem reliquit' (ibid., no. 74).

[92] Ibid., no. 128. The ambiguity in my translation is present in the Latin, although Mlle Fauroux's punctuation attaches the perpetual right to Robert, not, as is more likely, to the monks of St Wandrille.

transaction, recorded in a single charter, seems closely similar to the Anglo-Saxon charters which embody a royal grant to an individual of land or rights subsequently conveyed as a benefaction.[93] There are also two remarkable charters surviving only in later copies and not entirely unimpeachable, in which Osbern and Ansfrid, brothers-in-law of Duke Richard II, are recorded as granting to St Wandrille their estates in Montérolier, that is an alod 'as it was partitioned between them and Odelarius by allotment by cord on the order and authority' of the duke, the grant being confirmed by 'the lord Richard the second, chief of the Normans, of whom we hold all these things, who had our sister Papia to wife'.[94] These words may well mean that Duke Richard had indeed created this alodial property for his brothers-in-law.

But such evidence appears only occasionally in the ducal acts before 1066. The documents rarely indicate how alodial or inherited tenure had originated. Instead they reveal a dual process. First, ducal authority over alodial and inherited or heritable family land was being extended and defined, its emergence marked by references to service, or to tenurial dependence on the duke, and above all by the recourse to the duke for confirmation or attestation. Second, with every ducal confirmation the *jus hereditarium* was strengthened, the *alodum* stood out in sharper contrast to the *beneficium*, and the succession to the inheritance was confirmed or canalised. It would be tempting to suggest that alodial tenure was derived from the Scandinavian settlement of Normandy were it not that it could scarcely be defined except through the interplay between the dukes and their vassals and the interest of both in monastic foundation and endowment which are recorded in the early Norman charters. One thing is certain: the charters create no ground at all for thinking that the complex notions they record were all of ducal creation. To transfer the English experience after 1066, in which King William created fiefs for his men as feudal lord of all the land, to Normandy before 1066, in which Duke William was building up a superiority over his men's inherited family holdings, which were described in a language which was older than the surviving documentation, would be quite wrong. Heritable title and feudal authority grew togther.

This can be demonstrated quite simply. In Norman England the heir can be regarded simply as having a prior claim on his feudal lord. He had to establish his claim and be put in by his lord after the performance of homage and fealty. But this mechanism should not be allowed to obscure the fact that both in England after the Conquest and in Normandy before, the heir was known far more often than not.

[93] Stenton, *Latin Charters*, 59–60.
[94] *R.A.D.N.*, nos. 46, 46 *bis*.

In charter after charter he attested his predecessor's grants or participated as the son in the benefactions of the father. Acts of benefaction specifically precluded subsequent contravention by the heir. Even before he succeeded his claim could be weighed against cash and bought off. In short, he had a status which could be increased by ducal and royal approval but which was antecedent thereto and independent thereof. The heir continued to enjoy this status, indeed to tend it, even when disinherited. Disinheritance cannot be understood except as its contradiction. The duke might regard the heir's claim as permissive. The vassal regarded it as title, clearly and early expressed, if we may transgress the boundaries of Normandy, by Ivo, count of Beaumont sur Oise, in a benefaction to St Wandrille of 1039: 'I Count Ivo with my son of the same name, who is a clerk and canon, to whom *jure hereditario* I concede my castle of Conflent after the passing of my death.'[95] Orderic Vitalis wrote of the dispositions of some of the great Norman families in closely similar terms.[96] Family ties, not ducal power, defined the prior claim. The duke might override it, just as a father might deny his eldest son, but the claim was there, nevertheless, even if ignored or turned aside.

The arrangements of pre-Conquest Normandy were still a far cry from the enfeoffments of Bury St Edmunds and the expanding fortunes of the Cockfields a century later. *Hereditas, jus hereditarium* were words which echoed down the decades, but with some changes of meaning, and discontinuously, with periods of almost total silence. One important change concerned the question—who are the heirs? The descent of the Cockfield estates went by primogeniture; it seems that collaterals to the main line were allotted under-tenancies;[97] this became the predominant convention and very soon the rule within a generation or so of the Conquest. It had nowhere near so powerful a hold in Normandy before the Conquest; the further back in time, the weaker primogeniture appears. On the surface there were many exact parallels between the two periods and places; in Normandy as at Bury, *patrimonium* with its restrictive connotation, was a very rare word indeed. But behind the language the pattern of succession changed fundamentally, from one involving partition among sons and perhaps even wider distribution within the family, in the early eleventh century, to systems of lineal descent, whether by primogeniture or *parage*, in the early twelfth century. The language survived these changes. Grants were made with the concurrence or consent of heirs in the

[95] Lot, *St Wandrille*, no. 24.

[96] Orderic Vitalis, *Ecclesiastical History*, ed. M. Chibnall, ii. 10 (Grandmesnil); ii. 98 (Hauteville); iii. 89 (Guiscard); iv. 184 (Évreux).

[97] For evidence of an under-tenancy by a junior line of the Cockfields see *Jocelin of Brakelond*, 139 and *The Kalendar of Abbot Samson*, 4.

early eleventh century. They were still made as concessions by the grantor and his heirs to the recipient and his heirs in the late twelfth century. But in the earlier period the heirs may appear in parallel as joint heirs; in the later they appear in series as successive heirs. Collaterals and distant heirs might figure under either system. This renders difficult, if not impossible, any statistical analysis along the lines attempted by Robert Fossier for Picardie.[98]

Nevertheless there is enough casual information to indicate that division of the inheritance was quite frequent. Later sources, chiefly Ordericus Vitalis, record examples of such successions from the second quarter of the eleventh century: Robert, archbishop of Rouen,[99] Robert of Grandmesnil,[100] Giroie,[101] William of Bellême,[102] and Ralph Tesson.[103] Moreover the language of inheritance was so deployed as to make no distinction between ancestors who were fathers and other antecedents, or between heirs who were direct descendents and collaterals. This open situation is well revealed in one of the earliest grants to St Wandrille, 996–1006, in which a certain Albert conveyed his estate in Livry which 'had been conceded to him by his ancestors by hereditary right'. His sons, nephews and eight named blood relatives, *consanguinei*, whose precise relationship was not defined, figured with him as 'possessors' of the estate and fellow grantors.[104] Men moved away from that primitive situation only slowly. Perhaps the main impetus to change came from the possession of castles, which could scarcely be partitioned and were not easily shared, and from a ducal interest in preserving service unfragmented. Nonetheless on into the middle years of the century an inheritance might still be held by brothers, whether jointly or by division,[105] and brothers might make or confirm benefactions in one and the same document.[106] One such operation, the endowment of St Évroul, was founded on the mutual support of the Grandmesnils and the sons of Giroie. Duke William's charter of confirmation of 1050 referred to 'the possessions which Robert and Hugh (de Grandmesnil) his brother and William (Giroie) and his brothers and sons, and other faithful Christians, had given or

[98] Robert Fossier, *La Terre et les Hommes en Picardie* (Paris, 1968), 262–73.

[99] Orderic Vitalis, ed. Chibnall, iii. 84.

[100] Ibid., ii. 40.

[101] Ibid., ii. 28, iv. 156; M. Chibnall, 'Les droits d'héritage selon Orderic Vital', *Revue historique de droit français et étranger*, 4th ser., xlviii (1970), 347.

[102] Orderic Vitalis, ed. Chibnall, ii. 362–5.

[103] L. Musset, 'Actes inédits du xie siècle. V. Autour des origines de St Étienne de Fontenay' *Bulletin de la Société des Antiquaires de Normandie*, lvi. (1961–2), 26–9.

[104] *R.A.D.N.*, no. 7.

[105] Ibid., nos. 19 (1006–17), 21 (1015–17), 46 (1017–26), 94 (1035–*c.* 1040).

[106] Ibid., nos. 24 (1017–23), 118 (*c.* 1049–1051), 119 (*c.* 1040–50), 147 (1060), 197 (*c.* 1050–66).

were to give from their inherited property, or which the same Robert had received for himself from his brother and his other co-heirs according to the agreed partition'[107] (*juxta complacitam parcium divisionem*). Similar arrangements were still in vogue both before and after the English expedition. Between 1051 and 1066 Richard and Roger, sons of Herluin the Seneschal, along with their mother, granted the church of Authevernes and other properties to La Trinité du Mont. That each brother in addition granted properties *e proprio jure* demonstrates that they had a common interest in the joint grant.[108] Something similar occurred in 1092 when Roger Tanetin and his sons and four brothers Helte, Reinfrey, Thurstan and Robert, 'firmly and hereditarily conceded and sold' to Arnulf abbot of St Martin of Troarn and his monks part of the church and all the land which they had in Guillerville in return for 30l. of Le Mans, apparently paid to them jointly.[109]

How far an ordered system of succession, giving priority to the eldest son and awarding other sons and collaterals appropriate precedence, had emerged by the time of the English expedition is a matter of guesswork. It would be convenient, but quite wrong, to take arrangements established in England after 1066 as an indication of how things stood in Normandy. Anglo-Norman and Norman succession soon parted company, the one accepting primogeniture, the other *parage*. Quite apart from that the Conquest added enormously to the acquisitions available to the participating families, and this must have facilitated and accelerated the establishment of lineal succession. Some of the divisions which occurred in Normandy before the Conquest can be interpreted as separations of inheritance from acquisition. The acquisition of land, whether by purchase or by grant, was common enough, but there are few references to acquisition *eo nomine* and none to suggest that the clear cut distinction between inheritance and acquisition stated in the *Leges Henrici Primi* already had the status of a clearly defined rule.[110] The rule, like the acquisitions themselves, was probably a product of the Conquest.

[107] Ibid., no. 122. Cf. Orderic Vitalis, ed. Chibnall, ii. 16–18, 32–40; Orderic Vitalis, ed. Le Prévost, v. 173–80. Compare the foundation of the priory of Maule (Orderic Vitalis, ed. Chibnall, iii. 172–4, 182–90).

[108] *R.A.D.N.*, no. 202.

[109] B.N., MS. Lat. 10086, f. lxxxxiiib–lxxxxiiii, R. Sauvage, *L'Abbaye de Saint-Martin de Troarn*, 143.

[110] In the Norman sources I have found nothing comparable to the precise contrast between inheritance and acquisition drawn in the agreement between Tescelinus, priest of Verri, and the monks of St. Florent-lès-Saumur 1055–70 (J. C. Holt, 'Politics and Property in early medieval England', *Past & Present*, 57 (1972), 14, n. 54). William fitz Osbern's endowment of Lyre included the tithes of all the lands and mills which he had acquired in the Bessin and 'the tithe of all things which he might acquire during the rest of his days', but the bulk of his grant was made from his inherited lands in Lyre, Breteuil and elsewhere (*R.A.D.N.*, no. 120). Ordericus Vitalis emphasised that the benefactions

The definition of the acquisition was merely one facet of a far larger problem. The counterpart of King William's feudal superiority over his new realm was that initially, certainly for the first generation, no land in England could have been held by the newcomers in inheritance: all was acquisition. There is therefore a real break in continuity, and that coincides with a real gap in the evidence. We may fill that gap if we like by imagining that William's enfeoffment of his followers was recorded in charters which happen all to have been lost, but that would be to credit the eleventh century with the practices of the twelfth. The plain fact is that at the point both in time and place at which inheritance ceased to provide a point of reference the documentation changed its tone. The language of inheritance which had been used so variously and so vigorously in Normandy scarcely appears at all in England in the first years after the Conquest. No-one held *jure hereditario*. No-one made endowments to be held *jure hereditario*. *Alodum* was now used to describe strange Anglo-Saxon forms of tenure. To be sure, these changes occurred amidst a broader terminological development. *Alodum* and *beneficium* were being replaced and to some degree amalgamated in *feodum*. Endowments to be held *jure hereditario* were being succeeded by grants in perpetuity in free and pure alms, a formula already deployed in the endowments of Richard of Clare before 1086.[111] Nevertheless the circumstances which followed the Conquest enforced change. The old security of tenure *jure hereditario* had gone, at least for the time being.

The change is revealed most clearly in the benefactions of those families with maintained houses both in Normandy and England. The language in which Roger de Montgomery announced his foundation of the abbey of Troarn was unequivocal—'I grant my own property of my inheritance' or 'I have determined to give a considerable part of my inheritance'.[112] In 1083 this same Roger promised to found the abbey of Shrewsbury. Neither in his spurious foundation charter nor in the almost equally unsatisfactory confirmation of his son Hugh, nor in Hugh's authentic confirmation of 1094–8, is there any reference to tenure *jure hereditario*, although Hugh's authentic confirmation was made in pure and perpetual alms.[113] Between 1051 and 1066 Roger de Bully sold to Rainer, abbot of La Trinité du Mont, the tithe of the

---

of Roger of Montgomery to Troarn, Séez and other houses were made from his acquisitions not from his paternal inheritance and he returned to this theme in discussing the foundation of Shrewsbury (ed. Chibnall, iii. 142, 144). Cf., however, below, 214.

[111] *Select Documents of the English Lands of the Abbey of Bec*, ed. M. Chibnall (Camden 3rd Ser., lxxiii, 1951), 21–2.

[112] R. N. Sauvage, *L'Abbaye de Saint-Martin de Troarn*, 347, 352; *R.A.D.N.*, no. 144.

[113] *The Cartulary of Shrewsbury Abbey*, nos. 2–5.

vill of Bully in that it belonged to him by hereditary right.[114] In 1088 this same Roger founded the priory of St Mary of Blyth. His various benefactions recorded in the foundation charter were made *in perpetuum*. There was no reference to tenure *jure hereditario*.[115] It is plain that the English and continental possessions of these two men did not merit the same language. Even more important, it was not that the language was forgotten. It is rather that it was held in abeyance because it did not fit English circumstances.

That brings us finally to the way in which those terms came to be used in the twelfth century, to the hereditary tenure of the Cockfields, to enfeoffment *in feodo et hereditate*, to tenure *jure hereditario*, and to the *cartae hereditariae* of William of Diss. The Cockfield evidence by itself, and many other similar collections, could easily be interpreted each as a story of hereditary title gradually emerging in a strongly seignorial context which emphasised service and feudal superiority. But long before this happened the relevant legal terms had already undergone prolonged and varied usage. That all this was forgotten, that it might have been necessary to start from scratch as it were, is improbable, indeed scarcely imaginable. There are enough indications that it was not forgotten. Ordericus Vitalis has been criticised for presenting the eleventh century as seen through the spectacles of the twelfth, in exaggerating, for example, the role of primogeniture.[116] But that apart, he wrote of hereditary title in the eleventh century in terms closely similar to those used to describe it in contemporary documents. Estates are held by hereditary right; inheritances pass to nephews and cousins,[117] to sons-in-law *jure uxoris*,[118] to sisters in the absence of male heirs,[119] as well as to direct male descendents. Rightful heirs may be disinherited.[120] Indeed disinheritance is a denial of justice, a cause of protest[121] or of feud,

[114] *R.A.D.N.*, no. 200.

[115] *The Cartulary of Blyth Priory*, ed. R. T. Timson (Thoroton Soc., Record ser., xxvii, 1973), no. 325.

[116] See Chibnall in Orderic Vitalis, ii. xxxvi–xxxvii; 'Les droits d'héritage selon Orderic Vital'.

[117] Orderic Vitalis, ed. Chibnall, ii. 80, 358; iii. 200; iv. 216.

[118] Ibid., iii. 116; vi. 42, 176. See also Orderic's statement that Duke Richard II conveyed to Giroie in hereditary tenure the lands which had been held by Heugon, father of his betrothed, even though she died before marriage (ibid., ii. 22).

[119] Ibid., ii. 116.

[120] Ibid., ii. 282; iv. 158, 302; vi. 33. See especially the vision of the knight William of Glos who had taken up a poor man's mill in return for a loan and disinherited the lawful heir by leaving it to his own heirs (ibid., iv. 244).

[121] See especially the protest of Ascelin son of Arthur that the body of the Conqueror should not be 'covered with his soil or laid in his inheritance' (iv. 106). The story was also known to William of Malmsbury (*Gesta Regum*, ed. W. Stubbs (Rolls ser., 1889), 337). It reveals that a sense of injustice might lie hidden behind transactions which are

war and rebellion.[122] We could as well charge Ordericus with conserving this language and projecting these conditions into his own age. In reality he simply demonstrates that the language and the imagery were unbroken.[123]

That interpretation gains support from the manner in which these terms were deployed in England, in charters of endowment or enfeoffment, once inheritance came about with the passage of time and the succession of generations. It is very remarkable that the notion of inheritance appears suddenly on the scene in its fully developed form with very little indication of tentative experiment. In Normandy, over a period of half a century or more, men had worked their way by an inexorable logic from fact to expectancy, from the notion of inherited right to heritable claim. In England from the start the terms are used to express intention, often stated very precisely. Bishop Ranulf Flambard's enfeoffment of William son of Ranulf in Houghall and elsewhere in 1114–16 comprised *terras jure hereditario possidendas*.[124] A redrafted version of the same grant of 1116–19 stated that the lands were granted to William and his heirs who would succeed him *per hereditariam successionem*.[125] Almost universally this was the sense of hereditary tenure in the charters surviving in increasing numbers from the 1120s, '30s and '40s in which grants were made from the grantor and his heirs to the recipient and his heirs to be held *in feodo et hereditate*. Such tenure could be created from scratch.[126] *Hereditas* could be an

---

recorded simply as sales. For the record evidence see *Les Actes de Guillaume le Conquérant et de la Reine Mathilde pour les Abbayes Caennaises*, ed. L. Musset (Mémoires de la Société des Antiquaires de Normandie, xxxvii, 1967), no. 14 and pp. 45–6.

[122] Orderic Vitalis, v. 156; vi. 196, 220, 372.

[123] Orderic, however, gave the language his own special nuances which are not shared by the documentary evidence. He had a very strong sense, not infrequently expressed, of 'natural' or 'genuine' heirs, by which he meant heirs of the blood or rightful heirs (ii. 96, 130, 190; iv. 76; ii. 304). He also used *patrimonium*, which occurs only very rarely in records, quite frequently as a loose literary synonym for a paternal inheritance. Sometimes he deployed the word in a more pointed way to emphasise a claim in inheritance (ii. 122) or to contrast inheritance with acquisition (iii. 262; vi. 328–30, 402). But he could also use it very loosely and inconsequentially. See his comment that the refounder of Crowland Abbey, Thurketel, possessed 60 manors 'de patrimonio parentum suorum' (ii. 342). In a different vein compare Robert Curthose's promise to his followers of 'plurima quoque patrimoniis eorum augmenta' (ibid., iii. 102).

[124] *Durham Episcopal Charters 1071–1152*, ed. H. S. Offler (Surtees Soc., clxxix, 1968), no. 11.

[125] Ibid., no. 12.

[126] Grant by William Peverel of Dover, 1121–2, to his steward, Thurstan, 'tenendas in feodo et hereditate' (F. M. Stenton, *First Century of English Feudalism*, Oxford, 1961, 274; cf. *Regesta Regum Anglo-Normannorum*, ii., ed. C. Johnson and H. A. Cronne, Oxford, 1956, no. 1295). Grant by Osbert of Arden *c.* 1130 to Gerard and Nicholas, sons of Thomas 'in feudo et hereditate' (Stenton, *First Century*, p. 280). For a variant formula of land to be held 'jure hereditario' see the grant by William, earl of Lincoln, *c.* 1145 to

expectancy to which the heir had yet to succeed.[127] Men could be deprived of their hereditary lands and yet return to claim them.[128] Claim in hereditary title could be precluded from tenements held for life. In 1136–9 Theobald, archbishop of Canterbury, stated that the manor of Stisted had been violently usurped by John son of Anfrid after the death of his predecessor William of Corbeuil in 1136; John's father, Anfrid, had held the land at farm in the time of Archbishop Anselm and his son, said Theobald, never had *aliquam hereditatem sive aliquod feodum*.[129] That illustrates the violence which might lie behind the establishment of hereditary tenure. But it also contains in its denial a clear-cut notion of heritable title.

Who is speaking to us in these and similar passages? Here perhaps Theobald himself, but in the great majority of the documents we simply do not know. Very few are as specific as William de Briouze's charter of 1080 to St Florent-lès-Saumur which states that it was composed and drafted by Primaldus his clerk.[130] It must be allowed that the words and phrases which have made up the ammunition for my argument came immediately not from the authors of the acts from which they are drawn but from clerks, sometimes from beneficiaries, sometimes from superior authorities both lay and ecclesiastical. But that scarcely weakens the argument. Bishops and abbots were noblemen's brothers and cousins. And if it is argued, for example, that beneficiaries played a large part in the drafting of these documents then it follows that a large role must be given to all those monks of Norman and French houses who invaded England to establish the dependent cells which were the most immediate expression of the thanks which their secular patrons felt were due to God and the saints after the victory of 1066. Patron and beneficiary alike were familiar with the terms of Norman endowments. Hence it may be that these intricate concerns do not matter very much for the present argument.

There is finally one document, the greatest of them all, where there

---

Peter of Goxhill (*Documents illustrative of the social and economic history of the Danelaw*, ed. F. M. Stenton, British Academy, 1920, no. 490). See also a grant by Peter son of William *c.* 1125 to William son of Reinfrey and his heirs 'in feodo et hereditate', which illustrates the intimate connection between inheritance and lordship, with William son of Reinfrey and his heirs to hold in perpetuity 'quia ipse inde meus homo est' (*Sir Christopher Hatton's Book of Seals*, ed. L. C. Loyd and D. M. Stenton (Oxford, 1950), no. 528).

[127] Such is the implication of charters embodying the 'reddidisse' formula. For examples see Stenton, *First Century*, 272.

[128] *Charters of the Honour of Mowbray 1107–1191*, ed. D. E. Greenaway (British Academy, Records of Social and Economic History, new ser., I, 1972), no. 3, p. 10, discussed above, 5th ser., xxxii (1982), 211–12.

[129] A. Saltman, *Theobald Archbishop of Canterbury* (1956), 271–2.

[130] M. P. Marchegay, *Chartes normandes . . . de St. Florent*, 680.

is no doubt about who is speaking. The charter of liberties of Henry I has become something of a puzzle when set against all that has been written in recent years on the insecurity of title and inheritance. For just as private Anglo-Norman charters present tenure *in feodo et hereditate* fully grown, so Henry's charter projects a world in which all the incidents and trappings of such tenure were already in full operation. Rufus may have forced his vassals to ransom their lands, but the charter is clear evidence that there was a notion of a just and lawful relief applicable both to the king's barons and to their men, Widows were entitled to dower and marriage portions, and children, both male and female, might be in wardship. In the end the case can be left to depend on a single word. The central sentence of chapter 3 runs:

> And if when a baron or other man of mine dies a daughter remains as heir, I will give her with her land by the advice of my barons.

This assumes that in the ordinary course the heir would be known. Her identity was not determined by the king's court. It was recognised by the king's court by reference to a set of social conventions which had grown both within and outside it.[131] But it was from her husband to whom he gave her that the king took homage. That was the final recognition and warranty of title.[132] But how then could the king accept that the land might be described as *hers* not only before marriage but even before it had been decided to whom she might be married? In jurisdictional terms she had no title, yet the phrase is *cum terra sua*. That *sua* derived not from jurisdiction but from the social conventions within which the jurisdiction was set to work. These affected king and heiress alike. It is he who allows, not she who claims, that the land is 'hers'. They were at one.

The first known ancestor of the Cockfields, Lemmer, was to go by his name, Leofmaer, an Englishman. How he established himself among the Norman knightly tenants of Bury St Edmunds we can only guess. One thing is certain: as his descendants established their varied heritable title in the following generations they drew not only on the developing resources of the courts of the abbot and the king but also on notions which had deep roots in the Norman past. Without them the family's title deeds might have taken a very different form: *landbocs*, for example. But without them there might have been no Norman conquest.

[131] I do not intend to preclude here the possibility that in particular cases the king might adjudicate between the competing claims of heiresses or allocate and define the rights of seniority between co-heiresses.

[132] S. F. C. Milsom, 'Inheritance by women in the twelfth and early thirteenth centuries', *On the Laws and Customs of England*, ed. M. S. Arnold, T. A. Green, S. A. Scully, S. D. White (Chapel Hill, N.C., 1981), 60–89, esp. 62–5.

Note

In all that has been written of the enfeoffment of the King William's knight, Peter, by Abbot Baldwin of Bury St Edmunds, it has been assumed rather too easily that the sole piece of documentary evidence, of which the earliest copy comes from the late thirteenth century, is a standard charter of enfeoffment as such were known in the late eleventh century.[133] This is not so. The document has some of the characteristics of a notification, but whether it was intended as more than a memorandum for the abbot and convent is an open question. Stenton, who described it as a 'memorandum', was properly cautious of such a 'ill-drafted record'.[134] Moreover, the wording, even if assumed to be an accurate record to an authentic eleventh-century original, can scarcely bear the construction which it has been made to carry. It is difficult to follow Douglas in arguing that it reflects the supervision of local feudal institutions by the king or that the king was here endowing one of his followers.[135] The document simply seeks to define the duties of a vassal of the abbot who was also in the service of the king. The interpretation frequently placed on it, that it provides evidence that feudal military service was ill-defined in the generations following the Conquest is insubstantial, for the simple reason that the document does not clearly state, as has been claimed, that Peter was to serve 'within the kingdom with three or four knights'.[136] It is better construed as follows:

> If, before he is summoned on behalf of the king, he is summoned on behalf of the abbot, Peter promises to serve within the realm in keeping guard, either before or after the royal campaign, with three or four knights at his own expense. If, as the abbot's attorney, he pleads within the realm he shall be sustained at his own expense. But if the abbot takes him with him anywhere, it shall be at the abbot's expense. In addition to this he shall provide a knight as the abbot's own, within or without the realm, where and when the abbot wishes to have one.

Read thus, the service of three or four knights, which has occasioned so much discussion because of its vagueness, must be taken to refer to service *in custodia* not *in expeditione*. Moreover, the document can now be seen to face up not only to the problem of arranging the feudal

[133] D. C. Douglas, 'A Charter of Enfeoffment under William the Conqueror', *E.H.R.*, xlii (1929), 245; cf. *Feudal Documents of Bury St. Edmunds*, 15; C. W. Hollister, *The Military Organisation of Norman England* (Oxford, 1965), 50–2; R. A. Brown, *Origins of English Feudalism* (1973), 90, 138.

[134] Stenton, *First Century*, 154, 170.

[135] 'A Charter of Enfeoffment', 246.

[136] R. A. Brown, *Origins*, 138.

service of a vassal who was also a royal knight, but also to the stark fact that no feudal lord could expect personal service *in custodia* and *in expeditione* at one and the same time. The document does not define service *in expeditione*, presumably because Peter would then be in the king's not the abbot's service. It may be that the final sentence was aimed at repairing this deficiency.

THE ROYAL HISTORICAL SOCIETY

REPORT OF COUNCIL, SESSION 1982–1983

THE Council of the Royal Historical Society has the honour to present the following report to the Anniversary Meeting.

A conference on 'Crime and Punishment' was held at the University of Kent at Canterbury from 16 to 18 September 1982. The papers read were:

'The Origins of the Crime of Conspiracy', by Professor A. Harding.
'Crime, Punishment, and Social Control in Late Medieval English Towns', by Mr A.F. Butcher.
'Riot prevention and control in early Stuart London', by Dr K.J. Lindley.
'Sir John Fielding and the problem of criminal investigation in eighteenth-century England', by Mr J.A. Styles.
'The New Police, Crime and People in England and Wales, 1829–1888', by Dr D.J.V. Jones.

Thirty-seven members of the Society and seventeen guests attended. A private visit to Canterbury Cathedral on 16 September was followed by a joint reception given by the Mayor of Canterbury and the Dean. The University of Kent gave a reception on 17 September. The next conference will be held at Winchester from 14 to 18 July 1986 to mark the 900th aniversary of Domesday Book.

An evening party was held for members and guests at University College London on Wednesday 7 July 1982 for which 147 acceptances were received.

The representation of the Society upon various bodies was as follows: Professor F.M.L. Thompson and Mr A.T. Milne on the Joint-Anglo American Committee exercising a general supervision over the production of the *Bibliographies of British History*; Professor G.W.S. Barrow, Dr P. Chaplais, Mr M. Roper and Professor P.H. Sawyer on the Joint Committee of the Society and the British Academy established to prepare an edition of Anglo-Saxon charters; Professor E.B. Fryde on a committee to regulate British co-operation in the preparation of a new repertory of medieval sources to replace Potthast's *Bibliotheca Historica Medii Aevi*; Professor H.R. Loyn on a committee to promote the publication of photographic records of the more significant collections of British coins; Professor H.G. Koenigsberger on the Advisory Council on the Export of Works of Art; the President and Professor J.J. Scarisbrick on the British National Committee of the International Historical Congress; Dr G.H. Martin on the Council of the British Records Association; Mr M.R.D. Foot on the

Committee to advise the publishers of *The Annual Register*; Professor K. Cameron on the Lincoln Archaeological Trust; Professor C.J. Holdsworth on History at the Universities Defence Group, and Dr C.R.J. Currie on the British Standards Institution Sub-Committee for drafting a new British standard (now completed) for citing unpublished documents by bibliographical references. Council received reports from its representatives.

Professor W.N. Medlicott represents the Society on the Court of the University of Exeter, Professor J.A.S. Grenville on the Court of the University of Birmingham, Professor Glanmor Williams on the Court of the University College of Swansea; Professor C.N.L. Brooke on the British Sub-Commission of the Commission Internationale d'Histoire Ecclésiastique Comparée, and Dr A.I. Doyle has been appointed to represent the Society on the newly-established Anthony Panizzi Foundation.

As in the previous year, Council had to consider a number of questions of public policy. Representations were made concerning the National Heritage Act, and the Data Protection and Public Records (Amendment) Bills (struck down by the Dissolution of Parliament). Amendments incorporated in the National Heritage Act met a number of Council's points. Council protested to the Greater London Council against projected cuts in the budget of the Survey of London. Council submitted written evidence to the House of Commons Select Committee on Arts, Science and Education about the Government's response to the Wilson Report on Public Records. Council again asserted its opposition to charges imposed on users in the Gloucestershire and North Yorkshire county record offices, as well as to the fee imposed upon non-Oxonian users of the Bodleian Library. The Honorary Secretary attended a conference on 'Access to Records' organised by the Records Users' Group and the British Association for Local History, when the possibility of formulating a national policy for archives was mooted.

In order to encourage the study of history in schools, Council instituted prizes of £25 for the best performance at A-level in each of the 10 examining boards in the United Kingdom, to be awarded for the first time in 1983. In view of the enhanced value of the Whitfield Prize (awarded annually) and to encourage young historians Council decided to widen the field, opening it to any work of English or Welsh history published in the United Kingdom by an author under 40 years of age: the first award will be made for a book published in 1983.

The Vice-Presidents retiring under By-law XVI were Professor J.H. Burns and Dr R.F. Hunnisett. Professor R. Ashton and Professor H.R. Loyn were elected to replace them. The members of Council retiring under By-law XIX were Professor J.D. Hargreaves, Dr G.H. Martin,

Professor J.J. Scarisbrick and Professor P. Smith. Dr M.T. Clanchy, Professor A. Harding, Dr K.O. Morgan and Professor W.R. Ward were elected to fill the vacancies. Messrs Beeby, Harmar and Co. were appointed auditors for the year 1982–83 under By-law XXXVIII.

Publications and Papers read

Transactions, Fifth Series, volume 33 and *Texts and Calendars II, 1957–1982* (Guides and Handbooks series, no. 12) went to press during the session and are due to be published in early November 1983. The following works were published during the session: *The Devonshire Diary: Memoranda on State of Affairs 1759–1762* (Camden Fourth Series, volume 27); *Barrington Family Letters 1628–1632* (Camden Fourth Series, volume 28); the *Annual Bibliography of British and Irish History* (1981 publications); and six volumes in the STUDIES IN HISTORY series: *Estate Management in Eighteenth-Century England*, by J.R. Wordie (volume 30); *Merchant Shipping and War*, by M. Doughty (volume 31); *Faith by Statute: Parliament and the Settlement of Religion 1559*, by N. Jones (volume 32); *Britain, Greece and the Politics of Sanctions: Ethiopia 1935–1936*, by James Barros (volume 33); *Heresy and Reformation in South-East England, 1520–1529*, by J. Davis (volume 34); *Law, Litigants and the Legal Profession*, by E. Ives and T. Manchester (volume 36).

At the ordinary meetings of the Society the following papers were read:

'History and the Irish Question', by Dr R.F. Foster (15 October 1982).

'The Social Context of the Templars', by Dr M.C. Barber (4 February 1983).

'Early Nineteenth-Century Reactions to Benthamism', by Dr J.R. Dinwiddy (18 March 1983).

'Justice, Authority and the Creation of the Ancien Régime in Italy', by Dr Judith A. Hook (22 April 1983).

'The myth of Norman efficiency', by Professor W.L. Warren (6 July 1983: Prothero Lecture).

At the Anniversary Meeting on 26 November 1982, the President, Professor J.C. Holt, delivered an address on 'Feudal Society and the Family in early medieval England: II: Notions of Patrimony'.

The Alexander Prize was awarded to Mr A.G. Rosser for his essay 'The essence of medieval urban communities: the vill of Westminster 1200–1540', which was read on 20 May 1983.

The Whitfield Prize was awarded to Dr Norman Jones for his *Faith by Statute: Parliament and the Settlement of Religion 1559*.

Membership

Council records with regret the deaths of Professor A. Sapori, a Corresponding Fellow, and of 17 Fellows and 1 Associate. Among these Council would mention especially Professor D.C. Douglas, a former Vice-President, Sir Michael Postan, Professor R.B. Pugh and Professor Dorothy Whitelock, former members of Council. The resignations of 8 Fellows, 6 Associates and 17 Subscribing Libraries were received. 52 Fellows and 5 Associates were elected and 3 Libraries were admitted. One Library was reinstated. The membership of the Society on 30 June 1983 comprised 1,479 Fellows (including 77 Life Fellows and 97 Retired Fellows), 37 Corresponding Fellows, 163 Associates and 738 Subscribing Libraries (1,452, 38, 165, 751 respectively on 30 June 1982). The Society exchanged publications with 12 societies, British and foreign.

Finance

In a year of continued uncertainty in the markets and generally falling interest rates there was a modest fall in overall income and only minor changes were made in the Society's investments. A gradual improvement in income from royalties on the sale of the Society's publications, particularly the *Annual Bibliography*, is evident. Slight rescheduling of the publications programme for the year kept expenditure under this heading broadly in line with subscription income for the year, in accordance with Council's policy, and also contributed to the substantial fall in overall expenditure.

A final contribution from the estate of the late Andrew Browning, in the form of a payment of back tax by the Inland Revenue of more than £17,000 on the residual estate, came as a welcome addition to the Sinking Fund.

ROYAL HISTORICAL SOCIETY

Balance Sheet as at 30 June 1983

30.6.82 £	£	£	ACCUMULATED FUNDS	£	£	£
			General Funds			
	96,235		As at 1 July 1982		102,353	
	6,118		*Add* Excess of Income over Expenditure		8,024	
	102,353				110,377	
102,353	—		*Less* Loss of sale of Investments		1,772	108,605
			Sir George Prothero Bequest			
	16,043		As at 1 July 1982		16,043	
16,043	—		*Less* Loss on sale of Investments		149	15,894
			Reddaway Fund			
5,000			As at 1 July 1982			5,000
			Andrew Browning Fund			
	85,945		As at 1 July 1982		85,945	
85,945	—		*Less* Loss on sale of Investments		5,783	80,162
			Sinking Fund			
	63,568		As at 1 July 1982		67,215	
	—		Addition to Fund—Inland Revenue Tax Claim 1975/82		17,008	
	3,647		*Add* Interest, Dividends and Tax recoverable		6,465	
	—		*Add* Surplus on sale of Investments		2,979	
			Transfer from Miss E. M. Robinson Bequest—			
67,215	—		accumulated income		17,256	110,923
			Miss E. M. Robinson Bequest			
	32,425		As at 1 July 1982		36,027	
	3,602		*Add* Interest, Dividends and Tax recoverable		2,692	
	36,027				38,719	
36,027	—		*Less* Transfer to Sinking Fund		17,256	21,463
			A. S. Whitfield Prize Fund			
	11,020		As at 1 July 1982		11,347	
	927		*Add* Interest, Dividends and Tax recoverable		795	
	11,947				12,142	
		600	*Less* Prize Awarded	600		
11,347	600	—	*Less* Loss on sale of Investments	1,370	1,970	10,172
			Studies in History Account			
	13,931		As at 1 July 1982		12,658	
	650		Contributions received in year		400	
	1,531		Interest received		1,047	
	60		Royalties received		2,519	
	16,172				16,624	
12,658	3,514		*Less* Expenditure		3,086	13,538
£336,588						£365,757
			REPRESENTED BY:			
			Investments			
	239,746		Quoted Securities—at cost		264,383	
			Market Values £475,646 (1982: £322,757)			
	5,424		Local Authority Bond		—	
	50,500		Money at Call		77,000	
295,901	231		Due from Stockbrokers		395	341,778
			Current Assets			
			Balances at Bank:			
	8,797		Current Accounts	11,138		
	62,528		Deposit Accounts	54,202		
	23		Cash in hand	—		
	5,427		Income Tax repayable	2,004		
	811		Payments and Accruals in advance	434		
	—		Sundry Debtors	15		
82,146	4,560		Stock of Paper in hand	2,142	69,935	

contd

£	£	£		£	£	£
			Less Current Liabilities			
		3,410	Subscriptions in advance	4,967		
		453	Conference receipts in advance	—		
		1,719	Sundry Creditors	4,893		
		—	Sundry Accruals	46		
40,687	41,459	35,877	Provision for Publications in hand	36,050	45,956	23,979
£336,588						£365,757

ROYAL HISTORICAL SOCIETY

Income & Expenditure Account for the Year Ended 30 June 1983

30.6.82 £	£		£	£	£
		INCOME			
	598	Subscriptions for 1982/83: Associates		593	
	10,152	Libraries		10,478	
23,377	12,627	Fellows		13,060	24,131
		(The Society also had 77 Life Fellows at 30 June 1983)			
1,008		Tax recovered on Covenanted Subscriptions			1,215
1,738		Arrears of Subscriptions received in year			1,658
27,291		Interest and Dividends received and Tax recovered			24,633
931		Royalties and Reproduction Fees			903
1,259		Donations and Sundry Receipts			2,073
£55,604					£54,613
		EXPENDITURE			
		Secretarial and Administrative Expenses			
	12,406	Salaries, Pension contributions and National Insurance		13,442	
	1,037	General Printing and Stationery		2,061	
	2,188	Postage, Telephone and Sundries		2,126	
	1,029	Accountancy and Audit		1,075	
	854	Office Equipment		568	
	254	Insurance		260	
18,777	1,009	Meetings and Conference Expenses (Net Cost)		1,564	21,096
		Publications			
	540	Directors' Expenses		405	
		Publishing Costs in year:			
		Transactions, Fifth Series, Vol. 32	9,815		
		Camden, Fourth Series, Vol. 26	110		
		Camden, Fourth Series, Vol. 27	7,009		
		Camden, Fourth Series, Vol. 28	8,808		
			25,742		
	(4,709)	*Less* Provision made 30 June 1982	8,900	16,842	
		Provision for Publications in progress:			
		Transactions, Fifth Series, Vol. 33	9,600		
		Guides and Handbooks No. 10, Vol 2	14,850		
		Texts and Calendars II	11,600		
	33,350		36,050		
	—	*Less* Provision made 30 June 1982	24,450	11,600	
	3,135	*Handbook of Dates* (reprint)		—	
		Preparation of *Annual Bibliography*	1,214		
	(537)	*Less* Royalties received	(2,352)	(1,138)	
	245	Storage and Insurance of Stock		576	
	—	Advertising		15	
	32,024	*Carried forward*		28,300	

30.6.82 £	£	EXPENDITURE (contd.)	£	£
		Brought forward		
29,285	2,739	*Less* Sales of Publications	4,318	23,982
		LIBRARY AND ARCHIVES		
	1,136	Purchase of Books and Publications	1,395	
	38	Library Assistance	32	
	1,174		1,427	
1,174	—	*Less* Sale of Books	100	1,327
		OTHER CHARGES		
	143	Alexander Prize and Medal	73	
	32	Subscriptions to other bodies	36	
250	75	Prothero Lecture fee	75	184
£49,486				£46,589
55,604		TOTAL INCOME		54,613
49,486		TOTAL EXPENDITURE		46,589
£6,118		EXCESS OF INCOME OVER EXPENDITURE FOR THE YEAR		£8,024

J. C. HOLT, *President.*
C. J. KITCHING, *Treasurer.*

We have examined the foregoing Balance Sheet and Income and Expenditure Account which have been prepared under the Historical Cost Convention with the books and vouchers of the Society. We have verified the Investments and Bank Balances appearing in the Balance Sheet. In our opinion the foregoing Balance Sheet and Income and Expenditure Account are properly drawn up so as to exhibit a true and fair view of the state of affairs of the Society according to the best of our information and the explanation given to us and as shown by the books of the Society.

BEEBY, HARMAR & CO.,
Chartered Accountants

79 Leonard Street,
London, EC2A 4QS.
11th July 1983

THE DAVID BERRY TRUST

Receipts and Payments Account for the Year Ended 30 June 1983

30.6.82 £	£	RECEIPTS	£	£
		Balances in Hand 1 July 1982:		
		Cash at Bank:		
	3	Current Account	2	
	639	Deposit Account	856	
1,172	530	483.63 Shares Charities Official Investment Fund	530	1,388
	136	Dividends on Investment per Charity Commissioners	149	
216	80	Interest on Deposit Account	68	
			217	
—		Bank Charge refunded	1	218
£1,388				£1,606

30.6.82 £	£	PAYMENTS	£	£
—		Examiner's Fee		15
		Balances in Hand 30 June 1983:		
		Cash at Bank:		
	2	Current Account	3	
	856	Deposit Account	1,073	
	530	483.63 Shares Charities Official Investment Fund at cost (Market Value 30.6.83—£1,118)	530	
	1,388		1,606	
1,388	—	*Less* Due to Royal Historical Society	15	1,591
£1,388				£1,606

We have examined the above account with the books and vouchers of the Trust and find it to be in accordance therewith.

BEEBY, HARMAR & CO.,
Chartered Accountants

79 Leonard Street,
London, EC2A 4QS.
11th July 1983

The late David Berry, by his will dated 23rd day of April 1926, left £1,000 to provide in every three years a gold medal and prize money for the best essay on the Earl of Bothwell or, at the discretion of the Trustees, on Scottish History of the James Stuarts I to VI, in memory of his father, the late Rev. David Berry.

The Trust is regulated by a scheme sanctioned by the Chancery Division of the High Court of Justice dated 23rd day of January 1930, and made in an action 1927 A1233 David Anderson Berry deceased, Hunter and another *v.* Robertson and another and since modified by an order of the Charity Commissioners made on 11th January 1978, removing the necessity to provide a medal.

The Royal Historical Society is now the Trustee. The Investment held on Capital Account consists of 634 Charities Official Investment Fund Shares (Market Value £1,466).

The Trustee will in every second year of the three-year period advertise, inviting essays.

ALEXANDER PRIZE

The Alexander Prize was established in 1897 by L. C. Alexander, F.R.Hist.S. It consists of a silver medal awarded annually for an essay upon some historical subject. Candidates may select their own subject provided such subject has been previously submitted to and approved by the Literary Director. The essay must be a genuine work of original research, not hitherto published, and one which has not been awarded any other prize. It must not exceed 6,000 words in length and must be sent in on or before 1 November of any year. The detailed regulations should be obtained in advance from the Secretary.

LIST OF ALEXANDER PRIZE ESSAYISTS (1898–1983)[1]

1898. F. Hermia Durham ('The relations of the Crown to trade under James I').
1899. W. F. Lord, BA ('The development of political parties during the reign of Queen Anne').
1901. Laura M. Roberts ('The Peace of Lunéville').
1902. V. B. Redstone ('The social condition of England during the Wars of the Roses').
1903. Rose Graham ('The intellectual influence of English monasticism between the tenth and the twelfth centuries').
1904. Enid W. G. Routh ('The balance of power in the seventeenth century').
1905. W. A. P. Mason, MA ('The beginnings of the Cistercian Order').
1906. Rachel R. Reid, MA ('The Rebellion of the Earls, 1569').
1908. Kate Hotblack ('The Peace of Paris, 1763').
1909. Nellie Nield, MA ('The social and economic condition of the unfree classes in England in the twelfth and thirteenth centuries').
1912. H. G. Richardson ('The parish clergy of the thirteenth and fourteenth centuries').
1917. Isobel D. Thornely, BA ('The treason legislation of 1531–1534').
1918. T. F. T. Plucknett, BA ('The place of the Council in the fifteenth century').
1919. Edna F. White, MA ('The jurisdiction of the Privy Council under the Tudors').
1920. J. E. Neale, MA ('The Commons Journals of the Tudor Period').
1922. Eveline C. Martin ('The English establishments on the Gold Coast in the second half of the eighteenth century').
1923. E. W. Hensman, MA ('The Civil War of 1648 in the east midlands').
1924. Grace Stretton, BA ('Some aspects of mediæval travel').
1925. F. A. Mace, MA ('Devonshire ports in the fourteenth and fifteenth centuries').
1926. Marian J. Tooley, MA ('The authorship of the *Defensor Pacis*').

[1] No award was made in 1900, 1907, 1910, 1911, 1913, 1914, 1921, 1946, 1948, 1956, 1969, 1975, and 1977. The Prize Essays for 1909 and 1919 were not published in the *Transactions*. No Essays were submitted in 1915, 1916 and 1943.

1927. W. A. Pantin, BA ('Chapters of the English Black Monks, 1215–1540').
1928. Gladys A. Thornton, BA, PhD ('A study in the history of Clare, Suffolk, with special reference to its development as a borough').
1929. F. S. Rodkey, AM, PhD ('Lord Palmerston's policy for the rejuvenation of Turkey, 1839–47').
1930. A. A. Ettinger, DPhil ('The proposed Anglo-Franco-American Treaty of 1852 to guarantee Cuba to Spain').
1931. Kathleen A. Walpole, MA ('The humanitarian movement of the early nineteenth century to remedy abuses on emigrant vessels to America').
1932. Dorothy M. Brodie, BA ('Edmund Dudley, minister of Henry VII').
1933. R. W. Southern, BA ('Ranulf Flambard and early Anglo-Norman administration').
1934. S. B. Chrimes, MA, PhD ('Sir John Fortescue and his theory of dominion').
1935. S. T. Bindoff, MA ('The unreformed diplomatic service, 1812–60').
1936. Rosamund J. Mitchell, MA, BLitt ('English students at Padua, 1460–1475').
1937. C. H. Philips, BA ('The East India Company "Interest", and the English Government, 1783–4').
1938. H. E. I. Philips, BA ('The last years of the Court of Star Chamber, 1630–41').
1939. Hilda P. Grieve, BA ('The deprived married clergy in Essex, 1553–61').
1940. R. Somerville, MA ('The Duchy of Lancaster Council and Court of Duchy Chamber').
1941. R. A. L. Smith, MA, PhD ('The *Regimen Scaccarii* in English monasteries').
1942. F. L. Carsten, DPhil ('Medieval democracy in the Brandenburg towns and its defeat in the fifteenth century').
1944. Rev. E. W. Kemp, BD ('Pope Alexander III and the canonization of saints').
1945. Helen Suggett, BLitt ('The use of French in England in the later middle ages').
1947. June Milne, BA ('The diplomacy of John Robinson at the court of Charles XII of Sweden, 1697–1709').
1949. Ethel Drus, MA ('The attitude of the Colonial Office to the annexation of Fiji').
1950. Doreen J. Milne, MA, PhD ('The results of the Rye House Plot, and their influence upon the Revolution of 1688').
1951. K. G. Davies, BA ('The origins of the commission system in the West India trade').
1952. G. W. S. Barrow, BLitt ('Scottish rulers and the religious orders, 1070–1153').
1953. W. E. Minchinton, BSc (Econ) ('Bristol—metropolis of the west in the eighteenth century').
1954. Rev. L. Boyle, OP ('The *Oculus Sacerdotis* and some other works of William of Pagula').
1955. G. F. E. Rudé, MA, PhD ('The Gordon riots: a study of the rioters and their victims').
1957. R. F. Hunnisett, MA, DPhil ('The origins of the office of Coroner').
1958. Thomas G. Barnes, AB, DPhil ('County politics and a puritan *cause célèbre*: Somerset churchales, 1633').

1959. Alan Harding, BLitt ('The origins and early history of the Keeper of the Peace').
1960. Gwyn A. Williams, MA, PhD ('London and Edward I').
1961. M. H. Keen, BA ('Treason trials under the law of arms').
1962. G. W. Monger, MA, PhD ('The end of isolation: Britain, Germany and Japan, 1900–1902').
1963. J. S. Moore, BA ('The Domesday teamland: a reconsideration').
1964. M. Kelly, PhD ('The submission of the clergy').
1965. J. J. N. Palmer, BLitt ('Anglo-French negotiations, 1390–1396').
1966. M. T. Clanchy, MA, PhD ('The Franchise of Return of Writs').
1967. R. Lovatt, MA, DPhil, PhD ('The *Imitation of Christ* in late medieval England').
1968. M. G. A. Vale, MA, DPhil ('The last years of English Gascony, 1451–1453').
1970. Mrs Margaret Bowker, MA, BLitt ('The Commons Supplication against the Ordinaries in the light of some Archidiaconal Acta').
1971. C. Thompson, MA ('The origins of the politics of the Parliamentary middle groups, 1625–1629').
1972. I. d'Alton, BA ('Southern Irish Unionism: A study of Cork City and County Unionists, 1884–1914').
1973. C. J. Kitching, BA, PhD ('The quest for concealed lands in the reign of Elizabeth I').
1974. H. Tomlinson, BA ('Place and Profit: an Examination of the Ordnance Office, 1660–1714').
1976. B. Bradshaw, MA, BD ('Cromwellian reform and the origins of the Kildare rebellion, 1533–34').
1978. C. J. Ford, BA ('Piracy or Policy: The Crisis in the Channel, 1400–1403').
1979. P. Dewey, BA, PhD ('Food Production and Policy in the United Kingdom, 1914–1918').
1980. Ann L. Hughes, BA, PhD ('Militancy and Localism: Warwickshire Politics and Westminster Politics, 1643–1647').
1981. C. J. Tyerman, MA ('Marino Sanudo Torsello and the Lost Crusade: Lobbying in the Fourteenth Century').
1982. E. Powell, BA, DPhil ('Arbitration and the Law in England in the Late Middle Ages').
1983. A. G. Rosser, MA ('The essence of medieval urban communities: the vill of Westminster 1200–1540').

DAVID BERRY PRIZE

The David Berry Prize was established in 1929 by David Anderson-Berry in memory of his father, the Reverend David Berry. It consists of a money prize awarded every three years for Scottish history. Candidates may select any subject dealing with Scottish history within the reigns of James I to James VI inclusive, provided such subject has been previously submitted to and approved by the Council of the Royal Historical Society. The essay must be a genuine work of original research not hitherto published, and one which has not been awarded any other prize. The essay should be between 6,000 and 10,000 words, excluding footnotes and appendices. It must be sent in on or before 31 October 1985.

LIST OF DAVID BERRY PRIZE ESSAYISTS (1937–76)[1]

1937. G. Donaldson, MA ('The polity of the Scottish Reformed Church *c.* 1460–1580, and the rise of the Presbyterian movement').

1943. Rev. Prof. A. F. Scott Pearson, DTh, DLitt ('Anglo-Scottish religious relations, 1400–1600').

1949. T. Bedford Franklin, MA, FRSE ('Monastic agriculture in Scotland, 1440–1600').

1955. W. A. McNeill, MA ('"Estaytt" of the king's rents and pensions, 1621').

1958. Prof. Maurice Lee, PhD ('Maitland of Thirlestane and the foundation of the Stewart despotism in Scotland').

1964. M. H. Merriman ('Scottish collaborators with England during the Anglo-Scottish war, 1543–1550').

1967. Miss M. H. B. Sanderson ('Catholic recusancy in Scotland in the sixteenth century').

1970. Athol Murray, MA, LLB, PhD ('The Comptroller, 1425–1610').

1973. J. Kirk, MA, PhD ('Who were the Melvillians: A study in the Personnel and Background of the Presbyterian Movement in late Sixteenth-century Scotland').

1976. A. Grant, BA, DPhil ('The Development of the Scottish Peerage').

[1] No essays were submitted in 1940 and 1979. No award was made in 1946, 1952, 1961 and 1982.

WHITFIELD PRIZE

The Whitfield Prize was established by Council in 1976 as a money prize of £400 out of the bequest of the late Professor Archibald Stenton Whitfield: in May 1981 Council increased the prize to £600. Until 1982 the prize was awarded annually to the STUDIES IN HISTORY series. From 1983 the prize, value £600, will be awarded annually to the best work of English or Welsh history by an author under 40 years of age, published in the United Kingdom. The award will be made by Council in the Spring of each year in respect of works published in the preceding calendar year. Authors or publishers should send one copy (non-returnable) of a book eligible for the competition to the Society to arrive not later than 31 December of any year.

LIST OF WHITFIELD PRIZE WINNERS (1977–1982)

1977. K. D. Brown, MA, PhD (*John Burns*).
1978. Marie Axton, MA, PhD (*The Queen's Two Bodies: Drama and the Elizabethan Succession*).
1979. Patricia Crawford, MA, PhD (*Denzil Holles, 1598–1680: A study of his Political Career*).
1980. D. L. Rydz (*The Parliamentary Agents: A History*).
1981. Scott M. Harrison (*The Pilgrimage of Grace in the Lake Counties 1536–7*).
1982. Norman L. Jones (*Faith by Statute: Parliament and the Settlement of Religion 1559*).

THE ROYAL HISTORICAL SOCIETY

(INCORPORATED BY ROYAL CHARTER)

OFFICERS AND COUNCIL—1982

Patron
HER MAJESTY THE QUEEN

President
PROFESSOR J. C. HOLT, MA, DPhil, FBA, FSA.

Honorary Vice-Presidents

Professor C. R. Cheney, MA, DLitt, LittD, FBA.
Professor A. G. Dickens, CMG, MA, DLit, DLitt, LittD, FBA, FSA.
Professor G. R. Elton, MA, PhD, LittD, DLitt, DLitt, DLit, FBA.
Professor P. Grierson, MA, LittD, FBA, FSA.
Sir John Habakkuk, MA, FBA.
Professor Sir Keith Hancock, KBE, MA, DLitt, FBA.
Professor D. Hay, MA, DLitt, FBA.
Professor R. A. Humphreys, OBE, MA, PhD, DLitt, LittD, DLitt, DUniv.
Miss Kathleen Major, MA, BLitt, LittD, FBA, FSA.
The Hon Sir Steven Runciman, MA, DPhil, LLD, LittD, DLitt, LitD, DD.
Sir Richard Southern, MA, DLitt, LittD, DLitt, FBA.
Professor C. H. Wilson, CBE, MA, LittD, DLitt, DLitt, DLitt, FBA.

Vice-Presidents

Professor J. H. Burns, MA, PhD.
R. F. Hunnisett, MA, DPhil.
Professor R. L. Storey, MA, PhD.
Professor Glanmor Williams, MA, DLitt.
Professor P. H. Sawyer, MA.
K. V. Thomas, MA, FBA.
Professor G. W. S. Barrow, MA, BLitt, DLitt, FBA, FRSE.
Professor H. G. Koenigsberger, MA, PhD.

Council

PROFESSOR J. D. HARGREAVES, MA.
G. H. MARTIN, MA, DPhil.
PROFESSOR J. J. SCARISBRICK, MA, PhD.
PROFESSOR P. SMITH, MA, DPhil.
P. F. CLARKE, MA, PhD.
G. L. HARRISS, MA, DPhil.
PROFESSOR RAGNHILD M. HATTON, PhD.
PROFESSOR K. G. ROBBINS, MA, DPhil.
U.P. BURKE, MA.
PROFESSOR R. B. DOBSON, MA, DPhil.
PROFESSOR G. S. HOLMES, MA, DLitt.
PROFESSOR D. E. LUSCOMBE, MA, PhD.
PROFESSOR H. HEARDER, BA, PhD.
PROFESSOR C. J. HOLDSWORTH, MA, PhD, FSA.
PROFESSOR OLWEN HUFTON, BA, PhD.
MISS S. M. G. REYNOLDS, MA.

Honorary Secretary

PROFESSOR M. H. PORT, MA, BLitt, FSA.

Literary Director

I. ROY, MA, DPhil.

Assistant Literary Director

D. E. GREENWAY, MA, PhD.

Honorary Treasurer

C. J. KITCHING, BA, PhD, FSA.

Honorary Librarian

A. G. WATSON, MA, DLit, BLitt, FSA.

Honorary Solicitor

PROFESSOR R. M. GOODE, LLD.

Executive Secretary

MRS J. CHAPMAN.

Library and Offices

University College London, Gower Street, London WC1E 6BT.

Bankers

Barclay's Bank P.L.C.

STANDING COMMITTEES 1982

Finance Committee

PROFESSOR D. C. COLEMAN, BSc(Econ.), PhD, FBA.
P. J. C. FIRTH.
PROFESSOR H. R. LOYN, MA, FBA, FSA.
DR. G. H. MARTIN.
K. V. THOMAS.
And the Officers.

Publications Committee

DR. P. F. CLARKE.
C. R. ELRINGTON, MA, FSA
DR. G. L. HARRISS.
PROFESSOR RAGNHILD HATTON.
PROFESSOR C. J. HOLDSWORTH.
PROFESSOR OLWEN HUFTON.
PROFESSOR J. R. POLE, MA, PhD.
PROFESSOR K. ROBBINS.
And the Officers.

Library Committee

PROFESSOR J. H. BURNS.
PROFESSOR P. COLLINSON, MA, PhD, FBA.
PROFESSOR D. E. LUSCOMBE.
PROFESSOR P. SMITH, MA, DPhil.
And the Officers.

LIST OF FELLOWS OF THE ROYAL HISTORICAL SOCIETY

Names of Officers and Honorary Vice-Presidents are printed in capitals. Those marked have compounded for their annual subscriptions.*

Abbott, A. W., CMG, CBE, Frithys Orchard, West Clandon, Surrey.
Abramsky, Professor Chimen A., MA, Dept of Hebrew and Jewish Studies, University College London, Gower Street, London WC1E 6BT.
Abulafia, D. S. H., MA, PhD, Gonville and Caius College, Cambridge CB2 1TA.
Adair, Professor J. E., MA, PhD, Newlands Cottage, 41 Pewley Hill, Guildford, Surrey.
Adam, Professor R. J., MA, Easter Wayside, Hepburn Gardens, St Andrews KY16 9LP.
Adamthwaite, Professor A. P., BA, PhD, Dept of History, The University, Loughborough LE11 3TU.
Addison, P., MA, DPhil, Dept of History, The University, William Robertson Building, George Square, Edinburgh EH8 9JY.
Akrigg, Professor G. P. V., BA, PhD, FRSC, 4633 West 8th Avenue, Vancouver, B.C., V6R 2A6, Canada.
Alcock, Professor L., MA, FSA, 29 Hamilton Drive, Glasgow G12 8DN.
Alder, G. J., BA, PhD, Dept of History, The University, Whiteknights, Reading RG6 2AA.
Alderman, G., MA, DPhil, 172 Colindeep Lane, London NW9 6EA.
Allan, D. G. C., MSc(Econ), PhD, c/o Royal Society of Arts, John Adam Street, London WC2N 6EZ.
Allen, D. F., BA, PhD, School of History, The University, P.O. Box 363, Birmingham B15 2TT.
Allen, D. H., BA, PhD, 105 Tuddenham Avenue, Ipswich, Suffolk IP4 2HG.
Allmand, C. T., MA, DPhil, FSA, 111 Menlove Avenue, Liverpool L18 3HP.
Alsop, J. D., MA, PhD, School of History, The University, P.O. Box 147, Liverpool L69 3BX.
Altholz, Professor J., PhD, Dept of History, University of Minnesota, 614 Social Sciences Building, Minneapolis, Minn. 55455, U.S.A.
Altschul, Professor M., PhD, Case Western Reserve University, Cleveland, Ohio 44106, U.S.A.
Anderson, Professor M. S., MA, PhD, London School of Economics, Houghton Street, London WC2A 2AE.
Anderson, Mrs O. R., MA, BLitt, Westfield College, London NW3 7ST.
Anderson, Miss S. P., MA, BLitt, 17–19 Chilworth Street, London W2 3QU.
Andrew, C. M., MA, PhD, Corpus Christi College, Cambridge CB2 1RH.
Anglesey, The Most Hon., The Marquess of, FSA, FRSL, Plas-Newydd, Llanfairpwll, Anglesey LL61 6DZ.
Anglo, Professor S., BA PhD, FSA, Dept of History of Ideas, University College, Swansea SA2 8PP.
Annan, Lord, OBE, MA, DLitt, DUniv, 16 St John's Wood Road, London NW8 8RE.

Annis, P. G. W., BA, 65 Longlands Road, Sidcup, Kent DA15 7LQ.
Appleby, J. S., Little Pitchbury, Brick Kiln Lane, Great Horkesley, Colchester, Essex CO6 4EU
Armstrong, Miss A. M., BA, 7 Vale Court, Mallord Street, London SW3.
Armstrong, C. A. J., MA, FSA, Gayhurst, Lincombe Lane, Boars Hill, Oxford OX1 5DZ.
Armstrong, Professor F. H., PhD, University of Western Ontario, London 72, Ontario, Canada.
Armstrong, W A., BA, PhD, Eliot College, The University, Canterbury, Kent CT2 7NS.
Arnstein, Professor W. L., PhD, Dept of History, University of Illinois at Urbana-Champaign, 309 Gregory Hall, Urbana, Ill. 61801, U.S.A.
Artibise, Professor Alan F. J., Inst. of Urban Studies, University of Winnipeg, 515 Portage Avenue, Winnipeg, Canada R3B 2E9.
Ash, Marinell, BA, MA, PhD., 42 Woodburn Terrace, Edinburgh EH10 4ST.
Ashton, Professor R., PhD, The Manor House, Brundall, near Norwich NOR 86Z.
Ashworth, Professor W., BSc(Econ), PhD, Flat 14, Wells Court, Wells Road, Ilkley, W. Yorks. LS29 9LG.
Aston, Margaret, MA, DPhil, Castle House, Chipping Ongar, Essex.
Aston, T. H., MA, FSA, Corpus Christi College, Oxford OX1 4JF.
Austin, M. R., BD, MA, PhD, The Glead, 2a Louvain Road, Derby DE3 6BZ.
Axelson, Professor E. V., DLitt, Box 15, Constantia, 7848, S. Africa.
*Aydelotte, Professor W. O., PhD, State University of Iowa, Iowa City, U.S.A.
Aylmer, G. E., MA, DPhil, FBA, St Peter's College, Oxford OX1 2DL.

Bahlman, Professor Dudley W. R., PhD, Dept of History, Williams College, Williamstown, Mass. 01267, U.S.A.
Bailie, The Rev. W. D., MA, BD, PhD, DD, Kilmore Manse, 100 Ballynahinch Road, Crossgar, Downpatrick, N. Ireland BT30 9HT.
Bailyn, Professor B., MA, PhD, LittD, LHD, Widener J., Harvard University, Cambridge, Mass. 02138, U.S.A.
Baker, D., BSc, PhD, Dept of History, Christ Church College, Canterbury, Kent CT1 1QU.
Baker, J. H., LLD, PhD, MA, St Catharine's College, Cambridge CB2 1RL.
Baker, L. G. D., MA, BLitt, Christ's Hospital, Horsham, West Sussex.
Baker, T. F. T., BA, Camden Lodge, 50 Hastings Road, Pembury, Kent.
Ballhatchet, Professor K.A., MA, PhD, 11 The Mead, Ealing, London W13.
Banks, Professor J. A., MA, Dept of Sociology, The University, Leicester LE1 7RH.
Barber, M. C., BA, PhD, Dept of History, The University, Whiteknights, Reading, Berks. RG6 2AA.
Barber, R. W., MA, PhD, FSA, Stangrove Hall, Alderton, near Woodbridge, Suffolk IP12 3BL.
Barker, E. E., MA, PhD, FSA, 60 Marina Road, Little Altcar, Formby, Merseyside L37 6BP.
Barker, Professor T. C., MA, PhD, Minsen Dane, Brogdale Road, Faversham, Kent.
Barkley, Professor the Rev. J. M., MA, DD, 2 College Park, Belfast, N. Ireland.
*Barlow, Professor F., MA, DPhil, FBA, Middle Court Hall, Kenton, Exeter.
Barnard, T. C., MA, DPhil, Hertford College, Oxford OX1 3BW.

Barnes, Miss P. M., PhD, Public Record Office, Chancery Lane, London WC2A 1LR.
Barnes, Professor T. G., AB, DPhil, University of California, Berkeley, Calif. 94720, U.S.A.
Barratt, Miss D. M., DPhil, The Corner House, Hampton Poyle, Kidlington, Oxford.
Barratt, Professor G. R. de V., PhD, 197 Belmont Avenue, Ottawa, Canada K1S OV7.
Barron, Mrs C. M., MA, PhD, 35 Rochester Road, London NW1.
Barrow, Professor G. W. S., MA, BLitt, DLitt, FBA, FRSE, The Old Manse, 19 Westfield Road, Cupar, Fife KY15 5AP.
Bartlett, Professor C. J., PhD, Dept of Modern History, The University, Dundee DD1 4HN.
Batho, Professor G. R., MA, Dept of Education, The University, 48 Old Elvet, Durham DH1 3JH.
Baugh, Professor Daniel A., PhD, Dept of History, McGraw Hall, Cornell University, Ithaca, N.Y. 14853, U.S.A.
Baxter, Professor S. B., PhD, 608 Morgan Creek Road, Chapel Hill, N.C. 27514, U.S.A.
Baylen, Professor J. O., MA, PhD, 41 Victoria Street, Brighton, E. Sussex BN1 3FQ.
Beachey, Professor R. W., BA, PhD, 1 Rookwood, De La Warr Road, Milford-on-Sea, Hampshire.
Beales, D. E. D., MA, PhD, Sidney Sussex College, Cambridge CB2 3HU.
Bealey, Professor F., BSc(Econ), Dept of Politics, The University, Taylor Building, Old Aberdeen AB9 2UB.
Bean, Professor J. M. W., MA, DPhil, 622 Fayerweather Hall, Columbia University, New York, N.Y. 10027, U.S.A.
Beardwood, Miss Alice, BA, BLitt, DPhil, 415 Miller's Lane, Wynnewood, Pa, U.S.A.
Beasley, Professor W. G., PhD, FBA, 172 Hampton Road, Twickenham, Middlesex TW2 5NJ.
Beattie, Professor J. M., PhD, Dept of History, University of Toronto, Toronto M5S 1A1, Canada.
Beaumont, H., MA, Silverdale, Severn Bank, Shrewsbury.
Beckerman, John S., PhD, 225 Washington Avenue, Hamden, Ct. 06518, U.S.A.
Beckett, I. F. W., BA, PhD., 11 Tolpuddle Way, Yateley, Camberley, Surrey GU17 7BH.
Beckett, Professor J. C., MA, 19 Wellington Park Terrace, Belfast 9, N. Ireland.
Beckett, J. V., BA, PhD, Dept of History, The University, Nottingham NG7 2RD.
Bedarida, Professor F., CBE, 13 rue Jacob, 75006 Paris, France.
Beddard, R. A., MA, DPhil, Oriel College, Oxford OX1 4EW.
Beeler, Professor J. H., PhD, 1302 New Garden Road, Greensboro, N.C. 27410, U.S.A.
*Beer, E. S. de, CBE, MA, DLitt, FBA, FSA, 65 Century Court, Grove End Road, London NW8 9LD.
Beer, Professor Samuel H., PhD, Faculty of Arts & Sciences, Harvard University, Littauer Center G-15, Cambridge, Mass. 02138, U.S.A.
Behrens, Miss C. B. A., MA, Dales Barn, Barton, Cambridge.
Bell, P. M. H., BA, BLitt, School of History, The University, P.O. Box 147, Liverpool L69 3BX.

Beloff, Lord, DLitt, FBA, Flat No. 9, 22 Lewes Crescent, Brighton BN2 1GB.
Benedikz, B. S., MA, PhD, Main Library, University of Birmingham, P.O. Box 363, Birmingham B15 2TT.
Bennett, Capt. G. M., RN (ret.), DSC, Stage Coach Cottage, 57 Broad Street, Ludlow, Shropshire SY8 1NH.
Bennett, Rev. G. V., MA, DPhil, FSA, New College, Oxford OX1 3BN.
Bennett, M. J., BA, PhD, History Dept, University of Tasmania, Box 252C, G.P.O., Hobart, Tasmania 7001, Australia.
Bennett, R. F., MA, Magdalene College, Cambridge CB3 0AG.
Benson, J., BA, MA, PhD, The Polytechnic, Wolverhampton WV1 1LY.
Bentley, M., BA, PhD, Dept of History, The University, Sheffield S10 2TN.
Bernard, G.W., MA, DPhil, 92 Bassett Green Village, Southampton.
Best, Professor, G. F. A., MA, PhD, 12 Florence Street, London N1 2DZ.
Bhila, H. H. K., BA, MA, PhD, Dept. of History, University of Zimbabwe, P.O. Box MP 167, Mount Pleasant, Harare, Zimbabwe.
Biddiss, Professor M. D., MA, PhD, Dept of History, The University, Whiteknights, Reading RG6 2AA.
Biddle, M., MA, FSA, Christ Church, Oxford OX1 1DP.
Bidwell, Brigadier R. G. S., OBE, 8 Chapel Lane, Wickham Market, Woodbridge, Suffolk IP13 0SD.
Bill, E. G. W., MA, DLitt, Lambeth Palace Library, London SE1
Binfield, J. C. G., MA, PhD, 22 Whiteley Wood Road, Sheffield S11 7FE.
Binney, J. E. D., DPhil, 6 Pageant Drive, Sherborne, Dorset.
Birch, A., MA, PhD, University of Hong Kong, Hong Kong.
Bishop, A. S., BA, PhD, 44 North Acre, Banstead, Surrey SM7 2EG.
Bishop, T. A. M., MA, The Annexe, Manor House, Hemingford Grey, Hunts.
Black, Professor Eugene C., PhD, Dept of History, Brandeis University, Waltham, Mass. 02154, U.S.A.
Blake, E. O., MA, PhD, Roselands, Moorhill Road, Westend, Southampton SO3 3AW.
Blake, Professor J. W., CBE, MA, DLitt, 141 Seacoast Road, Limavady, Co Londonderry, N. Ireland.
Blake, Lord, MA, FBA, The Queen's College, Oxford OX1 4AW.
Blakemore, H., PhD, 43 Fitzjohn Avenue, Barnet, Herts.
*Blakey, Professor R. G., PhD, c/o Mr Raymond Shove, Order Dept, Library, University of Minnesota, Minneapolis, Minn., U.S.A.
Blakiston, H. N., BA, 6 Markham Square, London SW3.
Blanning, T. W. C., MA, PhD, Sidney Sussex College, Cambridge CB2 3HU.
Blaxland, Major W. G., Lower Heppington, Street End, Canterbury, Kent CT4 7AN.
Blewett, Professor N., BA, DipEd, MA, DPhil, School of Social Sciences, Flinders University of S. Australia, Bedford Park, S. Australia 5042.
Blomfield, Mrs K., 8 Elmdene Court, Constitution Hill, Woking, Surrey GU22 7SA.
Blunt, C. E., OBE, FBA, FSA, Ramsbury Hill, Ramsbury, Marlborough, Wilts.
*Bolsover, G. H., OBE, MA, PhD, 7 Devonshire Road, Hatch End, Middlesex HA5 4LY.
Bolton, Miss Brenda, BA, Dept of History, Westfield College, London NW3 7ST.
Bolton, Professor G. C., MA, DPhil, Australian Studies Centre, 27 Russell Square, London WC1B 5DS.
Bond, B. J., BA, MA, Dept of War Studies, King's College, London WC2R 2LS.

Bond, M. F., CB, OBE, MA, FSA, 19 Bolton Crescent, Windsor, Berks.
Booker, J. M. L., BA, MLitt, Braxted Place, Little Braxted, Witham, Essex CM8 3LD.
Boon, G.C., BA, FSA, FRNS, National Museum of Wales, Cardiff CF1 3NP.
Borrie, M. A. F., BA, 142 Culford Road, London N1.
Bossy, Professor J. A., MA, PhD, Dept of History, University of York, Heslington, York YO1 5DD.
Bottigheimer, Professor Karl S., Dept of History, State University of New York at Stony Brook, Long Island, N.Y., U.S.A.
Bourne, Professor K., BA, PhD, London School of Economics, Houghton Street, London WC2A 2AE.
Bowker, Mrs M., MA, BLitt, The Cottage, Bailrigg Lane, Lancaster.
Bowyer, M. J. F., 32 Netherhall Way, Cambridge.
*Boxer, Professor C. R., DLitt, FBA, Ringshall End, Little Gaddesden, Berkhamsted, Herts.
Boyce, D. G., BA, PhD, Dept of Political Theory and Government, University College of Swansea, Swansea SA2 8PP.
Boyle, Professor the Rev. L. E., DPhil, STL, Pontifical Institute of Mediaeval Studies, 59 Queen's Park, Toronto 181, Canada.
Boyle, T., Cert.Ed, BA, MPhil, Jersey Cottage, Mark Beech, Edenbridge, Kent TN8 5NS.
Boynton, L. O. J., MA, DPhil, FSA, Dept of History, Westfield College, London NW3 7ST.
Brading, D. A., MA, PhD, 28 Storey Way, Cambridge.
Bradshaw, B., MA, BD, PhD, Queens' College, Cambridge CB3 9ET.
Brand, P. A., MA, DPhil, Faculty of Law, University College Dublin, Belfield, Dublin 4, Ireland.
Brandon, P. F., BA, PhD, Greensleeves, 8 St Julian's Lane, Shoreham-by-Sea, Sussex BN4 6YS.
Breck, Professor A. D., MA, PhD, LHD, DLitt, University of Denver, Denver, Colorado 80210, U.S.A.
Brentano, Professor R., DPhil, University of California, Berkeley 4, Calif., U.S.A.
Brett, M., MA, DPhil, 7 Bardwell Road, Oxford OX2 6SU.
Bridge, F. R., PhD, The Poplars, Rodley Lane, Rodley, Leeds.
Bridges, R. C., BA, PhD, Dept of History, University of Aberdeen, King's College, Aberdeen AB9 2UB.
Briggs, Lord, BSc(Econ), MA, DLitt, FBA, Provost, Worcester College, Oxford OX1 2HB.
Briggs, J. H. Y., MA, Dept of History, University of Keele, Staffs. ST5 5BG.
Briggs, R., MA, All Souls College, Oxford OX1 4AL.
Brock, M. G., MA, Nuffield College, Oxford OX1 1NF.
Brock, Professor W. R., MA, PhD, 49 Barton Road, Cambridge CB3 9LG.
Brogan, D. H. V., MA, Dept of History, University of Essex, Colchester CO4 3SQ.
*Bromley, Professor J. S., MA, Merrow, Dene Close, Chilworth, Southampton SO1 7HL.
*Brooke, Professor C. N. L., MA, LittD, FBA, FSA, Faculty of History, West Road, Cambridge CB3 9EF.
Brooke, J., BA, 63 Hurst Avenue, Chingford, London E4 8DL.
Brooke, Mrs R. B., MA, PhD, c/o Faculty of History, West Road, Cambridge CB3 9EF.
Brooks, N. P., MA, DPhil, The University, St Andrews, Fife KY16 9AJ.

Brown, Professor A. L., MA, DPhil, Dept of History, The University, Glasgow G12 8QQ.
Brown, G. S., PhD, 1720 Hanover Road, Ann Arbor, Mich. 48103, U.S.A.
Brown, Judith M., MA, PhD, 10 The Downs, Cheadle, Cheshire SK8 1JL.
Brown, K. D., BA, MA, PhD, Dept of Economic and Social History, The Queen's University, Belfast BT7 1NN, N. Ireland.
Brown, Miss L. M., MA, PhD, 93 Church Road, Hanwell, London W7.
Brown, Professor M. J., MA, PhD, 350 South Candler Street, Decatur, Georgia 30030, U.S.A.
Brown, P. D., MA, 18 Davenant Road, Oxford OX2 8BX.
Brown, P. R. L., MA, FBA, Hillslope, Pullen's Lane, Oxford.
Brown, R. A., MA, DPhil, DLitt, FSA, King's College, London WC2R 2LS.
Bruce, J. M., ISO, MA, FRAeS, 6 Albany Close, Bushey Heath, Herts. WD2 3SG.
Brundage, Professor J. A., Dept of History, University of Wisconsin at Milwaukee, Milwaukee, Wisconsin, U.S.A.
Bryant, Sir Arthur (W. M.), CH, CBE, LLD, Myles Place, 68 The Close, Salisbury, Wilts.
Bryson, Professor W. Hamilton, School of Law, University of Richmond, Richmond, Va. 23173, U.S.A.
Buchanan, R. A., MA, PhD, School of Humanities and Social Sciences, The University, Claverton Down, Bath BA2 7AY.
Buckland, P. J., MA, PhD, 6 Rosefield Road, Liverpool L25 8TF.
Bueno de Mesquita, D. M., MA, PhD, 283 Woodstock Road, Oxford OX2 7NY.
Buisseret, Professor D. J., MA, PhD, The Newberry Library, 60 West Walton Street, Chicago, Ill. 60610, U.S.A.
Bullock, Lord, MA, DLitt, FBA, St Catherine's College, Oxford OX1 3UJ.
Bullock-Davies, Constance, BA, PhD, Dept of Classics, University College of North Wales, Bangor, Gwynedd LL57 2DG.
Bullough, Professor D. A., MA, FSA, Dept of Mediaeval History, 71 South Street, St Andrews, Fife KY16 9AJ.
Burke, U. P., MA, Emmanuel College, Cambridge CB2 3AP.
Burleigh, The Rev. Professor J. H. S., BD, 21 Kingsmuir Drive, Peebles, EH45 9AA.
Burns, Professor J. H., MA, PhD, 39 Amherst Road, London W13.
Burroughs, P., PhD, Dalhousie University, Halifax, Nova Scotia, Canada B3H 3J5.
Burrow, J. W., MA, PhD, Sussex University, Falmer, Brighton BN1 9QX.
Bury, J. P. T., MA, LittD, Corpus Christi College, Cambridge CB2 1RH.
Butler, R. D'O., CMG, MA, All Souls College, Oxford OX1 4AL.
Byerly, Professor B. F., BA, MA, PhD, Dept of History, University of Northern Colorado, Greeley, Colorado 80631, U.S.A.
Bythell, D., MA, DPhil, Dept of Economic History, University of Durham, 23–26 Old Elvet, Durham City DH1 3HY.

Cabaniss, Professor J. A., PhD, University of Mississippi, Box No. 253, University, Mississippi 38677, U.S.A.
Callahan, Professor Thomas, Jr., PhD, Dept of History, Rider College, Lawrenceville, N.J. 08648, U.S.A.
Calvert, Brigadier J. M. (ret.), DSO, MA, 33a Mill Hill Close, Haywards Heath, Sussex.
Calvert, P. A. R., MA, PhD, AM, Dept of Politics, University of Southampton, Highfield, Southampton SO9 5NH.

Cameron, A., BA, 35 Trevor Road, West Bridgford, Nottingham.
Cameron, Professor J. K., MA, BD, PhD, St Mary's College, University of St Andrews, Fife KY16 9JU.
Cameron, Professor K., PhD, FBA, Dept of English, The University, Nottingham NG7 2RD.
Campbell, Professor A. E., MA, PhD, School of History, University of Birmingham, P.O. Box 363, Birmingham B15 2TT.
Campbell, J., MA, Worcester College, Oxford OX1 2HB.
*Campbell, Professor Mildred L., PhD, Vassar College, Poughkeepsie, N.Y., U.S.A.
Campbell, Professor R. H., MA, PhD, University of Stirling, Stirling FK9 4LA.
Cannadine, D. N., BA, DPhil, Christ's College, Cambridge CB2 3BU.
Canning, J. P., MA, PhD, Dept of History, University College of North Wales, Bangor, Gwynedd LL57 2DG.
Cannon, Professor J. A., MA, PhD, Dept of History, The University, Newcastle upon Tyne NE1 7RU.
Canny, Professor N. P., MA, PhD, Dept of History, University College, Galway, Ireland.
Cant, R. G., MA, DLitt, 2 Kinburn Place, St Andrews, Fife KY16 9DT.
Cantor, Professor N. F., PhD, New York University, Dept of History, 19 University Place, New York, N.Y. 10003, U.S.A.
Capp, B. S., MA, DPhil, Dept of History, University of Warwick, Coventry, Warwickshire CV4 7AL.
Carey, P. B. R., DPhil, Trinity College, Oxford OX1 3BH.
*Carlson, Leland H., PhD, Huntington Library, San Marino, California 91108, U.S.A.
Carlton, Professor Charles, Dept of History, North Carolina State University, Raleigh, N.C. 27607, U.S.A.
Carman, W. Y., FSA, 94 Mulgrave Road, Sutton, Surrey.
Carpenter, M. Christine, MA, PhD, New Hall, Cambridge CB3 0DF.
Carr, A. D., MA, PhD, Dept of Welsh History, University College of North Wales, Bangor, Gwynedd LL57 2DG.
Carr, A. R. M., MA, FBA, St Antony's College, Oxford OX2 6JF.
Carr, W., PhD, 22 Southbourne Road, Sheffield S10 2QN.
Carrington, Miss Dorothy, 3 Rue Emmanuel Arene, 20 Ajaccio, Corsica.
Carter, Mrs A. C., MA, 12 Garbrand Walk, Ewell, Epsom, Surrey.
Carter, Jennifer J., BA, PhD, Johnston Hall, College Bounds, Old Aberdeen AB9 2TT.
Carwardine, R. J., MA, DPhil, Dept of History, The University, Sheffield S10 2TN.
Casey, J., BA, PhD, School of Modern Languages and European History, University of East Anglia, Norwich NR4 7TJ.
Catto, R. J. A. I., MA, Oriel College, Oxford OX1 4EW.
Cazel, Professor Fred A., Jr., Dept of History, University of Connecticut, Storrs, Conn. 06268, U.S.A.
Chadwick, Professor W. O., DD, DLitt, FBA, Selwyn Lodge, Cambridge CB3 9DQ.
Challis, C. E., MA, PhD, 14 Ashwood Villas, Headingley, Leeds 6.
Chalmers, C. D., Public Record Office, Kew, Richmond, Surrey TW9 4DU.
Chambers, D. S., MA, DPhil, Warburg Institute, Woburn Square, London WC1H 0AB.
Chandaman, Professor C. D., BA, PhD, 23 Bellamy Close, Ickenham, Uxbridge UB10 8SJ.

Chandler, D. G., MA, Hindford, Monteagle Lane, Yately, Camberley, Surrey.
Chaplais, P., PhD, FBA, FSA, Lew Lodge, Mount Owen Road, Bampton, Oxford.
Charles-Edwards, T. M., DPhil, Corpus Christi College, Oxford OX1 4JF.
*CHENEY, Professor C. R., MA, DLitt, LittD, FBA, 236 Hills Road, Cambridge CB2 2QE.
Cheney, Mrs. M., MA, Lucy Cavendish College, Cambridge.
Chibnall, Mrs. Marjorie, MA, DPhil, FBA, 6 Millington Road, Cambridge CB3 9HP.
Child, C. J., OBE, MA, PhM, 94 Westhall Road, Warlingham, Surrey CR3 9HB.
Childs, J. C. R., BA, PhD, School of History, The University, Leeds LS2 9JT.
Childs, Wendy R., MA, PhD, School of History, The University, Leeds LS2 9JT.
Chrimes, Professor S. B., MA, PhD, LittD, 24 Cwrt-y-Vil Road, Penarth, South Glam. CF6 2HP.
Christianson, Assoc. Professor P. K., PhD, Dept of History, Queen's University, Kingston, Ontario K7L 3N6, Canada.
Christie, Professor I. R., MA, FBA, 10 Green Lane, Croxley Green, Herts. WD3 3HR.
Church, Professor R. A., BA, PhD, School of Social Studies, University of East Anglia, Norwich NOR 88C.
Cirket, A. F., 71 Curlew Crescent, Bedford.
Clanchy, M. T., MA, PhD, FSA, Medieval History Dept, The University, Glasgow G12 8QQ.
Clark, A. E., MA, 32 Durham Avenue, Thornton Cleveleys, Blackpool FY5 2DP.
Clark, Professor Dora Mae, PhD, 134 Pennsylvania Ave., Chambersburg, Pa. 17201, U.S.A.
Clark, P. A., MA, Dept of Economic and Social History, The University, Leicester LE1 7RH.
Clarke, P. F., MA, PhD, St John's College, Cambridge CB2 1TP.
Clementi, Miss D., MA, DPhil, Flat 7, 43 Rutland Gate, London SW7 1BP.
Clemoes, Professor P. A. M., BA, PhD, Emmanuel College, Cambridge CB2 3AP.
Cliffe, J. T., BA, PhD, 263 Staines Road, Twickenham, Middx. TW2 5AY.
Clive, Professor J. L., PhD, 38 Fernald Drive, Cambridge, Mass. 02138, U.S.A.
Clough, C. H., MA, DPhil, FSA, School of History, The University, P.O. Box 147, Liverpool L69 3BX.
Cobb, H. S., MA, FSA, 1 Child's Way, London NW11.
Cobban, A. B., MA, PhD, School of History, The University, P.O. Box 147, Liverpool L69 3BX.
Cockburn, J. S., LLB, LLM, PhD, c/o Public Record Office, Chancery Lane, London WC2A 1LR.
Cocks, E. J., MA, Middle Lodge, Ardingly, Haywards Heath Sussex RH17 6TS.
Cohn, H. J., MA, DPhil, University of Warwick, Coventry CV4 7AL.
Cohn, Professor N., MA, DLitt, FBA, 61 New End, London NW3.
Coleman, B. I., MA, PhD, Dept of History, The University, Exeter EX4 4QH.

Coleman, Professor D. C., BSc(Econ.), PhD, LittD, FBA, Over Hall, Cavendish, Sudbury, Suffolk.

Coleman, Professor F. L., MA, PhD, Dept of Economics & Economic History, Rhodes University, P.O. Box 94, Grahamstown 6140, S. Africa.

Collier, W. O., MA, FSA, 34 Berwyn Road, Richmond, Surrey.

Collinge, J. M., BA, Institute of Historical Research, Senate House, Malet Street, London WC1E 7HU.

Collini, S. A., MA, PhD, 35 Fulbrooke Road, Cambridge CB3 9EE.

Collins, B. W., MA, PhD, Dept of Modern History, The University, Glasgow G12 8QQ.

Collins, Mrs I., MA, BLitt, School of History, The University, P.O. Box 147, Liverpool L69 3BX.

Collinson, Professor P., MA, PhD, FBA, Keynes College, The University, Canterbury, Kent CT2 7NS.

Colvin, H. M., CBE, MA, FBA, St. John's College, Oxford OX1 3JP.

Colyer, R. J., BSc, PhD, Inst. of Rural Sciences, University College of Wales, Aberystwyth, Dyfed.

Conacher, Professor J. B., MA, PhD, 151 Welland Avenue, Toronto 290, Ontario, Canada.

Congreve, A. L., MA, FSA, Galleons Lap, Sissinghurst, Kent TN17 2JG.

Connell-Smith, Professor G. E., PhD, 7 Braids Walk, Kirkella, Hull, Yorks. HU10 7PA.

Constable, G., PhD, Dumbarton Oaks, 1703 32nd Street, Washington, D.C. 20007, U.S.A.

Contamine, Professor P., DèsL., 12 Villa Croix-Nivert, 75015 Paris, France.

Conway, Professor A. A., MA, University of Canterbury, Christchurch 1, New Zealand.

Cook, A. E., MA, PhD, 20 Nicholas Road, Hunter's Ride, Henley-on-Thames, Oxon.

Cook, C. P., MA, DPhil, Dept of History, The Polytechnic of North London, Prince of Wales Road, London NW5 3LB.

Cooke, Professor, J. J., PhD., Dept of History, College of Liberal Arts, University of Mississippi, University, Miss. 38677, U.S.A.

Coolidge, Professor R. T., MA, BLitt, History Dept, Loyola Campus, Concordia University, 7141 Sherbrooke Street West, Montreal, Quebec H4B 1R6, Canada.

Cope, Professor Esther S., PhD, Dept of History, Univ. of Nebraska, Lincoln, Neb. 68508, U.S.A.

Corfield, Penelope J., MA, PhD, 99 Salcott Road, London SW11 6DF.

Cornell, Professor Paul G., PhD, Dept of History, University of Waterloo, Waterloo, Ontario, Canada N2L 3G1.

Cornford, Professor J. P., MA, The Brick House, Wicken Bonhunt, Saffron Walden, Essex CB11 3UG.

Cornwall, J. C. K., MA, 1 Orchard Close, Copford Green, Colchester, Essex.

Corson, J. C., MA, PhD, Mossrig, Lilliesleaf, Melrose, Roxburghshire.

Coss, P. R., BA, PhD, 7 Alexandra Way, Hall Close Chase, Cramlington, Northumberland.

Costeloe, M. P., BA, PhD, Dept of Hispanic and Latin American Studies, The University, 83 Woodland Road, Bristol BS8 1RJ.

Cowan, I. B., MA, PhD, University of Glasgow, Glasgow G12 8QQ.

Coward, B., BA, PhD, Dept of History, Birkbeck College, Malet Street, London WC1E 7HX.

Cowdrey, Rev. H. E. J., MA, St Edmund Hall, Oxford OX1 4AR.

Cowie, Rev. L. W., MA, PhD, 38 Stratton Road, Merton Park, London SW19 3JG.

Cowley, F. G., PhD, 17 Brookvale Road, West Cross, Swansea, W. Glam.

Cox, D. C., BA, PhD, 9 Mount Way Pontesbury, Shrewsbury SY5 0RB.

Craig, R. S., BSc(Econ), 27 Ridgmount Gardens, Bloomsbury, London WC1E 7AS.

Cramp, Professor Rosemary, MA, BLitt, FSA, Department of Archaeology, The Old Fulling Mill, The Banks, Durham.

Crampton, R. J., BA, PhD, Rutherford College, The University, Canterbury, Kent CT2 7NP.

Craton, Professor M. J., BA, MA, PhD, Dept of History, University of Waterloo, Waterloo, Ontario, Canada N2L 3G1.

Crawford, Patricia M., BA, MA, PhD, Dept of History, University of Western Australia, Nedlands, Western Australia 6009.

*Crawley, C. W., MA, 1 Madingley Road, Cambridge.

Cremona, His Hon Chief Justice Professor J. J., KM, DLitt, PhD, LLD, DrJur, 5 Victoria Gardens, Sliema, Malta.

Cressy, D. A., 231 West Sixth Street, Claremont, Calif. 91711, U.S.A.

Crimmin, Patricia K., MPhil, BA, Dept of History, Royal Holloway College, Englefield Green, Surrey TW20 0EX.

Crisp, Olga, BA, PhD, 'Zarya', 1 Millbrook, Esher, Surrey.

Croft, Pauline, MA, DPhil, Dept of History, Royal Holloway College, Englefield Green, Surrey TW20 0EX.

Crombie, A. C., BSc, MA, PhD, Trinity College, Oxford OX1 3BH.

Cromwell, Miss V., MA, University of Sussex, Falmer, Brighton, Sussex BN1 9QX.

Crook, D., MA, PhD, Public Record Office, Chancery Lane, London WC2A 1LR.

Cross, Miss M. C., MA, PhD, Dept of History, University of York, York YO1 5DD.

Crowder, Professor C. M. D., DPhil, Queen's University, Kingston, Ontario, Canada K7L 3N6.

Crowder, Professor M., MA, Dept of History, University of Botswana, P.B. 0022, Gaborone, Botswana.

Crowe, Miss S. E., MA, PhD, 112 Staunton Road, Headington, Oxford.

Cruickshank, C. G., MA, DPhil, 15 McKay Road, Wimbledon Common, London SW20.

Cruickshanks, Eveline G., PhD, 46 Goodwood Court, Devonshire Street, London W1N 1SL.

Cumming, Professor A., MA, DipMA, PGCE, PhD, Centre for Education Studies, University of New England, Armidale, Australia 2351.

Cumming, I., MEd, PhD, 672A South Titirangi Road, Titirangi, Auckland, New Zealand.

Cummins, Professor J. S., PhD, University College London, Gower Street, London WC1E 6BT.

Cumpston, Miss I. M., MA, DPhil, Birkbeck College, Malet Street, London WC1E 7HX.

Cunliffe, Professor M. F., MA, BLitt, DHL, Room 102, T Building, George Washington University, 2110 G. Street N.W., Washington, D.C., 20052, U.S.A.

Cunningham, Professor A. B., MA, PhD, Simon Fraser University, Burnaby 2, B.C., Canada.

Currie, C. R. J., MA, DPhil, Institute of Historical Research, Senate House, Malet Street, London WC1E 7HU.

Curtis, Professor L. Perry, PhD, Dept of History, Brown University, Providence, R.I. 02912, U.S.A.

Curtis, Timothy C., PhD (address unknown).

Cushner, Rev. N. P., SJ, MA (address unknown).

*Cuttino, Professor G. P., DPhil, FSA, Department of History, Emory University, Atlanta, Ga., 30322, U.S.A.

Cuttler, Asst. Professor Simon H., BA, MA, DPhil, 6550 Sherbrooke West, Apt. 1302, Montreal, Canada H4B 1N6.

*Dacre, Lord, MA, FBA, Peterhouse, Cambridge CB2 1RD.

Dakin, Professor D., MA, PhD, 20 School Road, Apperley, Gloucester GL19 4DJ.

D'Arcy, F. A., BA, MA, PhD, Dept of Modern History, University College, Belfield, Dublin 4, Ireland.

Daunton, M. J., BA, PhD, Dept of History, University College London, Gower Street, London WC1E 6BT.

Davenport, Professor T. R. H., MA, PhD, Dept of History, Rhodes University, P.O. Box 94, Grahamstown 6140, South Africa.

Davies, C. S. L., MA, DPhil, Wadham College, Oxford OX1 3PN.

Davies, Canon E. T., BA, MA, 11 Tŷ Brith Gardens, Usk, Gwent.

Davies, I. N. R., MA, DPhil, 22 Rowland Close, Wolvercote, Oxford.

Davies, P. N., MA, PhD, Cmar, Croft Drive, Caldy, Wirral, Merseyside.

Davies, R. G., MA, PhD, Dept of History, The University, Manchester M13 9PL.

Davies, Professor R. R., BA, DPhil, University College of Wales, Dept of History, 1 Laura Place, Aberystwyth SY23 2AU.

Davies, Wendy, BA, PhD, Dept of History, University College London, Gower Street, London WC1E 6BT.

*Davis, G. R. C., CBE, MA, DPhil, 214 Somerset Road, London SW19 5JE.

Davis, Professor R. H. C., MA, FBA, FSA, 56 Fitzroy Avenue, Harborne, Birmingham B17 8RJ.

Davis, Professor Richard W., Dept of History, Washington University, St Louis, Missouri 63130, U.S.A.

*Dawe, D. A., 46 Green Lane, Purley, Surrey.

Deane, Miss Phyllis M., MA, 4 Stukeley Close, Cambridge CB3 9LT.

*Deeley, Miss A. P., MA, 41 Linden Road, Bicester, Oxford.

de la Mare, Miss A. C., MA, PhD, Bodleian Library, Oxford.

Denham, E. W., MA, 27 The Drive, Northwood, Middx. HA6 1HW.

Dennis, P. J., MA, PhD, Dept of History, Royal Military College, Duntroon, A.C.T. 2600, Australia.

Denton, J. H., BA, PhD, Dept of History, The University, Manchester M13 9PL.

Devine, T. M., BA, Viewfield Cottage, 55 Burnbank Road, Hamilton, Strathclyde Region.

Dewey, P. E., BA, PhD, Dept of History, Royal Holloway College, Englefield Green, Surrey TW20 0EX.

Dewhurst, K., MD, DPhil, Manor House, Sandford-on-Thames, Oxford OX4 4YN.

DICKENS, Professor A. G., CMG, MA, DLit, DLitt, LittD, FBA, FSA, Institute of Historical Research, University of London, Senate House, London WC1E 7HU.

Dickinson, H. T., MA, PhD, Dept of Modern History, The University, Edinburgh EH8 9YL.

Dickinson, Rev. J. C., MA, DLitt, FSA, Yew Tree Cottage, Barngarth, Cartmel, South Cumbria.
Dickson, P. G. M., MA, DPhil, St Catherine's College, Oxford, OX1 3UJ.
Diké, Professor K. O., MA, PhD, Dept of History, Harvard University, Cambridge, Mass. 02138, U.S.A.
Dilks, Professor D. N., BA, Dept of International History, The University, Leeds LS2 9JT.
Dilworth, Rev. G. M., OSB, MA, PhD, Columba House, 16 Drummond Place, Edinburgh EH3 6PL.
Dinwiddy, J. R., PhD, Dept of History, Royal Holloway College, Englefield Green, Surrey TW20 0EX.
Ditchfield, G. McC, BA, PhD, Eliot College, University of Kent, Canterbury, Kent CT2 7NP.
Dobson, Professor R. B., MA, DPhil, Dept of History, The University, York YO1 5DD.
Dockrill, M. L., MA, BSc(Econ), PhD, King's College, Strand, London WC2R 2LS.
*Dodwell, Miss B., MA, The University, Reading RG6 2AH.
Dodwell, Professor C. R., MA, PhD, FSA, History of Art Department, The University, Manchester M13 9PL.
Dolley, R. H. M., BA, MRIA, FSA, Mavis Bank, Higher Brimley, Teignmouth, Devon.
Don Peter, The Rt. Revd. Monsignor W. L. A., MA, PhD, Aquinas University College, Colombo 8, Sri Lanka.
*Donaldson, Professor G., MA, PhD, DLitt, DLitt, FRSE, FBA, 6 Pan Ha', Dysart, Fife KY1 2TL.
Donaldson, Professor P. S., MA, PhD, Dept of Humanities, 14n-422, Massachusetts Institute of Technology, Cambridge, Mass. 02139, U.S.A.
*Donaldson-Hudson, Miss R., BA, (address unknown).
Donoughue, B., MA, DPhil, 7 Brookfield Park, London NW5 1ES.
Dore, R. N., MA, Holmrook, 19 Chapel Lane, Hale Barns, Altrincham, Cheshire WA15 0AB.
Downer, L. J., MA, LLB, Dept of Mediaeval Studies, Australian National University, Box 4, P.O., Canberra, Australia.
Doyle, A. I., MA, PhD, University College, The Castle, Durham.
Doyle, Professor W., MA., DPhil, Dept of History, The University, Nottingham NG7 2RD.
Driver, J. T., MA, BLitt, 25 Abbot's Grange, Chester CH2 1AJ.
*Drus, Miss E., MA, The University, Southampton SO9 5NH.
Duckham, Professor B. F., MA, Dept of History, St David's University College, Lampeter, Dyfed SA48 7ED.
Duggan, C., PhD, King's College, Strand, London WC2R 2LS.
Dugmore, The Rev. Professor C. W., DD, Thame Cottage, The Street, Puttenham, Guildford, Surrey GU3 1AT.
Duke, A. C., MA, Dept of History, The University, Southampton SO9 5NH
Duly, L. C., PhD, Bemidji State University, Bemidji, Minn. 56601, U.S.A.
Dumville, D. N., MA, PhD, Dept of Anglo-Saxon, Norse and Celtic, 9 West Road, Cambridge CB3 9DP.
Dunbabin, J. P. D., MA, St Edmund Hall, Oxford OX1 4AR.
Duncan, Professor A. A. M., MA, The University, Dept of History, Glasgow G12 8QQ.
Dunn, Professor R. S., PhD, Dept of History, The College, University of Pennsylvania, Philadelphia, Pa. 19104, U.S.A.

Dunning, R. W., BA, PhD, FSA, Musgrove Manor East, Barton Close, Taunton TA1 4RU.

Durack, Mrs I. A., MA, PhD, University of Western Australia, Crawley, Western Australia.

Durie, A. J., MA, PhD, Dept of Economic History, Edward Wright Building, The University, Aberdeen AB9 2TY.

Dykes, D. W., MA, Cherry Grove, Welsh St Donats, nr Cowbridge, Glam. CF7 7SS.

Dyson, Professor K. H. F., BSc(Econ), MSc(Econ), PhD, Undergraduate School of European Studies, The University, Bradford BD7 1DP.

Earle, P., BSc(Econ), PhD, Dept of Economic History, London School of Economics, Houghton Street, London WC2A 2AE.

Eastwood, Rev. C. C., PhD, Heathview, Monks Lane, Audlem, Cheshire CW3 0HP.

Eckles, Professor R. B., PhD, Apt 2, 251 Brahan Blvd., San Antonio, Texas 78215, U.S.A.

Edbury, P. W., MA, PhD, Dept of History, University College, P.O. Box 78, Cardiff CF1 1XL.

Ede, J. R., CB, MA, Palfreys, East Street, Drayton, Langport, Somerset TA10 0JZ.

Edmonds, Professor E. L., MA, PhD, University of Prince Edward Island, Charlottetown, Prince Edward Island, Canada.

Edwards, F. O., SJ, BA, FSA, 114 Mount Street, London W1Y 6AH.

Edwards, O. D., BA, Dept of History, William Robertson Building, The University, George Square, Edinburgh EH8 9YL.

Edwards, Professor R. W. D., MA, PhD, DLitt, 21 Brendan Road, Donnybrook, Dublin 4, Ireland.

Ehrman, J. P. W., MA, FBA, FSA, The Mead Barns, Taynton, Nr Burford, Oxfordshire OX8 5UH.

Eisenstein, Professor Elizabeth L., PhD, 82 Kalorama Circle N.W., Washington D.C. 20008, U.S.A.

Eldridge, C. C., PhD, Dept of History, Saint David's University College, Lampeter, Dyfed SA48 7ED.

Eley, G. H., BA, DPhil, MA, Dept of History, University of Michigan, Ann Arbor, Michigan 48109, U.S.A.

Elliott, Professor J. H., MA, PhD, FBA, King's College, Strand, London WC2R 2LS.

Ellis, R. H., MA, FSA, Cloth Hill, 6 The Mount, London NW3.

Ellis, S. G., BA, MA, PhD, Dept of History, University College, Galway, Ireland.

Ellul, M., BArch, DipArch, 'Pauline', 55 Old Railway Road, Birkirkara, Malta.

Elrington, C. R., MA, FSA, Institute of Historical Research, Senate House, London WC1E 7HU.

ELTON, Professor G. R., MA, PhD, LittD, DLitt, DLitt, DLit, FBA, 30 Millington Road, Cambridge CB3 9HP.

Elvin, L., FSA, FRSA, 10 Almond Avenue, Swanpool, Lincoln LN6 0HB.

*Emmison, F. G., MBE, PhD, DUniv, FSA, 8 Coppins Close, Chelmsford, Essex CM2 6AY.

Emsley, C., BA, MLitt, Arts Faculty, The Open University, Walton Hall, Milton Keynes MK7 6AA.

d'Entrèves, Professor A. P., DPhil, Strada Ai Ronchi 48, Cavoretto 10133, Torino, Italy.

Erickson, Charlotte, J., PhD, London School of Economics, Houghton Street, London WC2A 2AE.
*Erith, E. J., Shurlock House, Shurlock Row, Berkshire.
Erskine, Mrs A. M., MA, BLitt, FSA, 44 Birchy Barton Hill, Exeter EX1 3EX.
Evans, Mrs A. K. B., PhD, FSA, White Lodge, 25 Knighton Grange Road, Leicester LE2 2LF.
Evans, Sir David (L.), OBE, BA, DLitt, 2 Bay Court, Doctors Commons Road, Berkhamsted, Herts.
Evans, E. J., MA, PhD, Dept of History, Furness College, University of Lancaster, Bailrigg, Lancaster LA1 4YG.
Evans, Gillian R., PhD, Sidney Sussex College, Cambridge CB2 3HU.
Evans, R. J., MA, DPhil, School of European Studies, University of East Anglia, Norwich NR4 7TJ.
Evans, R. J. W., MA, PhD, Brasenose College, Oxford OX1 4AJ.
Evans, The Very Rev. S. J. A., CBE, MA, FSA, The Old Manor, Fulbourne, Cambs.
Everitt, Professor A. M., MA, PhD, The University, Leicester LE1 7RH.
Eyck, Professor U. F. J., MA, BLitt, Dept of History, University of Calgary, Alberta T2N IN4, Canada.

Fage, Professor J. D., MA, PhD, Centre of West African Studies, The University, Birmingham B5 2TT.
Fagg, J. E., MA, 47 The Avenue, Durham DH1 4ED.
Fairs, G. L., MA, Thornton House, Bear Street, Hay-on-Wye, Hereford HR3 5AN.
Falkus, M. E., BSc(Econ), Dept of History, London School of Economics, Houghton Street, London WC2A 2AE.
Farmer, D. F. H., BLitt, FSA, The University, Reading RG6 2AH.
Farr, M. W., MA, FSA, 12 Emscote Road, Warwick.
Fell, Professor C. E., MA, Dept of English, The University, Nottingham NG7 2RD.
Fenlon, Revd. D. B., BA, PhD, St Edmunds, 21 Westgate Street, Bury St Edmunds, Suffolk IP33 1QG.
Fenn, Rev. R. W. D., MA, BD, FSAScot, The Ditch, Bradnor View, Kington, Herefordshire.
Ferguson, Professor A. B., PhD, Dept of History, 6727 College Station, Duke University, Durham, N.C. 27708, U.S.A.
Fernandez-Armesto, F. F. R., DPhil, 16 Walton Street, Oxford.
Feuchtwanger, E. J., MA, PhD, Highfield House, Dean Sparsholt, nr Winchester, Hants.
Fieldhouse, D. K., MA, Nuffield College, Oxford OX1 1NF.
Finer, Professor S. E., MA, All Souls College, Oxford OX1 4AL.
Fines, J., MA, PhD, 119 Parklands Road, Chichester.
Finlayson, G. B. A. M., MA, BLitt, 11 Burnhead Road, Glasgow G43 2SU.
Finley, Professor Sir Moses, MA, PhD, DLitt, FBA, 12 Adams Road, Cambridge CB3 9AD.
Fisher, Professor Alan W., PhD, Dept of History, Michigan State University, East Lansing, Michigan 48824, U.S.A.
Fisher, D. J. V., MA, Jesus College, Cambridge CB3 9AD.
Fisher, Professor F. J., MA, London School of Economics, Houghton Street, London WC2A 2AE.
Fisher, F. N., Holmelea, Cromford Road, Wirksworth, Derby DE4 4FR.

Fisher, J. R., BA, MPhil, PhD, School of History, The University, P.O. Box 147, Liverpool L69 3BX.
Fisher, R. M., MA, PhD, Dept of History, University of Queensland, St Lucia, Queensland, Australia 4067.
Fisher, Professor S. N., PhD, 221 St Antoine, Worthington, Ohio 43085, U.S.A.
Fitch, Dr M. F. B., FSA, 37 Avenue de Montoie, 1007 Lausanne, Switzerland.
Fletcher, A. J., MA, 16 Southbourne Road, Sheffield S10 2QN.
*Fletcher, The Rt Hon The Lord, PC, BA, LLD, FSA, The Barn, The Green, Sarratt, Rickmansworth, Herts. WD3 6BP.
Fletcher, R. A., MA, Dept of History, The University, York YO1 5DD.
Flint, Professor J. E., MA, PhD, Dalhousie University, Halifax, Nova Scotia B3H 3J5, Canada.
Flint, Valerie I. J., MA, DPhil, Dept of History, The University, Private Bag, Auckland, New Zealand.
Floud, Professor R. C., MA, DPhil, Dept of History, Birkbeck College, Malet Street, London WC1E 7HX.
Fogel, Professor Robert W., PhD, Center for Population Economics, University of Chicago, 1101 East 58th Street, Chicago, Illinois 60637, U.S.A.
Foot, M. R. D., MA, BLitt, 88 Heath View, London N2 0QB.
Forbes, D., MA, 89 Gilbert Road, Cambridge.
Forbes, Thomas R., BA, PhD, FSA, 86 Ford Street, Hamden, Conn. 06517, U.S.A.
Ford, W. K., BA, 48 Harlands Road, Haywards Heath, West Sussex RH16 1LS.
Forster, G. C. F., BA, FSA, The University, Leeds LS2 9JT.
Foster, Professor Elizabeth R., AM, PhD, 205 Strafford Avenue, Wayne, Pa. 19087, U.S.A.
Foster, R. F., MA, PhD, Dept of History, Birkbeck College, Malet Street, London WC1E 7HX.
Fowler, Professor K. A., BA, PhD, 2 Nelson Street, Edinburgh 3.
Fowler, P. J., MA, PhD, 1a Althorp Road, St Albans, Herts. AL1 3AH.
Fox, L., OBE, DL, LHD, MA, FSA, FRSL, Silver Birches, 27 Welcombe Road, Stratford-upon-Avon.
Fox, R., MA, DPhil, The University, Bailrigg, Lancaster LA1 4YG.
Frame, R. F., MA, PhD, Dept of History, The University, 43 North Bailey, Durham DH1 3HP.
Francis, A. D., CBE, MVO, MA, 21 Cadogan Street, London SW3.
Franklin, R. M., BA, Baldwins End, Eton College, Windsor, Berks.
*Fraser, Miss C. M., PhD, 39 King Edward Road, Tynemouth, Tyne and Wear NE30 2RW.
Fraser, Professor D., BA, MA, PhD, 12 Primley Park Avenue, Leeds LS17 7JA.
Fraser, Professor Peter, MA, PhD, The Priory, Old Mill Lane, Marnhull, Dorset DT10 1JX.
Freeden, M. S., DPhil, Mansfield College, Oxford OX1 3TF.
Frend, Professor W. H. C., MA, DPhil, DD, FRSE, FSA, Marbrae, Balmaha, Stirlingshire.
Fritz, Professor Paul S., BA, MA, PhD, Dept of History, McMaster University, Hamilton, Ontario, Canada.
Fryde, Professor E. B., DPhil, Preswylfa, Trinity Road, Aberystwyth, Dyfed.
Fryde, Natalie M., BA, DrPhil, Preswylfa, Trinity Road, Aberystwyth, Dyfed.

*Fryer, Professor C. E., MA, PhD, (address unknown).
Fryer, Professor W. R., BLitt, MA, 68 Grove Avenue, Chilwell, Beeston, Notts. NG9 4DX.
Frykenberg, Professor R. E., MA, PhD, 1840 Chadbourne Avenue, Madison, Wis. 53705, U.S.A.
Fuidge, Miss N. M., 13 Havercourt, Haverstock Hill, London NW3.
*Furber, Professor H., MA, PhD, History Department, University of Pennsylvania, Philadelphia, Pa., U.S.A.
Fussell, G. E., DLitt, 55 York Road, Sudbury, Suffolk CO10 6NF.
Fyrth, H. J., BSc(Econ), 72 College Road, Dulwich, London SE21.

Gabriel, Professor A. L., PhD, FMAA, CFIF, CFBA, P.O. Box 578, University of Notre Dame, Notre Dame, Indiana 46556, U.S.A.
*Galbraith, Professor J. S., BS, MA, PhD, University of California, Los Angeles, Calif. 90024, U.S.A.
Gale, Professor H. P. P., OBE, PhD, 38 Brookwood Avenue, London SW13.
Gale, W. K. V., 19 Ednam Road, Goldthorn Park, Wolverhampton WV4 5BL.
Gann, L. H., MA, BLitt, DPhil, Hoover Institution, Stanford University, Stanford, Calif. 94305, U.S.A.
Gash, Professor N., MA, BLitt, FBA, Old Gatehouse, Portway, Langport, Somerset TA10 0NQ.
Gee, E. A., MA, DPhil, FSA, 28 Trentholme Drive, The Mount, York YO2 2DG.
Geggus, D. P., MA, DPhil, Dept of History, The University, Southampton SO9 5NH.
Genet, J., Ph., Agrégé d'Histoire, 147 Avenue Parmentier, Paris 75010, France.
Gentles, Professor I., BA, MA, PhD, Dept of History, Glendon College, 2275 Bayview Avenue, Toronto M4N 3M6, Canada.
Gerlach, Professor D. R., MA, PhD, University of Akron, Akron, Ohio 44325, U.S.A.
Gibbs, G. C., MA, Birkbeck College, Malet Street, London WC1E 7HX.
Gibbs, Professor N. H., MA, DPhil, All Souls College, Oxford OX1 4AL.
Gibson, Margaret T., MA, DPhil, School of History, The University, P.O. Box 147, Liverpool L69 3BX.
Gifford, Miss D. H., PhD, FSA, Public Record Office, Chancery Lane, London WC2A 1LR.
Gilbert, Professor Bentley B., PhD, Dept of History, University of Illinois at Chicago Circle, Box 4348, Chicago, Ill. 60680, U.S.A.
Gilley, S. W., BA, DPhil, Dept of Theology, University of Durham, Abbey House, Palace Green, Durham DH 1 3RS.
Ginter, Professor D. E., AM, PhD, Dept of History, Sir George Williams University, Montreal 107, Canada.
Girtin, T., MA, Butter Field House, Church Street, Old Isleworth, Mddx.
Gleave, Group Capt. T. P., CBE, RAF (ret.), Willow Bank, River Gardens, Bray-on-Thames, Berks.
*Glover, Professor R. G., MA, PhD, 2937 Tudor, Victoria, B.C. V8N IM2.
*Godber, Miss A. J., MA, FSA, Mill Lane Cottage, Willington, Bedford.
*Godfrey, Professor J. L., MA, PhD, 231 Hillcrest Circle, Chapel Hill, N.C., U.S.A.
Goldsmith, Professor M. M., PhD, Dept of Politics, University of Exeter, Exeter EX4 4RJ.
Gollin, Professor A., DLitt, University of California, Dept of History, Santa Barbara, Calif. 93106, U.S.A.

Gooch, John, BA, PhD, Dept of History, The University, Bailrigg, Lancaster LA1 4YG.
Goodman, A. E., MA, BLitt, Dept of Medieval History, The University, Edinburgh EH8 9YL.
Goodspeed, Professor D. J., BA, 164 Victoria Street, Niagara-on-the-Lake, Ontario, Canada.
*Gopal, Professor S., MA, DPhil, 30 Edward Elliot Road, Mylapore, Madras, India.
Gordon, Professor P., BSc(Econ), MSc(Econ), PhD, 241 Kenton Road, Kenton, Harrow HA3 0HJ.
Gordon-Brown, A., Velden, Alexandra Road, Wynberg, CP., South Africa.
Goring, J. J., MA, PhD, Little Iwood, Rushlake Green, Heathfield, East Sussex TN21 9QS.
Gorton, L. J., MA, 41 West Hill Avenue, Epsom, Surrey.
Gosden, P. H. J. H., MA, PhD, School of Education, The University, Leeds LS2 9JT.
Gough, Professor Barry M., PhD, History Dept, Wilfrid Laurier University, Waterloo, Ontario, Canada N2L 3C5.
Gowing, Professor Margaret, MA, DLitt, BSc(Econ), FBA, Linacre College, Oxford OX1 1SY.
*Graham, Professor G. S., MA, PhD, DLitt, LLD, Hobbs Cottage, Beckley, Rye, Sussex.
Gransden, Mrs A., MA, PhD, FSA, Dept of History, The University, Nottingham NG7 2RD.
Grattan-Kane, P., 12 St John's Close, Helston, Cornwall.
Graves, Professor Edgar B., PhD, LLD, LHD, 318 College Hill Road, Clinton, New York 13323, USA.
Gray, Professor J. R., MA, PhD, School of Oriental and African Studies, University of London, London WC1E 7HP.
Gray, J. W., MA, Dept of Modern History, The Queen's University of Belfast, Belfast BT7 1NN, N. Ireland.
Gray, Miss M., MA, BLitt, 68 Dorchester Road, Garstang, Preston PR3 1HH.
Greaves, Professor Richard L., PhD, 910 Shadowlawn Drive, Tallahassee, Florida 32312, U.S.A.
Greaves, Mrs R. L., PhD, 1920 Hillview Road, Lawrence, Kansas 66044, U.S.A.
Green, H., BA, 16 Brands Hill Avenue, High Wycombe, Bucks. HP13 5QA.
Green, I. M., MA, DPhil, Dept of Modern History, The Queen's University of Belfast, Belfast BT7 1NN, N. Ireland.
Green, Professor Thomas A., BA, PhD, JD, Legal Research Building, University of Michigan Law School, Ann Arbor, Michigan 48109, U.S.A.
Green, Rev. V. H. H., MA, DD, Lincoln College, Oxford OX1 3DR.
Greene, Professor Jack P., Dept of History, Johns Hopkins University, Baltimore, Md. 21218, U.S.A.
Greengrass, M., MA, DPhil, Dept of History, The University, Sheffield S10 2TN.
Greenhill, B. J., CMG, DPh, FSA, National Maritime Museum, Greenwich, London SE10 9FN.
Greenleaf, Professor W. H., BSc(Econ), PhD, University College of Swansea, Singleton Park, Swansea SA2 8PP.
Greenslade, M. W., JP, MA, FSA, 20 Garth Road, Stafford ST17 9JD.
GREENWAY, D. E., MA, PhD (*Assistant Literary Director*), Institute of Historical Research, Senate House, Malet Street, London WC1E 7HU.

Gregg, E., MA, PhD, Dept of History, University of South Carolina, Columbia, S.C. 29208, U.S.A.
Grenville, Professor J. A. S., PhD, University of Birmingham, P.O. Box 363, Birmingham B15 2TT.
Gresham, C. A., BA, DLitt, FSA, Bryn-y-deryn, Criccieth, Gwynedd, LL52 0HR.
GRIERSON, Professor P., MA, LittD, FBA, FSA, Gonville and Caius College, Cambridge CB2 1TA.
Grieve, Miss H. E. P., BA, 153 New London Road, Chelmsford, Essex.
Griffiths, Professor R. A., PhD, University College, Singleton Park, Swansea SA2 8PP.
Grimble, I. A. M., PhD, 10 Cumberland Road, London SW13.
Grisbrooke, W. J., MA, St Marys, Oscott College, Chester Road, Sutton Coldfield, West Midlands B73 5AA.
*Griscom, Rev. Acton, MA (address unknown).
Gruner, Professor Wolf D., Wilhelmshohenstrasse 6a, D-8130 Starnberg, West Germany.
Gum, Professor E. J., PhD, 2043 N.55th Street, Omaha, Nebraska 68104, U.S.A.
Guy, J. A., PhD, Dept of History, The University, Wills Memorial Building, Queens Road, Bristol BS8 1RJ.

HABAKKUK, Sir John (H.), MA, FBA, Jesus College, Oxford OX1 3DW.
Haber, Professor F. C., PhD, 3026 2R Street NW, Washington, D.C. 20007, U.S.A.
Hackett, Rev. M. B., OSA, BA, PhD, Austin Friars School, Carlisle CA3 9PB.
Haffenden, P. S., PhD, 36 The Parkway, Bassett, Southampton.
Haigh, C. A., MA, PhD, Christ Church, Oxford OX1 1DP.
Haight, Mrs M. Jackson, PhD, 3 Wolger Road, Mosman, N.S.W. 2088, Australia.
Haines, R. M., MA, MLitt, DPhil, FSA, Dalhousie University, Dept of History, Nova Scotia, Canada B3H 3J5.
Hainsworth, D. R., MA, PhD, University of Adelaide, Dept of History, North Terrace, Adelaide, South Australia 5001.
Hair, Professor P. E. H., MA, DPhil, School of History, The University, P.O. Box 147, Liverpool L69 3BX.
Hale, Professor J. R., MA, FBA, FSA, University College London, Gower Street, London WC1E 6BT.
Haley, Professor K. H. D., MA, BLitt, 15 Haugh Lane, Sheffield 11.
Hall, Professor A. R., MA, PhD, DLitt, FBA, 14 Ball Lane, Tackley, Oxford OX5 3AG.
Hall, B., MA, PhD, FSA, DD, 2 Newton House, Newton St Cyres, Devon EX5 5BL.
Hallam, Elizabeth M., BA, PhD, Public Record Office, Chancery Lane, London WC2A 1LR.
Hallam, Professor H. E., MA, PhD, University of Western Australia, Nedlands 6009, Western Australia.
Hamer, Professor D. A., MA, DPhil, History Dept, Victoria University of Wellington, Private Bag, Wellington, New Zealand.
Hamilton, B., BA, PhD, The University, Nottingham NG7 2RD.
Hammersley, G. F., BA, PhD, University of Edinburgh, William Robertson Building, George Square, Edinburgh EH8 9JY.
Hampson, Professor N., MA, Ddel'U, 305 Hull Road, York YO1 3LB.

Hand, Professor G. J., MA, DPhil, Faculty of Law, University of Birmingham, P.O. Box 363, Birmingham B15 2TT.

Handford, M. A., MA, MSc, 6 Spa Lane, Hinckley, Leicester LE10 1JB.

Hanham, Dean H. J., MA, PhD, School of Humanities and Social Science, Massachusetts Institute of Technology, Cambridge, Mass. 02139, U.S.A

Hannah, L., MA, DPhil, Business History Unit, Lionel Robbins Building, 10 Portugal Street, London WC2A 2HD.

Harcourt, Freda, PhD, Dept of History, Queen Mary College, Mile End Road, London E1 4NS.

Harding, Professor A., MA, BLitt, School of History, The University, P.O. Box 147, Liverpool L69 3BX.

Harding, H. W., BA, LLD, 39 Annunciation Street, Sliema, Malta.

Haren, M. J., DPhil, 5 Marley Lawn, Dublin 16, Ireland.

Hargreaves, Professor J. D., MA, 'Balcluain', Raemoir Road, Banchory, Kincardineshire.

Harkness, Professor D. W., MA, PhD, Dept of Irish History, The Queen's University, Belfast BT7 1NN, N. Ireland.

Harman, Rev. L. W., 72 Westmount Road, London SE9.

Harper-Bill, C., BA, PhD, 15 Cusack Close, Strawberry Hill, Twickenham, Middlesex.

Harris, G., MA, 4 Lancaster Drive, London NW3.

Harris, Mrs J. F., BA, PhD, 30 Charlbury Road, Oxford OX1 3UJ.

Harris, Professor J. R., MA, PhD, The University, P.O. Box 363, Birmingham B15 2TT.

Harrison, B. H., MA, DPhil, Corpus Christi College, Oxford OX1 4JF.

Harrison, C. J., BA, PhD, The University, Keele, Staffs. ST5 5BG.

Harrison, Professor Royden, MA, DPhil, 4 Wilton Place, Sheffield S10 2BT.

Harriss, G. L., MA, DPhil, Magdalen College, Oxford OX1 4AU.

Hart, C. J. R., MA, MB, DLitt, Goldthorns, Stilton, Peterborough PE7 3RH.

Hart, Mrs J. M., MA, St Anne's College, Oxford OX2 6HF.

Harte, N. B., BSc(Econ), Dept of History, University College London, Gower Street, London WC1E 6BT.

Hartley, T. E., BA, PhD, Dept of History, The University, Leicester LE1 7RH.

Harvey, Miss B. F., MA, BLitt, FBA, Somerville College, Oxford OX2 6HD.

Harvey, Margaret M., MA, DPhil, St Aidan's College, Durham DH1 3LJ.

Harvey, Professor P. D. A., MA, DPhil, FSA, Dept of History, The University, Durham DH1 3EX.

Harvey, Sally P. J., MA, PhD, Sint Hubertuslaan 7, 1980 Tervuren, Brussels, Belgium.

Haskell, Professor F. J., MA, FBA, Trinity College, Oxford OX1 3BH.

Haskins, Professor G. L., AB, LLB, JD, MA, University of Pennsylvania, The Law School, 3400 Chestnut Street, Philadelphia, Pa. 19104 U.S.A.

Haslam, Group Captain E. B., MA, RAF (retd), 27 Denton Road, Wokingham, Berks. RG11 2DX.

Hassall, W. O., MA, DPhil, FSA, The Manor House, 26 High Street, Wheatley, Oxford OX9 1XX.

Hast, Adele, PhD, Marquis Who's Who, Inc., 200 E. Ohio Street, Chicago, Ill. 60611, U.S.A.

Hatcher, M. J., BSc(Econ), PhD, Corpus Christi College, Cambridge CB2 1RH.

Hatley, V. A., BA, ALA, 6 The Crescent, Northampton NN1 4SB.

Hatton, Professor Ragnhild M., PhD, 49 Campden Street, London W8.

Havighurst, Professor A. F., MA, PhD, 11 Blake Field, Amherst, Mass. 01002, U.S.A.

Havinden, M. A., MA, BLitt, Dept of Economic History, Amory Building, The University, Exeter EX4 4QH.

Havran, Professor M. J., MA, PhD, Corcoran Dept of History, Randall Hall, University of Virginia, Charlottesville, Va. 22903, U.S.A.

HAY, Professor D., MA, DLitt, FBA, Dept of History, The University, Edinburgh EH8 9JY.

Hayes, P. M., MA, DPhil, Keble College, Oxford OX1 3PG.

Hazlehurst, G. C. L., BA, DPhil, FRSL, Research School of Social Sciences, Institute of Advanced Studies, Australian National University, P.O. Box 4, A.C.T. 2600, Australia.

Hearder, Professor H., BA, PhD, University College, P.O. Box 78, Cardiff CF1 1XL.

Heath, P., MA, Dept of History, The University Hull HU6 7RX.

Heathcote, T. A., BA, PhD, Cheyne Cottage, Birch Drive, Hawley, Camberley, Surrey.

Helmholz, R. H., PhD, LLB, The Law School, University of Chicago, 1111 East 60th Street, Chicago, Ill. 60637, U.S.A.

Hembry, Mrs. P. M., BA, PhD, Pleasant Cottage, Crockerton, Warminster, Wilts. BA12 8AJ.

Hendy, M. F., MA, Dept of History, The University, P.O. Box 363, Birmingham B15 2TT.

Henning, Professor B. D., PhD, History of Parliament, 34 Tavistock Square, London WC1H 9EZ.

Hennock, Professor E. P., MA, PhD, School of History, University of Liverpool, P.O. Box 147, Liverpool L69 3BX.

Heppell, Muriel, BA, MA, PhD, 104 Eton Hall, Eton College Road, London NW3 2DF.

Hernon, Professor J. M., PhD, Dept of History, University of Massachusetts, Amherst, Mass. 01002, U.S.A.

Hexter, Professor J. H., PhD, Dept of History, 237 Hall of Graduate Studies, Yale University, New Haven, Conn. 06520, U.S.A.

Highfield, J. R. L., MA, DPhil, Merton College, Oxford OX1 4JD.

Hill, B. W., BA, PhD, School of English and American Studies, University of East Anglia, Norwich NR4 7TJ.

Hill, J. E. C., MA, DLitt, FBA, Woodway, Sibford Ferris, nr. Banbury, Oxfordshire OX15 5RA.

Hill, Professor L. M., AB, MA, PhD, 5066 Berean Lane, Irvine, Calif. 92664, U.S.A.

*Hill, Miss M. C., MA, Crab End, Brevel Terrace, Charlton Kings, Cheltenham, Glos.

*Hill, Professor Rosalind M. T., MA, BLitt, FSA, Westfield College, Kidderpore Avenue, London NW3 7ST.

Hilton, Professor R. H., DPhil, FBA, University of Birmingham, P.O. Box 363, Birmingham B15 2TT.

Himmelfarb, Professor Gertrude, PhD, The City University of New York, Graduate Center, 33 West 42 St, New York, N.Y. 10036, U.S.A.

Hind, R. J., BA, PhD, Dept of History, University of Sydney, Sydney, N.S.W. 2006, Australia.

*Hinsley, Professor F. H., MA, St John's College, Cambridge CB2 1TP.

Hirst, Professor D. M., PhD, Dept of History, Washington University, St Louis, Missouri, U.S.A.

Hockey, The Rev. S. F., BA, Quarr Abbey, Ryde, Isle of Wight PO33 4ES.

*Hodgett, G. A. J., MA, FSA, King's College, Strand, London WC2R 2LS.
Holdsworth, Professor C. J., MA, PhD, FSA, 5 Pennsylvania Park, Exeter EX4 6HD.
Hollaender, A. E. J., PhD, FSA, 119 Narbonne Avenue, South Side, Clapham Common, London SW4 9LQ.
Hollis, Patricia, MA, DPhil, 30 Park Lane, Norwich NOR 47F.
Hollister, Professor C. Warren, MA, PhD, University of California, Santa Barbara, Calif. 93106, U.S.A.
Holmes, Professor Clive A., MA, PhD, Dept of History, McGraw Hill, Cornell University, N.Y. 14853, U.S.A.
Holmes, G. A., MA, PhD, 431 Banbury Road, Oxford.
Holmes, Professor G. S., MA, DLitt, Tatham House, Burton-in-Lonsdale, Carnforth, Lancs.
Holroyd, M. de C. F., 85 St Mark's Road, London W10.
HOLT, Professor J. C., MA, DPhil, FBA, FSA (*President*), Fitzwilliam College, Cambridge CB3 0DG.
Holt, Professor P. M., MA, DLitt, FBA, School of Oriental and African Studies, Malet Street, London WC1E 7HP.
Honey, Professor, J. R. de S., MA, DPhil, 5 Woods Close, Oadby, Leicester LE2 4FJ.
Hook, Mrs Judith, MA, PhD, Dept of History, Taylor Building, King's College, Old Aberdeen AB9 2UB.
Hope, R. S. H., 25 Hengistbury Road, Bournemouth, Dorset BH6 4DQ.
Hopkins, E., MA, PhD, 77 Stevens Road, Stourbridge, West Midlands DY9 0XW.
Hoppen, K. T., MA, PhD, Dept of History, The University, Hull HU6 7RX.
Horwitz, Professor H. G., BA, DPhil, Dept of History, University of Iowa, Iowa City, Iowa 52242, U.S.A.
Houlbrooke, R. A., MA, DPhil, Faculty of Letters and Social Sciences, The University, Reading RG6 2AH.
Housley, N. J., MA, PhD, School of History, The University, P.O. Box 147, Liverpool L69 3BX.
*Howard, C. H. D., MA, 15 Sunnydale Gardens, London NW7 3PD.
*Howard, Professor M. E., CBE, MC, DLitt, FBA, Oriel College, Oxford OX1 4EW.
Howarth, Mrs J. H., MA, St Hilda's College, Oxford OX4 1DY.
Howat, G. M. D., MA, MLitt, Old School House, North Moreton, Didcot, Oxfordshire OX11 9BA.
Howell, Miss M. E., MA, PhD, 10 Blenheim Drive, Oxford OX2 8DG.
Howell, Professor R., MA, DPhil, Dept of History, Bowdoin College, Brunswick, Maine 04011, U.S.A.
Howells, B. E., MA, Whitehill, Cwm Ann, Lampeter, Dyfed.
Hudson, Miss A., MA, DPhil, Lady Margaret Hall, Oxford OX2 6QA.
Hufton, Professor Olwen H., BA, PhD, 40 Shinfield Road, Reading, Berks.
Hughes, J. Q., BArch, PhD, 10a Fulwood Park, Liverpool L17 5AH.
Hull, F., BA, PhD, Roundwell Cottage, Bearsted, Maidstone, Kent ME14 4EU.
HUMPHREYS, Professor R. A., OBE, MA, PhD, DLitt, LittD, DLitt, DUniv, 5 St James's Close, Prince Albert Road, London NW8 7LG.
Hunnisett, R. F., MA, DPhil, 23 Byron Gardens, Sutton, Surrey SM1 3QG.
Hunt, Professor K. S., PhD, MA, Dept of History, Rhodes University Grahamstown 6140, South Africa.
Hurst, M. C., MA, St John's College, Oxford OX1 3JP.

Hurt, J. S., BA, BSc(Econ), PhD, 66 Oxford Road, Moseley, Birmingham B13 9SQ.

*Hussey, Professor Joan M., MA, BLitt, PhD, FSA, Royal Holloway College, Englefield Green, Surrey TW20 0EX.

Hutton, R. E., BA, DPhil, Dept of History, The University, Queen's Road, Bristol BS8 1RJ.

Hyams, P. R., MA, DPhil, Pembroke College, Oxford OX1 1DW.

*Hyde, H. Montgomery, MA, DLit, Westwell House, Tenterden, Kent.

Hyde, Professor J. K., MA, PhD, The University, Manchester M13 9PL.

Ingham, Professor K., OBE, MA, DPhil, The Woodlands, 94 West Town Lane, Bristol BS4 5DZ.

Ingram Ellis, Professor E. R., MA, PhD, Dept of History, Simon Fraser University, Burnaby, B.C., VSA IS6, Canada.

Ives, E. W., PhD, 214 Myton Road, Warwick.

Jack, Professor R. I., MA, PhD, University of Sydney, Sydney, N.S.W., Australia.

Jack, Mrs. S. M., MA, BLitt, University of Sydney, Sydney, N.S.W., Australia.

Jackman, Professor S. W., PhD, FSA, 1065 Deal Street, Victoria, British Columbia, Canada.

Jacob, Professor Margaret C., 40 Highbury Hill, Flat C, London N5.

Jagger, Rev. P. J., MA, MPhil, St Deiniol's Library, Hawarden, Deeside, Clwyd CH5 3DF.

Jalland, Patricia, PhD, MA, BA, Dept of History, School of Social Sciences, Western Australian Institute of Technology, South Bentley, Western Australia 6102.

James, Edward, MA, DPhil, Dept of History, The University, Heslington, York YO1 5DD.

James, M. E., MA, University of Durham, 43–45 North Bailey, Durham DH1 3HP.

James, R. Rhodes, MP, MA, FRSL, The Stone House, Great Gransden, nr Sandy, Beds.

Jeffs, R. M., MA, DPhil, FSA, 6a Gladstone Road, Sheffield S10 3GT.

Jenkins, Professor D., MA, LLM, LittD, Adeilad Hugh Owen, Penglais, Aberystwyth SY23 3DY.

Jeremy, D. J., BA, MLitt, PhD, 16 Britannia Gardens, Westcliff-on-Sea, Essex SS0 8BN.

Jewell, Miss H. M., MA PhD, School of History, The University, P.O. Box 147, Liverpool L69 3BX.

John, E., MA, The University, Manchester M13 9PL.

Johnson, D. J., BA, 41 Cranes Park Avenue, Surbiton, Surrey.

Johnson, Professor D. W. J., BA, BLitt, University College London, Gower Street, London WC1E 6BT.

*Johnson, J. H., MA, Whitehorns, Cedar Avenue, Chelmsford, Essex.

Johnston, Professor Edith M., MA, PhD, Dept of History, Macquarie Univ., North Ryde, N.S.W. 2113, Australia.

Johnston, Professor S. H. F., MA, Fronhyfryd, Llanbadarn Road, Aberystwyth, Dyfed.

Jones, D. J. V., BA, PhD, Dept of History, University College of Swansea, Singleton Park, Swansea SA2 8PP.

Jones, Dwyryd W., MA, DPhil, Dept of History, The University, Heslington, York YO1 5DD.

Jones, Revd. F., BA, MSc, PhD, 4a Castlemain Avenue, Southbourne, Bournemouth BH6 5EH.
Jones, G. A., MA, PhD, Dept of History, University of Reading, Whiteknights, Reading, Berks. RG6 2AH.
Jones, G. E., MA, PhD, MEd, 130 Pennard Drive, Pennard, Gower, West Glamorgan.
Jones, Professor G. Hilton, PhD, Dept of History, Eastern Illinois University, Charleston, Ill. 61920, U.S.A.
Jones, G. J., MPhil, The Croft, Litchard Bungalows, Bridgend, Glam.
Jones, Professor G. W., BA, MA, DPhil, Dept of Government, London School of Economics, Houghton Street, London WC2A 2AE.
Jones, Professor I. G., MA, 12 Laura Place, Aberystwyth, Dyfed.
Jones, J. D., MA, PhD, Carisbrooke Castle Museum, Newport, Isle of Wight PO30 1XY.
Jones, Professor, J. R., MA., PhD, School of English and American Studies, University Plain, Norwich NOR 30A.
Jones, Professor M. A., MA, DPhil, Dept of History, University College London, Gower Street, London WC1E 6BT.
Jones, Mrs Marian H., MA, Glwysgoed, Caradog Road, Aberystwyth, Dyfed.
Jones, M. C. E., MA, DPhil, FSA, Dept of History, The University, Nottingham NG7 2RD.
Jones, The Rev. Canon O. W., MA, The Vicarage, Builth Wells, Powys LD2 3BS.
Jones, P. J., DPhil, Brasenose College, Oxford OX1 4AJ.
Jones, Professor W. J., PhD, Dept of History, The University of Alberta, Edmonton T6G 2E1, Canada.
Jones-Parry, Sir Ernest, MA, PhD, 3 Sussex Mansions, Old Brompton Road, London SW7.
Judd, D., BA, PhD, Dept of History and Philosophy, Polytechnic of North London, Prince of Wales Road, London NW6.
Judson, Professor Margaret A., PhD, 8 Redcliffe Avenue, Highland Park, N.J. 08904, U.S.A.
Jukes, Rev. H. A. Ll., MA, STh, 1 St Mary's Court, Ely, Cambs. CB7 4HQ.

Kaeuper, Professor R. W., MA., PhD, 151 Village Lane, Rochester, New York 14610, USA.
Kamen, H. A. F., MA, DPhil, The University, Warwick, Coventry CV4 7AL.
Kanya-Forstner, A. S., PhD, Dept of History, York University, 4700 Keele Street, Downsview, Ontario M3J 1P3, Canada.
*Kay, H., MA, 68 Alwoodley Lane, Leeds LS17 7PT.
Kedward, H. R., MA, MPhil, 137 Waldegrave Road, Brighton BN1 6GJ.
Keeler, Mrs Mary F., PhD, 302 West 12th Street, Frederick, Maryland 21701, U.S.A.
Keen, L. J., MPhil, Dip Archaeol, FSA, 7 Church Street, Dorchester, Dorset.
Keen, M. H., MA, Balliol College, Oxford OX1 3BJ.
Kellas, J. G., MA, PhD, Dept of Politics, Glasgow University, Adam Smith Building, Glasgow G12 8RT.
Kellaway, C. W., MA, FSA, 2 Grove Terrace, London NW5.
Kellett, J. R., MA, PhD, Dept of Economic History, University of Glasgow, Glasgow G12 8QQ.
Kelly, Professor T., MA, PhD, FLA, Oak Leaf House, Ambleside Road, Keswick, Cumbria CA12 4DL.
Kemp, Miss B., MA, FSA, St Hugh's College, Oxford OX2 6LE.
Kemp, B. R., BA, PhD, 12 Redhatch Drive, Earley, Reading, Berks.

Kemp, The Right Rev. E. W., DD, The Lord Bishop of Chichester, The Palace, Chichester, Sussex PO19 1PY.
Kemp, Lt-Commander P. K., RN, Malcolm's, 51 Market Hill, Maldon, Essex.
Kennedy, J., MA, 14 Poolfield Avenue, Newcastle-under-Lyme ST5 2NL.
Kennedy, Professor P. M., BA, DPhil, School of English and American Studies, University of East Anglia, Norwich NOR 88C.
Kent, Professor C. A., DPhil, Dept of History, University of Saskatchewan, Saskatoon, Sask. S7N 0WO, Canada.
Kent, Professor J. H. S., MA, PhD, Dept of Theology, University of Bristol, Senate House, Bristol BS8 1TH.
Kent, Miss M. R., PhD, BA, School of Social Sciences, Deakin University, Geelong, Victoria, Australia.
Kenyon, Professor J. P., PhD, Dept of Modern History, St Salvator's College, St Andrews, Fife KY16 9AL.
Kerridge, E. W. J., PhD, 6 Llys Tudur, Myddleton Park, Denbigh LL16 4AL.
Kettle, Miss A. J., MA, FSA, Dept of Mediaeval History, 71 South Street, St Andrews, Fife.
Keynes, S. D., MA, PhD, Trinity College, Cambridge CB2 1TQ.
Khanna, Kahan Chand, MA, PhD, Ravensdale, Simla-2, India.
Kiernan, Professor V. G., MA, 27 Nelson Street, Edinburgh EH3 6LJ.
*Kimball, Miss E. G., BLitt, PhD, 200 Leeder Hill Drive, Apt 640, Hamden, Conn. 06517, U.S.A.
King, E. J., MA, PhD, Dept of History, The University, Sheffield S10 2TN.
King, P. D., BA, PhD, Lancaster View, Bailrigg, Lancaster.
Kirby, D. P., MA, PhD, Manoraven, Llanon, Dyfed.
Kirby, J. L., MA, FSA, 209 Covington Way, Streatham, London SW16 3BY.
Kirk, J., MA, PhD, Dept of Scottish History, University of Glasgow, Glasgow G12 8QQ.
Kishlansky, Professor Mark, Dept of History, University of Chicago, 1126 East 59th Street, Chicago, Illinois 60637, U.S.A.
Kitchen, Professor Martin, BA, PhD, Dept of History, Simon Fraser University, Burnaby, B.C. V5A 1S6, Canada.
KITCHING, C. J., BA, PhD, FSA (*Hon. Treasurer*), 11 Creighton Road, London NW6 6EE.
Klibansky, Professor R., MA, PhD, DPhil, FRSC, 608 Leacock Building, McGill University, P.O. Box 6070, Station A, Montreal H3C 3G1, Canada.
Knafla, Professor L. A., BA, MA, PhD, Dept of History, University of Calgary, Alberta, Canada.
Knecht, R. J., MA, 22 Warwick New Road, Leamington Spa, Warwickshire.
Knowles, C. H., PhD, University College, P.O. Box 78, Cardiff CF1 1XL.
Koch, H. W., BA, Dept of History, University of York, Heslington, York YO1 5DD.
Kochan, L. E., MA, PhD, 237 Woodstock Road, Oxford OX2 7AD.
Koenigsberger, Dorothy M. M., BA, PhD, 41a Lancaster Avenue, London NW3.
Koenigsberger, Professor H. G., MA, PhD, Dept of History, King's College, Strand, London WC2R 2LS.
Kohl, Professor Benjamin G., AB, MA, PhD, Dept of History, Vassar College, Poughkeepsie, New York, 12601, U.S.A.
Korr, Charles P., MA, PhD, College of Arts and Sciences, Dept of History, University of Missouri, 8001 Natural Bridge Road, St Louis, Missouri 63121, U.S.A.

Koss, Professor S. E., Dept of History, Columbia University, New York, N.Y. 10027, U.S.A.

Kossmann, Professor E. H., DLitt, Rijksuniversiteit te Groningen, Groningen, The Netherlands.

Kouri, E. I., PhD, Institut für Neuere Geschichte, Franz-Joseph-Strasse 10, D-8000 München, W. Germany.

Lake, P., BA, PhD, Dept of History, Bedford College, Regent's Park, London NW1 4NS.

Lambert, The Hon. Margaret, CMG, PhD, 39 Thornhill Road, Barnsbury Square, London N1 1JS.

Lambert, W. R., BA, PhD, 11 Pinnocks Way, Botley, Oxford OX2 9DD.

Lamont, W. M., PhD, Manor House, Keighton Road, Denton, Newhaven, Sussex BN9 0AB.

Lander, J. R., MA, MLitt, Social Science Centre, University of Western Ontario, London, Ont. N6A 5C2, Canada.

Landes, Professor D. S., PhD, Widener U, Harvard University, Cambridge, Mass. 02138, U.S.A.

Landon, Professor M. de L., MA, PhD, Dept of History, The University, Mississippi 38677 U.S.A.

Langford, P., MA, DPhil, Lincoln College, Oxford OX1 3DR.

Langhorne, R. T. B., MA, 15 Madingley Road, Cambridge.

Lapidge, M., BA, MA, PhD, Dept of Anglo-Saxon, Norse and Celtic, 9 West Road, Cambridge CB3 9DP.

Larkin, Rev J. F., CSV, PhD, 1212 East Euclid Street, Arlington Heights, Illinois 60004, U.S.A.

Larner, J. P., MA, The University, Glasgow G12 8QQ.

Lasko, Professor P. E., BA, FSA, Courtauld Institute of Art, 20 Portman Square, London W1H 0BE.

Latham, R. C., CBE, MA, FBA, Magdalene College, Cambridge CB3 0AG.

Lawrence, Professor C. H., MA, DPhil, Bedford College, Regent's Park, London NW1 4NS.

Laws, Captain W. F., BA, MLitt, 9 The Glebe, Thorverton, Devon EX5 5LS.

Leddy, J. F., MA, BLitt, DPhil, University of Windsor, Windsor, Ontario, Canada.

Lee, Professor J. M., MA, BLitt, Dept of Politics, University of Bristol, 77/79 Woodland Road, Bristol BS8 1UT.

Legge, Professor M. Dominica, MA, DLitt, FBA, 191a Woodstock Road, Oxford OX2 7AB.

Lehmann, Professor J. H., PhD, De Paul University, 25e Jackson Blvd., Chicago, Illinois 60604, U.S.A.

Lehmberg, Professor S. E., PhD, Dept of History, University of Minnesota, Minneapolis, Minn. 55455, U.S.A.

Leinster-Mackay, D. P., MA, MEd, PhD, Dept of Education, University of Western Australia, Nedlands, Western Australia 6009.

Lenman, B. P., MA, MLitt, FSA(Scot), 'Cromalt', 50 Lade Braes, St Andrews, Fife KY16 9DA.

Leslie, Professor R. F., BA, PhD, Market House, Church Street, Charlbury, Oxford OX7 3PP.

Lester, Professor M., PhD, Dept of History, Davidson College, Davidson, N.C. 28036, U.S.A.

Levine, Professor Joseph M., Dept of History, Syracuse University, Syracuse, New York 13210, U.S.A.

Levine, Professor Mortimer, PhD, 529 Woodhaven Drive, Morgantown, West Va. 26505, U.S.A.
Levy, Professor F. J., PhD, University of Washington, Seattle, Wash. 98195, U.S.A.
Lewin, G. R., BA, Camilla House, Forest Road, East Horsley, Surrey KT24 5BB.
Lewis, Professor A. R., MA, PhD, History Dept, University of Massachusetts, Amherst, Mass. 01003, U.S.A.
Lewis, Professor B., PhD, FBA, Near Eastern Studies Dept, Jones Hall, The University, Princeton, N.J. 08540, U.S.A.
Lewis, C. W., BA, FSA, University College, P.O. Box 78, Cardiff CF1 1XL.
Lewis, P. S., MA, All Souls College, Oxford OX1 4AL.
Lewis, R. A., PhD, University College of North Wales, Bangor, Gwynedd LL57 2DG.
Leyser, K., MA, Magdalen College, Oxford OX1 4AU.
Liddle, P. H., BA, MLitt, 'Dipity Cottage', 20 Lime Street, Waldridge Fell, nr Chester-le-Street, Co Durham.
*Lindsay, Mrs H., MA, PhD, (address unknown).
Lindsay, Lt.Col. Oliver, MBIM, Brookwood House, Brookwood, nr Woking, Surrey.
Linehan, P. A., MA, PhD, St John's College, Cambridge CB2 1TP.
Lipman, V. D., CVO, MA, DPhil, FSA, 9 Rotherwick Road, London NW11 9DG.
Livermore, Professor H. V., MA, Sandycombe Lodge, Sandycombe Road, St Margarets, Twickenham, Middx.
Lloyd, H. A., BA, DPhil, The University, Cottingham Road, Hull HU6 7RX.
Loach, Mrs J., MA, Somerville College, Oxford OX2 6HD.
Loades, Professor D. M., MA, PhD, University College of North Wales, Bangor, Gwynedd LL57 2DG.
Lobel, Mrs M. D., BA, FSA, 16 Merton Street, Oxford.
Lockie, D. McN., MA, Chemin de la Panouche, Saint-Anne, 06130 Grasse, France.
Lockyer, R. W., MA, Dept of History, Royal Holloway College, Englefield Green, Surrey TW20 0EX.
Logan, F. D., MA, MSD, Emmanuel College, 400 The Fenway, Boston, Mass. 02115, U.S.A.
Logan, O. M. T., MA, PhD, 18 Clarendon Road, Norwich NR2 2PW.
London, Miss Vera C. M., MA, 55 Churchill Road, Church Stretton, Shropshire SY6 6EP.
Longley, D. A., MA, PhD, Dept of History, King's College, The University, Old Aberdeen AB9 2UB.
Longmate, N. R., MA, 30 Clydesdale Gardens, Richmond, Surrey.
Loomie, Rev. A. J., SJ, MA, PhD, Fordham University, New York, N.Y. 10458, U.S.A.
Loud, G. A., DPhil, School of History, The University, Leeds LS2 9JT.
Lourie, Elena, MA, DPhil, Dept of History, University of The Negev, P.O. Box 4653, Beer Sheva, Israel.
Lovatt, R. W., MA, DPhil, Peterhouse, Cambridge CB2 1RD.
Lovell, J. C., BA, PhD, Eliot College, University of Kent, Canterbury CT2 7NS.
Lovett, A. W., MA, PhD, 26 Coney Hill Road, West Wickham, Kent BR4 9BX.

Lowe, P. C., BA, PhD, The University, Manchester M13 9PL.
Lowerson, J. R., BA, MA, Centre for Continuing Education, University of Sussex, Brighton.
Loyn, Professor H. R., MA, FBA, FSA, Westfield College, Kidderpore Avenue, London NW3 7ST.
Lucas, C. R., MA, DPhil, Balliol College, Oxford OX1 3BJ.
Lucas, P. J., MA, PhD, University College, Belfield, Dublin 4, Ireland.
Luft, Rev. Canon H. M., MA, MLitt, Highfurlong, 44 St Michael's Road, Blundellsands, Liverpool L23 7UN.
*Lumb, Miss S. V., MA, Torr-Colin House, 106 Ridgway, Wimbledon, London SW19.
Lunn, D. C. J., STL, MA, PhD, 25 Cornwallis Avenue, Clifton, Bristol BS8 4PP.
Lunt, Major-General J. D., MA, Hilltop House, Little Milton, Oxfordshire OX9 7PU.
Luscombe, Professor D. E., MA, PhD, 4 Caxton Road, Broomhill, Sheffield S10 3DE.
Luttrell, A. T., MA, DPhil, Dept of History, The University of Malta, Msida, Malta.
Lyman, Professor Richard W., PhD, 350 East 57th Street, Apt 14-B, New York, N.Y. 10022, U.S.A.
Lynch, Professor J., MA, PhD, Inst. of Latin American Studies, 31 Tavistock Square, London WC1H 9HA.
Lynch, M., MA, PhD, Dept of Scottish History, The University, 50 George Square, Edinburgh EH8 9YW.
Lyon, Professor Bryce D., PhD, Dept of History, Brown University, Providence, Rhode Island 02912, U.S.A.
Lyttelton, The Hon. N. A. O., BA, St Antony's College, Oxford OX2 6JF.

Mabbs, A. W., 14 Acorn Lane, Cuffley, Hertfordshire.
Macaulay, J. H., MA, PhD, 6 Hamilton Drive, Hillhead, Glasgow G12 8DR.
McBriar, Professor A. M., BA, DPhil, FASSA, Dept of History, Monash University, Clayton, Victoria 3168, Australia.
MacCaffrey, Professor W. T., PhD, 745 Hollyoke Center, Harvard University, Cambridge, Mass. 02138, U.S.A.
McCann, W. P., BA, PhD, 41 Stanhope Gardens, Highgate, London N6.
McCaughan, Professor R. E. M., MA, BArch, Hon DSc, FSA, FRAnthl, FRIBA, 'Rowan Bank', Kingsley Green, Fernhurst, West Sussex GU27 3LL.
McConica, Professor J. K., CSB, MA, DPhil, Pontifical Institute of Mediaeval Studies, 59 Queen's Park, Toronto, Ontario, Canada M5S 2C4.
McCord, Professor N., PhD, 7 Hatherton Avenue, Cullercoats, North Shields, Northumberland.
McCracken, Professor J. L., MA, PhD, 79 Ballaghmore Road, Bushmills, Co Antrim, N. Ireland.
MacCulloch, D. N. J., Wesley College, Henbury Road, Westbury-on-Trym, Bristol BS10 7QD.
MacCurtain, Margaret B., MA, PhD, Dept of History, University College, Belfield, Dublin 4, Ireland.
McCusker, J. J., MA, PhD, Dept of History, University of Maryland, College Park, Maryland 20742, U.S.A.
MacDonagh, Professor O., MA, PhD, Research School of Social Sciences, Institute of Advanced Studies, Australian National University, P.O. Box 4, A.C.T. 2600, Australia.

Macdonald, Professor D. F., MA, DPhil, 11 Arnhall Drive, Dundee.
McDonald, Professor T. H., MA, PhD, R. R. 1, Site 1A, Peachland, B.C., VOH 1XO, Canada.
McDowell, Professor R. B., PhD, LittD, Trinity College, Dublin, Ireland.
Macfarlane, A., MA, DPhil, PhD, King's College, Cambridge CB2 1ST.
Macfarlane, L. J., PhD, FSA, King's College, University of Aberdeen, Aberdeen AB9 1FX.
McGrath, Professor P. V., MA, University of Bristol, Bristol BS8 1RJ.
MacGregor, D. R., MA, ARIBA, FSA, 99 Lonsdale Road, London SW13 9DA.
McGurk, J. J. N., BA, MPhil, PhD, Conway House, 10 Stanley Avenue, Birkdale, Southport, Merseyside.
McGurk, P. M., PhD, Birkbeck College, Malet Street, London WC1E 7HX.
Machin, G. I. T., MA, DPhil, Dept of Modern History, University of Dundee, Dundee DD1 4HN.
MacIntyre, A. D., MA, DPhil, Magdalen College, Oxford OX1 4AU.
McKendrick, N., MA, Gonville and Caius College, Cambridge CB2 1TA.
McKenna, Professor J. W., MA, PhD, 1444 Old Gulph Road, Villanova, Pa. 19085, U.S.A.
Mackesy, P. G., MA, DPhil, DLitt, Pembroke College, Oxford OX1 1DW.
McKibbin, R. I., MA, DPhil, St John's College, Oxford OX1 3JP.
McKinley, R. A., MA, 42 Boyers Walk, Leicester Forest East, Leicester.
McKitterick, Rosamond D., MA, PhD, Newnham College, Cambridge CB3 9DF.
Maclagan, M., MA, FSA, Trinity College, Oxford OX1 3BH.
MacLeod, Professor R. M., AB, PhD, Dept of Science Education, Institute of Education, Bedford Way, London WC1H 0AL.
*McManners, Professor J., MA, DLitt, FBA, Christ Church, Oxford OX1 1DP.
MacMichael, N. H., FSA, 2b Little Cloister, Westminster Abbey, London SW1.
McMillan, J. F., MA, DPhil, Dept of History, The University, Heslington, York YO1 5DD.
MacNiocaill, Professor G., PhD, DLitt, Dept of History, University College, Galway, Ireland.
McNulty, Miss P. A., BA, 84b Eastern Avenue, Reading RG1 5SF.
Macpherson, Professor C. B., BA, MSc(Econ), DSc(Econ), DLitt, LLD, FRSC, University of Toronto, Toronto M5S 1A1, Canada.
Madariaga, Miss Isabel de, PhD, 25 Southwood Lawn Road, London N6.
Madden, A. F., DPhil, Nuffield College, Oxford OX1 1NF.
Maddicott, J. R., MA, DPhil, Exeter College, Oxford OX1 3DP.
Maehl, Professor W. H., PhD, College of Liberal Studies, Office of the Dean, 1700 Asp Avenue, Suite 226, Norman, Oklahoma 73037, U.S.A.
Maffei, Professor Domenico, MLL, DrJur, Via delle Cerchia 19, 53100 Siena, Italy.
Magnus-Allcroft, Sir Phillip, Bt., CBE, FRSL, Stokesay Court, Craven Arms, Shropshire SY7 9BD.
Maguire, W. A., MA, PhD, 18 Harberton Park, Belfast, N. Ireland BT9 6TS.
Mahoney, Professor T. H. D., AM, PhD, MPA, Massachusetts Institute of Technology, Cambridge, Mass. 02138, U.S.A.
*MAJOR, Miss K., MA, BLitt, LittD, FBA, FSA, 21 Queensway, Lincoln LN2 4AJ.
Mallett, Professor M. E., MA, DPhil, University of Warwick, Coventry CV4 7AL.

Malone, Professor J. J., PhD, 110-4th Street N.E., Washington, D.C. 20002, U.S.A.
Mann, Miss J. de L., MA, The Cottage, 462 Bowerhill, Melksham, Wilts.
Manning, Professor A. F., Bosweg 27, Berg en Dal, The Netherlands.
Manning, Professor B. S., MA, DPhil, New University of Ulster, Coleraine, Co Londonderry, Northern Ireland BT52 1SA.
Manning, Professor R. B., PhD, 2848 Coleridge Road, Cleveland Heights, Ohio 44118, U.S.A.
Mansergh, Professor P. N. S., OBE, MA, DPhil, DLitt, LittD, FBA, The Master's Lodge, St John's College, Cambridge.
Maprayil, C., BD, LD, DD, MA, PhD, c/o Institute of Historical Research, Senate House, London WC1E 7HU.
Marchant, The Rev Canon R. A., PhD, BD, Laxfield Vicarage, Woodbridge, Suffolk IP13 8DT.
Marett, W. P., BSc(Econ), BCom, MA, PhD, 20 Barrington Road, Stoneygate, Leicester LE2 2RA.
Margetts, J., MA, DipEd, DrPhil, 5 Glenluce Road, Liverpool L19 9BX.
Markus, Professor R. A., MA, PhD, The University, Nottingham NG7 2RD.
Marriner, Sheila, MA, PhD, Dept of Economic History, P.O. Box 147, Liverpool L69 3BX.
Marsh, Professor Peter T., PhD, Dept of History, Syracuse University, Syracuse, New York 13210, U.S.A.
Marshall, J. D., PhD, Brynthwaite, Charney Road, Grange-over-Sands, Cumbria LA11 6BP.
Marshall, Professor P. J., MA, DPhil, King's College, Strand, London WC2R 2LS.
Martin, E. W., Crossways, 41 West Avenue, Exeter EX4 4SD.
Martin, G. H., MA, DPhil, Public Record Office, Chancery Lane, London WC2A 2LR.
Martin, Professor Miguel, P.O. Box 1696, Zone 1, Panama, Republic of Panama.
Martindale, Jane M., MA, DPhil, School of English and American Studies, University of East Anglia, Norwich NR4 7TJ.
Marwick, Professor A. J. B., MA, BLitt, Dept of History, The Open University, Walton Hall, Milton Keynes, Bucks MK7 6AA.
Mason, E. Emma, BA, PhD, Dept of History, Birkbeck College, Malet Street, London WC1E 7HX.
Mason, F. K., Beechwood, Watton, Norfolk IP25 6AB.
Mason, J. F. A., MA, DPhil, FSA, Christ Church, Oxford OX1 1DP.
Mason, T. W., MA, DPhil, St Peter's College, Oxford OX1 2DL.
Mather, F. C., MA, 69 Ethelburt Avenue, Swaythling, Southampton.
Mathias, Professor P., MA, FBA, All Souls College, Oxford OX1 4AL.
*Mathur-Sherry, Tikait Narain, BA, LLB, 3/193-4 Prem-Nagar, Dayalbagh, Agra-282005 (U.P.), India.
Matthew, Professor D. J. A., MA, DPhil, Dept of History, The University, Reading RG6 2AA.
Matthew, H. C. G., MA, DPhil, Christ Church, Oxford OX1 1DP.
Mattingly, Professor H. B., MA, Dept of Ancient History, The University, Leeds LS2 9JT.
Mayr-Harting, H. M. R. E., MA, DPhil, St Peter's College, Oxford OX1 2DL.
Mbaeyi, P. M., BA, DPhil, Alvan Ikoku College of Education, Dept of History, PMB 1033, Owerri, Imo State, Nigeria.

Medlicott, Professor W. N., MA, DLit, DLitt, LittD, 172 Watchfield Court, Sutton Court Road, Chiswick, London W4 4NE.
Meek, Christine E., MA, DPhil, 3145 Arts Building, Trinity College, Dublin 2, Ireland.
Meek, D. E., MA, BA, Dept of Celtic, University of Edinburgh, George Square, Edinburgh EH8 9JX.
Meller, Miss Helen E., BA, PhD, 2 Copenhagen Court, Denmark Grove, Alexandra Park, Nottingham NG3 4LF.
Merson, A. L., MA, The University, Southampton SO9 5NH.
Mettam, R. C., BA, MA, PhD, Dept of History, Queen Mary College, Mile End Road, London E1 4NS.
Mews, Stuart, PhD, Dept of Religious Studies, Cartmel College, Bailrigg, Lancaster.
Micklewright, F. H. A., MA, PhD, 228 South Norwood Hill, London SE25.
Midgley, Miss L. M., MA, 84 Wolverhampton Road, Stafford ST17 4AW.
Miller, Professor A., BA, MA, PhD, Dept of History, University of Texas, Houston, Texas, U.S.A.
Miller, E., MA, LittD, 36 Almoners Avenue, Cambridge CB1 4PA.
Miller, Miss H., MA, University College of North Wales, Bangor, Gwynedd LL57 2DG.
Miller, J., MA, PhD, Dept of History, Queen Mary College, Mile End Road, London E1 4NS.
Milne, A. T., MA, 9 Frank Dixon Close, London SE21 7BD.
Milne, Miss D. J., MA, PhD, King's College, Aberdeen.
Milsom, Professor S. F. C., MA, FBA, 23 Bentley Road, Cambridge CB2 2AW.
Minchinton, Professor W. E., BSc(Econ), The University, Exeter EX4 4PU.
Mingay, Professor G. E., PhD, Mill Field House, Selling Court, Selling, nr Faversham, Kent.
Mitchell, C., MA, BLitt, LittD, Woodhouse Farmhouse, Fyfield, Abingdon, Berks.
Mitchell, L. G., MA, DPhil, University College, Oxford OX1 4BH.
Mitchison, Mrs R. M., MA, Great Yew, Ormiston, East Lothian EH35 5NJ.
Momigliano, Professor A. D., DLitt, FBA, University College London, Gower Street, London WC1E 6BT.
Mommsen, Professor Dr W. J., German Historical Institute, 42 Russell Square, London WC1B 5DA.
Mondey, D. C., 175 Raeburn Avenue, Surbiton, Surrey KT5 9DE.
Money, Professor J., PhD, 912 St Patrick Street, Victoria, B.C., Canada V8S 4X5.
Moody, Professor T. W., MA, PhD, Trinity College, Dublin, Ireland.
Moore, B. J. S., BA, University of Bristol, 67 Woodland Road, Bristol BS8 1UL.
Moore, Professor Cresap, 1 Richdale Avenue, Unit 15, Cambridge, Mass. 02140, U.S.A.
Moore, R. I., MA, Dept of History, The University, Sheffield S10 2TN.
*Moorman, Mrs M., MA, 22 Springwell Road, Durham DH1 4LR.
Morey, Rev. Dom R. Adrian, OSB., MA, DPhil, LittD, Benet House, Mount Pleasant, Cambridge CB3 0BL.
Morgan, B. G., BArch, PhD, Tan-y-Fron, 43 Church Walks, Llandudno, Gwynedd.
Morgan, David R., MA, PhD, Dept of Politics, The University, P.O. Box 147, Liverpool L69 3BX.
Morgan, K. O., MA, DPhil, The Queen's College, Oxford OX1 4AW.

Morgan, Miss P. E., 1A The Cloisters, Hereford HR1 2NG.
Morgan, Victor, BA, School of English and American Studies, University of East Anglia, Norwich NR4 7TJ.
*Morrell, Professor W. P., CBE, MA, DPhil, 20 Bedford Street, St Clair, Dunedin SW1, New Zealand.
Morrill, J. S., MA, DPhil, Selwyn College, Cambridge CB3 9DQ.
Morris, The Rev. Professor C., MA, 53 Cobbett Road, Bitterne Park, Southampton SO2 4HJ.
Morris, G. C., MA, King's College, Cambridge CB2 1ST.
Mortimer, R., PhD, 124 Trent Road, Beeston, Nottingham NG2 1LQ.
Morton, Miss C. E., MA, FSA, The Studio, Chaldon Herring, nr Dorchester, Dorset DT2 8DN.
Mosse, Professor W. E. E., MA, PhD, Dawn Cottage, Ashwellthorpe, Norwich, Norfolk.
Mullins, E. L. C., OBE, MA, Institute of Historical Research, University of London, Senate House, London WC1E 7HU.
Murdoch, D. H., MA, School of History, The University, Leeds LS2 9JT.
Murray, A., MA, BA, BPhil, University College, Oxford OX1 4BH.
Murray, Athol L., MA, LLB, PhD, 33 Inverleith Gardens, Edinburgh EH3 5PR.
Myerscough, J., BA, 60 Campden Street, London W8 7EL.
Myres, J. N. L., CBE, MA, LLD, DLitt, Dlit, FBA, FSA, The Manor House, Kennington, Oxford OX1 5PH.

Naidis, Professor M., PhD, 10847 Canby Avenue, Northridge, California 91324, U.S.A.
Nef, Professor J. U., PhD, 2726 N Street NW, Washington, D.C. 20007, U.S.A.
Nelson, Janet L., BA, PhD, Dept of History, King's College, London WC2R 2LS.
Neveu, Dr Bruno, Maison Française, Norham Road, Oxford OX2 6SE.
New, Professor J. F. H., Dept of History, Waterloo University, Waterloo, Ontario, Canada.
Newitt, M. D. D., BA, PhD, Queen's Building, University of Exeter, EX4 4QH.
Newman, A. N., MA, DPhil, 33 Stanley Road, Leicester.
Newsome, D. H., MA, LittD, Master's Lodge, Wellington College, Crowthorne, Berks. RG11 7PU.
Nicholas, Professor David, PhD, Dept of History, University of Nebraska, Lincoln, Nebraska 68588, U.S.A.
Nicholas, Professor H. G., MA, FBA, New College, Oxford OX1 3BN.
Nicol, Mrs A., MA, BLitt, Public Record Office, Chancery Lane, London WC2A 1LR.
Nicol, Professor D. M., MA, PhD, King's College, London WC2R 2LS.
Noakes, J. D., MA, DPhil, Queen's Bldg., The University, Exeter EX4 4QH.
Nordmann, Professor Claude J., 5 rue du Sergant Hoff, Paris 17, 75017 France.
Norman, E. R., MA, PhD, Peterhouse, Cambridge CB2 1RD.

Obolensky, Professor Dimitri, MA, PhD, DLitt, FBA, FSA, Christ Church, Oxford OX1 1DP.
O'Day, A., MA, PhD, Polytechnic of North London, Prince of Wales Road, London NW5.

O'Day, Mrs M. R., BA, PhD, Open University, Faculty of Arts, Milton Keynes MK7 6AA.
*Offler, Professor H. S., MA, 28 Old Elvet, Durham DH1 3HN.
O'Gorman, F., BA, PhD, The University, Manchester M13 9PL.
O'Higgins, The Rev J., SJ., MA, DPhil, Campion Hall, Oxford.
Olney, R. J., MA, DPhil, Historical Manuscripts Commission, Quality Court, Chancery Lane, London WC2A 1HP.
Orde, Miss A., MA, PhD, 8 Wearside Drive, Durham DH1 1LE.
Orme, N. I., MA, DPhil, The University, Exeter EX4 4QH.
*Orr, J. E., MA, ThD, DPhil, 11451 Berwick Street, Los Angeles, Calif. 90049, U.S.A.
Ó Tuathaigh, M. A. G., MA, Dept of History, University College, Galway, Ireland.
Otway-Ruthven, Professor A. J., MA, PhD, 7 Trinity College, Dublin, Ireland.
Outhwaite, R. B., MA, PhD, Gonville and Caius College, Cambridge CB2 1TA.
Ovendale, R., MA, DPhil, Dept of International Politics, University College of Wales, Aberystwyth SY23 3DB.
Owen, A. E. B., MA, 35 Whitwell Way, Coton, Cambridge CB3 7PW.
Owen, Mrs D. M., MA, FSA, 35 Whitwell Way, Coton, Cambridge CB3 7PW.
Owen, G. D., MA, PhD, 4 St Aubyn's Mansions, Kings Esplanade, Hove, Sussex.
Owen, J. B., BSc, MA, DPhil, Lincoln College, Oxford OX1 3DR.

Pagden, A. R. D., BA, Girton College, Cambridge CB3 0JG.
Palgrave, D. A., MA, CChem, FRSC, FSG, 210 Bawtry Road, Doncaster, S. Yorkshire DN4 7BZ.
Palliser, D. M., MA, DPhil, FSA, 14 Verstone Croft, Birmingham B31 2QE.
Pallister, Anne, BA, PhD, Dept of History, The University, Reading, Berks. RG6 2AA.
Palmer, J. J. N., BA, BLitt, PhD, 59 Marlborough Avenue, Hull.
Paret, Professor P., Dept of History, Stanford University, Palo Alto, California, U.S.A.
Parish, Professor P. J., BA, Dept of Modern History, The University, Dundee DD1 4HN.
Parker, N. G., MA, PhD, LittD, Dept of Modern History, St Salvator's College, The University, St Andrew's, Fife KY16 9AJ.
Parker, R. A. C., MA, DPhil, The Queen's College, Oxford OX1 4AW.
Parker, The Rev. Dr T. M., MA, DD, FSA, Flat 2, Ritchie Court, 380 Banbury Road, Oxford OX2 7PW.
Parkes, M. B., BLitt, MA, FSA, Keble College, Oxford OX1 3PG.
*Parkinson, Professor C. N., MA, PhD, Anneville Manor, Rue Anneville, Vale, Guernsey, C.I.
Parris, H. W., MA, PhD, 15 Murdoch Road, Wokingham, Berks. RG11 2DG.
Parsloe, C. G., MA, 1 Leopold Avenue, London SW19 7ET.
Patrick, Rev. J. G., MA, PhD, DLitt, 7920 Teasdale Court, University City, St Louis, Missouri 63130, U.S.A.
Patterson, Professor A. T., MA, 14 Cresta Court, Eastern Parade, Southsea PO4 9RB.
Pavlowitch, Stevan K., MA, LesL, Dept of History, The University, Southampton SO9 5NH.

Payne, Professor Peter L., BA, PhD, 14 The Chanonry, Old Aberdeen AB2 1RP.

Peake, Rev. F. A., DD, DSLitt, 234 Wilson Street, Sudbury, Ontario P3E 2S2, Canada.

Pearl, Mrs Valerie, MA, DPhil, FSA, New Hall, Cambridge CB3 0DF.

Peek, Miss H. E., MA, FSA, FSAScot, Taintona, Moretonhampstead, Newton Abbot, Devon TQ13 8LG.

Peel, Lynnette J., BAgrSc, MAgrSc, PhD, 49 Oaklands, Hamilton Road, Reading RG1 5RN.

Peele, Miss Gillian R., BA, BPhil, Lady Margaret Hall, Oxford OX2 6QA.

Pennington, D. H., MA, Balliol College, Oxford OX1 3BJ.

Perkin, Professor H. J., MA, Borwicks, Caton, Lancaster LA2 9NB.

Peters, Professor E. M., PhD, Dept of History, University of Pennsylvania, Philadelphia 19174, U.S.A.

Petti, Professor A. G. R., MA, DLit, FSA, Dept of English, University of Calgary, Alberta T2N 1N4, Canada.

Philips, Professor Sir Cyril (H.), MA, PhD, DLitt, 3 Winterstoke Gardens, London NW7.

Phillips, Sir Henry (E. I.), CMG, MBE, MA, 34 Ross Court, Putney Hill, London SW15.

Phillips, J. R. S., BA, PhD, FSA, Dept of Medieval History, University College, Dublin 4, Ireland.

Phythian-Adams, C. V., MA, Dept of English Local History, The University, Leicester LE1 7RH.

Pierce, Professor G. O., MA, Dept of History, University College, P.O. Box 95, Cardiff CF1 1XA.

Pitt, H. G., MA, Worcester College, Oxford OX1 2HB.

Platt, C. P. S., MA, PhD, FSA, 24 Oakmount Avenue, Highfield, Southampton.

Platt, Professor D. C. St M., MA, DPhil, St Antony's College, Oxford OX2 6JF.

Plumb, Professor J. H., PhD, LittD, FBA, FSA, Christ's College, Cambridge CB2 3BU.

Pocock, Professor J. G. A., PhD, Johns Hopkins University, Baltimore, Md. 21218, U.S.A.

Pole, Professor J. R., MA, PhD, St Catherine's College, Oxford OX1 3UJ.

Pollard, A. J., BA, PhD, 22 The Green, Hurworth-on-Tees, Darlington, Co Durham DL2 2AA.

Pollard, Professor S., BSc(Econ), PhD, Dept of Economic History, The University, Sheffield S10 2TN.

Polonsky, A. B., BA, DPhil, Dept of International History, London School of Economics, Houghton Street, London WC2A 2AE.

PORT, Professor M. H., MA, BLitt, FSA (*Hon. Secretary*), Queen Mary College, Mile End Road, London E1 4NS.

Porter, A. N., MA, PhD, Dept of History, King's College, London WC2R 2LS.

Porter, B. E., BSc(Econ), PhD, Dept of International Politics, University College of Wales, Aberystwyth, Dyfed SY23 3DB.

Porter, H. C., MA, PhD, Faculty of History, West Road, Cambridge CB3 9EF.

Post, J., MA, PhD, Public Record Office, Chancery Lane, London WC2A 1LR.

Potter, J., BA, MA(Econ), London School of Economics, Houghton Street, London WC2A 2AE.

Powell, W. R., BLitt, MA, FSA, 2 Glanmead, Shenfield Road, Brentwood, Essex.

Powicke, Professor M. R., MA, University of Toronto, Toronto M5S 1AI, Canada.

Prall, Professor Stuart E., MA, PhD, Dept of History, Queens College, C.U.N.Y., Flushing, N.Y. 11367, U.S.A.

Prest, W. R., MA, DPhil, Dept of History, University of Adelaide, North Terrace, Adelaide 5001, S. Australia.

Preston, P., MA, DPhil, Dept of History, Queen Mary College, Mile End Road, London E1 4NS.

*Preston, Professor R. A., MA, PhD, Duke University, Durham, N.C., U.S.A.

Prestwich, J. O., MA, 18 Dunstan Road, Old Headington, Oxford OX3 9BY.

Prestwich, Mrs M., MA, St Hilda's College, Oxford OX4 1DY.

Prestwich, M. C., MA, DPhil, Dept of History, 43/46 North Bailey, Durham DH1 3EX.

Price, A. W., 19 Bayley Close, Uppingham, Leicestershire LE15 9TG.

Price, Rev. D. T. W., MA, St David's University College, Lampeter, Dyfed SA48 7ED.

Price, F. D., MA, BLitt, FSA, Keble College, Oxford OX1 3PG.

Price, Professor Jacob M., AM, PhD, University of Michigan, Ann Arbor, Michigan 48104, U.S.A.

Price, R. D., BA, School of Modern Languages & European History, University of East Anglia, Norwich NR4 7TJ.

Prichard, Canon T. J., MA, PhD, The Rectory, London Road, Neath, W. Glam. SA11 1LE.

Prins, G. I. T., MA, PhD, Emmanuel College, Cambridge CB2 3AP.

Pritchard, Professor D. G., PhD, 11 Coed Mor, Sketty, Swansea, W. Glam. SA2 8BQ.

Pronay, N., BA, School of History, The University, Leeds LS2 9JT.

Prothero, I. J., BA, PhD, The University, Manchester M13 9PL.

Pugh, T. B., MA, BLitt, 28 Bassett Wood Drive, Southampton SO2 3PS.

Pullan, Professor B. S., MA, PhD, Dept of History, The University, Manchester M13 9PL.

Pulman, M. B., MA, PhD, History Dept, University of Denver, Colorado 80210, U.S.A.

Pulzer, P. G. J., MA, PhD, Christ Church, Oxford OX1 1DP.

Quinn, Professor D. B., MA, PhD, DLit, DLitt, LLD, DHL, 9 Knowsley Road, Liverpool L19 0PF.

Quintrell, B. W., MA, PhD, School of History, The University, P.O. Box 147, Liverpool L69 3BX.

Rabb, Professor T. J., MA, PhD, Princeton University, Princeton, N.J. 08540, U.S.A.

Radford, C. A. Ralegh, MA, DLitt, FBA, FSA, Culmcott, Uffculme, Cullompton, Devon EX15 3AT.

*Ramm, Miss A, MA, DLitt, Metton Road, Roughton, Norfolk NR11 8QT.

*Ramsay, G. D., MA, DPhil, 15 Charlbury Road, Oxford OX2 6UT.

Ramsden, J. A., BA, DPhil, Dept of History, Queen Mary College, Mile End Road, London E1 4NS.

Ramsey, Professor P. H., MA, DPhil, Taylor Building, King's College, Old Aberdeen AB9 1FX.

Ranft, Professor B. McL., MA, DPhil. 16 Eliot Vale, London SE3.

Ransome, D. R., MA, PhD, 10 New Street, Woodbridge, Suffolk.

Ratcliffe, D. J., MA, BPhil, Dept of History, The University, 43 North Bailey, Durham DH1 3EX.

Rawcliffe, Carole, BA, PhD, 24 Villiers Road, London NW2.

Rawley, Professor J. A., PhD, University of Nebraska, Lincoln, Nebraska 68508, U.S.A.

Ray, Professor R. D., BA, BD, PhD, University of Toledo, 2801 W. Bancroft Street, Toledo, Ohio 43606, U.S.A.

Read, Professor D., BLitt, MA, PhD, Darwin College, University of Kent at Canterbury, Kent CT2 7NY.

Reader, W. J., BA, PhD, 46 Gough Way, Cambridge CB3 9LN.

Reeves, Professor A. C., MA, PhD, Dept of History, Ohio University, Athens, Ohio 45701, U.S.A.

Reeves, Miss M. E., MA, PhD, 38 Norham Road, Oxford OX2 6SQ.

Reid, Professor L. D., MA, PhD, 200 E. Brandon Road, Columbia, Mo. 65201, U.S.A.

Reid, Professor W. S., MA, PhD, University of Guelph, Guelph, Ontario, Canada.

Renold, Miss P., MA, 24 Kirk Close, Oxford OX2 8JN.

Renshaw, P. R. G., MA, Dept of History, The University, Sheffield S10 2TN.

Reuter, T. A., MA, DPhil, Monumenta Germaniae Historica, Ludwigstrasse 16, 8 München 34, West Germany.

Reynolds, Miss S. M. G., MA, 26 Lennox Gardens, London SW1.

Richards J. M., MA, Dept of History, The University, Bailrigg, Lancaster LA1 4YG.

Richards, Rev. J. M., MA, BLitt, STL, Heythrop College, 11-13 Cavendish Square, London W1M 0AN.

Richardson R. C., BA, PhD, King Alfred's College, Winchester.

Richardson, Professor W. C., MA, PhD, 4263 Sweetbriar Street, Baton Rouge, Louisiana 70808, U.S.A.

Richmond, C. F., DPhil, 59 The Covert, The University, Keele, Staffs. ST5 5BG.

Richter, Professor M., DrPhil, Dept of Medieval History, University College, Dublin 4, Ireland.

Riley, P. W. J., BA, PhD, The University, Manchester M13 9PL.

Riley-Smith, Professor J. S. C., MA, PhD, Tandem House, North Street, Winkfield, Windsor, Berks. SL4 4TB.

Rimmer, Professor W. G., MA, PhD, University of N.S.W., P.O. Box 1, Kensington, N.S.W. 2033, Australia.

Ritcheson, Professor C. R., DPhil, Dept of History, University of Southern California, Los Angeles 90007, U.S.A.

Rizvi, S. A. G., MA, DPhil, 7 Portland Road, Summertown, Oxford.

Roach, Professor J. P. C., MA, PhD, 1 Park Crescent, Sheffield S10 2DY.

Robbins, Professor Caroline, PhD, 815 The Chetwynd, Rosemont, Pa. 19010, U.S.A.

Robbins, Professor K. G., MA, DPhil, Dept of History, The University, Glasgow G12 8QQ.

Roberts, Professor J. M., MA, DPhil, The University, Southampton SO9 5NH.

Roberts, Professor M., MA, DPhil, DLit, FilDr, FBA, 38 Somerset Street, Grahamstown 6140, C.P., South Africa.

Roberts, P. R., MA, PhD, FSA, Keynes College, The University, Canterbury, Kent CT2 7NP.

Roberts, Professor R. C., PhD, 284 Blenheim Road, Columbus, Ohio 43214, U.S.A.

Roberts, Professor R. S., PhD, History Dept, University of Zimbabwe, P.O. Box MP 167, Harare, Zimbabwe.
Robinson, F. C. R., MA, PhD, 13 Grove Road, Windsor, Berkshire SL4 1JE.
Robinson, K.E., CBE, MA, DLitt, LLD, The Old Rectory, Church Westcote, Kingham, Oxford OX7 6SF.
Robinson, R. A. H., BA, PhD, School of History, The University, Birmingham B15 2TT.
Robinton, Professor Madeline R., MA, PhD, 210 Columbia Heights, Brooklyn 1, New York, U.S.A.
Rodger, N. A. M., MA, DPhil, 97 Speldhurst Road, London W4.
*Rodkey, F. S., AM, PhD, 152 Bradley Drive, Santa Cruz, Calif., U.S.A.
Rodney, Professor W., MA, PhD, Royal Roads Military College, FMO, Victoria, B.C., VoS 1Bo, Canada.
Roe, F. Gordon, FSA, 19 Vallance Road, London N22 4UD.
Roebuck, Peter, BA, PhD, Dept of History, New University of Ulster, Coleraine, N. Ireland BT48 7JL.
Rogers, Professor A., MA, PhD, FSA, New University of Ulster, Coleraine, N. Ireland BT52 1SA.
Rogister, J. M. J., BA, DPhil, 4 The Peth, Durham DH1 4PZ.
Rolo, Professor P. J. V., MA, The University, Keele, Staffordshire ST5 5BG.
Rompkey, R. G., MA, BEd, PhD, Dept of English, University of Lethbridge, 4401 University Drive, Lethbridge, Alberta T1K 3M4, Canada.
Roots, Professor I. A., MA, FSA, Dept of History, University of Exeter, Exeter EX4 4QH.
Roper, M., MA, Public Record Office, Ruskin Avenue, Kew, Richmond, Surrey TW9 4DU.
Rose, P. L., MA, D.enHist (Sorbonne), Dept of History, James Cook University, Douglas, Queensland 4811, Australia.
Rosenthal, Professor Joel T., PhD, State University, Stony Brook, New York 11794, U.S.A.
Roseveare, H. G., PhD, King's College, Strand, London WC2R 2LS.
Roskell, Professor J. S., MA, DPhil, FBA, The University, Manchester M13 9PL.
Ross, Professor C. D., MA, DPhil, Wills Memorial Building, Queen's Road, Bristol BS8 1RJ.
Ross, K. G. M., MA, School of History, The University, Leeds LS2 9JT.
Rothney, Professor G. O., PhD, St John's College, University of Manitoba, Winnipeg R3T 2M5, Canada.
Rothblatt, Professor Sheldon, PhD, Dept of History, University of California, Berkeley, Calif. 94720, U.S.A.
Rothrock, Professor G. A., MA, PhD, Dept of History, University of Alberta, Edmonton, Alberta T6G 2H4, Canada.
Rousseau, P. H., MA, DPhil, 44 Bellevue Avenue, Northcote, Auckland 9, New Zealand.
*Rowe, Miss B. J. H., MA, BLitt, St Anne's Cottage, Winkton, Christchurch, Hants.
Rowe, W. J., DPhil, Rock Mill, Par, Cornwall PL25 2SS.
Rowse, A. L., MA, DLitt, DCL, FBA, Trenarren House, St Austell, Cornwall.
ROY, I., MA, DPhil (*Literary Director*), Dept of History, King's College, Strand, London WC2R 2LS.
Roy, Professor R.H., MA, PhD, 2841 Tudor Avenue, Victoria, B.C., Canada.
Royle, E., MA, PhD, Dept of History, The University, Heslington, York YO1 5DD.

Rubens, A., FRICS, FSA, 16 Grosvenor Place, London SW1.

Rubini, D. A., DPhil, Temple University, Philadelphia 19122, Penn., U.S.A.

Rubinstein, Professor N., PhD, Westfield College, London NW3 7ST.

Ruddock, Miss A. A., PhD, FSA, Wren Cottage, Heatherwood, Midhurst, W. Sussex GU29 9LH.

Rudé, Professor G. F. E., MA, PhD, The Oast House, Hope Farm, Beckley, nr Rye, E. Sussex.

Rule, Professor John C., MA, PhD, Ohio State University, 230 West 17th Avenue, Columbus, Ohio 43210, U.S.A.

*RUNCIMAN, The Hon. Sir Steven, MA, DPhil, LLD, LittD, DLitt, LitD, DD, DHL, FBA, FSA, Elshieshields, Lockerbie, Dumfriesshire.

Runyan, Professor Timothy J., Cleveland State University, Cleveland, Ohio 44115, U.S.A.

Rupp, Professor the Rev. E. G., MA, DD, FBA, 42 Malcolm Place, King Street, Cambridge CB1 1LS.

Russell, Professor C. S. R., MA, Yale University, New Haven, Conn. 06520, U.S.A.

Russell, Mrs J. G., MA, DPhil, St Hugh's College, Oxford OX2 6LE.

Russell, Professor P. E., MA, FBA, 23 Belsyre Court, Woodstock Road, Oxford OX2 6HU.

Ryan, A. N., MA, School of History, University of Liverpool, P.O. Box 147, Liverpool L69 3BX.

Rycraft, P., BA, Dept of History, The University, Heslington, York YO1 5DD.

Ryder, A. F. C., MA, DPhil, Dept of History, Wills Memorial Building, Queen's Road, Bristol BS8 1RJ.

Sachse, Professor W. L., PhD, 4066 Whitney Avenue, Mt. Carmel, Conn. 06518, U.S.A.

Sainty, J. C., MA, 22 Kelso Place, London W8.

*Salmon, Professor E. T., MA, PhD, 36 Auchmar Road, Hamilton, Ontario LPC 1C5, Canada.

Salmon, Professor J. H. M., MA, MLitt, DLit, Bryn Mawr College, Bryn Mawr, Pa. 19101, U.S.A.

*Saltman, Professor A., MA., PhD, Bar Ilan University, Ramat Gan, Israel.

Sammut, E., KM, MA, LLD, 4 Don Rua Street, Sliema, Malta.

Samuel, E. R., BA, MPhil, 8 Steynings Way, London N12 7LN.

Sanderson, Professor G. N., MA, PhD, Dept of Modern History, Royal Holloway College, Englefield Green, Surrey TW20 0EX.

Sar Desai, Professor Damodar R., MA, PhD, Dept of History, University of California, Los Angeles, Calif. 90024, U.S.A.

Saunders, A. D., MA, FSA, 12 Ashburnham Grove, London SE10 8UH.

Saville, Professor J., BSc(Econ), Dept of Economic and Social History, The University, Hull HU6 7RX.

Sawyer, Professor P. H., MA, Viktoriagatan 18, 441 33 Alingsas, Sweden.

Sayers, Miss J. E., MA, BLitt, PhD, FSA, 17 Sheffield Terrace, Campden Hill, London W8.

Scammell, G. V., MA, Pembroke College, Cambridge CB2 1RF.

Scammell, Mrs Jean, MA, Clare Hall, Cambridge.

Scarisbrick, Professor J. J., MA, PhD, 35 Kenilworth Road, Leamington Spa, Warwickshire.

Schofield, A. N. E. D., PhD, 15 Westergate, Corfton Road, London W5 2HT.

Schofield, R. S., MA, PhD, 27 Trumpington Street, Cambridge CB2 1QA.

Schreiber, Professor Roy E., PhD, Dept of History, Indiana University, P.O.B. 7111, South Bend, Indiana 46634, U.S.A.
Schweizer, Karl W., MA, PhD, 4 Harrold Drive, Bishop's University, Lennoxville, Quebec, Canada.
Schwoerer, Professor Lois G., PhD, 7213 Rollingwood Drive, Chevy Chase, Maryland 20015, U.S.A.
Scott, H. M., MA, PhD, Dept of Modern History, The University, St Salvator's College, St Andrews, Fife.
Scouloudi, Miss I., MSc(Econ), FSA, 67 Victoria Road, London W8 5RH.
Scribner, R. W., MA, PhD, Clare College, Cambridge CB2 1TL.
Seaborne, M. V. J., MA, Chester College, Cheyney Road, Chester CH1 4BJ.
Searle, A., BA, MPhil, Dept of Manuscripts, British Library, London WC1B 3DG.
Searle, Professor Eleanor, AB, PhD, 431 S. Parkwood Avenue, Pasadena, Calif. 91107, U.S.A.
Searle, G. R., MA, PhD, School of English and American Studies, University of East Anglia, Norwich NR4 7TJ.
Seary, Professor E. R., MA, PhD, LittD, DLitt, FSA, 537 Topsail Road, St Johns, Newfoundland A1E 2C6, Canada.
Seaver, Professor Paul S., MA, PhD, Dept of History, Stanford University, Stanford, Calif. 94305, U.S.A.
Seddon, P. R., BA, PhD, Dept of History, The University, Nottingham NG7 2RD.
Sell, Rev. A. P. F., BA, BD, MA, PhD, 40 Hobart Drive, Walsall WS5 3NL.
Sellar, W. D. H., BA, LLB, 6 Eildon Street, Edinburgh EH3 5JU.
Semmel, Professor Bernard, PhD, Dept of History, State University of New York at Stony Brook, Stony Brook, N.Y. 11790, U.S.A.
Serjeant, W. R., BA, 51 Derwent Road, Ipswich IP3 0QR.
Seton-Watson, C. I. W., MC, MA, Oriel College, Oxford OX1 4EW.
Seton-Watson, Professor G. H. N., MA, FBA, Dept of Russian History, School of Slavonic Studies, London WC1E 7HU.
Shackleton, R., MA, DLitt, LittD, DUniv, FBA, FSA, FRSL, All Souls College, Oxford OX1 4AL.
Shannon, Professor R. T., MA, PhD, Dept of History, University College of Swansea, Swansea SA2 8PP.
Sharp, Mrs M., MA, PhD, (address unknown).
Sharpe, J. A., MA, DPhil, Dept of History, The University, Heslington, York YO1 5DD.
Sharpe, K. M., MA, DPhil, Dept of History, University of Southampton, Southampton SO9 5NH.
Shaw, I. P., MA, 3 Oaks Lane, Shirley, Croydon, Surrey CR0 5HP.
Shead, N. F., MA, BLitt, 8 Whittliemuir Avenue, Muirend, Glasgow G44 3HU.
Sheils, W. J., PhD, 186 Stockton Lane, York YO3 0EY.
Shennan, Professor J. H., PhD, Dept of History, University of Lancaster, Bailrigg, Lancaster LA1 4YG.
Sheppard, F. H. W., MA, PhD, FSA, 55 New Street, Henley-on-Thames, Oxon RG9 2BP.
Sherborne, J. W., MA, 26 Hanbury Road, Bristol BS8 2EP.
Sherwood, R. E., 22 Schole Road, Willingham, Cambridge CB4 5JD.
Simpson, D. H., MA, Royal Commonwealth Society, 18 Northumberland Avenue, London WC2.
Simpson, G. G., MA, PhD, FSA, Taylor Building, King's College, Old Aberdeen AB9 2UB.

Sinar, Miss J. C., MA, 60 Wellington Street, Matlock, Derbyshire DE4 3GS.
Siney, Professor Marion C., MA, PhD, 2676 Mayfield Road, Cleveland Heights, Ohio 44106, U.S.A.
Singhal, Professor D. P., MA, PhD, University of Queensland, St Lucia, Brisbane, Queensland 4067, Australia.
Skidelsky, Professor R. J. A., BA, PhD, 32 Gt Percy Street, London WC1.
Skinner, Professor Q. R. D., MA, Christ's College, Cambridge CB2 3BU.
Slack, P. A., MA, DPhil, Exeter College, Oxford OX1 3DP.
Slade, C. F., PhD, FSA, 28 Holmes Road, Reading, Berks.
Slater, A. W., MSc(Econ), 146 Castelnau, London SW13 9ET.
Slatter, Miss M. D., MA, 12 Dunstall Close, Tilehurst, Reading, Berks. RG3 5AY.
Slavin, Professor A. J., PhD, College of Arts & Letters, University of Louisville, Louisville, Kentucky 40268, U.S.A.
Smail, R. C., MBE, MA, PhD, FSA, Sidney Sussex College, Cambridge CB2 3HU.
*Smalley, Miss B., MA, PhD, FBA, 5c Rawlinson Road, Oxford OX2 6UE.
Smith, A. G. R., MA, PhD, 5 Cargil Avenue, Kilmacolm, Renfrewshire.
Smith, A. Hassell, BA, PhD, School of English and American Studies, University of East Anglia, Norwich NR4 7TJ.
Smith, B. S., MA, FSA, Historical Manuscripts Commission, Quality Court, Chancery Lane, London WC2A 1HP.
Smith, Charles Daniel, PhD, 114 Sims, Syracuse University, Syracuse, N.Y. 13210, U.S.A.
Smith, D. M., MA, PhD, FSA, Borthwick Institute of Historical Research, St Anthony's Hall, York YO1 2PW.
Smith, E. A., MA, Dept of History, Faculty of Letters, The University, Whiteknights, Reading RG6 2AH.
Smith, F. B., MA, PhD, Research School of Social Sciences, Institute of Advanced Studies, Australian National University, A.C.T. 2600, Australia.
Smith, Professor Goldwin A., MA, PhD, DLitt, Wayne State University, Detroit, Michigan 48202, U.S.A.
Smith, J. Beverley, MA, University College, Aberystwyth SY23 2AX.
Smith, Joseph, BA, PhD, Dept of History, The University, Exeter EX4 4QH.
Smith, Professor L. Baldwin, PhD, Northwestern University, Evanston, Ill. 60201, U.S.A.
Smith, Professor P., MA, DPhil, Dept of History, The University, Southampton So9 5NH.
Smith, R. S., MA, BA, 7 Capel Lodge, 244 Kew Road, Kew, Surrey TW9 3JU.
Smith, S., BA, PhD, Les Haies, 40 Oatlands Road, Shinfield, Reading, Berks.
Smith, W. H. C., BA, PhD, Flat A, 110 Blackheath Hill, London SE10 8AG.
Smith, W. J., MA, 5 Gravel Hill, Emmer Green, Reading, Berks. RG4 8QN.
*Smyth, Rev. Canon C. H. E., MA, 12 Manor Court, Pinehurst, Cambridge.
Snell, L. S., MA, FSA, FRSA, 27 Weoley Hill, Selly Oak, Birmingham B29 4AA.
Snow, Professor V. F., MA, PhD, Dept of History, Syracuse University, 311 Maxwell Hall, Syracuse, New York 13210, U.S.A.
Snyder, Professor H. L., MA, PhD, 4646 Woodside Drive, Baton Rouge, La. 70808, U.S.A.
Soden, G. I., MA, DD, Buck Brigg, Hanworth, Norwich, Norfolk.

Somers, Rev. H. J., JCB, MA, PhD, St Francis Xavier University, Antigonish, Nova Scotia, Canada.
Somerville, Sir Robert, KCVO, MA, FSA, 3 Hunt's Close, Morden Road, London SE3 0AH.
SOUTHERN, Sir Richard (W.), MA, DLitt, LittD, DLitt, FBA, The President's Lodgings, St John's College, Oxford OX1 3JP.
Southgate, D. G., BA, DPhil, 40 Camphill Road, Broughty Ferry, Dundee.
Spalding, Miss R., MA, 34 Reynards Road, Welwyn, Herts.
Speck, Professor W. A., MA, DPhil, The University, Cottingham Road, Hull HU6 7RX.
Spencer, B. W., BA, FSA, 6 Carpenters Wood Drive, Chorleywood, Herts.
Spiers, E. D., MA, PhD, 487 Street Lane, Leeds, West Yorkshire LS17 6LA.
Spooner, Professor F. C., MA, PhD, The University, 23 Old Elvet, Durham DH1 3HY.
Spring, Professor D., PhD, Dept of History, Johns Hopkins University, Baltimore, Md. 21218, U.S.A.
Spufford, Mrs H. M., MA, PhD, Walnut Tree House, 36 High Street, Haddenham, Cambs. CB6 3XB.
Spufford, P., MA, PhD, Queens' College, Cambridge CB3 9ET.
Squibb, G. D., QC, FSA, The Old House, Cerne Abbas, Dorset DT2 7JQ.
Stacpoole, Dom Alberic J., OSB, MA, Saint Benet's Hall, Oxford OX1 3LN.
Stanley, The Hon. G. F. G., MA, BLitt, DPhil, The Office of Lieutenant-Governor, Fredericton, New Brunswick, Canada.
Stansky, Professor Peter, PhD, Dept of History, Stanford University, Stanford, Calif. 94305, U.S.A.
Steele, E. D., MA, PhD, School of History, The University, Leeds LS2 9JT.
Steinberg, J., MA, PhD, Trinity Hall, Cambridge CB2 1TJ.
Steiner, Mrs Zara S., MA, PhD, New Hall, Cambridge CB3 0DF.
Stephens, W. B., MA, PhD, FSA, 37 Batcliffe Drive, Leeds 6.
Steven, Miss M. J. E., PhD, 3 Bonwick Place, Garran, A.C.T. 2605, Australia.
Stevenson, D., BA, PhD, Dept of History, Taylor Building, King's College, Old Aberdeen AB1 0EE.
Stevenson, Miss J. H., BA, c/o Institute of Historical Research, Senate House, Malet Street, London WC1E 7HU.
Stevenson, J., MA, DPhil, Dept of History, The University, Sheffield S10 2TN.
Stewart, A. T. Q., MA, PhD, Dept of Modern History, The Queen's University, Belfast BT7 1NN.
Stitt, F. B., BA, BLitt, William Salt Library, Stafford.
Stockwell, A. J., MA, PhD, Dept of History, Royal Holloway College, Englefield Green, Surrey TW20 0EX.
Stone, E., MA, DPhil, FSA, Keble College, Oxford OX1 3PG.
Stone, Professor L., MA, Princeton University, Princeton, N.J. 08540, U.S.A.
*Stones, Professor E. L. G., PhD, FBA, FSA, 34 Alexandra Road, Parkstone, Poole, Dorset BH14 9EN.
Storey, Professor R. L., MA, PhD, 19 Elm Avenue, Beeston, Nottingham NG9 1BU.
Storry, J. G., Woodland View, Huntercombe End, Nettlebed, nr Henley-on-Thames, Oxon. RG9 5RR.
Story, Professor G. M., BA, DPhil, 335 Southside Road, St John's, Newfoundland, Canada.
*Stoye, J. W., MA, DPhil, Magdalen College, Oxford OX1 4AU.
Street, J., MA, PhD, 6 Thulborn Close, Teversham, Cambridge.
Strong, Mrs F., MA, South Cloister, Eton College, Windsor SL4 6DB.

Strong, Sir Roy, BA, PhD, FSA, Victoria & Albert Museum, London SW7.
Stuart, C. H., MA, Christ Church, Oxford OX1 1DP.
Studd, J. R., PhD, Dept of History, The University, Keele, Staffs. ST5 5BG.
Sturdy, D. J., BA, PhD, Dept of History, New University of Ulster, Coleraine, N. Ireland BT52 1SA.
Supple, Professor B. E., BSc (Econ), PhD, MA, Christ's College, Cambridge CB2 3BU.
Surman, Rev. C. E., MA, 352 Myton Road, Leamington Spa CV31 3NY.
Sutcliffe, Professor A. R., MA, DU, Dept of Economic and Social History, The University, 21 Slayleigh Avenue, Sheffield S10 3RA.
Sutherland, Professor D. W., DPhil, State University of Iowa, Iowa City, Iowa 52240, U.S.A.
Sutherland, N. M., MA, PhD, Bedford College, London NW1 4NS.
Swanson, R. N., MA, PhD, School of History, The University, P.O. Box 363, Birmingham B15 2TT.
Swanton, M. J., BA, PhD, FSA, Queen's Building, The University, Exeter EX4 4QH.
Swart, Professor K. W., PhD, LittD, University College London, Gower Street, London WC1E 6BT.
Sweet, D. W., MA, PhD, Dept of History, The University, 43 North Bailey, Durham.
Swinfen, D. B., MA, DPhil, 14 Cedar Road, Broughty Ferry, Dundee.
Sydenham, M. J., PhD, Carleton University, Ottawa 1, Canada.
Syrett, Professor D., PhD, 46 Hawthorne Terrace, Leonia, N.J., 07605, U.S.A.

Taft, Barbara, PhD, 3101 35th Street, Washington, D.C. 20016, U.S.A.
Talbot, C. H., PhD, BD, FSA, 47 Hazlewell Road, London SW15.
Tamse, Coenraad Arnold, DLitt, De Krom, 12 Potgieterlaan, 9752 Ex Haren (Groningen), The Netherlands.
Tanner, J. I., CBE, MA, PhD, DLitt, Flat One, 57 Drayton Gardens, London SW10 9RU.
Tarling, Professor P. N., MA, PhD, LittD, University of Auckland, Private Bag, Auckland, New Zealand.
Tarn, Professor J. N., B.Arch, PhD, FRIBA, Dept of Architecture, The University, P. O. Box 147, Liverpool L69 3BX.
Taylor, Arnold J., CBE, MA, DLitt, FBA, FSA, Rose Cottage, Lincoln's Hill, Chiddingfold, Surrey GU8 4UN.
Taylor, Professor Arthur J., MA, The University, Leeds LS2 9JT.
Taylor, J., MA, School of History, The University, Leeds LS2 9JT.
Taylor, J. W. R., 36 Alexandra Drive, Surbiton, Surrey KT5 9AF.
Taylor, P. M., BA, PhD, School of History, The University, Leeds LS2 9JT.
Taylor, R. T., MA, PhD, Dept of Political Theory and Government, University College of Swansea, Swansea SA2 8PP.
Taylor, W., MA, PhD, FSAScot, 25 Bingham Terrace, Dundee.
Teichova, Professor Alice, BA, PhD, University of East Anglia, University Plain, Norwich NR4 7TJ.
Temperley, H., BA, MA, PhD, School of English and American Studies, University of East Anglia, Norwich NR4 7TJ.
Temple, Nora C., BA, PhD, University College, P.O. Box 78, Cardiff CF1 1XL.
Templeman, G., CBE, MA, DCL, DL, FSA, Barton Corner, 2A St Augustine's Road, Canterbury, Kent.
Thackray, Professor Arnold W., PhD, E. F. Smith Hall D-6, University of Pennsylvania, Philadelphia 19104, U.S.A.

Thirsk, Mrs I. Joan, PhD, FBA, St Hilda's College, Oxford OX4 1DY.
Thistlethwaite, Professor F., CBE, DCL, LHD, 15 Park Parade, Cambridge CB5 8AL.
Thomas, Professor A. C., MA, DipArch, FSA, MRIA, Lambessow, St Clement, Truro, Cornwall.
Thomas, D. O., MA, PhD, Orlandon, 31 North Parade, Aberystwyth, Dyfed SY23 2JN.
Thomas of Swynnerton, Lord, MA, 29 Ladbroke Grove, London W11 3BB.
Thomas, Rev. J. A., MA, PhD, 164 Northfield Lane, Brixham, Devon TQ5 8RH.
Thomas, J. H., BA, PhD, Dept of Historical and Literary Studies, Portsmouth Polytechnic, Southsea, Portsmouth PO5 3AT.
Thomas, K. V., MA, FBA, St John's College, Oxford OX1 3JP.
Thomas, Professor P. D. G., MA, PhD, University College, Aberystwyth SY23 2AU.
Thomas, W. E. S., MA, Christ Church, Oxford OX1 1DP.
Thomis, Professor M. I., MA, PhD, University of Queensland, St Lucia, Brisbane 4067, Australia.
Thompson, A. F., MA, Wadham College, Oxford OX1 3PN.
Thompson, Mrs D. K. G., MA, School of History, The University, P.O. Box 363, Birmingham B15 2TT.
Thompson, D. M., MA, PhD, Fitzwilliam College, Cambridge CB3 0DG.
Thompson, E. P., MA, Wick Episcopi, Upper Wick, Worcester.
Thompson, Professor F. M. L., MA, DPhil, FBA, Institute of Historical Research, Senate House, London WC1E 7HU.
Thomson, J. A. F., MA, DPhil, The University, Glasgow G12 8QQ.
Thomson, R. M., MA, PhD, Dept of History, University of Tasmania, Box 252C, GPO, Hobart, Tasmania 7001, Australia.
Thorne, C., BA, School of European Studies, University of Sussex, Brighton BN1 9QX.
Thornton, Professor A. P., MA, DPhil, University College, University of Toronto, Toronto M5S 1A1, Canada.
*Thrupp, Professor S. L., MA, PhD, University of Michigan, Ann Arbor, Mich. 48104, U.S.A.
Thurlow, The Very Rev. A. G. G., MA, FSA, 2 East Pallant, Chichester, West Sussex PO19 1TR.
Tomkeieff, Mrs O. G., MA, LLB, 88 Moorside North, Newcastle upon Tyne NE4 9DU.
Tomlinson, H. C., BA, 10 Connaught Close, Wellington College, Crowthorne, Berkshire RG11 7PU.
Townshend, C. J. N., MA, DPhil, The Hawthorns, Keele, Staffordshire.
Toynbee, Miss M. R., MA, PhD, FSA, 22 Park Town, Oxford OX2 6SH.
Trebilcock, R. C., MA, Pembroke College, Cambridge CB2 1RF.
Tsitsonis, S. E., PhD, 6 Foskolou Street, Halandri, Athens, Greece.
Tyacke, N. R. N., MA, DPhil, 1A Spencer Rise, London NW5.
Tyler, P., BLitt, MA, DPhil, University of Western Australia, Nedlands, Western Australia 6009.

Ugawa, Professor K., BA, MA, PhD, 1008 Ikebukuro, 2 Chome, Toshimaku, Tokyo 171, Japan.
Underdown, Professor David, MA, BLitt, DLitt, Dept of History, Brown University, Providence, Rhode Island 02912, U.S.A.
Upton, A. F., MA, 5 West Acres, St Andrews, Fife.

Vaisey, D. G., MA, FSA, 12 Hernes Road, Oxford.
Vale, M. G. A., MA, DPhil, St John's College, Oxford OX1 3JP.
Van Caenegem, Professor R. C., LLD, PhD, Veurestraat 18, 9821 Afsnee, Belgium.
Van Roon, Professor Ger, Dept of Contemporary History, Vrije Universiteit, Amsterdam, Koningslaan 31-33, The Netherlands.
Vann, Professor Richard T., PhD, Dept of History, Wesleyan University, Middletown, Conn. 06457, U.S.A.
*Varley, Mrs J., MA, FSA, 164 Nettleham Road, Lincoln.
Vaughan, Sir (G.) Edgar, KBE, MA, 27 Birch Grove, West Acton, London W3 9SP.
Veale, Elspeth M., BA, PhD, 31 St Mary's Road, Wimbledon, London SW19 7BP.
Véliz, Professor C., BSc, PhD, Dept. of Sociology, La Trobe University, Melbourne, Victoria 3083, Australia.
Vessey, D. W. T. C., MA, PhD, 10 Uphill Grove, Mill Hill, London NW7.
Villiers, Lady de, MA, BLitt, 4 Church Street, Beckley, Oxford.
Virgoe, R., BA, PhD, University of East Anglia, School of English and American Studies, Norwich NR4 7TJ.

Waddell, Professor D. A. G., MA, DPhil, University of Stirling, Stirling FK9 4LA.
*Wagner, Sir Anthony (R.), KCVO, MA, DLitt, FSA, College of Arms, Queen Victoria Street, London EC4.
Waites, B. F., MA, FRGS, 6 Charter Road, Oakham, Leics. LE15 6RY.
Walcott, R., MA, PhD, 14 Whig Street, Dennis, Mass. 02638, U.S.A.
Waley, D. P., MA, PhD, Dept of Manuscripts, British Library, London WC1B 3DG.
Walford, A. J., MA, PhD, FLA, 45 Parkside Drive, Watford, Herts.
Walker, Rev. Canon D. G., DPhil, FSA, University College of Swansea, Swansea SA2 8PP.
Wallace, Professor W. V., MA, Institute of Soviet and East European Studies, University of Glasgow, Glasgow G12 8LQ.
Wallace-Hadrill, Professor J. M., MA, DLitt, FBA, All Souls College, Oxford OX1 4AL.
Wallis, Miss H. M., MA, DPhil, FSA, 96 Lord's View, St John's Wood Road, London NW8 7HG.
Wallis, P. J., MA, 27 Westfield Drive, Newcastle upon Tyne NE3 4XY.
Walne, P., MA, FSA, County Record Office, County Hall, Hertford.
Walsh, T. J., MA, PhD, MB, BCh, LittD, (Hon.) FFA, RCSI, 5 Lower George Street, Wexford, Ireland.
Walvin, J., BA, MA, DPhil, Dept of History, The University, Heslington, York YO1 5DD.
Wangermann, E., MA, DPhil, School of History, The University, Leeds LS2 9JT.
Wanklyn, M. D., BA, MA, PhD, Dept of Arts, The Polytechnic, Wulfruna Street, Wolverhampton, West Midlands.
*Ward, Mrs G. A., PhD, FSA, Unsted, 51 Hartswood Road, Brentwood, Essex.
Ward, Jennifer C., MA, PhD, 22 The Priory, Priory Park, London SE3 9XA.
Ward, Professor J. T., MA, PhD, Dept of History, McCance Bldg., University of Strathclyde, 16 Richmond Street, Glasgow G1 1XQ.
Ward, Professor W. R., DPhil, University of Durham, 43 North Bailey, Durham DH1 3HP.

*Warmington, Professor E. H., MA, 48 Flower Lane, London NW7.
Warner, Professor G., MA Dept of History, The University, Leicester LE1 7RH.
Warren, Professor W. L., MA, DPhil, FRSL, Dept of Modern History, The Queen's University, Belfast, N. Ireland BT7 1NN.
Wasserstein, B. M. J., MA, DPhil, The Tauber Institute, Brandeis University, Waltham, Mass. 02254, U.S.A.
*Waterhouse, Professor E. K., CBE, MA, AM, FBA, Overshot, Badger Lane, Hinksey Hill, Oxford.
*Waters, Lt-Commander D. W., RN, FSA, Jolyons, Bury, nr Pulborough, West Sussex.
Watkin, The Rt. Rev. Abbot Aelred, OSB, MA, FSA, St Benet's, Beccles, Suffolk NR34 9NR.
WATSON, A. G., MA, DLit, BLitt, FSA (*Hon Librarian*), University College London, Gower Street, London WC1E 6BT.
Watson, D. R., MA, BPhil, Dept of Modern History, The University, Dundee DD1 4HN.
Watson, J. S., MA, DLitt, DHL, DH, The University College Gate, North Street, St Andrews, Fife KY16 9AJ.
Watt, Professor D. C., MA, London School of Economics, Houghton Street, London WC2A 2AE.
Watt, Professor D. E. R., MA, DPhil, Dept of Mediaeval History, St Salvator's College, St Andrews, Fife KY16 9AJ.
Watt, Professor J. A., BA, PhD, Dept of History, The University, Newcastle upon Tyne NE1 7RU.
Watts, M. R., BA, DPhil, Dept of History, The University, Nottingham NG7 2RD.
Webb, Professor Colin de B., BA, MA, Dept of History, University of Cape Town, Rondebosch 7700, South Africa.
Webb, J. G., MA, 11 Blount Road, Pembroke Park, Old Portsmouth, Hampshire PO1 2TD.
Webb, Professor R. K., PhD, 3307 Highland Place NW., Washington, D.C. 20008, U.S.A.
Webster (A.) Bruce, MA, FSA, 5 The Terrace, St Stephens, Canterbury.
Webster, C., MA, DSc, Corpus Christi College, Oxford OX1 4JF.
Wedgwood, Dame (C.) Veronica, OM, DBE, MA, LittD, DLitt, LLD, Whitegate, Alciston, nr Polegate, Sussex.
Weinbaum, Professor M., PhD, 133–33 Sanford Avenue, Flushing, N.Y. 11355, U.S.A.
Weinstock, Miss M. B., MA, 26 Wey View Crescent, Broadway, Weymouth, Dorset.
Wells, R. A. E., BA, DPhil, Dept of Humanities, Brighton Polytechnic, Falmer, Brighton, Sussex.
Wendt, Professor Bernd-Jürgen, DrPhil, Beim Andreasbrunnen 8, 2 Hamburg 20, West Germany.
Wernham, Professor R. B., MA, Marine Cottage, 63 Hill Head Road, Hill Head, Fareham, Hants.
*Weske, Mrs Dorothy B., AM, PhD, Oakwood, Sandy Spring, Maryland 20860, U.S.A.
West, Professor F. J., PhD, Deakin University Interim Council, Cnr. Fenwick and Little Ryrie Streets, Geelong, Victoria 3220, Australia.
Weston, Professor Corinne C., PhD, 200 Central Park South, New York, N.Y. 10019, U.S.A.
Wheatley, R. R. A., MA, BLitt, Library and Records Dept, Foreign and

Commonwealth Office, Cornwall House, Stamford Street, London SE1.
Whelan, The Rt. Rev. Abbot C. B., OSB, MA, Belmont Abbey, Hereford HR2 9RZ.
White, Professor B. M. I., MA, DLit, FSA, 3 Upper Duke's Drive, Eastbourne, Sussex BN20 7XT.
White, Rev. B. R., MA, DPhil, 55 St Giles', Regent's Park College, Oxford.
Whiteman, Miss E. A. O., MA, DPhil, FSA, Lady Margaret Hall, Oxford OX2 6QA.
Whiting, J. R. S., MA, DLitt, 15 Lansdown Parade, Cheltenham, Glos.
Whittam, J. R., MA, BPhil, PhD, Dept of History, University of Bristol, Senate House, Bristol BS8 1TH.
Wiener, Professor J. H., BA, PhD, City College of New York, Convent Avenue at 138th Street, N.Y. 10031, U.S.A.
Wilkie, Rev. W., MA, PhD, Dept of History, Loras College, Dubuque, Iowa 52001, U.S.A.
Wilks, Professor M. J., MA, PhD, Dept of History, Birkbeck College, Malet Street, London WC1E 7HX.
*Willan, Professor T. S., MA, DPhil, 3 Raynham Avenue, Didsbury, Manchester M20 0BW.
Williams, D., MA, PhD, DPhil, University of Calgary, Calgary, Alberta T2N 1N4, Canada.
Williams, Sir Edgar (T.), CB, CBE, DSO, MA, 94 Lonsdale Road, Oxford OX2 7ER.
Williams, Professor Glanmor, MA, DLitt, University College of Swansea, Swansea SA2 8PP.
Williams, Professor Glyndwr, BA, PhD, Queen Mary College, Mile End Road, London E1 4NS.
Williams, Professor G. A., MA, PhD, University College, Cardiff CF1 1XL.
Williams, J. A., MA, BSc(Econ), 44 Pearson Park, Hull, HU5 2TG.
Williams, J. D., BA, MA, PhD, 56 Spurgate, Hutton Mount, Brentwood, Essex CM13 2JT.
Williams, P. H., MA, DPhil, New College, Oxford OX1 3BN.
Williams, T. I., MA, DPhil, 20 Blenheim Drive, Oxford OX2 8DG.
WILSON, Professor C. H., CBE, LittD, DLitt, DLitt, DLitt, FBA, Jesus College, Cambridge CB5 8BL.
Wilson, D. M., MA, LittD, FilDr, DrPhil, FBA, FSA, The Director's Residence, The British Museum, London WC1B 3DG.
Wilson, H. S., BA, BLitt, Dept of History, The University, York YO1 5DD.
Wilson, K. M., MA, DPhil, 8 Woodland Park Road, Headingley, Leeds 6.
Wilson, R. G., BA, PhD, University of East Anglia, School of Social Studies, University Plain, Norwich NR4 7TJ.
Wilson, Professor T., MA, DPhil, Dept of History, University of Adelaide, Adelaide, South Australia.
Winks, Professor R. W. E., MA, PhD, 648 Berkeley College, Yale University, New Haven, Conn. 06520, U.S.A.
Winter, J. M., BA, PhD, Pembroke College, Cambridge CB2 1RF.
Wiswall, Frank L., Jr., BA, JuD, PhD, Meadow Farm, Castine, Maine 04421, U.S.A.
Withrington, D. J., MA, MEd, Centre for Scottish Studies, University of Aberdeen, King's College, Old Aberdeen AB9 2UB.
Wolffe, B. P., MA, DPhil, DLitt, Highview, 19 Rosebarn Avenue, Exeter EX4 6DY.

Wong, John Yue-Wo, BA, DPhil, Dept of History, University of Sydney, N.S.W., Australia 2006.
*Wood, Rev. A. Skevington, PhD, Cliff House, Calver, Sheffield S30 1XG.
Wood, I. N., MA, DPhil, School of History, The University, Leeds LS2 9JT.
Wood, Mrs S. M., MA, BLitt, St Hugh's College, Oxford OX2 6LE.
Woodfill, Professor W. L., PhD, 762 Creston Road, Berkeley, Calif. 94708, U.S.A.
Woods, J. A., MA, PhD, School of History, The University, Leeds LS2 9JT.
Woolf, Professor S. J., MA, DPhil, University of Essex, Wivenhoe Park, Colchester CO4 3SQ.
Woolrych, Professor A. H., BLitt, MA, Patchetts, Caton, nr Lancaster.
Worden, A. B., MA, DPhil, St Edmund Hall, Oxford OX1 4AR.
Wormald, B. H. G., MA, Peterhouse, Cambridge CB2 1RD.
Wormald, Jennifer M., MA, PhD, Dept of Scottish History, The University, Glasgow G12 8QQ.
Wortley, The Rev. J. T., MA, PhD, History Dept, University of Manitoba, Winnipeg, Manitoba R3T 2N2, Canada.
Wright, A. D., MA, DPhil, School of History, The University, Leeds LS2 9JT.
Wright, C. J., MA, PhD, 8 Grove Road, East Molesey, Surrey KT8 9JS.
Wright, Professor E., MA, Institute of United States Studies, 31 Tavistock Square, London WC1H 9EZ.
Wright, Rev. Professor J. Robert, DPhil, General Theological Seminary, 175 Ninth Avenue, New York, N.Y. 10011, U.S.A.
Wright, L. B., PhD, 3702 Leland Street, Chevy Chase, Md. 20015, U.S.A.
Wright, Maurice, BA, DPhil, Dept of Government, Dover Street, Manchester M13 9PL.
Wroughton, J. P., MA, 6 Ormonde House, Sion Hill, Bath BA1 2UN.

Yates, W. N., MA, Kent Archives Office, County Hall, Maidstone, Kent ME14 1XH.
Yost, Professor John K., MA, STB, PhD, Dept of History, University of Nebraska, Lincoln, Neb. 68508, U.S.A.
Youings, Professor Joyce A., BA, PhD, Dept of History, The University, Exeter EX4 4QH.
Youngs, Professor F. A., Jr., Dept of History, Louisiana State University, Baton Rouge, Louisiana 70803, U.S.A.

Zagorin, Professor P., PhD, Dept of History, College of Arts and Sciences, University of Rochester, River Campus Station, Rochester, N.Y. 14627, U.S.A.
Zeldin, T., MA, DPhil, St Antony's College, Oxford OX2 6JF.
Ziegler, P. S., FRSL, 22 Cottesmore Gardens, London W8.

ASSOCIATES OF THE ROYAL HISTORICAL SOCIETY

Adams, S. L., BA, MA, DPhil, 4 North East Circus Place, Edinburgh EH3 6SP.
Addy, J., MA, PhD, 66 Long Lane, Clayton West, Huddersfield HD8 9PR.
Aitken, Rev. Leslie R., MBE, The Rectory, Alvechurch, Birmingham B48 7SB.
Ashton, Ellis, MBE, FRSA, 1 King Henry Street, London N16.
Ayrton, Lt. Col. M. McI., HQ Mess, The School of Signals, Blandford Camp, Dorset DT11 8RH.

Baird, Rev. E. S., BD, (address unknown).
Begley, M. R., 119 Tennyson Avenue, King's Lynn, Norfolk.
Bird, E. A., 29 King Edward Avenue, Rainham, Essex RN13 9RH.
Blackwood, B., FRIBA, FRTPI, FSAScot, Ebony House, Whitney Drive, Stevenage SG1 4BL.
Boyes, J. H., 129 Endlebury Road, Chingford, London E4 6PX.
Brake, Rev. G. Thompson, 19 Bethell Avenue, Ilford, Essex.
Bratt, C., 65 Moreton Road, Upton, Merseyside L49 4NR.
Bridge, A. E., 115 Ralph Road, Saltley, Birmingham B8 1NA.
Brocklesby, R., BA, The Elms, North Eastern Road, Thorne, Doncaster, S. Yorks. DN8 4AS.
Bryant, W. N., MA, PhD, College of S. Mark and S. John, Derriford Road, Plymouth, Devon.
Burton, Commander R. C., RN (ret.), Great Streele Oasthouse, Framfield, Sussex.
Butler, Mrs M. C., MA, 4 Castle Street, Warksworth, Morpeth, Northumberland NE65 0UW.

Cable, J. A., MA, MEd, ALCM, 21 Malvern Avenue, York YO2 5SF.
Cairns, Mrs W. N., MA, Alderton House, New Ross, Co. Wexford, Ireland.
Carter, F. E. L., CBE, MA, 8 The Leys, London N2 0HE.
Cary, Sir Roger, Bt, BA, 23 Bath Road, London W4.
Chappell, Rev. M. P., MA, Greymouth Close, Hartburn, Stockton-on-Tees, Cleveland TS18 5LF.
Cobban, A. D., 11 Pennyfields, Warley, Brentwood, Essex CM14 5JP.
Coleby, A. M., BA, Lincoln College, Oxford OX1 3DR.
Condon, Miss M. M., BA, 56 Bernard Shaw House, Knatchbull Road, London NW10.
Cooksley, P. G., 14 Wallington Court, Wallington, Surrey SM6 0HG.
Cooper, Miss J. M., MA, PhD, 1 William Street, New Marston, Oxford OX3 0ES.
Cox, A. H., Winsley, 11A Bagley Close, West Drayton, Middlesex.
Cox, Benjamin G., Fairways, 3 St Leonards Avenue, Blandford Forum, Dorset DT11 7NZ.
Creighton-Williamson, Lt-Col. D., 2 Church Avenue, Farnborough, Hampshire.

d'Alton, Ian, MA, PhD, 30 Kew Park Avenue, Lucan, Co Dublin, Ireland.

Daniels, C. W., MEd, FRSA, 'Brookfield', St John's Royal Latin School, Buckingham MK18 1AX.
Davies, G. J., BA, PhD, FSA, 16 Melcombe Avenue, Weymouth, Dorset DT4 7TH.
Davies, P. H., BA, 64 Hill Top, Hampstead Garden Suburb, London NW11.
Downie, W. F., BSc, CEng, FICE, FINucE, MIES, 10 Ryeland Street, Strathaven, Lanarkshire ML10 6DL.
Dowse, Rev. I. R., St Paul's Rectory, 8 Auchnacloich Road, Rothesay, Isle of Bute, Scotland.
Draffen of Newington, George, MBE, KLJ, MA, Meadowside, Balmullo, Leuchars, Fife KY16 0AW.
Dunster, E. R., BA, LCP, 5 Brittania Road, Southsea, Hampshire.

Elliott, Rev. W., BA, The Vicarage, Far Forest, nr Kidderminster, Worcs. DY 14 9TT.
Emberton, W. J., Firs Lodge, 13 Park Lane, Old Basing, Basingstoke, Hampshire.
Emsden, N., Strathspey, Lansdown, Bourton-on-the-Water, Cheltenham, Glos. GL54 2AR.

Foster, J. M., MA, 3 Marchmont Gardens, Richmond, Surrey TW 10 6ET.
Franco de Baux, Don Victor, KCHS, KCN, 10b Rumsey Road, London SW9 0TR.
Frazier, R. Ll., BA, Dept of History, The University, Nottingham NG7 2RD.
Freeman, Miss J., 11 St Georges Avenue, London N7.

Granger, E. R., Bluefield, Blofield, Norfolk.
Grant, A., BA, DPhil, Dept of History, The University, Lancaster LA1 4YG.
Greatrex, Professor Joan G., MA, The Highlands, Great Donard, Symonds Yat, Herefordshire HR9 6DY.
Green, P. L., MA, 9 Faulkner Street, Gate Pa, Tauranga, New Zealand.
Grosvenor, Ian D., BA, 40 Waterloo Road, Kingsheath, Birmingham.
Gurney, Mrs. S. J., 'Albemarle', 13 Osborne Street, Wolverton, Milton Keynes MK12 5HH.
Guy, Rev. J. R., BA, Selden End, Ash, nr Martock, Somerset TA12 6NS.

Hall, P. T., Accrington and Rosendale College, Sandy Lane, Accrington, Lancs. BB25 2AW.
Hanawalt, Mrs B. A., MA, PhD, Indiana University, Ballantine Hall, Bloomington, Indiana 47401, U.S.A.
Harfield, Major A. G., Little Beechwood, Childe Okeford, Dorset DT11 8EH.
Harmar, A. P., FCA, Pear Tree Cottage, Dene Street, Dorking, Surrey RH4 2BZ.
Hawkes, G. I., BA, MA, PhD, Linden House, St Helens Road, Ormskirk, Lancs.
Hawtin, Miss G., BA, PhD, FSAScot, FRSAI, Honey Cottage, 5 Clifton Road, London SW19 4QX.
Heal, Mrs F., PhD, Jesus College, Oxford OX1 3DW.
Henderson-Howat, Mrs A. M. D., 8 Dove House Close, Wolvercote, Oxford OX2 8BG.
Hillman, L. B., BA, 18 Creswick Walk, Hampstead Garden Suburb, London NW11.
Hoare, E. T., 70 Addison Road, Enfield, Middx.
Hodge, Mrs G., 85 Hadlow Road, Tonbridge, Kent.

Hope, R. B., MA, MEd, PhD, 5 Partis Way, Newbridge Hill, Bath, Avon BA1 3QG.

Jackson, A., BA, 14 Latimer Lane, Guisborough, Cleveland.
James, T. M., BA, MA, PhD, 26 St Michael's Close, Crich, Matlock, Derbyshire DE4 5DN.
Jarvis, L. D., Middlesex Cottage, 86 Mill Road, Stock, Ingatestone, Essex.
Jennings, T. S., GTCL, 'Hillcrest', High Land, Haslemere, Surrey GU27 1AZ.
Jermy, K. E., MA, Cert. Archaeol, FRSA, MIM, FISTC, 8 Thelwall New Road, Thelwall, Warrington, Cheshire WA4 3JF.
Jerram-Burrows, Mrs L. E., Parkanaur House, 88 Sutton Road, Rochford, Essex.
Johnston, F. R., MA, 20 Russell Street, Eccles, Manchester.
Johnstone, H. F. V., 96 Wimborne Road, Poole, Dorset BH15 2DA.
Jones, Dr N. L., Dept of History & Geography, Utah State University, UMC 07, Logan, Utah 84322, U.S.A.

Keefe, T. K., BA, PhD, Dept of History, Appalachian State University, Boone, North Caroline 28608, U.S.A.
Keir, Mrs G. I., BA, BLitt, 17 Old Harpenden Road, St Albans AL3 6AX.
Kennedy, M. J., BA, Dept of Medieval History, The University, Glasgow G12 8QQ.
Knight, G. A., BA, PhD, DAA, MIInfSc, 36 Trinder Way, Wickford, Essex SS12 0HQ.
Knowlson, Rev. G. C. V., 21 Wilton Crescent, Alderley Edge, Cheshire SK9 7RE.

Lea, R. S., MA, 29 Crestway, London SW15.
Lead, P., BA, 3 Montrose Court, Holmes Chapel, Cheshire CW4 7JJ.
Leckey, J. J., MSc(Econ), LCP, FRSAI, Vestry Hall, Ballygowan, Co Down, N. Ireland BT23 6HQ.
Lee, Professor M. du P., PhD, Douglass College, Rutgers University, NB, NJ 08903, U.S.A.
Lewin, Mrs J., MA, 3 Sunnydale Gardens, Mill Hill, London NW7.
Lewis, J. B., MA, CertEd, FRSA, 16 Rushfield Road, Westminster Park, Chester CH4 7RE.
Lewis, Professor N. B., MA, PhD, 79 Old Dover Road, Canterbury, Kent CT1 3DB.

McIntyre, Miss S. C., BA, DPhil, West Midlands College of Higher Education, Walsall, West Midlands.
McKenna, Rev. T. J., P.O. Box 509, Quean Beyaw, Australia 2620.
McLeod, D. H., BA, PhD, Dept of Theology, The University, P.O. Box 363, Birmingham B15 2TT.
Meatyard, E., BA, DipEd, Guston, Burial Lane, Church Lane, Llantwit Major, S. Glam.
Metcalf, D. M., MA, DPhil, 40 St Margaret's Road, Oxford OX2 6LD.
Mills, H. J., BSc, MA, Headington, Brockenhurst, Hants.
Morgan, D. A. L., MA, Dept of History, University College London, Gower Street, London WC1E 6BT.
Munson, K. G., 'Briar Wood', 4 Kings Ride, Seaford, Sussex BN25 2LN.

Nagel, L. C. J., BA, 61 West Kensington Court, London W14.

Newman, L. T., LRIC, CEng, MIGasE, AMInstF, 27 Mallow Park, Pinkneys Green, Maidenhead, Berks.
Noonan, J. A., BA, MEd, HDE, St Patrick's Comprehensive School, Shannon, Co Clare, Ireland.

Oldham, C. R., MA, Te Whare, Walkhampton, Yelverton, Devon PL20 6PD.

Pam, D. O., 44 Chase Green Avenue, Enfield, Middlesex EN2 8EB.
Partridge, Miss F. L., BA, 17 Spencer Gardens, London SW14 7AH.
Pasmore, H. S., MB, BS, South Cottage, Ham Gate Avenue, Ham Common, Richmond, Surrey TW10 5HB.
Paton, L. R., 49 Lillian Road, Barnes, London SW13.
Paulson, E., BSc(Econ), 11 Darley Avenue, Darley Dale, Matlock, Derbys. DE4 2GB.
Perry, E., FSAScot, 28 Forest Street, Hathershaw, Oldham OL8 3ER.
Perry, K., MA, 14 Highland View Close, Colehill, Wimborne, Dorset.
Pitt, B. W. E., Merryfield House, Ilton, Ilminster TA19 9EX.
Porter, S., BA, MLitt, Dept of History, King's College, London WC2R 2LS.
Powell, Mrs A. M., Downing College, Cambridge CB2 1DQ.
Priestley, E. J., MA, MPhil, 33 Grange Road, Shrewsbury SY3 9DG.

Raban, Mrs S. G., MA, PhD, Dept of History, Homerton College, Cambridge.
Raspin, Miss A., London School of Economics, Houghton Street, London WC2A 2AE.
Reid, N. H., MA, 45 Roseburn Terrace, Edinburgh EH12 5NQ.
Rendall, Miss J., BA, PhD, Dept of History, University of York, Heslington, York YO1 5DD.
Richards, N. F., PhD, 376 Maple Avenue, St Lambert, Prov. of Quebec, Canada J4P 2S2.
Roberts, S. G., MA, DPhil, 23 Beech Avenue, Radlett, Herts. WD7 7DD.
Rosenfield, M. C., AB, AM, PhD, Box 395, Mattapoisett, Mass. 02739, U.S.A.
Russell, Mrs E., BA, c/o Dept of History, Yale University, New Haven, Conn. 06520, U.S.A.

Sabben-Clare, E. E., MA, 4 Denham Close, Abbey Hill Road, Winchester SO23 7BL.
Sainsbury, F., 16 Crownfield Avenue, Newbury Park, Ilford, Essex.
Saksena, D. N., D-105 Curzon Road Apts., New Delhi, 11-00 01, India.
Scannura, C. G., 1/11 St Dominic Street, Valletta, Malta.
Scott, The Rev. A. R., MA, BD, PhD, Ahorey Manse, Portadown, Co Armagh, N. Ireland.
Sellers, J. M., MA, 9 Vere Road, Pietermaritzburg 3201, Natal, S. Africa.
Shores, C. F., ARICS, 40 St Mary's Crescent, Hendon, London NW4 4LH.
Sibley, Major R. J., 8 Ways End, Beech Avenue, Camberley, Surrey.
Sloan, K., BEd, MPhil, 6 Netherwood Close, Fixby, Huddersfield, Yorks.
Sorensen, Mrs M. O., MA, 8 Layer Gardens, London W3 9PR.
Sparkes, I. G., FLA, 124 Green Hill, High Wycombe, Bucks.
Stafford, D. S., BA, 10 Highfield Close, Wokingham, Berks. RG11 1DG.

Thewlis, J. C., BA, PhD, Dept of History, The University, Hull HU6 7RX.

Thomas, D. L., BA, Public Record Office, Chancery Lane, London WC2A 1LR.

Thomas, Miss E. J. M., BA, 8 Ravenscroft Road, Northfield End, Henley-on-Thames, Oxon.

Thompson, C. L. F., MA, Orchard House, Stanford Road, Orsett, nr Grays, Essex RM16 3BX.

Thompson, L. F., Orchard House, Stanford Road, Orsett, nr Grays, Essex RM16 3BX.

Tracy, J. N., BA, MPhil, PhD, c/o P. Huth Esq, 6 Chaucer Court, 28 New Dover Road, Canterbury, Kent.

Tudor, Victoria M., BA, PhD, 33 Convent Close, Hitchin, Herts. SG5 1QN.

Waldman, T. G., MA, P.O. Box 53187, Philadelphia, Pa. 19105, U.S.A.

Walker, J. A., 1 Sylvanus, Roman Wood, Bracknell, Berkshire RG12 4XX.

Wall, Rev. J., BD, MA, PhD, 'Kinganton', 46 The Meadows, Sedgefield, Stockton-on-Tees TS21 2DH.

Warrillow, E. J. D., MBE, FSA, Hill-Cote, Lancaster Road, Newcastle, Staffs.

Weise, Selene H. C., PhD, 22 Hurd Street, Mine Hill, New Jersey 07801, U.S.A.

Wilkinson, F. J., 40 Great James Street, Holborn, London WC1N 3HB.

Williams, A. R., BA, MA, 5 Swanswell Drive, Granley Fields, Cheltenham, Glos.

Williams, C. L. Sinclair, ISO, The Old Vicarage, The Green, Puddletown, nr Dorchester, Dorset.

Williams, G., ALA, 32 St John's Road, Manselton, Swansea SA5 8PP.

Williams, P. T., FSAScot, FRSA, FFAS, Bryn Bueno, Whitford Street, Holywell, Clwyd.

Windeatt, M. C., (address unknown).

Windrow, M. C., West House, Broyle Lane, Ringmer, nr Lewes, Sussex.

Wood, A. W., 11 Blessington Close, London SE13.

Wood, J. O., BA, MEd, Flat 1, Lothian Lodge, Vauvert, St Peter Port, Guernsey, Channel Islands.

Woodall, R. D., BA, Bethel, 7 Wynthorpe Road, Horbury, nr Wakefield, Yorks. WF4 5BB.

Worsley, Miss A. V., BA, 3D St George's Cottages, Glasshill Street, London SE1.

Wright, J. B., BA, White Shutters, Braunston, Leicester LE15 8QT.

Zerafa, Rev. M. J., St Dominic's Priory, Valletta, Malta.

CORRESPONDING FELLOWS

Ajayi, Professor J. F. Ade, University of Ibadan, Ibadan, Nigeria, West Africa.

Berend, Professor T. Ivan, Hungarian Academy of Sciences, 1361 Budapest V, Roosevelt-tèr 9, Hungary.

Bischoff, Professor B., DLitt, 8033 Planegg C. München, Ruffini-Allee 27, West Germany.

Boorstin, Daniel J., MA, LLD, 3541 Ordway Street, N.W., Washington, DC 20016, U.S.A.

Braudel, Professor F., Commission des Archives Diplomatiques, Ministère des Affaires Étrangères, 37 Quai d'Orsay, 75007 Paris, France.

Cipolla, Professor Carlo M., University of California, Berkeley Campus, Berkeley, Calif. 94720, U.S.A.

Crouzet, Professor F. M. J., 6 rue Benjamin Godard, 75016 Paris, France.

Donoso, R., Presidente de la Sociedad Chilena de Historia y Geografia, Casilla 1386, Santiago, Chile.

Duby, Professor G., Collège de France, 11 Place Marcelin-Berthelot, 75005 Paris, France.

Garin, Professor Eugenio, via Giulio Cesare Vanini 28, 50129 Florence, Italy.

Gieysztor, Professor Aleksander, Polska Akademia Nauk, Wydzial I Nauk, Rynek Starego Miasta 29/31, 00-272 Warszawa, Poland.

Giusti, Rt Rev. Mgr M., JCD, Archivio Segreto Vaticano, Vatican City, Italy.

Glamann, Professor K., DrPhil, Frederiksberg, Bredegade 13A, 2000 Copenhagen, Denmark.

Gopal, Professor S., MA, DPhil, Centre for Historical Studies, Jawaharlal Nehru University, New Mehrauli Road, New Delhi-110067, India.

Gwynn, Professor the Rev. A., SJ, MA, DLitt, Milltown Park, Dublin 6, Ireland.

Hancock, Professor Sir Keith, KBE, MA, DLitt, FBA, Australian National University, Box 4, P.O., Canberra, ACT, Australia.

Hanke, Professor L. U., PhD, University of Massachusetts, Amherst, Mass. 01002, U.S.A.

Heimpel, Professor Dr H., DrJur, Dr Phil, former Direktor des Max Planck-Instituts für Geschichte, Gottingen, Dahlmannstr. 14, West Germany.

Hubatsch, Professor Walther, Neuere Geschichte, 53 Bonn, Konviktstrasse 11, West Germany.

Inalcik, Professor Halil, PhD, The University of Ankara, Turkey.

Kossmann, Professor E. H., DLitt, Rijksuniversiteit te Groningen, Groningen, The Netherlands.

Kuttner, Professor S., MA, JUD, SJD, LLD, Institute of Medieval Canon Law, University of California, Berkeley, Calif. 94720, U.S.A.

Ladurie, Professor E. B. LeRoy, Collège de France, 11 Place Marcelin-Berthelot, 75005 Paris, France.

Lyons, F. S. L., MA, PhD, LittD, FBA, 20 Alma Court, Alma Road, Monkstown, Co Dublin, Ireland.

McNeill, Professor William H., 1126 East 59th Street, Chicago, Illinois 60637, U.S.A.

Maruyama, Professor Masao, 2-44-5 Higashimachi, Kichijoji, Musashinoshi, Tokyo 180, Japan.

Michel Henri, 12 Rue de Moscou, 75008 Paris, France.

Peña y Cámara, J. M. de la, Avenida Reina, Mercedes 65, piso 7-B, Seville 12, Spain.

Rodrigues, Professor José Honório, Rua Paul Redfern 23, ap. C.O. 1, Rio de Janeiro, Gb. ZC-37, Brazil.

Slicher van Bath, Professor B. H., Gen. Fouldesweg 113, Wageningen, The Netherlands.

Thapar, Professor Romila, Dept of Historical Studies, Jawaharlal Nehru University, New Mehrauli Road, New Delhi-110067, India.

Thorne, Professor S. E., MA, LLB, LittD, LLD, FSA, Law School of Harvard University, Cambridge, Mass. 02138, U.S.A.

Van Houtte, Professor J. A., PhD, FBA, Termunkveld, Groeneweg 51, Egenhoven, Heverlee, Belgium.

Verlinden, Professor C., PhD, 3 Avenue du Derby, 1050 Brussels, Belgium.

Wolff, Professor Philippe, 3 rue Espinasse, 31000 Toulouse, France.

Woodward, Professor C. Vann, PhD, Yale University, 104 Hall of Graduate Studies, New Haven, Conn. 06520, U.S.A.

Zavala, S., LLD, Montes Urales 310, Mexico 10, D.F., Mexico.

TRANSACTIONS AND PUBLICATIONS

OF THE

ROYAL HISTORICAL SOCIETY

The publications of the Society consist of the *Transactions*, supplemented in 1897 by the *Camden Series* (formerly the Camden Society, 1838–97); since 1937 by a series of *Guides and Handbooks* and, from time to time, by miscellaneous publications. The Society also began in 1937 an annual bibliography of *Writings on British History*, for the continuation of which the Institute of Historical Research accepted responsibility in 1965; it publishes, in conjunction with the American Historical Association, a series of *Bibliographies of British History*.

List of series published

The following are issued in collaboration with the distributor/publisher indicated:

Annual Bibliography of British and Irish History	
All titles	Harvester Press
Bibliographies of British History	
All except 1485–1603, 1714–1789	Oxford University Press
1485–1603, 1714–1789	Harvester Press
Camden Series	
Old Series and New Series	Johnson Reprint
Third and Fourth Series*	Boydell and Brewer
Guides and Handbooks	
Main Series*	Boydell and Brewer
Supplementary Series*	Boydell and Brewer
Miscellaneous titles	Boydell and Brewer
Studies in History	
All titles	Swift Printers Ltd.
Transactions of the Royal Historical Society	
Up to *Fifth Series*, Vol. 19	Kraus Reprint
Fifth Series, Vol. 20 onwards*†	Boydell and Brewer
Writings on British History	
Up to 1946	Dawson Book Service
1946 onwards	Institute of Historical Research

Members' entitlements

Fellows and Subscribing Libraries receive free copies of new volumes of series marked*.

Corresponding Fellows, Retired Fellows and Associates receive free copies of new volumes of this series marked†.

Terms for members' purchase of individual titles are listed below.

Methods of Ordering Volumes

Institute of Historical Research—an invoice will be sent with volume.

In all other cases pre-payment is required. If correct price is not known, a cheque made payable to the appropriate supplier, in the form 'Not exceeding £   ' may be sent with the order. Otherwise a pro-forma invoice will be sent.

LIST OF TITLES
ARRANGED BY DISTRIBUTOR

BOYDELL & BREWER

Address for orders: P.O. Box 9, Woodbridge, Suffolk IP12 3DF.

Camden Third Series: All titles now available; a list can be sent on request. Prices range from £10 for original volumes to £30 for the largest reprinted volumes. (£7.50–£22.50 to Members).

Camden Fourth Series: The following titles are available price £10. (£7.50 to Members):

1. Camden Miscellany, Vol. XXII: 1. Charters of the Earldom of Hereford, 1095–1201. Edited by David Walker. 2. Indentures of Retinue with John of Gaunt, Duke of Lancaster, enrolled in Chancery, 1367–99. Edited by N. B. Lewis. 3. Autobiographical memoir of Joseph Jewell, 1763–1846. Edited by A. W. Slater. 1964.
2. Documents illustrating the rule of Walter de Wenlock, Abbot of Westminster, 1283–1307. Edited by Barbara Harvey. 1965.
3. The early correspondence of Richard Wood, 1831–41. Edited by A. B. Cunningham. 1966. (*Out of print.*)
4. Letters from the English abbots to the chapter at Cîteaux, 1442–1521. Edited by C. H. Talbot. 1967.
5. Select writings of George Wyatt. Edited by D. M. Loades. 1968.
6. Records of the trial of Walter Langeton, Bishop of Lichfield and Coventry (1307–1312). Edited by Miss A. Beardwood. 1969.
7. Camden Miscellany, Vol. XXIII: 1. The Account Book of John Balsall of Bristol for a trading voyage to Spain, 1480. Edited by T. F. Reddaway and A. A. Ruddock. 2. A Parliamentary diary of Queen Anne's reign. Edited by W. A. Speck. 3. Leicester House politics, 1750–60, from the papers of John second Earl of Egmont. Edited by A. N. Newman. 4. The Parliamentary diary of Nathaniel Ryder, 1764–67. Edited by P. D. G. Thomas. 1969.
8. Documents illustrating the British Conquest of Manila, 1762–63. Edited by Nicholas P. Cushner. 1971.
9. Camden Miscellany, Vol XXIV: 1. Documents relating to the Breton succession dispute of 1341. Edited by M. Jones. 2. Documents relating to the Anglo-French negotiations, 1439. Edited by C. T. Allmand. 3. John Benet's Chronicle for the years 1400 to 1462. Edited by G. L. Harriss. 1972.
10. Herefordshire Militia Assessments of 1663. Edited by M. A. Faraday. 1972.
11. The early correspondence of Jabez Bunting, 1820–29. Edited by W. R. Ward. 1972.
12. Wentworth Papers, 1597–1628. Edited by J. P. Cooper, 1973.
13. Camden Miscellany, Vol. XXV: 1. The Letters of William, Lord Paget. Edited by Barrett L. Beer and Sybil Jack. 2. The Parliamentary Diary of John Clementson, 1770–1802. Edited by P. D. G. Thomas. 3. J. B. Pentland's Report on Bolivia, 1827. Edited by J. V. Fifer, 1974.

14. Camden Miscellany, Vol. XXVI: 1. Duchy of Lancaster Ordinances, 1483. Edited by Sir Robert Somerville. 2. A Breviat of the Effectes devised for Wales. Edited by P. R. Roberts. 3. Gervase Markham, The Muster-Master. Edited by Charles L. Hamilton. 4. Lawrence Squibb, A Book of all the Several Offices of the Court of the Exchequer (1642). Edited by W. H. Bryson. 5. Letters of Henry St. John to Charles, Earl of Orrery, 1709–11. Edited by H. T. Dickinson. 1975.
15. Sidney Ironworks Accounts, 1541–73. Edited by D. W. Crossley. 1975.
16. The Account-Book of Beaulieu Abbey. Edited by S. F. Hockey. 1975.
17. A calendar of Western Circuit Assize Orders, 1629–48. Edited by J. S. Cockburn. 1976.
18. Four English Political Tracts of the later Middle Ages. Edited by J.-Ph. Genet. 1977.
19. Proceedings of the Short Parliament of 1640. Edited by Esther S. Cope in collaboration with Willson H. Coates. 1977.
20. Heresy Trials in the Diocese of Norwich, 1428–31. Edited by N. P. Tanner. 1977.
21. Edmund Ludlow: A Voyce from the Watch Tower (Part Five: 1660–1662). Edited by A. B. Worden. 1978.
22. Camden Miscellany, Vol. XXVII: 1. The Disputed Regency of the Kingdom of Jerusalem, 1264/6 and 1268. Edited by P. W. Edbury. 2. George Rainsford's *Ritratto d'Ingliterra* (1556). Edited by P. S. Donaldson. 3. The Letter-Book of Thomas Bentham, Bishop of Coventry and Lichfield, 1560–1561. Edited by Rosemary O'Day and Joel Berlatsky. 1979.
23. The Letters of the Third Viscount Palmerston to Laurence and Elizabeth Sulivan, 1804–63. Edited by Kenneth Bourne. 1979.
24. Documents illustrating the crisis of 1297–98 in England. Edited by M. Prestwich. 1980.
25. The Diary of Edward Goschen, 1900–1914. Edited by C. H. D. Howard. 1980.
26. English Suits before the Parlement of Paris, 1420–36. Edited by C. T. Allmand and C. A. J. Armstrong. 1982.
27. The Devonshire Diary, 1759–62. Edited by P. D. Brown and K. W. Schweizer. 1982.
28. Barrington Family Letters, 1628–1632. Edited by A. Searle. 1983.

Provisionally accepted by the Society for future publication:

The *Acta* of Archbishop Hugh of Rouen (1130–64). Edited by T. Waldman.
Cartularies of Reading Abbey. Edited by B. R. Kemp.
Correspondence of William Camden. Edited by Richard DeMolen.
Early Paget Correspondence. Edited by C. J. Harrison and A. C. Jones.
Documents on the origin of the British Association for the Advancement of Science 1828–31. Edited by A. W. Thackray and J. B. Morrell.
Vita Mariae Reginae Anglie. Edited by D. MacCulloch.
The Account of the Great Household of Humphrey, first Duke of Buckingham, for the year 1452–3. Edited by Mrs. M. Harris.
Letters of J. A. Blackwell concerning events in Hungary, 1848–9. Edited by A. Sked.
Supplementary Documents of the English Lands of the Abbey of Bec. Edited by Marjorie Chibnall.
Documents concerning the Anglo-French Treaty of 1550. Edited by D. L. Potter.

Despatch of the Count of Feria to Philip II, 1558. Edited by S. L. Adams and M. J. Rodriguez-Salgado.
Letters to Sir Reynold Bray. Edited by De Ll Guth and Miss M. Condon.
Clifford Letters, c. 1500–39. Edited by R. W. Hoyle.

Guides and handbooks

Main series

1. Guide to English commercial statistics, 1696–1782. By G. N. Clark, with a catalogue of materials by Barbara M. Franks. 1938. (*Out of print.*)
2. Handbook of British chronology. Edited by F. M. Powicke and E. B. Fryde, 1st edn. 1939; 2nd edn. 1961. (*Out of print.*)
3. Medieval libraries of Great Britain, a list of surviving books. Edited by N. R. Ker, 1st edn. 1941; 2nd edn. 1964. £8.00.
4. Handbook of dates for students of English history. By C. R. Cheney. 1982. £5.00.
5. Guide to the national and provincial directories of England and Wales, excluding London, published before 1856. By Jane E. Norton. 1950. (*Out of print.*)
6. Handbook of Oriental history. Edited by C. H. Philips. 1963. £5.00.
7. Texts and calendars: an analytical guide to serial publications. Edited by E. L. C. Mullins. 1st edn. 1958; 2nd edn. 1978. £8.00.
8. Anglo-Saxon charters. An annotated list and bibliography. Edited by P. H. Sawyer. 1968. £8.00.
9. A Centenary Guide to the Publications of the Royal Historical Society, 1868–1968. Edited by A. T. Milne. 1968. £5.00.
10. A Guide to the Local Administrative Units of England. Vol. I. Edited by F. A. Youngs, Jr. 1980; 2nd edn. 1981. £25.00.
11. A Guide to Bishops' Registers to 1646. Edited by D. M. Smith. 1981. £15.00.
12. Texts and Calendars: II: an analytical guide to serial publications 1957–1982. By E. L. C. Mullins.

Supplementary series

1. A Guide to the Papers of British Cabinet Ministers, 1900–1951. Edited by Cameron Hazlehurst and Christine Woodland. 1974. £4.50.
2. A Guide to the Reports of the U.S. Strategic Bombing Survey. Edited by Gordon Daniels. 1981. £12.00.

Provisionally accepted by the Society for future publication:

A Handbook of British Currency. Edited by P. Grierson and C. E. Blunt.
A Guide to the Records and Archives of Mass Communications. Edited by Nicholas Pronay.
A Guide to the Maps of the British Isles. Edited by Helen Wallis.
A Guide to the Local Administrative Units of England. Vol. II. Edited by F. A. Youngs, Jr.
Handlist of British Diplomatic Representatives, 1508–1688. Edited by G. Bell.
Scottish Texts and Calendars. Edited by D. and W. B. Stevenson.

Miscellaneous publications

Domesday Studies, 2 vols, Edited by P. E. Dove, 1886. £3.50. (Vol. I out of print.)
The *Domesday Monachorum* of Christ Church, Canterbury. 1944. £15.
The Royal Historical Society, 1868–1968. By R. A. Humphreys. 1969. £1.25.

Transactions, Fifth Series
Vol. 20 onwards. Price £8.50. (£6.38 to Members).

DAWSON BOOK SERVICE

Address for orders: Cannon House, Folkstone, Kent.
Writings on British History to 1946. Prices on request.

HARVESTER PRESS

Address for orders: 17 Ship Street, Brighton, Sussex.
Annual Bibliography of British and Irish History (Editor: G. R. Elton)

1. Publications of 1975 (1976)
2. Publications of 1976 (1977)
3. Publications of 1977 (1978)
4. Publications of 1978 (1979)
5. Publications of 1979 (1980)
6. Publications of 1980 (1981)
7. Publications of 1981 (1982)

Prices on request.
Bibliography of British History: Tudor Period, 1485–1603. Edited by Conyers Read. 1st edn. 1933; 2nd edn. 1959; 3rd edn. 1978. Price £28.00.
Bibliography of British History: The Eighteenth Century, 1714–1789. Edited by S. Pargellis and D. J. Medley. 1st edn. 1951; 2nd edn. 1977. Price £18.95.

INSTITUTE OF HISTORICAL RESEARCH

Address for orders: University of London, Senate House, Malet Street, London WC1E 7HU.
Writings on British History, 1946–1948. Compiled by D. J. Munro. 1973. Price £15.00.
Writings on British History, 1949–1951. Compiled by D. J. Munro. 1975. Price £15.00.
Writings on British History, 1952–1954. Compiled by J. M. Sims. 1975. Price £15.00.
Writings on British History, 1955–1957. Compiled by J. M. Sims and P. M. Jacob. 1977. Price £15.00.
Writings on British History, 1958–1959. Compiled by H. J. Creaton. 1977. Price £15.00.
Writings on British History, 1960–1961. Compiled by C. H. E. Philpin and H. J. Creaton. 1978. Price £15.00.
Writings on British History, 1962–1964. Compiled by H. J. Creaton. 1979. Price £17.00.
Writings on British History, 1965–1966. Compiled by H. J. Creaton. 1981. Price £18.00.
Writings on British History, 1967–1968. Compiled by H. J. Creaton. 1982. Price £20.00.

JOHNSON REPRINT

Address for orders: 24–28 Oval Road, London NW1 7DX.
Camden Old and New Series. Prices on request.

KRAUS REPRINT

Address for orders: Route 100, Millwood, N.Y. 10546, U.S.A.
Transactions: Old, New, Third, Fourth, Fifth Series Vols. 1–19. Prices on request.

OXFORD UNIVERSITY PRESS

Method of ordering: through booksellers.
If members have difficulty in obtaining volumes at the special price, reference should be made to the Society.

Bibliography of English History to 1485. Based on the Sources and Literature of English History from earliest times by Charles Gross. Revised and expanded by Edgar B. Graves. 1975. Price £48 (£36 to Members).

Bibliography of British History: Stuart Period, 1603–1714. 2nd edn. Edited by Mary F. Keeler, 1970. Price £35.00 (£26.25 to Members).

Bibliography of British History: 1789–1851. Edited by Lucy M. Brown and Ian R. Christie. 1970. Price £38.00 (£28.50 to Members).

Bibliography of British History: 1851–1914. Edited by H. J. Hanham. 1976. Price £58.00 (£43.50 to Members).

In preparation

Supplement to Bibliography of British History: 1714–89. Edited by S. M. Pargellis and D. J. Medley. Edited by A. T. Milne and A. N. Newman.

SWIFT PRINTERS

Address for orders: 1–7 Albion Place, Britton Street, London EC1M 5RE.
Studies in History is a series of historical monographs, preferably of no more than 90,000 words, intended to help solve the increasing difficulties encountered by historians in getting their books accepted for publication, especially young scholars seeking first publication. Those interested in submitting works for consideration by the Editorial Board should write to the Editorial Assistant, c/o The Royal Historical Society, University College London, Gower Street, WC1E 6BT from whom further details can be obtained. No typescripts should be sent until asked for.

1. F. F. Foster: *The Politics of Stability: A Portrait of the Rulers in Elizabethan London.* 1977. £11.40 (£7.35 to Members).
2. Rosamond McKitterick, *The Frankish Church and the Carolingian Reforms 789–895.* 1977. £13.40 (£8.57 to Members).
3. K. D. Brown, *John Burns.* 1977. £9.50 (£6.14 to Members).
4. D. Stevenson, *Revolution and Counter Revolution in Scotland, 1644–1651.* 1977. £12.30 (£7.92 to Members).
5. Marie Axton, *The Queen's Two Bodies: Drama and the Elizabethan Succession.* 1978. £11.40 (£7.35 to Members).
6. Anne Orde: *Great Britain and International Security, 1920–1926.* 1978. £11.80 (£7.67 to Members).
7. J. H. Baker (ed), *Legal Records and the Historian* (Papers read to the 2nd Conference on Legal History, held at Cambridge in 1975). 1978. £11.40 (£7.37 to Members).

8. M. P. Costeloe: *Church and State in Independent Mexico: a study of the Patronage Debate, 1821–1857*. 1978. £12.70 8.12 to Members).
9. Wendy Davies: *An Early Welsh Microcosm: Studies in the Llandaff Charters*, 1978. £11.00 (£7.12 to Members).
10. Bernard Wasserstein: *The British in Palestine: The Mandatory Government and the Arab-Jewish Conflict, 1917–1929*. 1978. £13.60 (£8.89 to Members).
11. Michael McCahill: *Order and Equipoise: the Peerage and the House of Lords, 1783–1806*. 1979. £15.00 (£9.67 to Members).
12. Norman Etherington: *Preachers, Peasants and Politics in Southeast Africa 1835–1880. African Christian Communities in Natal, Pondoland and Zululand*. 1979. £14.00 (£8.87 to Members).
13. S. A. G. Rizvi: *Linlithgow and India: A Study of British Policy and the Political Impasse in India, 1936–1943*. 1979. £15.00 (£9.62 to Members).
14. David McLean: *Britain and her Buffer-state: The Collapse of the Persian Empire, 1890–1914*. 1979. £12.50 (£8.25 to Members).
15. Howard Tomlinson: *Guns and Government: The Ordnance Office under the later Stuarts*. 1979. £17.00 (£10.92 to Members).
16. Patricia Crawford: *Denzil Holles, 1598–1680: A study of his Political Career*. 1979. £15.60 (£10.34 to Members).
17. D. L. Rydz: *The Parliamentary Agents: A History*. 1979. £15.30 (£9.87 to Members).
18. Uri Bialer: *The Shadow of the Bomber: The Fear of Air Attack and British Politics 1932–1939*. 1980. £14.00 (£8.85 to Members).
19. David Parker: *La Rochelle and the French Monarchy: Conflict and Order in Seventeenth-Century France*. 1980. £16.50 (£10.42 to Members).
20. A. P. C. Bruce: *The Purchase System in the British Army, 1660–1871*. 1980. £14.00 (£8.87 to Members).
21. Stephen Gradish: *The Manning of the British Navy During the Seven Years War*. 1980. £15.25 (£9.62 to Members).
22. Alan Harding (ed.): *Lawmaking and Lawmakers in British History* (Papers presented to the Edinburgh Legal History Conference 1977). 1980. £15.25 (£9.62 to Members).
23. Diane Willen: *John Russell First Earl of Bedford*. 1981. £13.00 (£8.00 to Members).
24. Roy Schreiber: *The Political Career of Sir Robert Naunton, 1589–1635*. 1981. £15.40 (£9.35 to Members).
25. W. M. Mathew: *The House of Gibbs and the Peruvian Guano Monopoly*. 1981. £18.25 (£11.44 to Members).
26. D. M. Schurman: *Julian S. Corbett 1854–1922, Historian of British Maritime Policy from Drake to Jellicoe*. 1981. £15.75 (£9.91 to Members).
27. Scott M. Harrison: *The Pilgrimage of Grace in the Lake Counties 1536–7*. 1981. £13.00 (£8.00 to Members).
28. Angus MacKay: *Money, Prices and Politics in Fifteenth-Century Castile*. 1982. £14.52 (£8.87 to Members).
29. D. Duman: *The Judicial Bench in England 1727–1875: The Reshaping of a Professional Elite*. 1982. £16.02 (£8.89 to Members).
30. J. R. Wordie: *Estate Management in Eighteenth-Century England*. 1982. £20.02 (£12.46 to Members).
31. M. Doughty: *Merchant Shipping and War*. 1982. £15.77 (£9.93 to Members).
32. N. Jones: *Faith by Statute: Parliament and the Settlement of Religion 1559*. 1982. £17.52 (£10.62 to Members).
33. James Barros: *Britain, Greece and the Politics of Sanctions: Ethiopa 1935–1936*. 1982. £18.02 (£11.46 to Members).